# Date Due

| | | | |
|---|---|---|---|
| MAR 17 1989 | | | |
| JUN 2 1989 | | | |
| | | | |
| | | | |
| | | | |
| | | | |
| | | | |
| | | | |
| | | | |
| | | | |
| | | | |
| | | | |
| | | | |
| | | | |
| | | | |
| | | | |
| | | | |

BRODART, INC.          Cat. No. 23 233          Printed in U.S.A.

# Nonlinear System Theory

This is Volume 175 in
MATHEMATICS IN SCIENCE AND ENGINEERING
A Series of Monographs and Textbooks
Edited by RICHARD BELLMAN, *University of Southern California*

The complete listing of books in this series is available from the Publisher
upon request.

# NONLINEAR SYSTEM THEORY

## John L. Casti

*International Institute for Applied Systems Analysis*
*Laxenburg, Austria*

1985

ACADEMIC PRESS, INC.

(Harcourt Brace Jovanovich, Publishers)

Orlando   San Diego   New York   London
Toronto   Montreal   Sydney   Tokyo

COPYRIGHT © 1985, BY ACADEMIC PRESS, INC.
ALL RIGHTS RESERVED.
NO PART OF THIS PUBLICATION MAY BE REPRODUCED OR
TRANSMITTED IN ANY FORM OR BY ANY MEANS, ELECTRONIC
OR MECHANICAL, INCLUDING PHOTOCOPY, RECORDING, OR
ANY INFORMATION STORAGE AND RETRIEVAL SYSTEM, WITHOUT
PERMISSION IN WRITING FROM THE PUBLISHER.

ACADEMIC PRESS, INC.
Orlando, Florida 32887

*United Kingdom Edition published by*
ACADEMIC PRESS INC. (LONDON) LTD.
24–28 Oval Road, London NW1 7DX


Library of Congress Cataloging in Publication Data

Casti, J. L.
    Nonlinear system theory.

    (Mathematics in science and engineering)
    Includes bibliographical references and index.
    1. System analysis.  2. Nonlinear theories.  I. Title.
II. Series.
QA402.C38  1983       003       84-6463
ISBN 0-12-163452-3 (alk. paper)

# 10727024

12·23·85·10

PRINTED IN THE UNITED STATES OF AMERICA

85 86 87 88        9 8 7 6 5 4 3 2 1

*To V, with love and admiration for a living system that continues to defy analysis.*

# Contents

## Chapter 4   Reachability and Controllability

## Chapter 5   Observability, Realization, and Estimation

## Chapter 6   Stability Theory: Singularities, Bifurcations, and Catastrophes

# Preface

Wittgenstein's famous dictum, "whereof one cannot speak, thereof one must be silent," serves well as encapsulation of the state of mathematical system theory in most of the post-war period. Until very recently, it was mathematically impossible to speak meaningfully of the system-theoretic properties of nonlinear systems, since the necessary framework of concepts and results for even *linear* processes was still under development. This backcloth, against which the play of nonlinear phenomena must be acted out, is treated in detail in my previous book, "Dynamical Systems and Their Applications: Linear Theory" (Academic Press, 1977). This book is a sequel to that earlier volume and represents an attempt to satisfy Wittgenstein's criterion by showing that it is *now* possible to "speak" about nonlinear systems.

Considering the five principal problem areas comprising the subject matter of mathematical system theory—reachability–controllability, observability–reconstructibility, realization theory–identification, stability, and optimality—if a report card were to be issued on how things currently stand in regard to the completeness of analytic and computational results for the major questions of nonlinear systems in each area, it would look something like this:

| | |
|---|---|
| Reachability–Controllability | B+ |
| Observability–Reconstructibility | B |
| Realization–Identification | C+ |
| Stability Theory | A |
| Optimality | A− |

This is a pretty decent record, especially in view of the fact that when my earlier book was published, the first three subjects on the card would have hardly merited more than a gentlemanly C. There is good reason to suspect that a similar report issued say, five years from now, will show all areas to be in the $B^+$ category or higher.

Rather than engage in a boring and unnecessarily redundant recounting of what this book is and what it contains (a story obtainable much more painlessly anyway by a quick glance at the Table of Contents), let me say a few words about what the book is *not:*

(i) *It is not an introductory text.* Although the book contains a number of problems and exercises, it was written as a reference guide to the current status of nonlinear system theory. The problems given are decidely not textbook exercises, most of them coming from the current literature and requiring a substantial amount of background to solve. Furthermore, many of the results are stated without proof with only a citation to the literature for details.

(ii) *It is not a balanced view of the competing philosophies and methods of nonlinear analysis.* The book is resolutely algebraic and geometric in flavor, totally eschewing methods of classical and functional analysis for the study of nonlinear processes. I make no apologies for slighting analysis in favor of algebraic and geometrical approaches to the basic questions of system theory. Prejudices are prejudices, and mine are such that I feel algebraic–geometric ideas have much greater intrinsic potential for unlocking the mysteries of nonlinear processes than do the tools of analysis. Furthermore, while it must be confessed that it is a matter of taste, I feel that the algebraic–geometric view of systems presents the problems (and solutions) in a much cleaner, more elegant, and, generally speaking, more computable form than do the results arising from a more analytic treatment.

(iii) *It is not an encyclopedic reference.* Many important aspects of nonlinear processes are either ignored totally or given rather brief and superficial treatment. For instance, the book deals only with finite-dimensional problems, thereby excluding discussion of processes governed by partial differential, differential-delay, and other more exotic types of functional equations. Also with one or two minor exceptions, the book deals only with deterministic processes. Personally, I have always found probability theory and stochastic processes to be tediously and insanely boring and of little intellectual interest (this is not to deny their obvious practical utility, only their intrinsic value as an expression of the way things *are*) and have resolutely tried to avoid their suffocating and obfuscating effect whenever possible. One of the few joys of writing a book such as this is the freedom to pick and choose among topics having personal intellectual interest and to leave out those that do not. Hence, I cheerfully leave a treatment of stochastic nonlinear systems to more random spirits than me, wherever they may be. Finally, optimization theory and optimal control have been omitted entirely from the volume. In this case, it is not lack of intellectual interest or content, but instead the rather voluminous literature already extant on these subjects that accounts for their omission here.

The embryo from which this book emerged was a survey article on nonlinear system theory published in the *SIAM Review*. For their efforts in ensuring that this paper did not distort too seriously either the form or content of the main results in the field, I thank H. Hermes, A. Krener, J. Baillieul, R. Kalman, and most especially, E. Sontag. Support from H. Miser was helpful during this period. As always, my thanks (and sympathies) to the people who turn arcane and unintelligible scribble into recognizable English typescript. In this regard, a heartfelt thanks to Karen Williams, Nora Avedisian, Susan Stock, and Susie Riley. Finally, an Acknowledgment to the management of the International Institute for Applied Systems Analysis, whose remarkable views on the value of system theory and long-term theoretical systems research have served for years as a source of motivation for the production of this book.

JLC

# 1
## Perspectives and Problems of Nonlinear System Theory

### I. A NONLINEAR WORLD

**Question.** What do a rolling ship, a national economy, and a supersonic aircraft have in common?

*Answer.* They are all inherently nonlinear processes which are treated as linear phenomena until catastrophic events force managers and analysts alike to explicitly acknowledge the effect of the nonlinear structure on the system behavior.

One might wonder why the nonlinear model was not employed at the outset. The answer is quite simple: the tools of linear analysis are quite well developed, while those able to deal with nonlinear phenomena were, until rather recently, feeble and fragmentary at best. Nature, the Practical Joker, armed the systems analyst with a set of linear tools and then insisted upon creating a nonlinear world to tantalize and frustrate him. However, times change and sufficient progress has been made in mathematical system theory to now give some degree of confidence in approaching several classes of nonlinear problems. We shall present many of the most important results throughout the course of this book. But before entering into the mathematics, it is instructive to consider several examples of nonlinear processes in applied areas to focus attention on some of the characteristics distinguishing the linear from the nonlinear theory.

**Example A:  The Nonlinear Pendulum**

Consider the simple mechanical situation depicted in Fig. 1.1, in which a child of mass $m$ is sitting on a swing. To change the amplitude of the oscillation, the child can, in effect, move his mass up or down the supporting rod. For simplicity, we ignore the mass of the swing itself. The variables describing the oscillation of the swing are

$$\{(\theta, \dot{\theta}, l): 0 \leq \theta \leq \pi, |\dot{\theta}| < \infty \text{ and } 0 < l < l_0\}.$$

By equating the rate of change of the angular momentum about the support with the torque due to gravity, after a bit of algebra, we obtain the system of dynamical equations

$$\frac{d\theta}{dt} = \phi,$$

$$\frac{d\phi}{dt} = -\frac{1}{l}\sin\theta - 2u\phi/l,$$

$$\frac{dl}{dt} = u,$$

where $u\ (= dl/dt)$ is the control input which the child can utilize to modify the amplitude of the swing.

School yard experience shows that a question of interest in connection with the swing is whether or not it is possible to find *pumping modes*, which will maintain or increase a given amplitude of oscillation. In system-theoretic terms, this is a question of reachability whose answer can be obtained by the techniques we shall present in Chapter 4.

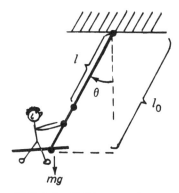

**FIG. 1.1**   Child on a swing.

**Example B:   Urban Population Migration**

We postulate a neighborhood with a housing capacity $N$, which is fixed. Suppose that initially the neighborhood is entirely composed of whites who possess sufficient resources to move from the neighborhood if they wish. Further, suppose that the neighborhood holds no attraction for similar whites elsewhere, but that there is a large black population which is initially located elsewhere and would be able and willing to move into the given neighborhood if vacant housing becomes available. Thus, no black can move in until a white moves out. Our goal is to model the migration process under the following assumptions:

(i)   the migration process is rapid enough that the natural birth and death rates can be ignored;

(ii)   the whites have a natural emigration rate $\mu$, with the goal of securing better housing;

(iii)   the blacks have a natural gross immigration rate, which is proportional to the vacant housing available $k_1(N - x_w(t) - x_b(t))$ with $k_1$ being the proportionality constant;

(iv)   because some of the whites have a bias against living near blacks, there is a specific bigotry emigration rate $v$, which is proportional to the fraction of the area which is black, i.e.,

$$v = k_2 \left[ \frac{x_b(t)}{x_b(t) + x_w(t)} \right].$$

Here, of course, $x_w(t)$ and $x_b(t)$ are the numbers of whites and blacks in the neighborhood at time $t$, respectively.

Under the preceding conditions, the appropriate migration dynamics are

$$\frac{dx_w}{dt} = -\left[ \mu + \frac{k_2 x_b(t)}{x_w(t) + x_b(t)} \right] x_w(t),$$

$$\frac{dx_b}{dt} = k_1 [N - x_w(t) - x_b(t)].$$

The initial conditions are $x_w(0) = N$, $x_b(0) = 0$.

An interesting feature of the above model is that the transition from an all-white to an all-black neighborhood is inevitable as long as the whites always have a positive net emigration rate. Thus, if we wish to achieve a permanently interracial neighborhood, then ways must be found to change the sign of $\mu$. Another interesting question that could arise from such a situation is the following: If it is possible to measure only the fraction of the area that is white, i.e., we are given

$$y(t) = \frac{x_w(t)}{x_w(t) + x_b(t)},$$

can we always *uniquely* determine the total number of blacks and whites in the neighborhood? This is a problem of nonlinear observability which will be considered in Chapter 5.

### Example C:  Neutron Transport in a Rod

A thin rod of length $x$, $0 \le x \le a$, is regarded as a primitive nuclear reactor. Between collisions with atoms of the reactor, neutrons are assumed to move with unit velocity along the rod with no neutron–neutron interaction. When a neutron interacts with an atom of the rod, the outcome is instantaneous replacement of the original neutron by $0, 1, \ldots, N$ neutrons, with respective probabilities $c_0, c_1, \ldots, c_N$. The neutrons arising from a collision are equally likely to be moving to the left or right with unit velocity. The expected number of neutrons arising from a collision is the factor

$$c = \sum_{k=1}^{N} kc_k.$$

Collisions of neutrons with atoms are assumed to be governed by the Poisson law, i.e., in an infinitesimal interval $(x, x + \Delta)$, there is a probability $\sigma\Delta$ of a collision, where $\sigma$ is the reciprocal of the mean free path. The probability of no collision in a path of length $b$ is thus $e^{-\sigma b}$. When a neutron reaches either end of the rod, it is absorbed.

A single trigger neutron moving to the right is introduced at point $x$ at time $t = 0$. If we let $u(x)$ denote the probability that at least one neutron is *alive* at $t = \infty$, with $v(x)$ denoting the similar quantity for a neutron initially moving to the left, then a particle-counting argument shows that

$$1 - u(x) = e^{-(a-x)\sigma} + \int_x^a e^{-(y-x)\sigma}\sigma p(y)\,dy,$$

where $p(y)$ is the probability of all products of the collision in $(y, y + dy)$ becoming extinct. Clearly,

$$p(y) = \sum_{k=0}^{N} c_k p_k(y),$$

where $p_k(y) = $ probability that none of the $k$ neutrons generated yield a chain reaction. Of the $k$ neutrons produced, there is a probability $\binom{k}{p}(\frac{1}{2})^k$ that $p$ will

move to the right and the rest to the left; the corresponding extinction
probability is $[1 - u(y)]^p[1 - v(y)]^{k-p}$. Thus,

$$1 - u(x) = e^{-(a-x)\sigma} + \int_x^a \sigma e^{-(y-x)\sigma} \sum_{k=0}^N c_k \sum_{p=0}^N \binom{k}{p}(\tfrac{1}{2})^k$$

$$\times [1 - u(y)]^p[1 - v(y)]^{k-p}\, dy.$$

A similar equation holds for $v(x)$. Upon setting

$$z(x) = [u(x) + v(x)]/2,$$

we obtain the equation for $z$ as

$$z(x) = \int_0^a E(x, y)G[z(y)]\, dy, \qquad 0 \le x \le a, \qquad (1.1)$$

where

$$E(x, y) = \tfrac{1}{2}\sigma e^{-\sigma|x-y|},$$

$$G(r) = cr - \sum_{k=2}^N c_k[(1 - r)^k - 1 + kr]$$

$$= 1 - \sum_{k=0}^N c_k(1 - r)^k.$$

Equation (1.1) represents a nonlinear relationship between the input (the
trigger neutrons moving to the left and right) and the output (the probability
that at least one neutron is alive). In view of the probabilistic definitions of $u$
and $v$, the nontrivial solutions of interest satisfy $0 \le z(x) \le 1$. For a number
of reasons, both analytical as well as computational, it is of interest to know
whether it is possible to express $z(x)$ as the solution of a differential equation
system, possessing the same input–output relationship as (1.1). With a modest
amount of work, it can be verified that Eq. (1.1) is indeed equivalent to the
nonlinear differential equation

$$-\frac{d^2z}{dx^2} + \sigma^2 z = \sigma^2 G[z(x)], \qquad 0 < x < a, \qquad (1.2)$$

with the boundary conditions

$$z'(0) - \sigma z(0) = 0, \qquad z'(a) + \sigma z(a) = 0 \qquad (1.3)$$

Equation (1.2), together with the boundary conditions (1.3), is termed a
*realization* of the nonlinear input–output description (1.1). Realization
problems form the very essence of mathematical model-building, and will be

examined in detail in Chapter 5. For now it suffices to note only the fact that not every integral equation (input–output relation) is equivalent to some *finite-order* differential system. Thus, the realization problem is nontrivial and it will be our task to identify those input–output maps for which finite-dimensional realizations are possible. Further, we have the additional task of providing algorithms for actually generating such a realization from numerical data.

**Example D:  Predator–Prey Relations**

A classical type of nonlinear system describes the temporal oscillations of a population of predators and their prey in a localized geographic region. Let us denote the prey population by $N_1(t)$ and the predator population by $N_2(t)$. We assume that the growth rate of prey, in the absence of predators, is $aN_1(t)$, while the predator multiplication rate is $bN_1(t)N_2(t)$. Further, we assume that the loss rate of prey is proportional to the numbers of prey and predators, i.e., loss rate of prey equals $\alpha N_1(t)N_2(t)$, while the loss rate of predators equals their death rate $2\beta N_2(t)$ (here the factor 2 is for mathematical convenience later on). Putting these remarks together, the dynamics of the predator–prey interaction are described by the Lotka–Volterra equations

$$\dot{N}_1(t) = aN_1 - \alpha N_1 N_2,$$
$$\dot{N}_2(t) = bN_1 N_2 - 2\beta N_2. \tag{1.4}$$

By the scaling of variables

$$\overline{N}_1 = \frac{1}{2}\frac{bN_1}{\beta}, \qquad \overline{N}_2 = \frac{\alpha N_2}{a}, \qquad \overline{t} = at,$$

it is a simple exercise to verify that the above dynamics obey the conservation law

$$H = (\overline{N}_1 - \log \overline{N}_1) + \frac{1}{2\beta}(\overline{N}_2 - \log \overline{N}_2) = \text{const.}$$

The point $N_1^* = 2\beta/b$, $N_2^* = a/\alpha$ is the only nontrivial equilibrium of the Lotka–Volterra system. Since the function $H$ is constant along orbits of the system, it is easy to verify that if the initial condition $(N_1(0), N_2(0) \neq (N_1^*, N_2^*))$, the trajectory is a closed orbit as depicted in Fig. 1.2. Thus, for any given initial condition, the populations of predator and prey will oscillate cyclically. Neither species will die out, nor will it grow indefinitely. Furthermore, except for the improbable initial state $(N_1^*, N_2^*)$, the populations will not remain constant.

The important point to note about the above example is that no amount of perturbation of either the initial state or the system parameters alters the qualitative structure of the system trajectory. Thus, the Lotka–Volterra system is stable relative to changes in the initial state and/or system parameters. The above type of behavior is vaguely reminiscent of the phase plane portrait of the classical harmonic oscillator, familiar from linear system theory, with the major exception that the harmonic oscillator can be highly sensitive to changes in system parameters.

By the imposition of an additional term in Eqs. (1.4) to account for a growth limitation, we can introduce a substantially different flavor into the system dynamics. In dimensionless variables, assume the modified dynamics are now

$$\dot{N}_1 = (a - bN_2 - \lambda N_1)N_1,$$
$$\dot{N}_2 = (cN_1 - d - \mu N_2)N_2,$$

where $a$, $b$, $c$, $d$, $\lambda$, $\mu$ are all positive constants. Some simple geometric arguments now show that if the two lines

$$L_1 = a - bN_2 - \lambda N_1 = 0,$$
$$L_2 = cN_1 - d - \mu N_2 = 0,$$

intersect at a point $z$ in the first quadrant, then either a trajectory approaches $z$ as $t \rightarrow \infty$, or else it spirals down to a limit cycle $\Gamma$. The general picture for $z$ is an equilibrium as in Fig. 1.3. Thus, any population obeying these quadratic growth limitations eventually settles down to either a constant or a periodic population. In addition, it can be shown that there is an upper bound $a/\lambda$ above which no population can go, regardless of the initial condition.

The appearance of a limit cycle $\Gamma$ is a strictly nonlinear phenomenon that is of great importance in understanding the dynamics of complex processes. In later chapters, we shall undertake an investigation of the birth and death

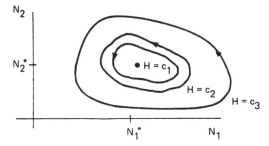

**FIG. 1.2**   Phase-plane portraits of Lotka–Volterra systems.

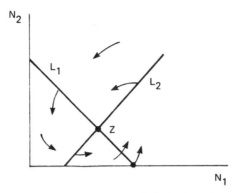

**FIG. 1.3**   Approach to equilibrium for growth limited predator–prey dynamics.

of such phenomena as parameters of the system change, as well as a consideration of even more *strange* attractors that appear when we pass to systems of dimension greater than two. All of these questions fall into the general category of *stability analysis*, forming one of the cornerstones of modern nonlinear system theory.

**Example E:   Missile Warfare**

Imagine two countries A and S, who may engage in nuclear warfare involving strategic weapons (missiles). We let

$M_A(t)$ = missile stocks held by A at time $t$,
$M_S(t)$ = missile stocks held by S at time $t$,
$C_A(t)$ = casualties in country A at time $t$,
$C_S(t)$ = casualties in country S at time $t$,
$u_A(t)$ = rate at which country A fires its missiles at time $t$,
$u_S(t)$ = rate at which country S fires its missiles at time $t$,
$\bar{u}_A(t)$ = proportion of missiles devoted to counterforce strikes by country A, i.e., proportion targeted at enemy missiles,
$\bar{u}_S(t)$ = proportion of missiles devoted to counterforce strikes by country S, i.e., proportion targeted at enemy missiles.

Using this notation, a simple model of the dynamics of a missile war is given by

$$\dot{M}_A = -u_A M_A - u_S \bar{u}_S M_S f_S,$$
$$\dot{M}_S = -u_S M_S - u_A \bar{u}_A M_A f_A,$$
$$\dot{C}_A = (1 - \bar{u}_S) u_S M_S v_S,$$
$$\dot{C}_S = (1 - \bar{u}_A) u_A M_A v_A,$$

(1.5)

where $f_A$ and $f_S$ are the number of S and A missiles destroyed by one A and S counterforce missile, respectively. That is, $f_A$ and $f_S$ represent the effectiveness of the counterforce missiles. Similarly, the quantities $v_A$ and $v_S$ represent the number of casualties inflicted by a single countervalue missile of A and S.

In model (1.5), strategic decisions in A and S concerning rates of fire are given by the control functions $u_A(t)$ and $u_S(t)$, while the strategic decisions concerning targets are summarized by the control functions $\bar{u}_A(t)$ and $\bar{u}_S(t)$. In general, the control functions are constrained by

$$0 \le u_A(t) \le U_A, \qquad 0 \le u_S(t) \le U_S,$$

$$0 \le \bar{u}_A(t) \le 1, \qquad 0 \le \bar{u}_S(t) \le 1,$$

where $U_A$ and $U_S$ are the maximum rates of fire of the two countries.

During wartime, each country must choose a firing and targeting strategy. Taking the viewpoint of country A, it is reasonable to assume that A seeks to maximize a payoff function dependent on the number of missiles and casualties in both countries at the end of the war at time $t = T$. Thus, we have a criterion

$$J_A = J_A(M_A, M_S, C_A, C_S),$$

where the termination time $T$ can be either fixed or determined by the evolution of the war itself, e.g., when one country has a low number of missiles or a large number of casualties. It is reasonable to assume that $J_A$ increases with $M_A(T)$, decreases with both $M_S(T)$ and $C_A(T)$, and can either increase or decrease with $C_S(T)$.

Maximizing $J_A$, subject to the above dynamics and constraints, given strategic decisions of S and missile effectiveness ratios, yields optimum strategies for A. In general, these optimum strategies are switching strategies, i.e.,

$$u_A^*(t) = \begin{cases} A, & 0 \le t \le \tau, \\ 0, & \tau \le t \le T. \end{cases}$$

Similarly, the optimum targeting is pure counterforce initially, followed by a switch to countervalue at a time $\tau'$, i.e.,

$$\bar{u}_A^*(t) = \begin{cases} 1, & 0 \le t \le \tau', \\ 0, & \tau' \le t \le T. \end{cases}$$

Thus, we see that the war can be divided into three phases:

(i)  Country A fires its missiles at the maximum rate and uses pure counterforce to reduce the missile force of S.

(ii)  If $\tau < \tau'$, then A switches to zero fire rate, keeping counterforce targeting, i.e., A threatens the force of S, but ceases fire; if $\tau > \tau'$, then A fires at maximum rate at the cities of S. This is the only phase during which casualties are inflicted on S.

(iii)   In the final phases of the war (when $t > \max\{\tau, \tau'\}$), A is firing at zero rate and has all of his missiles targeted at the cities of S.

The preceding example illustrates an optimization process in which a great deal of the structure of the optimal strategies is relatively insensitive to the precise form of the optimization criteria. This is an important aspect of system optimization, especially in those processes governed by nonlinear dynamics, as in the missile example just cited.

## II. THE CENTRAL QUESTIONS OF SYSTEM THEORY

Examples A–E each illustrate at least one major study area of modern system theory. We conveniently group the major questions into the following categories:

1. Realization–Identification,
2. Reachability–Controllability,
3. Observability–Reconstructibility,
4. Stability–Bifurcation,
5. Optimality.

Although each of these topics has been hinted at in the examples, the importance of each class of questions is so great that no harm can come from a bit of expository repetition. Consequently, as a prelude to the technical results of later chapters, let us now consider each of the five problem areas in more detail.

### A.  Realization–Identification

The *sine qua non* of system theory is the construction of a state-variable representation (internal model) for given input–output data (external model). The underlying idea is that the state-variable model provides an *explanation* of the observed data, since the connections and data paths from the input to the output are explicitly exhibited. In other words, the state-variable model represents the internal workings of the black box called *the system*.

There are several important issues surrounding the realization problem, not the least of which is the specification of the form of the input–output data, as well as the isolation of the class of internal models which the modeler wishes to use as his explanatory mechanism. For example, an input–output model which admits the representation

$$\dot{x} = f(x(t), t) + u(t)g(x(t), t),$$

$$y(t) = h(x(t)), \qquad f, g, h \in C^{\infty},$$

with $u(t)$ = input, $y(t)$ = output, $x(t)$ = state, requires, in principle, an *infinite* sequence of kernel functions $\{w_i(t_1, t_2, \ldots, t_i)\}_{i=1}^{\infty}$ for its specification. This is easily seen from the simple formula

$$y(t) = w_0(t) + \int_0^t w_1(t, s)u(s)ds$$

$$+ \int_0^t \int_0^{s_1} w_2(t, s_1, s_2)u(s_1)u(s_2)ds_1 ds_2$$

$$+ \cdots,$$

where the kernels can be computed recursively by the methods we shall develop later. The point is that the realization problem consists of being *given* the sequence of kernels with the task of *finding* the functions $f$, $g$, and $h$. Here we have chosen to specify the input–output data by the kernels $\{w_i\}$, while we have chosen what is called a *linear-analytic* structure for the internal model of the system.

A much more difficult situation arises if we are given only a *finite* string of measured numerical data $\{A_0, A_1, A_2, \ldots, A_m\}$, where the matrices $A_i$ are $p \times m$. We interpret element $(i, j)$ of the matrix $A_k$ to be the response measured at the $i$th output terminal at time $k$, due to a *pulse* input at terminal $j$. Here the *pulse* is the unit vector $e_j$ having a 1 at position $j$, 0 elsewhere, in discrete time. In continuous time, the pulse would be the Dirac delta function $\delta(t - t_j)$ at time $t_j$. Here the problem is that of identifying functions $f$, $g$, $h$, which may, in principle, require an infinite number of parameters for their specification, from a finite amount of information.

The difficulties inherent in the nonlinear realization problem are made more explicit when we compare to the linear case, i.e., when

$$f(x, t) = Fx, \qquad g(x, t) = G, \qquad h(x) = Hx,$$

$$A_k = He^{Ft_k}G,$$

with $F$, $G$, $H$ constant matrices. In this case, the class of models has been reduced to one for which each member of the class can be parameterized by a finite number of parameters: the elements of $F$, $G$, and $H$ (assuming, of course, that a finite-dimensional realization exists). Thus if we know the dimension of a realization, it is possible to reduce the problem to a manipulatory exercise in linear algebra involving the matrices $\{A_k\}$. No such luxury exists in the general nonlinear case since it is not even possible, in principle, to finitely parameterize a general function, even a smooth ($C^{\infty}$) function. Thus, even if the state space is finite dimensional, there can exist no general realization algorithm which is finitely computable.

As a result of the above observation, the only reasonable approach to a practically implementable nonlinear realization theory is to restrict attention to suitable subclasses of models. For a variety of practical as well as mathematical reasons, the most suitable classes of systems appear to be those which contain certain linear features, such as the bilinear models, or those which have other desirable analytic structure (e.g., polynomial, linear in the control). The key element is some sort of property which enables us to specify a model using only a finite number of parameters. We summarize the current status of the realization problem in Chapter 5.

## B. Reachability–Controllability

Having specified some type of internal model of the data at hand, the issue arises as to what sort of properties the model possesses, especially properties relating to the interaction of the model variables (states) with the external world (inputs and outputs). Here the question of reachability enters in an essential way.

In broad terms, reachability of a given state from another involves several interrelated factors:

(i)   the initial state $x_0$,
(ii)  the terminal state $x_T$,
(iii) the class of admissible inputs, and
(iv)  the time period during which the transfer $x_0 \to x_T$ is to take place.

Consider the following simple case.

Let the system be described by the dynamics

$$\dot{x} = Fx + u(t)gc'x(t),$$

where $u(\cdot)$ is a scalar function and $g$ and $c$ are nonzero column vectors. The linear system

$$\dot{x} = Fx + gv$$

is reachable in $R^n$ if and only if

$$\text{rank}\{g, Fg, F^2g, \ldots, F^{n-1}g\} = n.$$

Hence, if the linear system is reachable we might suppose that the above bilinear one is also, since if $v$ is a control which transfers $x_0$ to $x_T$, then the control

$$u(t) = v(t)/c'x(t)$$

would drive the bilinear system from $x_0$ to $x_T$. This argument is fallacious since $c'x(t)$ might vanish along the trajectory leaving $u(t)$ undefined. In particular, if $x_0 = 0$, then $x(t) \equiv 0$ and the most that we could hope for is that any $x_0 \neq 0$ could be transferred to any $x_T \neq 0$. Even this is too much to hope for, as we shall see in Chapter 4.

The conclusion to be drawn from this state of affairs is that the reachability problem, together with its counterpart the controllability question (where we have $x_0 \neq 0$, $x_T = 0$), is full of mathematical subtleties in the nonlinear case and cannot be resolved by elementary means. Nevertheless, many valuable results have been obtained in identifying those classes of systems which are reachable, and the techniques of Chapter 4 show how to deal with these problems.

Among some of the important questions related to reachability that we shall examine are

(i)   how to identify those pairs of states $(x_0, x_T)$ which can be joined by a system trajectory, given the input class and time interval;

(ii)   how to construct inputs which effect a theoretically feasible transfer;

(iii)   how to characterize mathematically the set of states reachable from $x_0$;

(iv)   how to determine the reachable set when the input class is subjected to natural restrictions, e.g., positivity, boundedness, *bang-bang*.

## C. Observability–Reconstructibility

The intuitive content of the observability problem is that of identifying the precise amount of information about the system state that is contained in the measured system output. In abstract terms, we are concerned with whether the output map $h: X \to Y$ is one-to-one, where $X$ and $Y$ are the system state and output spaces, respectively. In more specific terms, we are given the system

$$\dot{x} = f(x, u), \qquad x(0) = x_0,$$

$$y(t) = h(x),$$

and the input $u(\cdot)$ and must determine whether or not the state $x_0$ can be *uniquely* determined from the output $y(t)$ measured over any interval $0 < t \leq \tau$. If so, then we say that $x_0$ is an *observable* state.

In the linear case when $f(x, u) = Fx$, $h(x) = Hx$, the question of observability is easily answered in terms of properties of the matrix

$$\theta = [H' | H'F' | H'(F')^2 | \cdots | H'(F')^{n-1}].$$

However, the elementary scalar system

$$\dot{x} = 0, \qquad x(0) = x_0,$$

$$y = x^2(t),$$

shows that no amount of observation of $y(s)$, will suffice to uniquely identify $x_0$. The nonlinear structure introduces essential mathematical complications into the observability question, complications which require a surprising amount of mathematical sophistication to resolve.

In connection with observability issues, in Chapter 5 we shall consider questions of the following type:

(i)   what mathematical procedures may be employed to determine those states which are observable;

(ii)   how can we mathematically characterize the structure of the set of observable states;

(iii)   what connection exists, if any, between the concepts of reachability and observability for nonlinear processes;

(iv)   how do restrictions on the observing process influence the structure of the observable states.


## D.  Stability–Bifurcation

Any model of a real process is a mathematical idealization containing a number of approximations to reality such as point particles, lack of frictional and gravitational effects, perfect vacuums, and other physical fictions. In assessing the predictive merits of a given model, it is of considerable importance to know how the behavior of the model changes under various types of perturbations of its defining structure. This is the general problem of stability theory. The specific questions, however, take many forms depending on the mathematical description of the process, the type of perturbation acting on the system, and the particular behavior that the analyst wishes to investigate.

As an example of a typical stability problem, assume that we have a system described by the input–output map

$$f : \Omega \to \Gamma,$$

where $\Omega$ and $\Gamma$ are the input and output function spaces, respectively. One type of question that naturally occurs in this context is under what conditions on $f$ can we assert that $\Gamma$ will inherit properties of $\Omega$? That is to say, if $\Omega$ is, for instance, the space of essentially bounded functions on $[0, \infty]$, what conditions of $f$ will suffice to ensure that the outputs also remain bounded. This is the bounded input–bounded output (BIBO) stability problem. In Chapter 6, we shall see that if $f$ has additional structure (e.g., consists of several feedback loops), then rather detailed results are available on the BIBO problem.

Most stability and sensitivity problems occur not in the input–output setting, but rather within the context of an internal system model

$$\dot{x} = f(x, u), \qquad x(0) = x_0,$$

$$y = h(x).$$

The two most common stability issues surrounding such a system model involve perturbations in the initial state $x_0$ (classical Lyapunov stability) or perturbations in the dynamics $f$ (structural stability). In the case of Lyapunov-type stability we ask questions such as:

(i)  if $x_0 \neq 0$ and the origin is an equilibrium for the system, i.e., $f(0, \cdot) = 0$ for all $u$, does $x(t) \to 0$ as $t \to \infty$ (asymptotic stability);

(ii)  if $x(t) \nrightarrow 0$, does $x(t)$ remain in some neighborhood of 0 for all $t$ (the neighborhood size depending, of course, on the size of $x_0$);

(iii)  if $x(t) \to 0$, at what rate is the origin approached;

(iv)  how can we classify the region $D$ in state space such that $x(t) \to 0$ for all $x_0 \in D$

The foregoing questions form the basis for classical stability analyses in the event of no control, i.e., $u(t) \equiv 0$. If we allow for the modification of dynamical behavior by controls, then an entirely new set of questions arises involving the manner in which the control inputs affect the stability properties of the controlled system. For example, if the control is of feedback form, i.e., $u(t) = u(x(t))$, then the closed-loop system dynamics are

$$\dot{x} = f(x, u(x)),$$

and we can ask the same set of questions as those posed above for the case $u \equiv 0$. In the linear case $f(x, u) = Fx + Gu$, $u(t) = -Kx$, and it is well known that if the pair $(F, G)$ is reachable, then the closed-loop matrix $F - GK$ can have its characteristic values located at predefined positions by suitable selection of $K$ (Pole-Shifting theorem). Thus, the stability behavior of the original process can be arbitrarily altered by feedback control. In a similar vein, we are interested in to what extent the stability properties of the uncontrolled nonlinear system may be modified by feedback. In particular, the question as to whether the origin can be made globally stable for any nonlinear system by suitable feedback naturally arises.

Moving away from the classical *point* stability notions, we consider the effect on the system trajectory when the dynamics themselves, are perturbed. Thus, instead of the system equation being

$$\dot{x} = f(x)$$

the system is perturbed by a new function $\epsilon(x)$ and actually operates according to the dynamics

$$\dot{z} = f(z) + \epsilon(z).$$

An important question is: without knowing the precise form of the function $\epsilon(\cdot)$, but only qualitative properties such as degree of smoothness, norm, etc., what is the connection between the trajectories $x(t)$ and $z(t)$? Specifically, do

$x(t)$ and $z(t)$ have the same topological properties? This is clearly an important question in model construction apropos the earlier remarks on approximations to reality in mathematical modeling. Here, the function $\epsilon(\cdot)$ is supposed to account for the effect of the various simplifications and approximations in the model.

One important way in which the above *structural stability* problem arises is through changes in parameters in the process. We have a system

$$\dot{x} = f(x, a),$$

where $a$ is a vector of parameters which may change. We would like to know those critical values of $a$ at which the system trajectory $x = x(t, a)$ undergoes a qualitative change. Here such a change may show up as an equilibrium point changing its type from stable to unstable or from node to focus. Or a discontinuity may occur in the system trajectory for critical values of $a$. Another possibility is that the solution of the system equation may *bifurcate* into several distinct trajectories and so forth.

An interesting illustration of the preceding type of behavior is provided by the second-order system

$$\dot{x}_1 = x_2 - x_1^3 - ax_1,$$
$$\dot{x}_2 = -x_1$$

with $-1 \le a \le +1$. Here for each $a$, $-1 \le a \le 0$, all solutions are such that $x_1(t)$, $x_2(t) \to 0$ as $t \to \infty$. However, for $0 < a \le 1$, the system has a unique periodic solution $\Gamma$ (whose period depends on $a$) and the origin becomes a source (see Fig. 1.4). Thus, $a = 0$ is the bifurcation value of the parameter and the basic structure of the phase portrait of the system undergoes a dramatic change at the value $a = 0$: the origin changes its topological character from an attracting focus to an unstable source. We shall consider other Hopf-type bifurcations of this sort in the chapter on stability theory.

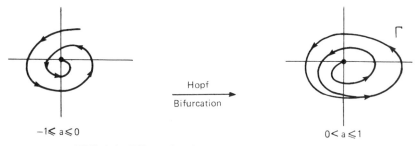

Hopf
Bifurcation

$-1 \le a \le 0$                                                      $0 < a \le 1$

**FIG. 1.4**  Bifurcation from a focus to a limit cycle.

Another type of bifurcation that has attracted considerable attention is when parametric changes in $a$ cause the system equilibrium to *discontinuously* shift from one fixed-point to another. More precisely, the correspondence $a \to x^*(a)$ defines a map from the parameter space into the system state space. The *theory of catastrophes*, developed by Thom, Arnol'd, Mather, and others, studies the properties of this map, especially the characterization of those critical hyper-surfaces in parameter space on which the map is discontinuous. We shall examine the interpretations of catastrophe theory in system-theoretic terms in a later chapter.

## E. Optimality

Instead of selecting the system input $u(t)$ to achieve some desired terminal state or to render the system stable in one sense or another, it may be desirable to superimpose an explicit criterion function upon the process and choose $u(t)$ to minimize this performance index. Classically, the situation would involve minimizing (over $u$)

$$J = \int_0^T L(x, u, t)\, dt,$$

where $x$ and $u$ are related by the differential equation

$$\dot{x} = f(x, u, t), \qquad x(0) = x_0.$$

Such problems are treated in the classical calculus of variations and in its modern reincarnation, optimal control theory. The role of system theory in such a problem is to critically examine the interconnections between optimality and the notions of reachability, observability, and stability. For example, if the dynamics are linear, $f(x, u) = Fx + Gu$, and the criterion function is quadratic, $L(x, u) = (Sx, Sx) + (u, Ru)$, then it is well known that if $T = \infty$, $R > 0$, $(S, F)$ observable, and $(F, G)$ reachable, then the optimal closed-loop feedback law $u^* = -K^*x$ will render the system asymptotically stable, i.e., the matrix $F - GK^*$ has all of its characteristic roots in the left-half plane. It is of considerable interest to examine to what extent this result extends to nonlinear dynamics and/or nonquadratic costs.

The classification of all criteria $L(x, u)$ for which a given feedback law $u^*(x, t)$ is optimal for fixed dynamics $f(x, u)$ comprises what is known as the Inverse Problem of Optimal Control. In the linear dynamics–quadratic costs (LQ) case, the problem is reasonably well understood; however, only partial results are available for the non-LQ situation. We shall examine the results and their implications for application in Chapter 6.

## III. CLASSES OF NONLINEAR PROCESSES

Without imposing a certain amount of structure on the dynamical processes we consider, it is virtually impossible to say anthing of mathematical interest. Consequently, throughout this volume we will consider only those dynamics $f(x, u)$ which possess enough smoothness to justify employment of various tools of geometry and algebra to answer some of the questions posed above. Generally speaking, this means that we shall have to assume that the dynamics are *smooth*, in the mathematical sense, i.e., infinitely differentiable in the $(x, u)$ region of interest (technically: $f$ is $C^\infty$ in $x$ and $u$). Occasionally, we shall have to invoke the even stronger assumption that the dynamics are real *analytic* in $x$ and/or $u$. In either case, the principal classes of specific nonlinear processes that we consider will satisfy the smoothness requirements. Let us briefly examine some of the major types of nonlinearities which are considered in the remainder of the book.

### A. Bilinear

Here the process is described by the equation

$$\dot{x} = Fx + Gu + \sum_{T=1}^{K} u_i N_i x,$$

where $u_i$ is the $i$th component of the input vector $u$ and $F, G, N_i$ are constant matrices. Many of the most important results from the linear theory carry over with modest additional algebraic effort to processes of the above sort.

### B. Multilinear

An obvious generalization of the bilinear case is to those processes which are linear in each component of the state and control, taken separately. These are the multilinear processes of which a simple second-order example is

$$\dot{x}_1 = a_{11}x_1 + a_{12}x_2 + c_{12}x_1x_2 + b_{11}u_1x_1 + b_{12}u_2x_1,$$
$$\dot{x}_2 = a_{21}x_1 + a_{22}x_2 + c_{21}x_1x_2 + b_{21}u_1x_2 + b_{22}u_2x_2.$$

Such processes can be described more compactly using tensor notation and inherit a great deal of structure from the purely linear case.

### C. Polynomial

Here we consider those dynamics which are polynomials in the state and/or the control, i.e.,

$$\dot{x} = P(x, u),$$

where $P(\cdot, \cdot)$ is a polynomial function in the components of $x$ and $u$. As might be suspected, study of the system-theoretic questions involved with such processes relies heavily upon elementary results from classical algebraic geometry, a subject devoted to the description and classification of manifolds given as the zero-set of sets of polynomial equations.

### D.  Linear in State–Linear in Control

It should be increasingly evident to the reader that the further a model departs from pure linearity, the more difficult its analysis and the less specific the statements that can be made regarding its dynamical behavior. Thus, an important type of nonlinear process is that in which either the control or the state appear linearly. In the first case, we have a system of the form

$$\dot{x} = p(x) + \sum_{T=1}^{m} u_i(t)\, g_i(x),$$

where $p$ and $g_i$ are smooth functions of $x$ alone. A substantial body of results is available on such processes, most of it relentlessly exploiting the fact that the control enters only linearly.

The situation in which the dynamics are linear while the control is non-linear is somewhat easier to deal with. The general setup is the system

$$\dot{x} = Fx + g(u), \tag{1.6}$$

where $g(\cdot)$ is a smooth nonlinear function of $u$. If $g(\cdot)$ is an invertible function on its range, then Eq. (1.6) obviously reduces to the purely linear situation through the new control vector $z = g(u)$. If $g(\cdot)$ is not invertible, it is still possible to employ the substitution to answer almost all interest system-theoretic questions about such a process.

The delineation of various classes and subclasses of nonlinear processes could go on almost indefinitely, but the ones we noted are probably those most often encountered in practice. Occasionally, we run into processes involving rational function dynamics, trigonometric forms, and so forth. In later chapters, we shall deal with interesting examples of these types, although most of our theoretical development shall focus on the types just discussed. At the bare minimum, they provide a solid basis for the construction of a comprehensive theory of nonlinear processes.

### IV.  LINEAR VERSUS NONLINEAR SYSTEM THEORY

Before setting forth in pursuit of results in nonlinear system theory rivaling those of the linear theory, it is instructive to examine some of the technical and computational hurdles that must be surmounted. In this way, a deeper appreciation can be obtained for the necessity to employ the *sophisticated* mathematical apparatus described in the next chapter.

The major mathematical obstacle to a complete theory of nonlinear processes is a lack of a superposition principle for general nonlinear systems. We recall that in the linear case, if $x_1(t)$ and $x_2(t)$ are two solutions of the uncontrolled linear equation $\dot{x} = Fx$, then so is $\alpha_1 x_1 + \alpha_2 x_2, \alpha_1, \alpha_2$ constants. Thus, the state space of such a process is a *subspace* of $R^n$. In the case of the controlled dynamics $\dot{x} = Fx + Gu$, it is fairly easy to see that the *reachable subset* of $R^n$ is also a subspace. Thus, if two states are reachable, so is any nontrivial linear combination of the states. The fact that the state space of a linear system is a vector space, coupled with the ability to parameterize any finite-dimensional linear system by a finite set of parameters (the elements of the matrices $F$, $G$, and $H$), enables us to employ the tools of *linear* algebra and matrix theory in analyzing the system-theoretic questions discussed earlier.

In the case of a general nonlinear system there is no superposition principle and no finite parameterization. This is not to say, however, that the state space has no interesting mathematical structure induced by the nonlinear dynamics. For instance, if the dynamics are multilinear, then it can be shown that the state space is an *affine variety*, a fact which may be exploited to transfer many of the results from the linear theory at the expense of a more elaborate algebraic setup than just linear vector spaces.

As an illustration of the type of difficulty which may be encountered even in simple nonlinear situations, consider the system of equations describing a *controllable* harmonic oscillator

$$\dot{x}_1 = x_2, \qquad\qquad x_1(0) = 1,$$
$$\dot{x}_2 = [-1 + u(t)]x_1, \qquad x_2(0) = 0,$$

where $|u(t)| \leq \epsilon \ll 1$. The reachable set at time $t = T$, for $T$ small, is the region depicted in Fig. 1.5a. However, for $T$ large enough, the reachable set encircles the origin. Thus, for large $T$, no states in a neighborhood of the origin are reachable and, in fact, the reachable set even fails to be convex, let alone a subspace of $R^2$. The difficulty in this particular problem is that the free motion of the system is an undamped oscillation. Intuitively, after a sufficiently long time the system can never reach the origin since the *damping factor* $u(t)$ is too small (by the constraint on $\epsilon$). If we want to classify those systems whose reachable sets are convex, then we shall have to adopt hypotheses which rule out this type of behavior.

As it turns out, an appropriate mathematical setting for consideration of nonlinear problems is the theory of differentiable manifolds. Since the state space of a nonlinear system is not globally *flat* (a Euclidean vector space), we must be content to work in a region which *locally* looks like $n$-dimensional Euclidean space and for which we can introduce a smooth, local coordinate system which enables us to do calculus in a consistent fashion. These requirements are the essence of the theory of differentiable manifolds, the basic aspects of which we outline in Chapter 2.

The algebraic cornerstone of linear system theory is the Cayley–Hamilton theorem, which asserts that every matrix satisfies its own characteristic equation. In particular, this implies that if $F$ is an $n \times n$ matrix, then

$$F^n = \sum_{i=1}^{n} \beta_i F^{n-i}, \qquad \beta_i \text{ constants,}$$

i.e., successive iterations of the operator $F$ yield *nothing new* after a finite number $n$ of iterations. Essential use of this fact is the basis for most of the algebraic results involving controllability, observability, and realization theory for linear systems. Unfortunately, for a general nonlinear transformation $f$, there is no analogue of the Cayley–Hamilton theorem. Consequently, there is no a priori upper bound on the number of times the transformation $f$ must be iterated to guarantee that no new *information* will be generated by further application of $f$. That is, if $x \in R^n$ is a fixed vector, then it may be that the elements $x, f(x), \ldots, f^{n-2}(x)$ are linearly independent, but $f^{n-1}(x), \ldots, f^{n+p-1}(x)$ are dependent on these elements, with $f^{n+p}(x)$ then being linearly independent for $p$ *arbitrarily large*, but finite.

A further algebraic complication is introduced by the fact that it is not possible to parameterize a general nonlinear transformation using only a finite set of numbers (parameters). For example, any linear transformation

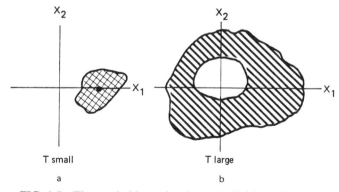

FIG. 1.5   The reachable set for the controllable oscillator.

$F: R^n \to R^n$ can be represented by a matrix of $n^2$ numbers, the elements of $F$. However, if $f: R^n \to R^n$ is a smooth transformation, all we can do, in general, is assert that $f$ is representable in a *neighborhood* of any point $x_0 \in R^n$, by an infinite series of parameters, the expansion coefficients in its multidimensional Taylor series about $x_0$. This fact introduces considerable complications into the search for *constructive* realization algorithms for nonlinear problems.

In view of these algebraic difficulties, two approaches suggest themselves:

(i)   restrict the class of nonlinear processes to those which are representable using only a finite number of parameters. Such processes include all of the multilinear and polynomial-type nonlinear processes introduced earlier;

(ii)   approximate the process under consideration by one with a finite number of parameters and provide various measures of error for the approximation. Such procedures lie at the heart of *linearization ideas*, whereby a given system is approximated by its linear part in a small neighborhood of a reference trajectory. More general approximations, using bilinear or polynomial systems, form a system-theoretic analogue of the classical Weierstrass theorem which enables us to uniformly approximate any continuous function on a closed, bounded interval by a polynomial of sufficiently high order.

These two approaches provide the theoretical (and computational) basis for consideration of general dynamical processes, and, to a large extent, justify our consideration of the special classes of nonlinear systems outlined earlier. As we shall see, an overwhelming majority of the nonlinear problems encountered in practice fall into the category of systems approximable by one or another of the types of nonlinearities that we will consider. Consequently, from a theoretical point of view, it is defensible to focus our attention on such systems.

The computational implications of the lack of a Cayley–Hamilton type of theorem are that we can no longer hope to characterize reachable sets, observable states, and so on with algorithms whose termination point can be determined *in advance* unless we impose special restrictions on the system. In addition, computation of optimal controls is hampered by the necessity to solve nonlinear two-point boundary value problems, due to the lack of a superposition principle relating the system state and co-state linearly. Finally, stability studies are complicated since system equilibria are no longer globally stable or unstable, as in the linear case. The existence of multiple equilibria, limit cycles, chaotic motion, and other *strange* attractors for nonlinear processes forces us to develop an entirely different set of computational methods for determining the location and type of such equilibria. We shall begin our analytical and computational attack on nonlinear systems in Chapter 4, following a brief survey of the relevant mathematics in Chapter 2 and a review of the linear theory in Chapter 3.

## NOTES AND REFERENCES

**Section 1.I** Nonlinear oscillations have been extensively treated in the analytical mechanics literature for at least two centuries. Good summaries of the current state of affairs are

V. I. Arnol'd, "Mathematical Methods of Classical Mechanics," Springer, Berlin, 1978.
R. Abraham and J. Marsden, "Foundations of Mechanics," 2nd Ed., Addison–Wesley, Reading, Massachusetts, 1978.

For an account of how nonlinear phenomena enter into human affairs, see

W. Weidlich and G. Haag, "Quantitative Sociology," Springer, Berlin, 1983.

Nonlinear processes arising in the theory of neutron transport and radiative transfer are discussed in

H. Kagiwada, R. Kalaba, and S. Ueno, "Multiple Scattering Processes: Inverse and Direct," Addison–Wesley, Reading, Massachusetts, 1975.

See also

G. M. Wing, "An Introduction to Transport Theory," Wiley, New York, 1962.
V. Kourganoff, "Basic Methods in Transfer Problems," Oxford Univ. Press, Oxford, 1952.

Predator–prey dynamics are extensively considered in numerous papers and volumes. A good starting point is

N. Goel, S. Maitra, and E. Montroll, On the Volterra and other nonlinear models of interacting populations, *Rev. Mod. Phys.* **43** (1971), 231–276.

and in Chapter 12 of

M. Hirsch and S. Smale, "Differential Equations, Dynamical Systems and Linear Algebra," Academic Press, New York, 1974.

Mathematical models of international conflict, including missile warfare, are considered in the works

J. V. Gillespie and D. A. Zinnes, eds., "Mathematical Systems in International Relations Research," Praeger, New York, 1977.
W. Hollist, ed., "Exploring Competitive Arms Processes," Dekker, New York, 1978.

**Section 1.II** A reasonably complete survey of the current (1983) status of nonlinear system theory is provided in

J. Casti, Recent developments and future perspectives in nonlinear system theory, *SIAM Rev.* **24** (1982), 301–331.

Nonlinear optimal control processes are treated in

S. Barnett, "Introduction to Mathematical Control Theory," Oxford Univ. Press, Oxford, 1975.

D. H. Jacobson, "Extensions of Linear-Quadratic Control, Optimization and Matrix Theory," Academic Press, New York, 1977.

**Section 1.III**    Some good general references on nonlinear phenomena and the mathematics needed to deal with them are

T. Saaty, and J. Bram, "Nonlinear Mathematics," McGraw-Hill, New York, 1964.
T. Saaty, "Modern Nonlinear Equations," McGraw-Hill, New York, 1967.
H. Davis, "Introduction to Nonlinear Differential and Integral Equations," Dover, New York, 1962.

# 2

# Mathematical Tools
# of Nonlinear System Theory

## I. INTRODUCTION

The theory of linear dynamical processes is, mathematically speaking, an advanced exercise in linear algebra and matrix theory. As shown in Chapter 3, the essential ingredients of linear theory involve various conditions concerning the ranks of certain matrices and the properties of certain polynomials. In short, no mathematics beyond the theory of vector spaces and linear operators is required for a rather complete account of linear system theory. When we extend our horizons to cover nonlinear processes, the situation changes noticeably. Due to the considerations partially outlined in Chapter 1, we can no longer make do with the relatively simple tools of linear mathematics. A much more sophisticated armada of mathematical weaponry ranging from differential topology to Lie algebras to algebraic geometry will be required to make a real dent in the problem of understanding nonlinear systems. Fortunately, it is not necessary to utilize all of the machinery of modern mathematics to say something substantial about processes of interest, so we shall devote this chapter to a summary of the essential aspects of algebra, geometry, and analysis, which prove to be of system-theoretic interest.

## II. ALGEBRAIC CONCEPTS

A great deal of a system theorist's daily activity has its basis in modern abstract algebra. In this section, we briefly review the idea of a group, ring, field, and module as background for their utilization in the study of system structure.

The concept of a *group* is an abstract outgrowth of the basic idea of addition of two real numbers. More specifically, given a set $G$ with a binary operation $\circ$, defined on it, we say $G$ is a group if the following properties hold:

  (i)  $g_1 \circ (g_1 \circ g_2) = (g_1 \circ g_2) \circ g_3$ for $g_1, g_2, g_3 \in G$ (*associativity*);
  (ii)  there exists an element $e \in G$, such that $g \circ e = e \circ g = g$ for all $g \in G$ (*existence of identity*);
  (iii)  for each $g \in G$, there exists an element $g^{-1} \in G$ such that $g \circ g^{-1} = g^{-1} \circ g = e$ (*existence of inverses*).

If, in addition, it turns out that $g_1 \circ g_2 = g_2 \circ g_1$ for all $g_1, g_2 \in G$, then we say that $G$ is an *abelian* group. We will often have occasion to consider only a subset $H$ of $G$ possessing properties (i)–(iii), in which case we call $H$ a *subgroup* of $G$.

It is of considerable interest to know when two groups $G$ and $F$ possess the same abstract structure. That is, given the operation $\circ$ in $G$ and the operation $*$ in $F$, when does the product $g_1 \circ g_2$ correspond in a 1–1 operation-preserving fashion to the product $f_1 * f_2$ in $F$? This leads to the concept of group homomorphisms and isomorphisms. More precisely, if $\alpha: G \to F$, we say $\alpha$ is a *group homomorphism* if

$$\alpha(g_1 \circ g_2) = \alpha(g_1) * \alpha(g_2)$$

for all $g_1, g_2 \in G$. If, in addition, $\alpha$ is 1–1, then we call $\alpha$ a *group isomorphism*.

**Example:   State-Space Isomorphism Theorem**

To illustrate the group-theoretic ideas introduced above, let $X$ be a group, with $C$ a subgroup of $X$. Further, let $U$ and $Y$ be two arbitrary sets with the maps $f: X \to X$, $g: U \to X$, $h: X \to Y$, with $h$ being 1–1 on the space $X/C$, the set of equivalence classes of $X$ relative to $C$. (Remark: $x_1, x_2 \in X$ belong to the same element of $X/C$ if and only if $x_1 - x_2 \in C$.) Let the system dynamics evolving on $X$ be described by the rule

$$x(k + 1) = g[u(k)] \circ f \circ x(k),$$
$$y(k) = h[x(k)]. \tag{$\Sigma$}$$

Thus, the nonlinear system $\Sigma$ evolves on the state space $X$, with the inputs from $U$ and outputs in $Y$ being determined by the maps $g$ and $h$. In the case of finite-dimensional linear systems, i.e., $X = R^n$, $U = R^m$, and $Y = R^p$, with $f$, $g$, and $h$ appropriate matrices, it is known that two canonical systems $\Sigma$ and $\hat{\Sigma}$ are equivalent through a state-space isomophism. That is, there exists an isomophism $t: X \rightarrow X$ such that

$$\hat{f} = t \cdot f \cdot t^{-1}, \qquad \hat{g} = t \cdot g, \qquad \hat{h} = h \cdot t^{-1}.$$

Corresponding to this result, we have the following:

**Theorem**  *Let $\Sigma$ and $\hat{\Sigma}$ be two systems whose state spaces are the finite groups $X$ and $\hat{X}$, respectively. Assume the dynamics*

$$x(k + 1) = g[u(k)] \circ f \circ x(k), \quad y = h[x(k)], \quad x(0) = e,$$

$$\hat{x}(k + 1) = \hat{g}[\hat{u}(k)] * \hat{f} * \hat{x}(k), \quad \hat{y} = \hat{h}[\hat{x}(k)], \quad \hat{x}(0) = \hat{e}$$

*define the same input–output map. Assume that $\Sigma$ and $\hat{\Sigma}$ are both controllable and observable (i.e., any state can be reached from any other and any two distinct states give rise to distinct outputs for some input string). Then $X$ and $\hat{X}$ are isomorphic as groups and the map*

$$z: \quad f \rightarrow \hat{f},$$

$$z: \quad g[u] \rightarrow \hat{g}[\hat{u}]$$

*can be extended to a group isomorphism $z: X \rightarrow \hat{X}$.*

Thus, we see that the state-space isomophism theorem from the linear theory really does not rely upon the linearity of the maps $f$, $g$, and $h$, nor upon the special properties of the Euclidean space $R^n$. Rather, the essential content of the theorem lies in the *algebraic* structure of the state space: it is a group. Results of this type form the basis for the so-called *algebraic theory of systems*, which we shall review in some detail in Chapter 3.

Imposing a second binary operation $*$, called multiplication, on the group $G$, we are led to the concept of a *ring*. To motivate the properties to impose on the operation $*$ to make it compatible with $\circ$, we return to the model of the real numbers with the operations of addition and multiplication. Thus, we define a set $R$ to be a *ring* if the following properties hold:

1. properties (i)–(iii) for a group relative to the operation $\circ$,
2. $r_1 * (r_2 * r_3) = (r_1 * r_2) * r_3$,
3. $r_1 * (r_2 \circ r_3) = (r_1 * r_2) \circ (r_1 * r_3)$ for all $r_1, r_2, r_3 \in R$.

If, in addition, $r_1 * r_2 = r_2 * r_1$ for all $r_1, r_2 \in R$, then we say $R$ is a *commutative ring*. Further, if there exists an element $z \in R$ such that $z * r = r * z = r$ for all $r \in R$, then $R$ is called a *ring with unit*.

The most important ring for system-theoretic purposes is the ring of polynomials in the indeterminate $z$ with coefficients in a field $k$, denoted $k[z]$. A typical element in $k[z]$ is

$$\sum_{i=0}^{p} \alpha_i z^i, \qquad \alpha_i \in k,$$

for some integer $p \geq 0$. The polynomial ring $k[z]$ possesses some important properties not shared by all commutative rings. For instance, if $p, q, r \in k[z]$, and if $p$ is not the zero polynomial, then the identity

$$pq = pr$$

implies $q = r$. This property is called *cancellation* and holds despite the fact that we cannot do division in $k[z]$. Any commutative ring having the cancellation property is called an *integral domain* or, more simply, a *domain*.

A second important property of $k[z]$ is that it forms what is called a *principal ideal domain*. To understand the implications of this fact, we first need a bit more terminology. Let $I$ be a subset of $R$ which is closed under both of the operations ∘ and ∗, i.e.,

$$i_1, i_2 \in I, \quad r_1, r_2 \in R \Rightarrow (r_1 * i_1) \circ (r_2 * i_2) \in I.$$

The set $I$ is called an *ideal* of $R$. Intuitively, any element of $I$ *absorbs* the product of itself with any element of $R$. In vector space terms, an ideal resembles a subspace, although it is important to note that an ideal is *not* the same thing as a *subring*, which has the following set of properties:

$S$ is a *subring* of $R$ if

  (i)   1, the multiplicative identity is in $S$ and
  (ii)  $s_1, s_2 \in S \Rightarrow (s_1 \circ s_2) \in S$ and $(s_1 * s_2) \in S$.

Now consider an element $r_1 \in R$. We say that $r_2 \in R$ divides $r_1$ if we can find an $r_3 \in R$ such that

$$r_1 = r_2 * r_3.$$

If there exists an $i \in I$ such that $i$ divides every $j \in I$, then we call $I$ a *principal ideal*. In analogy with vector spaces, a principal ideal resembles a subspace of dimension one. If $R$ is a domain such that every ideal of $R$ is a principal ideal, then we call $R$ a *principal ideal domain*. As noted earlier, $k[z]$ is an important example of such a ring.

The last important purely algebraic concept we shall need is the idea of an *R-module*. Essentially, this is a generalization of the idea of a vector space where instead of using a coefficient field such as the real or complex numbers, we let the coefficients be elements of a commutative ring $R$. More specifically, given a ring $R$ and an abelian group $G$, the $R$-module $M$ consists of the set of elements of $G$ satisfying

  (i)    $r(g_1 + g_2) = (rg_1) + (rg_2)$,
  (ii)   $(r_1 + r_2)g = (r_1 g) + (r_2 g)$,
  (iii)  $(r_1 r_2)g = r_1(r_2 g)$,
  (iv)   $1g = g$,

for all $r, r_1, r_2 \in R$, $g \in G$. (Note that here we have replaced the symbols ∘

and $*$ by the usual notation for addition and multiplication. This convention will remain throughout the book, unless explicit mention is made to the contrary.)

An important property of the $R$-module $M$ *not* shared by a vector space is the possibility that in $M$ we may have the product $rm = 0$, with $r \neq 0$ and $m \neq 0$. For instance, if $M$ is the group of infinitely differentiable real functions, taking $R$ to be the ring of polynomials in the derivative operator $D$, then $p(D)f = 0$ is equivalent to solving the linear differential equation

$$D^n f + a_1 D^{n-1} f + \cdots + a_n = 0,$$

a typical operation in applied engineering. Any function $f$ satisfying such an equation is called a *torsion* element of the module $M$. In general, $m \in M$, $m \neq 0$, is a torsion element if there exists some $r \in R, r \neq 0$, such that $rm = 0$.

An $R$-module $M$ is termed *finitely generated* if there is a subset $\{m_1, m_2, \ldots, m_n\}$ of $M$ with the property that any element $m \in M$ can be expressed as

$$m = \sum_{i=1}^{n} r_i m_i$$

for some set of elements $\{r_i\}$ in $R$. The elements $\{m_i\}$ are said to be *linearly independent* if

$$\sum_{i=1}^{n} r_i m_i = 0 \Rightarrow r_i = 0, \qquad i = 1, 2, \ldots, n.$$

If the set $\{m_i\}$ generates $M$ and if the $\{m_i\}$ are linearly independent, then we call $M$ a *free module* on the basis $\{m_i\}$. The *rank* of a free module equals the number of elements in any basis.

### Example:  Matrix Fractions

To tie some of the foregoing ideas together, let us consider the problem of determining two polynomial matrices $N(\lambda)$, $D(\lambda)$ such that a given transfer function matrix $Z(\lambda)$ may be expressed as

$$Z(\lambda) = N(\lambda)D^{-1}(\lambda)$$

with $N(\lambda)$ and $D(\lambda)$ having no matrix factors in common other than unimodular matrix factors (i.e., factors whose determinant equals 1). The importance of this problem in linear system theory is that the usual way of expressing the matrix $Z(\lambda)$ is

$$Z(\lambda) = A(\lambda)/b(\lambda),$$

where $b(\lambda)$ is a denominator polynomial which is always equal to the *minimal* polynomial of the system matrix $F$ in an internal realization $\Sigma = (F, G, H)$

of the transfer matrix $Z(\lambda)$. The problem is that the number of dynamical elements needed to realize $Z(\lambda)$ equals the degree of the *characteristic* polynomial $\chi_F(\lambda)$ of $F$ and $b(\lambda)$ is only a factor of $\chi_F(\lambda)$. Thus, the usual view of transfer matrices does not enable us to see by inspection how many dynamical elements are needed to realize it. The matrix fraction method overcomes this difficulty. Let us examine how the above algebraic apparatus can be employed to compute the factors $N(\lambda)$ and $D(\lambda)$.

We begin by selecting the ring $R$ to be $k[z]$, and identify

$$[b(\lambda)I]^{-1}A(\lambda) = N(\lambda)D^{-1}(\lambda).$$

We can express this equation in the free-module form

$$[-b(\lambda)I \ \ A(\lambda)]\begin{bmatrix} N(\lambda) \\ D(\lambda) \end{bmatrix} = [0],$$

i.e.,

$$T(\lambda)\begin{bmatrix} N(\lambda) \\ D(\lambda) \end{bmatrix} = [0].$$

In other words, each column of the matrix

$$\begin{bmatrix} N(\lambda) \\ D(\lambda) \end{bmatrix}$$

represents an element of the kernel ker $T(\lambda)$ of $T(\lambda)$. The problem of finding the elements $N(\lambda)$, $D(\lambda)$ of the matrix fraction has been reduced to finding a basis for $\ker[-b(\lambda)I \ A(\lambda)]$, i.e., to solving a linear equation on a free $k[z]$ − module.

As illustration of the preceding ideas, consider the case where

$$Z(\lambda) = \begin{bmatrix} \dfrac{2\lambda + 3}{(\lambda + 1)(\lambda + 2)} & \dfrac{1}{(\lambda + 1)(\lambda + 2)} \\ \dfrac{3\lambda + 4}{(\lambda + 1)(\lambda + 2)} & \dfrac{1}{\lambda + 1} \end{bmatrix}.$$

Then $b(\lambda) = (\lambda + 1)(\lambda + 2)$ and

$$A(\lambda) = \begin{bmatrix} 2\lambda + 3 & 1 \\ 3\lambda + 4 & \lambda + 2 \end{bmatrix}.$$

It is easy to compute the minimal realization of $Z(\lambda)$ as

$$F = \begin{bmatrix} -1 & 0 & 0 \\ 0 & -2 & 0 \\ 0 & 0 & -2 \end{bmatrix}, \quad G = \begin{bmatrix} 1 & 1 \\ 1 & 0 \\ 0 & 1 \end{bmatrix}, \quad H = \begin{bmatrix} 1 & 1 & -1 \\ 1 & 2 & 0 \end{bmatrix}$$

a system of dimension $3 > 2 = $ degree of $b(\lambda)$. Upon solving the corresponding matrix fraction problem sketched above, we find

$$N(\lambda) = \begin{bmatrix} 2\lambda + 3 & 4\lambda + 4 \\ 3\lambda + 4 & 6\lambda + 6 \end{bmatrix},$$

$$D(\lambda) = \begin{bmatrix} \lambda^2 + 3\lambda + 2 & (2\lambda + 1)(\lambda + 2) \\ 0 & \lambda + 2 \end{bmatrix}.$$

Since det $D(\lambda)$ is $k$-proportional to the characteristic polynomial $\chi_F(\lambda)$ of the minimal dimension system matrix realizing $Z(\lambda)$, we can verify from $D(\lambda)$ that the minimal realization must have dimension $3 = $ degree det $D(\lambda)$.

An important part of any mathematical modeling activity is knowing when and how to discard redundant information. In algebra, the idea of *factoring out* extraneous or repetitive data is accomplished through the concept of a *quotient set*. Intuitively, the notion of a quotient is nothing more than dividing the total set of objects under consideration into those which are of interest and those which are not. The rule of separating interesting objects from uninteresting is based on the idea of two elements being *equivalent*. Roughly speaking, we say two objects are equivalent if they differ only in details which are not important for the problem at hand. But, let us be more specific.

Let $S$ be some set. A binary relation $\lambda$ on $S$ is said to be an *equivalence relation* if the following properties hold:

(i)   $s \in S$, $(s, s) \in \lambda$ *(reflexive)*;
(ii)  $(s_1, s_2) \in \lambda$, $(s_2, s_1) \in \lambda$ for all $s_1, s_2 \in S$ *(symmetric)*;
(iii) $(s_1, s_2) \in \lambda$ and $(s_2, s_3) \in \lambda \Rightarrow (s_1, s_3) \in \lambda$ for $s_1, s_2, s_3 \in S$ *(transitive)*.

The importance of an equivalence relation is that it partitions the set $S$ into disjoint *equivalence classes* such that two elements of $S$ are in the same class if and only if they are equivalent, i.e., if an only if they are in the relation $\lambda$. We denote the set of equivalence classes by $S/\lambda$ and define the natural projection $\pi: S \to S/\lambda$, which acts to send every $s \in S$ onto its equivalence class in $S/\lambda$. The function $\pi$ is a mechanism whereby we can discard details of no particular interest.

The utility of the quotient concept is better understood if we consider an arbitrary function $f: S \to T$, where $T$ is another set. Further, let us assume that $f$ cannot distinguish the discarded information, i.e.,

$$(s_1, s_2) \in \lambda \Leftrightarrow f(s_1) = f(s_2).$$

Then, there exists a *unique* function

$$g: \quad S/\lambda \to T$$

such that $g \circ \pi = f$. Diagramatically,

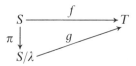

Thus, if we are interested in the calculation represented by $f$, then it suffices to make the corresponding calculation with $g$ on the set $S/\lambda$. Since $S/\lambda$ is usually a much smaller set than $S$, the use of $g$ instead of $f$ can result in a substantial computational advantage. We shall consider an important application of the foregoing ideas to controllability theory. But first let us consider how these ideas can be sharpened when we impose additional structure upon the set $S$, namely, if we let $S$ be a $k$-vector-space $V$.

Suppose that $V$ is a $k$-vector-space and that $W$ is a subspace of $V$. If we agree not to distinguish vectors if they differ only by an element in $W$, then we are led to the equivalence relation $\lambda_W$,

$$(v_1, v_2) \in \lambda_W \qquad \text{if and only if} \quad v_1 - v_2 \in W.$$

In this vector space setting, it is customary to denote $V/\lambda_W$ as $V/W$. In this case, the operations of addition and scalar multiplication in $V$ can be naturally extended to $V/W$ so that $V/W$ is a vector space in its own right. This is accomplished in the following way: if $[v]$ denotes the class of the element $v \in V$ in $V/W$, then

$$[v_1] + [v_2] = [v_1 + v_2], \qquad v_1, v_2 \in V,$$

and

$$[\alpha v] = \alpha[v], \qquad \alpha \in k.$$

Note that the kernel of the projection map $\pi \colon V \twoheadrightarrow V/W$ is just $W$, i.e., if $w \in W$, $[w]$ plays the role of the additive identity in $V/W$. Now let $L \colon V \twoheadrightarrow X$ be a linear map such that $W \subset \ker L$. Then for any $w \in W$ we have

$$L(v + w) = Lv,$$

i.e., $L$ respects the equivalence relation on $V$ and, as a result, there exists a unique linear map $\bar{L} \colon V/W \twoheadrightarrow X$ such that

$$\bar{L} \cdot \pi = L.$$

To see how the preceding considerations enable us to selectively discard information, we consider the set of equations

$$x_{i+1} = Ax_i, \qquad i = 0, 1, 2, \dots,$$

where $A \colon X \twoheadrightarrow X$ is a linear map on the $k$-vector-space $X$. Suppose that we wish to *discard* the subspace $U \subset X$. Utilizing the projection map $\pi: X \to X/U$, we have

$$\pi x_{i+1} = \pi A x_i, \qquad i = 0, 1, 2, \dots.$$

Our task is to convert this equation into one of the original form, but now in $X/U$ rather than in $X$. To do this, we must *pass* $\pi$ through the map $A$. This necessitates introducing the idea of an $A$-invariant subspace.

A subspace $W$ of $V$ is called *A-invariant* if

$$AW \subset W,$$

i.e., $A$ maps elements of $W$ into $W$. If $\pi: V \to V/W$ is the natural projection, then if $W$ is $A$-invariant,

$$(\pi \circ A)w = 0 \qquad \text{for} \quad w \in W.$$

In this event there exists a unique map $\bar{A}: V/W \to V/W$ which satisfies

$$\pi \circ A = \bar{A} \circ \pi.$$

This follows from the earlier discussion since $W \subset \ker(\pi \circ A)$. $\bar{A}$ is called the *induced map* of $A$ in $V/W$.

Continuing with the example, we now suppose that $U$ is an $A$-invariant subspace of $X$. Then we have

$$\pi x_{i+1} = (\bar{A} \circ \pi) x_i$$

or, using our earlier notation

$$[x_{i+1}] = \bar{A}[x_i], \qquad i = 0, 1, 2, \dots.$$

If $\dim X = n$ and $\dim U = p$, then it is easy to verify that $\bar{A}$ is an $(n - p \times (n - p)$ matrix, a reduction of dimension that may be crucial in some practical situations. Let us now examine a slightly more concrete application of these ideas involving quotient sets.

### Example: Controllability Subspaces

Consider the constant linear system

$$x_{i+1} = F x_i + G u_i, \qquad x_0 = 0, \qquad i = 0, 1, 2, \dots, \tag{$\Sigma$}$$

where $F: X \to X$ and $G: U \to X$ are linear maps and $X$ and $U$ are $n$- and $m$-dimensional $k$-vector-spaces, respectively. Let $\gamma = \operatorname{Im} G$, i.e., $\gamma$ is the subspace generated by the columns of $G$ and define

$$\langle F | \gamma \rangle = \gamma + F\gamma + F^2\gamma + \cdots + F^{n-1}\gamma.$$

As is well known from linear system theory, $\langle F | \gamma \rangle$ represents the subspace of reachable (or controllable) states in $X$. The system $\Sigma$ is completely reachable if $\langle F|\gamma \rangle = X$.

We wish to employ the quotient set ideas to show that the states not in $\langle F|\gamma \rangle$ are completely *cut off* from the control inputs $\{u_i\}$. The first step is to show that $\langle F|\gamma \rangle$ is an $F$-invariant subspace of $X$. We have

$$F\langle F|\gamma \rangle = F(\gamma + F\gamma + F^2\gamma + \cdots + {}^{n-1}\gamma) = F\gamma + F^2\gamma + \cdots + F^n\gamma$$

$$\subset (F\gamma + F^2\gamma + \cdots + F^{n-1}\gamma) + \langle F|\gamma \rangle = \langle F|\gamma \rangle,$$

where the containment step $F^n\gamma \subset \langle F|\gamma \rangle$ is justified by appeal to the Cayley–Hamilton theorem. Now we introduce the projection $\pi \colon X \to X/\langle F|\gamma \rangle$. Thus, we separate the states in $X$ which can be reached from those which cannot and discard the reachable states. Applying the projection $\pi$ to the system dynamics yields

$$\pi(x_{i+1}) = (\pi \circ F)x_i + (\pi \circ G)u_i$$

or, since $\pi \circ G = 0$ because $\langle F|\gamma \rangle = \ker \pi$ and $\gamma \subset \langle F|\gamma \rangle$,

$$[x_{i+1}] = \bar{F}[x_i], \qquad i = 0, 1, \ldots,$$

showing that in $X/\langle F|\gamma \rangle$ the control $u_i$ does not appear.

The quotient set idea in a vector space setting enables us to discard *linearity* in an extremely compact fashion by factoring out subspaces from a larger vector space. An analogue to this idea for nonlinear situations involves the concept of a *tensor product* space, which, in essence, is designed to discard *bilinearity* or, more generally, *multilinearity*. To understand the implications of tensor product spaces for system theory, we must first consider the concept of a bilinear map.

Let $V_1$, $V_2$, $V_3$, be $k$-vector-spaces. Then we say a map $B \colon V_1 \times V_2 \to V_3$ is *bilinear* if

(i)  $B(\alpha v + \beta w, y) = \alpha B(v, y) + \beta B(w, y)$,
(ii)  $B(v, \alpha y + \beta z) = \alpha B(v, y) + \beta B(v, z)$

for all $v, w \in V_1$, $y, z \in V_2$, $\alpha, \beta \in k$. Since the image $B$ is not, in general, a subspace of $V_3$ (in contrast with the case of a linear map), we call the smallest subspace of $V_3$ containing Im $B$, the *subspace generated by* Im $B$. Now we can define the tensor product of $V_1$ and $V_2$.

Given $k$-vector-spaces $V_1$, $V_2$, $V_3$, and $V_4$, together with the bilinear map $B \colon V_1 \times V_2 \to V_3$, we call $(V_3, B)$ a *tensor product* for $V_1$ and $V_2$ if

(i)   the subspace of $V_3$ generated by Im $B$ is $V_3$ itself;
(ii)  for each bilinear map $\hat{B} \colon V_1 \times V_2 \to V_4$, there is a *linear* map $\hat{\bar{B}} \colon V_3 \to V_4$ such that

$$\hat{B} = \hat{\bar{B}} \circ B.$$

The situation is depicted schematically using the standard notation $V_1 \otimes V_2$ for $V_3$:

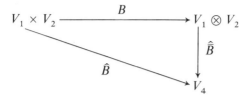

## Example

Let $V_1 = k^2$, $V_2 = k^3$, with $v_1 \in V_1$, $v_2 \in V_2$ being 2- and 3-dimensional vectors with components $v_1 = (a_1, a_2)$, $v_2 = (b_1, b_2, b_3)$ in the field $k$, respectively. Then if we write $v_1 \otimes v_2$, for the tensor product of $v_1$ and $v_2$, we can define

$$v_1 \otimes v_2 = \begin{bmatrix} a_1 b_1 & a_1 b_2 & a_1 b_3 \\ a_2 b_1 & a_2 b_2 & a_2 b_3 \end{bmatrix},$$

i.e., $v_1 \otimes v_2$ is a $2 \times 3$ matrix. The tensor product $V_1 \otimes V_2$ can then be taken to be all such arrays with the usual matrix operations of addition and scalar multiplication.

The most common use of the tensor product is to form the product of two linear maps. Let $V_1, V_2, V_3, V_4$ be $k$-vector-spaces with

$$L_1 : \quad V_1 \to V_2, \qquad L_2 : \quad V_3 \to V_4$$

linear maps. Then we can define a bilinear map $\hat{B} : V_1 \times V_3 \to V_2 \otimes V_4$ by

$$\hat{B}(v_1, v_3) = (L_1 v_1) \otimes (L_2 v_3).$$

We call the *unique* linear map $\hat{B}$ the tensor product of $L_1$ and $L_2$ and denote it by $L_1 \otimes L_2$. It is important to emphasize that $L_1 \otimes L_2$ is a *linear* map,

$$L_1 \otimes L_2 : \quad V_1 \otimes V_3 \to V_2 \otimes V_4.$$

In other words, we may study the action of the bilinear map $\hat{B}$, defined in terms of $L_1$ and $L_2$, by studying the action of the induced linear map $L_1 \otimes L_2$.

If we have bases $\{b_1, b_2, \ldots, b_m\}$ for $V_1$ and $\{c_1, c_2, \ldots, c_n\}$ for $V_2$, we can easily generate a basis $\{b_i \otimes c_j : i = 1, 2, \ldots, m; j = 1, 2, \ldots, n\}$ for $V_1 \otimes V_2$. Thus, if $\dim V_1 = m$, $\dim V_2 = n$, then $\dim V_1 \otimes V_2 = nm$. It is an easy exercise to verify that the matrix representation of $L_1 \otimes L_2$ is

$$[L_1 \otimes L_2]_{ij} = [L_1]_{ij} L_2, \qquad i = 1, 2, \ldots, n, \quad j = 1, 2, \ldots, m,$$

where $[M]_{ij}$ denotes the $(i, j)$ element of a matrix $M$.

## Example: Bilinear Functions of a Linear System

We have remarked that the tensor product operation allows us to study the properties of a bilinear function by forming an equivalent linear function. To make this notion more concrete, we consider the set of linear differential equations

$$\dot{x} = Fx,$$

where $F: X \to X$ is a linear map with $X$ a finite-dimensional real vector space. Suppose that $\hat{B}: X \times X \to R$ is a real bilinear map on $X$. The preceding discussion shows that $\hat{B}$ can be understood in terms of a unique linear map $\hat{\hat{B}}: X \otimes X \to R$. Thus, if we want to study $\hat{B}$ on the Cartesian product space $X \times X$, it suffices to study the time behavior of $(x \otimes x)(t)$ in $X \otimes X$. Forming the derivative of $x \otimes x$, we have

$$\frac{d}{dt}(x \otimes x) = (\dot{x} \otimes x) + (x \otimes \dot{x}) \qquad \text{(since } \otimes \text{ is bilinear)}$$

$$= Ax \otimes x + x \otimes Ax$$

$$= (Ax \otimes Ix) + (Ix \otimes Ax)$$

$$= (A \otimes I)(x \otimes x) + (I \otimes A)(x \otimes x)$$

$$= [(A \otimes I) + (I \otimes A)](x \otimes x).$$

Hence, we see that the dynamical behavior of the bilinear function $x \otimes x$ is also governed by a linear equation with the associated linear map being

$$(A \otimes I) + (I \otimes A): \quad X \otimes X \to X \otimes X.$$

## III. SOME IDEAS FROM DIFFERENTIAL GEOMETRY

### A. Differentiable Manifolds

The tools of abstract and linear algebra suffice for the description and analysis of virtually all problems arising in the study of *linear* systems. However, to study global properties of nonlinear systems it is necessary to piece together a collection of local results using procedures developed in the theory of differentiable manifolds and Lie algebras of vector fields. Here we consider the relevant concepts lying at the interface of algebra and geometry which are needed for our subsequent development.

A *differentiable manifold* is a set $M$ of elements equipped with a differentiable structure. By this we mean a triple $(M, \tau, \Phi)$, where $\tau$ is a topology on $M$ and $\Phi$ is a collection of homeomorphisms $M \to R^n$. The topology $\tau$ is assumed to be such that the topological space $(M, \tau)$ is both *Hausdorff* and *separable*.

The collection of maps $\Phi = \{\phi_i : M_i \to N_i, M_i \subset M, N_i \subset R^n\}$ is assumed to have the following properties:

(i)   the collection of open sets $\{M_i\}$ covers $M$, i.e., $M = \cup M_i$;

(ii)   $\phi_i$ maps its domain $M_i$ homeomorphically onto $N_i$, an open subset of $R^n$;

(iii)   if $M_i \cap M_j \neq \{\phi\}$, and if $\phi_i : M_i \cap M_j \to P_{ij}$ and $\phi_j : M_i \cap M_j \to Q_{ij}$, then $\phi_j \circ \phi_i^{-1}$ is a diffeomorphism of $P_{ij} \to Q_{ij}$ (see Fig. 2.1).

The locally defined maps $\phi_i$ are called *charts* and the collection $\Phi$ is called an *atlas*. In short, a differentiable manifold is a space upon which we can do differential calculus in a consistent way. In general, the space $M$ is some curved manifold like a sphere, torus, cylinder, etc., and it is necessary to introduce the maps $\Phi$ to transfer our local calculations from $M$ to $R^n$, where the usual operations associated with the differential calculus (addition, quotient, limits) are well defined. It is intuitively satisfying to think of an $n$-dimensional differentiable manifold $M$ as being a space which locally *looks* like $R^n$. We then make statements about the global object $M$ by piecing together the local information obtained for each $N_i$.

Let us consider some other interesting examples of differentiable manifolds.

## 1. The Unimodular Group

Let $M = R^{n^2}$, viewed as the space of all real $n \times n$ matrices, and let $\phi : R^{n^2} \to R$, be the determinant function. Then $\phi^{-1}(1)$ is the set of all $n \times n$ matrices of determinant 1.

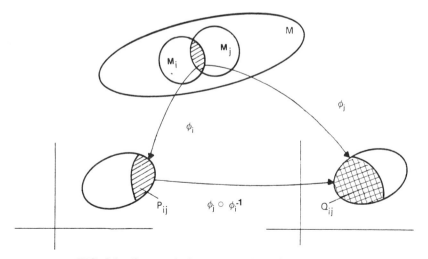

**FIG. 2.1**   Geometrical representation of two charts.

2. The Orthogonal Group

Let $M = R^{n^2}$ and let $\phi: R^{n^2} \to R^{n(n+1)/2}$ be the map which associates each $n \times n$ matrix $A$ with the symmetric matrix $AA'$. Define $M_0 = \phi^{-1}(I)$. Then $M_0$ is a differentiable manifold called the orthogonal group.

3. Differentiable (Analytic) Varieties in $R^n$

Here we let $\phi_1, \phi_2, \ldots \phi_m$ be $C^\infty$ (analytic) functions on $R^n$ and suppose that

$$\text{rank} [\text{grad } \phi_1, \text{grad } \phi_2, \ldots, \text{grad } \phi_m] = m$$

at each point on the set $M = \{x : \phi_i(x) = 0, i = 1, 2, \ldots, m\}$. Then the set $M$ can be given the structure of a differentiable (analytic) manifold.

## B. Vector Fields

Dynamical system theory is concerned with the behavior of the trajectory of a system as it moves on a state space which, generally speaking, is not a vector space but a manifold $M$. Loosely speaking, a vector field is a rule which assigns the *direction* and magnitude of the system trajectory at each point of $M$. Before formalizing this concept, we must first introduce the concept of a tangent vector at a point $m \in M$.

Let $M$ be an $n$-dimensional manifold and let $F(M)$ be the set of all $C^\infty$ functions on $M$, i.e.,

$$F(M) = \{ f : M \to R, f \in C^\infty \}.$$

A *tangent vector* at $m \in M$ is an operator $v : F(M) \to R^n$ such that

(i)   $v(f + g) = v(f) + v(g)$,
(ii)  $v(fg) = v(f) \cdot g(m) + v(g) \cdot f(m)$

for all $f, g \in F(M)$. To put this coordinate-free definition into more familiar terms, if $x_1, x_2, \ldots, x_n$ define a local coordinate system in the neighborhood of a point $m \in M$, then for each $i$, $v(f) = (\partial f/\partial x_i)_m$ defines a tangent vector to $M$ at $m$. The set of objects $(\partial f/\partial x_i)_m$ forms a basis for the set of all tangent vectors at $m$, i.e., for the *tangent space* at $m$, denoted $T_m(M)$ (see Fig. 2.2).

A vector field $v$ on $M$ is now understood to be a map $m \xrightarrow{v} T_m(M)$. But, since the elements $(\partial/\partial x_i)$ form a basis for $T_m(M)$, we can represent a $C^\infty$-vector field as

$$m \xrightarrow{v} f_1(m) \frac{\partial}{\partial x_i} + f_2(m) \frac{\partial}{\partial x_2} + \cdots + f_n(m) \frac{\partial}{\partial x_n},$$

where the functions $f_i(\cdot)$ are $C^\infty$ on $M$.

This notation makes the connection between the vector field $v$ and a set of differential equations

$$\dot{x}_1 = f_1(x_1, x_2, \ldots, x_n),$$
$$\dot{x}_2 = f_2(x_1, x_2, \ldots, x_n),$$
$$\vdots$$
$$\dot{x}_n = f_n(x_1, x_2, \ldots, x_n).$$

The functions $x_1(t), \ldots, x_n(t)$ satisfy this system of equations if and only if the curve

$$\gamma(t) = (x_1(t), \ldots, x_n(t))$$

is an integral manifold for the vector field

$$v = f_1 \frac{\partial}{\partial x_1} + f_2 \frac{\partial}{\partial x_2} + \cdots + f_n \frac{\partial}{\partial x_n}.$$

(Note that $\gamma$ is called an *integral manifold* for $v$ if the tangent vector to $\gamma$ at time $t$ is $v(\gamma(t))$ for each $t$.) As an example, consider the equations

$$\dot{x}_1 = x_1, \qquad \dot{x}_2 = x_2$$

having the solution $x_1(t) = c_1 e^t$, $x_2(t) = c_2 e^t$. The curve $\gamma(t) = (x_1(t), x_2(t)) = (c_1 e^t, c_2 e^t)$ is the integral manifold for the vector field

$$v = x_1 \frac{\partial}{\partial x_1} + x_2 \frac{\partial}{\partial x_2},$$

Since $x_2(t) = (c_2/c_1)x_1(t)$, we see that the only integral manifolds are the straight lines through the origin, plus the trivial case when $\gamma(t) = (0, 0)$ for all $t$.

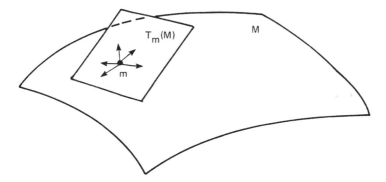

**FIG. 2.2**  The tangent space of $M$ at $m$.

When we speak of a differentiable dynamical system being on a manifold, what we mean is that at each point $m \in M$, we can choose local coordinates such that the vector field $v: M \to T_m(M)$ can be locally represented near $m$ by the differential equation

$$\dot{x} = f(x, t).$$

Thus, *locally* there is no difference between studying a differential equation on a manifold or studying it on $R^n$. It is only when we are concerned with the *global* properties of the system that the distinction becomes important as the next example illustrates.

**Example:    A Nonlinear Electrical Network**

Consider the RC-electrical circuit depicted schematically in Fig. 2.3. Here we assume the capacitor C is linear with constant characteristics, while the resistor R has the characteristic depicted in Fig. 2.4, i.e.,

$$i_R = f(v_R),$$

where $i_R$ is the current through R and $v_R$ is the voltage across R. (Since the function $f(\cdot)$ may not be linear, Ohm's Law is not assumed to hold). There are five variables in this circuit:

$$q(t) = \text{capacitor charge,}$$

$$v_R(t) = \text{resistor voltage,}$$

$$v_C(t) = \text{capacitor voltage,}$$

$$i_R(t) = \text{resistor current,}$$

$$i_C(t) = \text{capacitor current.}$$

The five basic variables are subject to three constraints:

(i)   *Branch characteristics,*

$$i_R = f(v_R), \qquad q = Cv_C.$$

(ii)   *Kirchoff's Laws,*

$$v_R - v_C = 0, \qquad i_R + i_C = 0.$$

(iii)   *Maxwell's Equations,*

$$\frac{dq}{dt} = i_C.$$

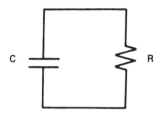

**FIG. 2.3**   An RC-circuit.

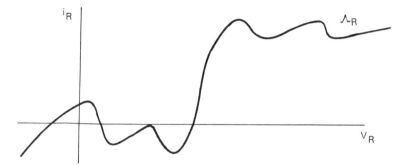

**FIG. 2.4**   The resistor characteristic.

Now consider Fig. 2.4. The pair $(v_R, i_R)$, is defined on $R^2$; however, the constraint $i_R = f(v_R)$ forces the pair to lie on $\Lambda_R$, a very small portion of $R^2$. In short, the pair $(v_R, i_R)$ must lie on the differentiable *manifold* $\Lambda_R$ (assuming the function $f(\cdot)$ is smooth). The other constraints of type (i) and (ii) are all linear, forcing the relevant variables to lie on appropriate *subspaces* of $R^2$. Define

$$\Lambda = \{(q, v_R, v_C, i_R, i_C) \in R^5 : i_R = f(v_R), \qquad q = Cv_C\},$$

$$K = \{(q, v_R, v_C, i_R, i_C) \in R^5 : v_R - v_C = 0, \qquad i_R + i_C = 0\}.$$

Since the five variables must simultaneously satisfy constraints (i), (ii), and (iii), we have the relation

$$(q, v_R, v_C, i_R, i_C) \in \Lambda \cap (R^1 \times K) \equiv M \subset R^5.$$

Thus, although the 5-tuple $(q, v_R, v_C, i_R, i_C)$ is defined in $R^5$, it is restricted to $M$, which is a small subset of $R^5$. In fact, $M$ is a one-dimensional submanifold, i.e., a *curve* in $R^5$. This is easily seen by the relation

$$\frac{dq}{dt} = -f\left(\frac{q}{C}\right).$$

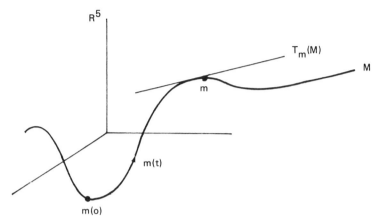

**FIG. 2.5**  The flow of $m(t)$ on $M$ and the tangent space of $M$ at $m$.

and the fact that the circuit is completely determined once $q(t)$ is known, e.g.,

$$v_R = q/C,$$
$$v_C = q/C,$$
$$i_R = -f(q/C),$$
$$i_C = f(q/C).$$

Thus, the point

$$m(t) = [q(t), v_R(t), v_C(t), i_R(t), i_C(t)]$$

will move in $R^5$, but be constrained to lie only on $M$. Hence, the dynamics of the circuit take place only on $M$ (see Fig. 2.5). By virtue of the fact that $q(t)$ determines the circuit, the vector field describing the flow $m(t)$ is determined by the differential equation $dq/dt = -f(q/C)$.

## C.  Lie Algebras of Vector Fields

Consider the dynamical system

$$\dot{x} = u_1(t)f(x) + u_2(t)g(x), \qquad x(0) = x_0, \tag{2.1}$$

where $f, g: R^n \to R^n$ are $C^\infty$-maps. If we employ the special choice of controls

$$u_1(s) = \begin{cases} -1, & t \leq s < 2t, \\ 0, & 0 \leq s < t, \quad 2t \leq s \leq 3t, \\ 1, & 3t \leq s < 4t, \end{cases}$$

$$u_2(s) = \begin{cases} -1, & 0 \leq s < t, \\ 0, & t \leq s < 2t, \quad 3t \leq s < 4t, \\ 1, & 2t \leq s < 3t, \end{cases}$$

then a slightly involved calculation shows that

$$x(4t) = x_0 + \left\{ \left[ \left( \frac{\partial f}{\partial x} \right) g(x) - \left( \frac{\partial g}{\partial x} \right) f(x) \right]_{x=x_0} \right\} t^2$$
$$+ O(t^3).$$

The quantity $(\partial f/\partial x)g(x) - (\partial g/\partial x)f(x)$ is usually written as

$$\left( \frac{\partial f}{\partial x} \right) g(x) - \left( \frac{\partial g}{\partial x} \right) f(x) \doteq [f, g](x)$$

and is called the *Lie bracket* of $f$ and $g$. A set of vector fields $f_i : R^n \to R^n$ is called *involutive* if the Lie bracket of any two is a linear combination of the $\{f_i\}$. The relevance of the Lie bracket operation to system-theoretic studies is that according to a theorem of Frobenius, the set of points near $x_0$ which can be reached along integral curves of Eq. (2.1), with $\{f, g\}$ involutive, can be expressed as

$$\phi_2(t_2, \phi_1(t_1, x_0)),$$

where $\phi_1(t, x)$ and $\phi_2(t, x)$ are the solutions of

$$\dot{x} = f(x), \qquad \dot{x} = g(x),$$

respectively. The reason that $\{f, g\}$ must be involutive is that otherwise the choice of $u_1(\cdot)$, $u_2(\cdot)$ given above will, for small $t$, surely lead out of the set of points expressible in the form $\phi_2(t_2, \phi_1(t_1, x_0))$. This result can be generalized to the case of $m$ inputs, as we shall see in Chapter 4.

Given a set of vector fields $f_i : R^n \to R^n$, the collection of all vector fields formed by taking Lie brackets of the $f_i$, as well as linear combinations of these elements is called the *Lie algebra* generated by the set $\{f_i\}$, denoted $\{f_i\}_{LA}$. This concept will play a central role in our study of reachability and observability for nonlinear systems.

**Example:   An Involutive System**

Consider the three analytic vector fields in $R^3$ given by

$$f_1(x) = \begin{bmatrix} 0 \\ x_3 \\ -x_2 \end{bmatrix}, \qquad f_2(x) = \begin{bmatrix} -x_3 \\ 0 \\ x_1 \end{bmatrix}, \qquad f_3(x) = \begin{bmatrix} x_2 \\ -x_1 \\ 0 \end{bmatrix}.$$

We have $[f_1, f_2] = f_3$, $[f_2, f_3] = f_1$, and $[f_3, f_1] = f_2$. Furthermore, at each point in $R^3 - \{0\}$, the set contains exactly two linearly independent elements since $x_1 f_1 + x_2 f_2 + x_3 f_3 = 0$. Thus, the set $\{f_1, f_2, f_3\}$ forms a Lie algebra of vector fields since it is closed under the Lie bracket operation (in fact, it is an involutive set of vector fields).

**Example:    The Matrix Commutator**

Let $A_1$ and $A_2$ be two $n \times n$ real matrices and consider the two vector fields $f_1(x) = A_1 x$ and $f_2(x) = A_2 x$. An easy calculation shows that

$$[f_1(x), f_2(x)] = (A_1 A_2 - A_2 A_1)x.$$

Thus, the Lie bracket of $f_1$ and $f_2$ is expressible as the commutator of the matrices $A_1$ and $A_2$. Hence, if the matrices $A_1$ and $A_2$ have the property that

$$(A_1 A_2 - A_2 A_1)x = \alpha_1 A_1 x + \alpha_2 A_2 x,$$

for some scalars $\alpha_1$, $\alpha_2$ and all $x \in R^n$, then the vector fields $f_1(x)$ and $f_2(x)$ form an involutive Lie algebra. Otherwise, they do not.


## IV. CONCEPTS FROM ALGEBRAIC GEOMETRY

According to one school of thought, the most efficient way to study constant linear systems is through the transfer matrix

$$Z(\lambda) = H(\lambda I - F)^{-1}G,$$

a rational matrix function in the complex variable $\lambda$. In quite another direction, the Thom theory of catastrophes suggests that the canonical structure of a wide class of nonlinear systems is represented by a process whose dynamics

$$\dot{x} = f(x, u)$$

are such that the function $f(\cdot, \cdot)$ is a polynomial of low degree in the variable $x$ and linear in $u$. In pursuing either of these lines of thought, we are led to consideration of the properties of polynomial or rational maps between vector spaces or manifolds. The study of rational maps is the cornerstone of modern algebraic geometry, the tools of which have only recently been applied for system-theoretic purposes. In this section we outline the main concepts from algebraic geometry needed for our subsequent development.

Let $C^n$ denote the set of complex $n$ vectors. We say a subset $W$ of $C^n$ is *algebraic* if there exists a set of polynomials $P_1(x), \ldots, P_n(x)$ such that

$$W = \{x \in C^n : P_i(x) = 0, \ i = 1, 2, \ldots, n\},$$

i.e., $W$ is the solution set of polynomial equations $P_i(x) = 0, i = 1, 2, \ldots, n$. A subset of $C^n$ is said to be *Zariski closed* if it is a finite union of algebraic subsets. The complement of a Zariski closed subset is said to be *Zariski open*. The Zariski open subsets define a topology for $C^n$ which, however, is non-Hausdorff so that some of our intuition about topology gained from the usual topology for real and complex numbers must be given up. Basically, we can think of Zariski open subsets as being *big*, while a Zariski closed subset is *small* in $C^n$.

A subset of $C^n$ is said to be *almost all* of $C^n$ if it contains a nonempty Zariski open subset. In classical algebraic geometry a property depending upon points of $C^n$ is called *generic* if the set of points where the property holds is almost all of $C^n$. For instance, the property that the determinant of an $n \times n$ complex matrix $A$ is nonzero is a generic property. A map

$$\phi: \quad X \to C^n,$$

where $X$ is an arbitrary set, is called *almost onto* if $\phi(X)$ is almost all of $C^n$.

A mapping

$$f: \quad C^n \to C,$$

$$x \mapsto p(x)/q(x),$$

where $p(x)$ and $g(x)$ are polynomial functions is called a *rational function* on $C^n$. If we remove from $C^n$ all those points at which $q(x) = 0$, we can regard f as a mapping of Zariski open subsets of $C^n \to C$. We let $\mathrm{RF}(C^n)$ denote the set of all rational functions on $C^n$, with $\mathrm{PF}(C^n)$ being the set of all polynomial functions on $C^n$.

We define a *rational mapping*

$$\phi: \quad C^n \to C^m$$

as an $m$ vector $(\phi_1(x), \ldots, \phi_m(x))'$, whose components are rational functions on $C^n$. Using the rational mapping $\phi$, we can define a ring homomorphism

$$\phi^*: \quad \mathrm{PF}(C^m) \to \mathrm{RF}(C^n)$$

by the rule

$$\phi^*(p) = p(\phi(x))$$

for a rational mapping $\phi$.

For example, if

$$\phi(x) = \left( \frac{x}{x^2 + 1}, \frac{x^2}{5x^3 + 3x + 2} \right), \qquad p(y_1, y_2) = 1 + y_1 + y_2^2,$$

$$\phi^*(p(x)) = p(\phi(x)) = 1 + \frac{x}{x^2 + 1} + \left( \frac{x^2}{5x^3 + 3x + 2} \right)^2.$$

We say a rational map $\phi$ is a *submersion* if the map $\phi^*: \mathrm{PF}(C^m) \to \mathrm{RF}(C^n)$ is 1–1. The basic result needed for system-theoretic studies is

**Theorem 2.1**  *Suppose $\phi$ is a submersion. Let $X$ be the set of points in $C^n$ at which $\phi$ is well defined. Then $\phi(x)$ is almost all of $C^m$, i.e., $\phi$ is almost onto.*

Intuitively, the theorem states that, except for a *negligible* set of $y$'s, the equations

$$\phi(x) = y, \quad x \in C^n, \quad y \in C^m$$

are solvable. Here negligible means a set of algebraic dimension $<m$. We note that Theorem 2.1 critically depends on the assumptions that $x$ and $y$ are complex. The result is not true for real $x$ and $y$ without further hypotheses, as the map

$$f: \quad R \to R,$$

$$x \to x^2$$

shows.

We would like to develop some simple, easily testable conditions under which a given map $\phi$ is a submersion. To this end, we consider the Jacobian matrix $J(x)$ of the map $\phi$,

$$J(x) = \left[\frac{\partial \phi_i}{\partial x_j}\right], \quad i = 1, 2, \ldots, n, \quad j = 1, 2, \ldots, m.$$

In terms of $J(x)$, we can give the following easy test for $\phi$ to be a submersion:

**Theorem 2.2** *If at some point* $x^* \in C^n$, *rank* $J(x^*) = m$, *then* $\phi$ *is a submersion.*

REMARK 1. In coordinate-free terminology, the role of $J(x)$ is taken on by the Frechet differential $d\phi$ of $\phi$, which is defined by the formula

$$d\phi(x^*)(x) = \frac{\partial}{\partial t} \phi(x^* + tx)\Big|_{t=0}.$$

The theorem is then stated in terms of the rank of $d\phi(x^*)$.

REMARK 2. Note that the rank condition needs to be verified at only a *single* point of $C^n$ for the theorem to hold.

REMARK 3. These results imply that the image of $\phi$ is such that not only does $C^m - \phi(X)$ have measure zero (in the Lebesgue sense), but it is contained in a finite union of algebraic sets of dimension less than $m$.

**Example:   Diagonalization of a Matrix**

To illustrate the utility of Theorems 2.1 and 2.2 in a familiar setting, consider the space $L(C^n, C^n)$ of $n \times n$ complex matrices. Let $D^n(C)$ be the space of $n \times n$ complex diagonal matrices. Define the rational map

$$\phi: \quad L(C^n, C^n) \times D^n(C) \to L(C^n, C^n),$$

$$(A, D) \mapsto ADA^{-1}.$$

We can regard $\phi$ as a rational map from $C^{n^2+n} \to C^{n^2}$ by making the usual identifications $L(C^n, C^n) \to C^{n^2}, D^n(C) \to C^n$.

As is typical with rational maps, $\phi$ is not defined everywhere, e.g., at those points of $C^{n^2}$ where $A$ is singular. To provide a domain for $\phi$ which is free of singularities, we consider $GL(n, C)$, the space of nonsingular $n \times n$ complex matrices. Let us examine the set

$$\phi(GL(n, C) \times D^n(C)) \subset L(C^n, C^n).$$

We know from linear algebra that this set is exactly the set of diagonalizable matrices. A subset is the set of matrices with *distinct* characteristic values. Let us show how to derive these conclusions from Theorems 2.1 and 2.2.

The Frechet differential of $\phi$ at a point $(A_0, D_0) \in GL(n, C) \times D^n(C)$ is

$$d\phi(A, D) = \frac{\partial}{\partial t}\left[(A_0 + tA)(D_0 + tD)(A_0 + tA)^{-1}\right]_{t=0}$$

$$= AD_0A_0^{-1} + A_0DA_0^{-1} - A_0D_0A_0^{-1}AA_0^{-1}.$$

We must find conditions such that $d\phi$ is *onto*. Consider the point $(I, \bar{D}) \in GL(n, C) \times D^n(C)$, where $\bar{D}$ is a diagonal matrix with distinct diagonal elements. Thus, with $A_0 = I, D_0 = \bar{D}$,

$$d\phi(A, D) = \{A\bar{D} + D - \bar{D}A : A \in L(C^n, C^n), D \in D^n(C)\}. \qquad (2.2)$$

To check whether the above set (2.2) represents all of $L(C^n, C^n)$, we multiply by an arbitrary $n \times n$ matrix $B$ and compute the inner product, *i.e.*, the trace. The existence of a nonzero $B$ which is orthogonal to the set $d\phi(A, D)$ is then a necessary and sufficient condition for $d\phi$ *not* to be onto. We have

$$\text{tr}[B(A\bar{D} - \bar{D}A + D)] = \text{tr}[\bar{D}BA - B\bar{D}A + BD] = \text{tr}\{[\bar{D}, B]A + BD\},$$

where $[X, Y] = XY - YX$ is the matrix commutator (or Lie bracket). For the above expression to vanish identically, we must have

$$[\bar{D}, B] = 0, \qquad \text{tr}(BD) = 0$$

for all $D \in D^n(C)$. It is easily verified that these two conditions imply $B \equiv 0$ if and only if $\bar{D}$ has distinct diagonal entries. Thus, there do exist points in $GL(n, C) \times D^n(C)$ at which $d\phi$ is onto; hence, $\phi$ is a submersion and we conclude that the image $\phi$ is almost onto, i.e., *almost every $n \times n$ complex matrix is diagonalizable*.

It is often desirable to consider nonlinear control systems of the form

$$\dot{x}(t) = Fx^{[p]} + \sum_{i=1}^{m} u_i(t)G_ix(t)^{[q_i]}, \qquad x(0) = x_0,$$

where $F$ is an $n \times \binom{n+p-1}{p}$ matrix and for each $i = 1, \ldots, m$, $G_i$ is an $n \times \binom{n+q_i-1}{q_i}$ matrix. Here the notation $x^{[p]}$ denotes the $\binom{n+p-1}{p}$-tuple of weighted $p$-forms in the components of $x$, i.e.,

$$x^{[p]} = (x_1^p, \alpha_1 x_1^{p-1} x_2, \alpha_2 x_1^{p-1} x_3, \ldots, x_n^p),$$

where the entries are ordered lexicographically and the weights are chosen so
that $\|x^{[p]}\| = \|x\|^p$. We define $x^{[0]} = 1$.

It is a surprising fact that the seemingly larger class of systems

$$\dot{x} = f(x(t)) + \sum_{i=1}^{m} u_i(t) g_i(x(t)) \tag{2.3}$$

with the components of the vector fields $f(x)$ and $g(x)$ being rational functions
of the components of $x$, is in reality equivalent to the polynomially nonlinear
system (2.3) as the following argument shows. We write the components of $f$
and the $g_i$'s in terms of a common denominator $G(x)$. Then

$$\dot{x}(t) = G(x)^{-1} \Big[ F(x) + \sum_{i=1}^{m} u_i(t) G_i(x) \Big],$$

where $G$ is a scalar-valued polynomial function of $x$ and $F$ and the $G_i$'s are
vector fields whose components are polynomials in $x$. Next, we introduce the
new state variable $v(t) = G(x)^{-1}$. Then the augmented state vector $\bar{x}(t) = \left( \begin{smallmatrix} x\,(t) \\ v\,(t) \end{smallmatrix} \right)$ is easily seen to satisfy the equation

$$\dot{\bar{x}}(t) = \bar{F}(\bar{x}) + \sum_{i=1}^{m} u_i(t) \bar{G}(\bar{x}),$$

where the components of $\bar{F}(\bar{x})$ and $\bar{G}_i(\bar{x})$ are polynomial functions of $x_1, x_2,$
$\ldots, x_n, v$. Finally, we introduce the new variable $w$ satisfying $\dot{w}(t) = 0$,
$w(0) = 1$. Suppose $p$ is the highest degree in any of the polynomial components of $\bar{F}(\bar{x})$. In each component, we multiply any term of degree $r < p$ by
$w^{p-r}$, so that each component becomes a homogeneous polynomial of degree
$p$ in the variables $x, v, w$. Similarly, let $q_i$ denote the highest degree of any of
the components of $\bar{G}_i(\bar{x})$ and multiply terms by powers of $w$ as needed so
that all components are homogeneous polynomials of degree $q_i$ in the
variable $x, v, w$. We now find that the $(n + 2)$ vector

$$z(t) = \begin{bmatrix} x(t) \\ v(t) \\ w(t) \end{bmatrix}$$

satisfies a differential system of the required form. We now introduce some
additional concepts from algebraic geometry which will prove useful for
studying homogeneous polynomial systems of the foregoing type.

Let $k[s_1, \ldots, s_n]$ denote the ring of polynomials in the indeterminates

$s_1, \ldots, s_n$ over the domain $k$, abbreviated $k[s]$. If $\mathscr{S} \subseteq k[s]$, we have an associated algebraic set

$$V(\mathscr{S}) = \{x \in k^n : f(x) = 0 \qquad \text{for all} \quad f \in \mathscr{S}\}.$$

Let $\mathscr{I}_{\mathscr{S}}$ denote the smallest ideal in $k[s]$ containing $\mathscr{S}$ as a subset. Then

$$V(\mathscr{S}) = V(\mathscr{I}_{\mathscr{S}}).$$

On the other hand, if $S \subseteq k^n$, we define the ideal

$$\mathscr{V}(S) = \{f \in k[s] : f(x) = 0 \qquad \text{for all} \quad x \in S\}$$

Clearly, $S \subseteq V(\mathscr{V}(S))$. We say that an algebraic set $V$ is *irreducible* if there do not exist algebraic sets $V_1$ and $V_2$ such that $V = V_1 \cup V_2$, with $V \neq V_i$. Irreducible algebraic sets are also called (*affine*) *algebraic varieties*.

If $f \in k(s)$, $x \in k^n$, the *differential* of $f$ at $x$ is defined as the linear function

$$d_x f: \quad k^n \to k$$

given by

$$d_x f(v) = \sum_{i=1}^{n} \left(\frac{\partial f}{\partial s_i}\right)(x) v_i.$$

Let $V$ be an algebraic variety defined by the equations $f_1(x) = \cdots = f_r(x) = 0$. Then the *tangent space* to $V$ at $x$, denoted $T_x V$, is the vector space of all $v \in k^n$ such that $d_x f_i(v) = 0$, $i = 1, 2, \ldots, r$. If $x \in V$ is such that $\dim T_x V = \min_y \dim T_y V$, $x$ is called a *simple point*. All other points of $V$ are called *singular* points.

We say that a point $\xi \in V$ is *generic* over $k$ if every polynomial equation $f(\xi) = 0$, which holds for $\xi$ also holds for all other points of $V$. Now let $\xi$ be a generic point of $V$ and assume that there are exactly $r$ algebraically independent elements among the components of $\xi$. The number $r$ is called the *algebraic dimension* of the variety $V$. The *geometric dimension* of a variety is defined to be the dimension of the tangent space at any simple point. If $k =$ complex numbers, the algebraic and geometric dimension coincide. In general, however,

$$\text{geometric dim } V \leq \text{algebraic dim } V.$$

Let us now show how these algebraic concepts can be employed to study polynomial differential equations of the form

$$\dot{x}(t) = Ax^{[p]}, \qquad x(0) = x_0 \qquad (2.4)$$

which may be thought of as the free (uncontrolled) motion of the nonlinear control system introduced earlier. Recall that the matrix $A$ is of size

$n \times \binom{n+p-1}{p}$. To deal with this system of equations, we introduce the auxiliary system

$$\frac{d}{dt} x(t)^{[r]} = A_{[r]} x(t)^{[p+r-1]}, \qquad r = 0, 1, \ldots .$$

The properties of the $\binom{n+r-1}{r} \times \binom{n+p+r-2}{p+r-1}$ matrix $A_{[r]}$ will prove essential for characterizing the solutions to the original problem, since if there exists a nonzero vector $v$ in $\mathcal{N}(A'_{[r]})$, the null space of $A'_{[r]}$, then $f(x) = v'x^{[r]}$ is a first integral for (2.4), i.e.,

$$d_x f(Ax^{[p]}) = \sum_m v'_m A_{[m]} x^{[p+m-1]} \equiv 0.$$

Hence, in seeking analytic first integrals of (2.4), we may confine our attention to homogeneous polynomials and calculate $\mathcal{N}(A'_{[m]})$, $m = 1, 2, \ldots$. This is a simple problem in linear algebra. The underlying motivation for this argument is the following result:

**Theorem 2.3**   *Let $f_1, \ldots, f_r$ be (homogeneous) polynomial first integrals of (2.4) and let $\mathscr{I}$ be the ideal they generate in $k[s]$. Suppose algebraic* dim $V(\mathscr{I}) = 1$. *Then the solution of (2.4) can be expressed explicitly in terms of automorphic functions of t.*

To see how to utilize Theorem 2.3 to construct solutions to (2.4), we sketch the proof. Let $x_0 = (x_1^0, \ldots, x_n^0)$ and let

$$y_i = f_i(x_0), \qquad i = 1, 2, \ldots, r.$$

Define $\mathscr{I}_1$ to be the ideal in $k[s]$ generated by the polynomials $f_i(s_1, \ldots, s_n) - y_i$, $i = 1, 2, \ldots, r$. Since dim $V(\mathscr{I}) = 1$, the dim $V(\mathscr{I}_1) = 0$ or 1. If dim $V(\mathscr{I}_1) = 0$, $V(\mathscr{I}_1)$ is a finite set and any solution starting in $V(\mathscr{I}_1)$ must remain there for all $T > 0$, i.e., the solution is a constant.

Now assume dim $V(\mathscr{I}_1) = 1$ and let $g_i(s_1, \ldots, s_n)$ be the $p$th degree homogeneous polynomial such that $g_i(x(t)) = i$th entry in $Ax^{[p]}$. Introduce the new indeterminate $\dot{s}_i$ and let $\hat{\mathscr{I}}$ be the smallest ideal containing both $\mathscr{I}_1$ and the polynomial $\dot{s}_i - g_i(s_1, \ldots, s_n)$ in $k[\dot{s}_i, s_1, \ldots, s_n]$. The algebraic dim $V(\hat{\mathscr{I}}) = 1$, hence there is a polynomial $f(\dot{s}_i, s_i) \in k[\dot{s}_i, s_i]$ such that $(x_{n+1}, x_1, \ldots, x_n) \in V(\hat{\mathscr{I}})$, $f(x_{n+1}, x_i) = 0$ ($f$ may be explicitly computed using elimination theory). This determines $\dot{x}_i(t)$ as an algebraic function of $x_i(t)$ and we denote the dependence as $\dot{x}_i = \dot{x}_i[x_i(t)]$. Write

$$\tau = \int^s \frac{d\sigma}{\dot{x}_i[\sigma]}$$

to find that $ds/d\tau = \dot{x}_i[s] = \dot{x}_i[s(\tau)]$, which shows that $s(t)$ is the solution of

$f(\dot{x}_i, x_i) = 0$. Since algebraic curves of the form $f(\dot{x}_i, x_i) = 0$ (in the $(\dot{x}_i,$ $x_i)$ = plane) are "uniformized" by automorphic functions, the theorem follows.

Since the steps in the proof are lengthy, let us summarize the solution recipe:

1. Compute $\mathcal{N}(A'_{[m]})$, $m = 1, 2, \ldots$.
2. If there is a nonzero vector $v \in \mathcal{N}(A'_{[r]})$, then $f(x) = v'x^{[r]}$ is an analytic first integral of (2.4).
3. Write all homogeneous polynomial first integrals of (2.4), say $f_1, \ldots, f_r$ and construct the ideal $\mathcal{I}$ which they generate. Check that algebraic dim $V(\mathcal{I}) = 1$.
4. Let $\mathcal{I}_1$ be the ideal generated by the polynomials $f_i(s_1, \ldots, s_n) - y_i$, $i = 1, 2, \ldots, r$, where $y_i = f_i(x_1^0, x_2^0, \ldots, x_n^0)$.
5. Define $\hat{\mathcal{I}}$ equal to the smallest ideal containing $\mathcal{I}_1$ and the polynomial $\dot{s}_i - g_i(s_1, \ldots, s_n)$, where $g_i(x_1, \ldots, x_n)$ is the $i$th entry in $Ax(t)^{[p]}$.
6. Use the equation for the first integrals, together with $s_i - g_i(x_1, \ldots, s_n)$ to determine $x_i[s]$ through the integral

$$\tau = \int^s \frac{d\sigma}{\dot{x}_i[\sigma]}$$

i.e., $ds/d\tau = \dot{x}_i[s]$. This yields a single algebraic relation between $\dot{x}_i$ and $x_i$.

To illustrate use of the procedure, we give some examples.

**Example 1**

Consider the 2nd degree homogeneous system

$$\dot{x}_1 - x_2^2(t), \qquad x_1(0) = a,$$
$$\dot{x}_2 = x_1(t)x_2(t), \qquad x_2(0) = b.$$

Here

$$A = \begin{bmatrix} 0 & 0 & 1 \\ 0 & 1 & 0 \end{bmatrix},$$

so we see that $\mathcal{N}(A') = \{0\}$. However,

$$A_{[2]} = \begin{bmatrix} 0 & 0 & 2\sqrt{3}/3 & 0 \\ 0 & -\sqrt{2}/3 & 0 & \sqrt{2} \\ 0 & 0 & -2\sqrt{3}/3 & 0 \end{bmatrix},$$

so that

$$\mathcal{N}(A'_{[2]}) = \begin{pmatrix} \alpha \\ 0 \\ \alpha \end{pmatrix} : \alpha \in R^1$$

Thus, $f(x_1, x_2) = x_1^2 + x_2^2$ is a first integral. Now we must consider the equations

$$s_1^2 + s_2^2 = c,$$
$$\dot{s}_1 - s_2^2 = 0, \tag{2.5}$$

since $g_1(x_1, x_2)$ equals the 1st entry in $Ax^{[2]} = x_2^2$. Eliminating $s_2$ from Eqs. (2.5) yields

$$\dot{s}_1 = c - s_1^2$$

and we must invert the integral

$$\tau = \int^s \frac{d\sigma}{c - \sigma^2}.$$

In other words, to obtain $x_1(t)$ we specialize the indeterminate $s_1$. After a bit of elementary algebra and calculus, we find

$$x_1(t) = \sqrt{c} \, \frac{(1 + a\sqrt{c})e^{\sqrt{c}t} - (1 - a\sqrt{c})e^{-\sqrt{c}t}}{(1 + a\sqrt{c})e^{\sqrt{c}t} + (1 - a\sqrt{c})e^{-\sqrt{c}t}},$$

$$x_2(t) = \frac{2b}{(1 + a\sqrt{c})e^{\sqrt{c}t} + (1 - a\sqrt{c})e^{-\sqrt{c}t}}.$$

**Example 2:  Euler's Equations for a Rigid Body**

Let

$$\dot{x}_1 = a_1 x_2(t) x_3(t),$$
$$\dot{x}_2 = a_2 x_1(t) x_3(t),$$
$$\dot{x}_3 = a_3 x_1(t) x_2(t).$$

Here

$$A = \begin{bmatrix} 0 & 0 & 0 & 0 & a_1 & 0 \\ 0 & 0 & a_2 & 0 & 0 & 0 \\ 0 & a_3 & 0 & 0 & 0 & 0 \end{bmatrix}.$$

Thus, $\mathcal{N}(A') = \{0\}$, But,

$$A_{[2]} = \sqrt{2/3}\begin{bmatrix} 0 & 0 & 0 & 0 & a_1 & 0 & 0 & 0 & 0 & 0 \\ 0 & 0 & a_2 & 0 & 0 & 0 & 0 & a_1 & 0 & 0 \\ 0 & a_3 & 0 & 0 & 0 & 0 & 0 & 0 & a_1 & 0 \\ 0 & 0 & 0 & 0 & a_2 & 0 & 0 & 0 & 0 & 0 \\ 0 & 0 & 0 & a_3 & 0 & a_2 & 0 & 0 & 0 & 0 \\ 0 & 0 & 0 & 0 & a_3 & 0 & 0 & 0 & 0 & 0 \end{bmatrix},$$

so that

$$\mathcal{N}\{A'_{[2]}\} = \{(\alpha_1, 0, 0, \alpha_2, 0, \alpha_3): a_1\alpha_1 + a_2\alpha_2 + a_3\alpha_3 = 0\}.$$

Choose $(\bar{\alpha}_1, \bar{\alpha}_2, \bar{\alpha}_3)$ and $(\hat{\alpha}_1, \hat{\alpha}_2, \hat{\alpha}_3)$ as any two linearly independent vectors satisfying the constraint

$$a_1\alpha_1 + a_2\alpha_2 + a_3\alpha_3 = 0.$$

Then we have the two first integrals

$$\bar{\alpha}_1 x_1^2 + \bar{\alpha}_2 x_2^2 + \bar{\alpha}_3 x_3^2$$

and

$$\hat{\alpha}_1 x_1^2 + \hat{\alpha}_2 x_2^2 + \hat{\alpha}_3 x_3^2.$$

Hence, we consider the equations

$$\bar{\alpha}_1 s_1^2 + \bar{\alpha}_2 s_2^2 + \bar{\alpha}_3 s_3^2 = c_1,$$

$$\hat{\alpha}_1 s_1^2 + \hat{\alpha}_2 s_2^2 + \hat{\alpha}_3 s_3^2 = c_2,$$

$$\dot{s}_1 - a_1 s_2 s_3 = 0$$

and eliminate $s_2$ and $s_3$, obtaining an equation of the form

$$\dot{s}_1^2 = \beta_0 + \beta_1 s_1 + \beta_2 s_1^2 + \beta_3 s_1^3 + \beta_4 s_1^4.$$

If the roots of the polynomial on the right side are all distinct, then this represents a curve in $(s_1, \dot{s}_1)$ space of genus 1 so that

$$\tau = \int^s \frac{d\sigma}{\dot{x}_1[\sigma]}$$

is an elliptic integral. This implies that $x_1(t)$ may be expressed in terms of elliptic functions of $t$. This is in agreement with the classical solution of Euler's equations in terms of Jacobian elliptic functions.

If the polynomial $\beta_0 + \beta_1 s_1 + \cdots + \beta_4 s_1^4$ has repeated roots, the genus of the $(s_1, \dot{s}_1)$ curve is 0 and $x_1(t)$ may be expressed in terms of elementary functions of $t$. It is easy to see that if

$$c_1 = \bar{\alpha}_j \quad \text{and} \quad c_2 = \hat{\alpha}_j \quad \text{for some} \quad j = 1, 2, \text{or } 3,$$

then this polynomial will have repeated roots. So, for all values of $(\alpha_1, \alpha_2, \alpha_3, \hat{\alpha}_1, \hat{\alpha}_2, \hat{\alpha}_3, c_1, c_2)$ lying in a Zariski open set in $k^8$, the polynomial has distinct roots.

We shall make much more use of these ideas later in our studies of reachability and observability.

## V. GRASSMANN MANIFOLDS
## AND THE CLASSIFICATION PROBLEM

Following in the footsteps of workers in ordinary differential equations and dynamical system theory, mathematical system theorists have increasingly been focusing attention on the *global structure* of system, rather than studying individual systems. Thus, the modern viewpoint is to consider an individual system as a member of a family of systems and to study the geometrical and algebraic properties of the entire class. One of the main approaches for this type of study in the case of linear systems is the concept of a Grassmann manifold.

Mathematically speaking, the notion of a Grassmann manifold is introduced to give us a way to attach coordinates to all the subspaces of fixed dimension of a given vector space $V$. More precisely, let $k$ be an arbitrary field, let $V$ be an $n$-dimensional vector space over $k$, and let $m$ be an integer such that $0 < m < n$. Then the Grassmann space $G^m(V)$ is the space, each of whose points represents an $m$-dimensional subspace of $V$.

We now show how to parameterize the elements of $G^m(V)$. First of all, fix a projection map

$$P: \quad V \to V$$

such that $\dim P(V) = m$. (Recall that $P$ is a *projection* if $P^2 = P$.) Next, choose an element $\gamma \in G^m(V)$ such that

$$\gamma \cap (I - P)(V) = \{0\}.$$

Now it can be shown that there exists a unique map $X_\gamma : V \to V$, satisfying the following conditions:

(i)   $X_\gamma^2 = 0$,
(ii)  $PX_\gamma = 0$,
(iii) $X_\gamma P = X_\gamma$,
(iv) $(X_\gamma + P)(V) = \gamma$.

Thus, the subspace $\gamma$ is parameterized by the maps (matrices) $P$ and $X_\gamma$. If we now set

$$V_1 = P(V), \qquad V_2 = (I - P)(V),$$

properties (ii) and (iii) show that

$$X_\gamma(V_1) \subset V_2, \qquad X_\gamma(V_2) = 0.$$

Hence, $X_\gamma$ is determined by its values on $V_1$ and there is an isomorphism between the space of $X$'s and $L(V_1, V_2)$, the space of linear maps $V_1 \to V_2$. Putting all these remarks together, we see that there is a 1–1 correspondence between $G^m(V)$ and $L(V_1, V_2)$.

Now let us examine how the parameterization of $\gamma$ changes when we let $GL(V)$ act on $G^m(V)$, i.e., we let an invertible linear transformation $A : V \to V$ act upon $G^m(V)$. Let

$$A_{11} = PAP,$$

$$A_{12} = PA(I - P),$$

$$A_{21} = (I - P)AP,$$

$$A_{22} = (I - P)A(I - P).$$

At the matrix level this corresponds to partitioning $A$ as

$$A = \begin{bmatrix} A_{11} & A_{12} \\ A_{21} & A_{22} \end{bmatrix},$$

where the blocks are of size $m \times m$, $(n - m) \times m$, $m \times (n - m)$, and $(n - m) \times (n - m)$, respectively. Suppose now that

$$\gamma = (P + X_\gamma)(V) \in G^m(V),$$

with $P$ and $X_\gamma$ as above and set

$$\gamma' = A\gamma.$$

Our task is to compute (if it exists) the map $X_{\gamma'}$ satisfying conditions (i)–(iii) such that

$$\gamma' = (P + X_{\gamma'})(V).$$

The key to finding $X_{\gamma'}$ is the observation that $A(P + X_\gamma) \in \ker(I - P - X_{\gamma'})$, for the relation $\gamma' = A\gamma$ to be satisfied. Thus,

$$(I - P - X_{\gamma'})A(P + X_\gamma) = 0$$

or

$$AP + AX_\gamma - PAP - PAX_\gamma - X_{\gamma'}AP - X_{\gamma'}AX_\gamma = 0. \qquad (2.6)$$

Now using the relations (i)–(iii), as well as the definitions of the $A_{ij}$, we have

$$AP = A_{11} + A_{21},$$

$$AX_\gamma = (A_{12} + A_{22})X_\gamma,$$

$$PAX_\gamma = A_{12}X_\gamma,$$

$$X_\gamma, AP = X_\gamma, A_{11},$$

$$X_\gamma, AX_\gamma = X_\gamma, A_{12}X_\gamma.$$

Thus, Eq. (2.6) takes the form

$$A_{21} + A_{22}X_\gamma - X_{\gamma'}A_{11} - X_{\gamma'}A_{12}X_\gamma = 0$$

or

$$X_{\gamma'} = (A_{21} + A_{22}X_\gamma)(A_{11} + A_{12}X_\gamma)^{-1}. \tag{2.7}$$

The relation (2.7) is a *generalized fractional linear transformation* which would define GL($V$) as a transformation group on $L(V_1, V_2)$ except that it is not defined for all $A \in \text{GL}(V)$ or all $X \in L(V_1, V_2)$. This is what is called a *local* transformation group action in Lie group theory. Note, however, that the map $X_\gamma \rightarrow \gamma$, which assigns the subspace $\gamma = (P + X_\gamma)(V)$ to each $X \in L(V_1, V_2)$ imbeds $L(V_1, V_2)$ as an open dense subset of $G^m(V)$.

**Example 1**

Let $V = R^n$ and let

$$\gamma = \{x \in V : x_i = 0, i = m + 1, m + 2, \ldots, n\}.$$

The simplest projection $P$ such that dim $P(R^n) = m$ is

$$P = \begin{array}{c} \\ m \\ n - m \end{array} \overset{\displaystyle \overset{m \quad\ n - m}{}}{\left[ \begin{array}{c|c} I & 0 \\ \hline 0 & 0 \end{array} \right]}. \tag{2.8}$$

It is a trivial exercise to verify that the unique matrix $X$ satisfying

$$X^2 = 0, \qquad PX = 0, \qquad XP = X,$$

is $X \equiv 0$. Hence, the parameterization for this *standard* $m$-dimensional subspace is the pair $(P, 0)$, where $P$ is the partitioned matrix (2.8).

While this example is trivial to compute, the next example will show its importance, since we can use the *standard* case to parameterize any other $m$-dimensional subspace using exactly the same $P$ as in (2.8).

**Example 2**

Let $V = R^3$ and let $\gamma' =$ subspace of $R^3$ generated by the vectors

$$\begin{pmatrix} 1 \\ 1 \\ 1 \end{pmatrix}, \quad \begin{pmatrix} 2 \\ 1 \\ 0 \end{pmatrix} \doteq \left\langle \begin{bmatrix} 1 \\ 1 \\ 1 \end{bmatrix}, \quad \begin{bmatrix} 2 \\ 1 \\ 0 \end{bmatrix} \right\rangle.$$

Here dim $\gamma' = 2$, so we choose

$$P = \left[ \begin{array}{cc|c} 1 & 0 & 0 \\ 0 & 1 & 0 \\ \hline 0 & 0 & 0 \end{array} \right]$$

and our task is to find a $3 \times 3$ matrix $X$ satisfying $X^2 = 0, PX = 0, XP = X$.
A frontal assault on this problem is tedious due to the quadratic nature of the
conditions on $X$. We employ another route, whereby we can make use of
Eq. (2.7).

Let $A$ be the matrix such that

$$A\gamma = \gamma',$$

where

$$\gamma = \left\langle \begin{bmatrix} 1 \\ 0 \\ 0 \end{bmatrix}, \quad \begin{bmatrix} 0 \\ 1 \\ 0 \end{bmatrix} \right\rangle$$

is equal to the standard 2-dimensional subspace of $R^3$. We also require

$$A\left\langle \begin{bmatrix} 0 \\ 0 \\ 1 \end{bmatrix} \right\rangle = R^3 - \gamma'.$$

A simple calculation shows that

$$A = \begin{bmatrix} 1 & 2 & 1 \\ 1 & 1 & -2 \\ 1 & 0 & 1 \end{bmatrix}.$$

We have already seen that a parameterization for $\gamma$ is

$$P = \begin{bmatrix} 1 & 0 & 0 \\ 0 & 1 & 0 \\ 0 & 0 & 0 \end{bmatrix}, \qquad X_\gamma = 0.$$

Keeping $P$ fixed, our task is to compute $X_{\gamma'}$ from Eq. (2.7). We have

$$A_{11} = PAP = \begin{bmatrix} 1 & 2 & 0 \\ 1 & 1 & 0 \\ 0 & 0 & 0 \end{bmatrix},$$

$$A_{12} = PA(I - P) = \begin{bmatrix} 0 & 0 & 1 \\ 0 & 0 & -2 \\ 0 & 0 & 0 \end{bmatrix},$$

$$A_{21} = (I - P)AP = \begin{bmatrix} 0 & 0 & 0 \\ 0 & 0 & 0 \\ 1 & 0 & 0 \end{bmatrix},$$

$$A_{22} = (I - P)A(I - P) = \begin{bmatrix} 0 & 0 & 0 \\ 0 & 0 & 0 \\ 0 & 0 & 1 \end{bmatrix}.$$

Since $X_{\gamma} = 0$, computing $X_{\gamma'}$, shows that

$$X_{\gamma'}A_{11} = A_{21}.$$

This equation gives

$$X_{\gamma'} = \begin{bmatrix} 0 & 0 & x_{13} \\ 0 & 0 & x_{23} \\ -1 & 2 & x_{33} \end{bmatrix}.$$

Now we use the condition $X_{\gamma'}^2 = 0$ to see that

$$x_{13} = x_{23} = x_{33} = 0.$$

Thus,

$$X_{\gamma'} = \begin{bmatrix} 0 & 0 & 0 \\ 0 & 0 & 0 \\ -1 & 2 & 0 \end{bmatrix}$$

which gives the parameterization of $\gamma'$ as

$$P = \begin{bmatrix} 1 & 0 & 0 \\ 0 & 1 & 0 \\ 0 & 0 & 0 \end{bmatrix}, \qquad X_{\gamma'} = \begin{bmatrix} 0 & 0 & 0 \\ 0 & 0 & 0 \\ -1 & 2 & 0 \end{bmatrix}.$$

We can check the computation by the condition that

$$(P + X_{\gamma'})(R^3) = \gamma'.$$

We have

$$(P + X_{\gamma'})\begin{bmatrix} x_1 \\ x_2 \\ x_3 \end{bmatrix} = \begin{bmatrix} x_1 \\ x_2 \\ -x_1 + 2x_2 \end{bmatrix} = x_1 \begin{bmatrix} 1 \\ 0 \\ -1 \end{bmatrix} + x_2 \begin{bmatrix} 0 \\ 1 \\ 2 \end{bmatrix}.$$

It is easy to verify that the vectors

$$\begin{bmatrix} 1 \\ 0 \\ -1 \end{bmatrix} \quad \text{and} \quad \begin{bmatrix} 0 \\ 1 \\ 2 \end{bmatrix}$$

span the same space as

$$\begin{bmatrix} 1 \\ 1 \\ 1 \end{bmatrix} \quad \text{and} \quad \begin{bmatrix} 2 \\ 1 \\ 0 \end{bmatrix},$$

which establishes the uniqueness of the parameterization.

The reader will note that the simplicity of the computation was a consequence of the simple form of $P$. Fortunately, such *canonical* projections can always be employed since the only requirement on $P$ is that dim $\gamma$ = dim $P(V)$.

It is of considerable system-theoretic interest to follow-up the preceding development by considering a continuously differentiable flow in GL($V$) and inquiring as to the differential equation which describes the orbit of this flow in $G^m(V)$ or, more precisely, in $L(V_1, V_2)$, the parameterization space of $G^m(V)$. The result of this inquiry leads us to the consideration of the matrix Riccati equation, one of the most ubiquitous and important equations in applied mathematics.

Suppose that $t \to A(t)$ is a flow in GL($V$) and let $t \to B(t) = (dA/dt)A(t)^{-1} \in L(V, V)$ be its infinitesimal generator, *i.e.*, $dA/dt = B(t)A(t)$. Consider the orbits

$$t \to \gamma(t) = A(t)\gamma,$$

$$t \to X_{\gamma}(t) = A(t)X_{\gamma}$$

of a smooth flow acting on $G^m(V)$ and $L(V_1, V_2)$. Our goal is to determine the differential equation satisfied by $X_{\gamma}(t)$.

We first compute the derivatives of $A_{ij}(t), i, j = 1, 2$.

$$\frac{d}{dt} A_{11}(t) = PBAP$$

$$= (PBP)(PAP) + (PB(I - P))((I - P)AP)$$

$$= B_{11}A_{11} + B_{12}A_{21}.$$

Similarly,

$$\frac{d}{dt} A_{12} = B_{11}A_{12} + B_{12}A_{22},$$

$$\frac{d}{dt} A_{21} = B_{21}A_{11} + B_{22}A_{21},$$

$$\frac{d}{dt} A_{22} = B_{21}A_{12} + B_{22}A_{22}.$$

Since

$$X_{\gamma'} = (A_{21}(t) + A_{22}(t)X_\gamma)(A_{11}(t) + A_{12}(t)X_\gamma)^{-1},$$

we compute the derivatives of each factor

$$\frac{d}{dt}(A_{21} + A_{22}X_\gamma) = B_{21}A_{11} + B_{22}A_{21} + (B_{21}A_{12} + B_{22}A_{22})X_\gamma$$

$$= B_{21}(A_{11} + A_{12}X_\gamma) + B_{22}(A_{21} + A_{22}X_\gamma),$$

$$\frac{d}{dt}(A_{11} + A_{12}X_\gamma)^{-1} = -(A_{11} + A_{12}X_\gamma)^{-1}(B_{11} + B_{12}X_\gamma).$$

Thus,

$$\frac{dX_\gamma}{dt} = B_{21} + B_{22}X_\gamma(t) - X_\gamma(t)[B_{11} + B_{12}X_\gamma(t)]. \tag{2.9}$$

Equation (2.9) is a *generalized Riccati equation* (or *matrix Riccati equation*) for the orbit curves $t \to X_\gamma(t)$ in $L(V_1, V_2)$. They naturally arise in the theory of optimal control.

These procedures enable us to uniquely attach parameters in a coordinate-free way to each subspace of a vector space $V$. Sometimes, however, it is instructive to carry out the procedure in a more classical fashion using coordinates. This approach enables us to construct an *algebraic set* each of whose points represents a subspace of $V$ of given dimension. Such a set is called a *Grassmann variety* and plays a role in the global theory of systems. Here we sketch the general procedure for constructing the Grassmann variety of $G^m(V)$.

Let $w_0, w_1, \ldots, w_m$ be a basis for an $(m + 1)$-dimensional subspace $W_{m+1} \in G^{m+1}(V)$. Suppose we have dim $V = n + 1$ and assume

$$w_i = (x_0^{(i)}, \ldots, x_n^{(i)}), \qquad i = 0, 1, \ldots, m$$

relative to some fixed basis in $V$. Set

$$\pi_{i_0, i_1, \cdots, i_m} = \det \begin{bmatrix} x_{i_0}^{(0)} & x_{i_1}^{(0)} & \cdots & x_{i_m}^{(0)} \\ \vdots & & & \vdots \\ x_{i_0}^{(m)} & x_{i_1}^{(m)} & \cdots & x_{i_m}^{(m)} \end{bmatrix},$$

where $0 \le i_j \le n$. Not all $\pi$'s are zero since the vectors $w_0, \ldots, w_m$ are linearly independent. Also, interchanging any two indices changes the sign of $\pi_{i_0 \cdots i_m}$ and if two indices are equal $\pi_{i_0 \cdots i_m} = 0$. Thus, these quantities are uniquely determined if we know those with $i_0 < i_1 < \cdots < i_m$. It can be shown that the numbers $\pi_{i_0 \cdots i_m}$ can be used as coordinates of a point in a projective space $P_N(k)$ ($k$ = any field) of dimension $N = \binom{n+1}{m+1} - 1$. Furthermore, this point only depends on the subspace $W_{m+1}$.

The definition of $\pi_{i_0 \cdots i_m}$ gives us a well-defined 1–1 map

$$\Psi : \quad (m+1)\text{-dimensional subspaces}$$

$$W_{m+1} \quad \text{of} \quad V \twoheadrightarrow P_N(k).$$

The quantities $\pi_{i_0 \cdots i_m}$ are called the *Plücker coordinates* of $W_{m+1}$.

**Question**   Is $\Psi$ onto?

*Answer.*   It is not!

The term $\Psi(G^{m+1}(V))$ is contained in a proper algebraic subset of $P_N(k)$. To describe this subset, introduce the new variables $z_{i_0 \cdots i_m}$, where $0 \le i_j \le n$. We impose the following conditions on the $z$'s.

(i)  $z_{i_0 \cdots i_m} = 0$ if two indices are the same;
(ii)  $z_{i_0 \cdots i_m}$ reverses sign if two indices are interchanged;

(iii)  $z_{i_0 \cdots i_m} z_{j_0 \cdots j_m} = \sum_{k=0}^{m} z_{j_k i_1 \cdots i_m} z_{j_0 \cdots j_{k-1} i_0 j_{k+1} \cdots j_m}.$

The quantities $z_{i_0 \cdots i_m}$ with $i_0 < i_1 < \cdots < i_m$ are homogeneous coordinates of a point in $P_N(k)$ (if all these quantities are not zero). Conditions (i)–(iii) constitute a set of homogeneous polynomial equations determining an algebraic set $A_{m+1}$ in $P_N(k)$. This algebraic set is called the *Grassmann variety* associated with the $(m+1)$-dimensional subspaces of $V$. $A_{m+1}$ consists of the points $(z_{i_0 \cdots i_m})$, $i_0 < i_1 < \cdots < i_m$, satisfying conditions (i)–(iii).

In general $A_{m+1}$ is a proper algebraic subset of $P_N(k)$. For example, in the case $m = 1$, $n = 3$, conditions (i)–(iii) reduce to the single equation

$$z_{01} z_{23} - z_{02} z_{13} + z_{03} z_{12} = 0.$$

We can regard this as a quadric in $P_5(k)$ since $N = 5$ and it is clearly a proper subset of $P_5(k)$.

It is a nontrivial step to prove that the map

$$\Psi: G^{m+1}(V) \to A_{m+1}$$

is onto. This fact, however, establishes a 1–1 onto correspondence between the points of $G^{m+1}(V)$ and $A_{m+1}$, allowing us to conclude that $A_{m+1}$ parameterizes $G^{m+1}(V)$.

### PROBLEMS AND EXERCISES

**1.** Consider the linear system $\Sigma$

$$\dot{x} = Fx + Gu, \qquad x \in R^n, \quad u \in R^m$$

and let $T: R^n \to R^n$, $V: R^m \to R^m$ be nonsingular linear transformations acting on $\Sigma$ in the following fashions:

$$(T, V) \circ (F, G) = (TFT^{-1}, TGV) = (\hat{F}, \hat{G}), \tag{2.10}$$

Show that the set of all pairs $(T, V)$ acting as in (2.10) on pairs $(F, G)$ forms a *group* under the operation $\circ$ defined as

$$(T_1, V_1) \circ (T_2, V_2) = (T_2 T_1, V_1 V_2).$$

**2.** (a) Show that for any square matrix $A$, the set of all solutions of $AX + XA' = 0$ forms a Lie algebra.

(b) Show that the set of $n \times n$ symmetric matrices do *not* form a Lie algebra and that the nonsingular symmetric matrices do not form a group.

**3.** Let $Y$ be a $k$-vector-space. By the *formal power series* in $x^{-1}$ over $Y$, we mean the additive abelian group

$$W = \left\{ \sum_{i=1}^{\infty} y_i x^{-i} : y_i \in Y \right\},$$

where addition is defined by

$$\left( \sum y_i x^{-i} \right) + \left( \sum \hat{y}_i x^{-i} \right) = \sum (y_i + \hat{y}_i) x^{-i}.$$

Here the additive identity is the series all of whose coefficients are zero in $Y$.

Show that the set of formal power series $W$ can be made into a $k[x]$-*module* using the scalar multiplication rule

$$p(x)W = \left( \sum_{j=0}^{r} k_j x^j \right) \left( \sum_{i=1}^{\infty} y_i x^{-i} \right) = \sum_{j=0}^{r} \sum_{i=1}^{\infty} (k_j y_i) x^{j-i},$$

where all terms involving powers of $x$ of nonnegative degree are discarded.

**4.**  Consider the space $S = \{(F, G, H): F = n \times n, G = n \times m, H = p \times n$ real matrices$\}$ of all constant linear systems of dimensions $n$ having $m$ inputs and $p$ outputs. Define a relation $\sim$ on $S$ by the rule $s \sim \bar{s}$ if and only if $s$ and $\bar{s}$ have the same transfer matrix, i.e.,

$$H(\lambda I - F)^{-1}G = \bar{H}(\lambda I - \bar{F})^{-1}\bar{G}$$

for all complex $\lambda$. Show that $\sim$ is an *equivalence relation* on $s$ if and only if $s$ and $\bar{s}$ are completely reachable and completely observable.

**5.**  Let $\langle F | G \rangle = X$ and let $V \subset X$ decompose $F$, i.e., $FV \subset V$ and $S \subset X$ with $FS \subset S$ and $V \otimes S = X$. If $Q$ is the projection on $V$ along $S$, show that $V = \langle F | QG \rangle$.

**6.**  Consider the set of fractional linear transformations of $R$ to itself

$$x \rightarrow \frac{ax + b}{cx + d}, \qquad a, b, c, d \in R.$$

Prove that this set forms a group

**7.**  Let $A$ be an arbitrary $n \times m$ matrix and let $\tau(A)$ be the operation of *stacking* the columns of $A$, i.e., $\tau(A)$ is a $nm \times 1$ vector. If $P$, $A$, and $Q$ are matrices so that the product $PAQ$ is well defined, prove that

$$\tau(PAQ) = (Q' \otimes P)\tau(A).$$

**8.**  Let $A$ and $B$ be real square matrices. Establish the Baker–Campbell–Hausdorff formula

$$C^A B e^{-A} = B + [A, B] + \frac{1}{2!}[A, [A, B]] + \frac{1}{3!}[A, [A, [A, B]]] + \cdots,$$

where $[\,,\,]$ is the matrix commutator.

**9.**  Let $M$ be a Riemannian manifold with metric $G = [g_{ij}]$ and let $\phi$ be a smooth function on $M$. The gradient of $\phi$, grad $\phi$, is defined to be the element of $TM$ given by

$$\text{grad } \phi(x) = \sum g_{ij}(x) \frac{\partial \phi}{\partial x_i} \frac{\partial}{\partial x_j}.$$

If we change coordinates in $M$ by $x \rightarrow \psi(x) = y$, show that the differential equation

$$\dot{x} = f(x) \rightarrow \dot{y} = \left(\frac{\partial \psi}{\partial x}\right) f(\psi^{-1}(y)),$$

while the metric $G(x)$ becomes

$$\left(\frac{\partial \psi}{\partial x}\right)^{-1} g_{ij}(x) \left(\frac{\partial \psi}{\partial x}\right)^{-1}.$$

Further, show that if $f(x) = \operatorname{grad} \psi$, then the new vector field is the gradient of $\phi(\psi^{-1}(y))$.

**10.** (a) Let $x_0$ be a point of a smooth manifold $M$. Two smooth maps $f_1$ and $f_2$ are defined in neighborhoods $U_1$ and $U_2$ of $x_0$. Define the relation $\sim_G$ as $f_1 \sim_G f_2$ if there is a third neighborhood $U_3$ of $x_0$ on which $f_1$ and $f_2$ agree, i.e., $f_1|_{U_3} = f_2|_{U_3}$. Show that $\sim_G$ is an equivalence relation. (If $f$ is any smooth function defined at $x_0$, the equivalence class of $f$ is called the *germ of f* at $x_0$).

(b) If $f$ is a smooth map at a point $x_0$, the *k-jet* of $f$ is the Taylor series of $f$ truncated at terms of degree $(k + 1)$ and higher. Let $J^k_{x_0}(M)$ be the space of $k$-jets of germs of diffeomorphisms of $M$ into $M$ leaving $x_0$ fixed. Show that $J^k_{x_0}(M)$ is a *group*.

**11.** Assume that $W(z) = p(z)/q(z) \in Z[[z^{-1}]]$, where $p$, $q$ are polynomials and $Z[[z^{-1}]]$ is the ring of formal power series in $z^{-1}$ with integer coefficients. Show that $W \in Z[[z^{-1}]]$ if and only if $p$ and $q$ are polynomials such that

(i) $\deg p < \deg q$;
(ii) $q$ is monic;
(iii) $p$ and $q$ have no common factors;
(iv) $p, q \in Z[z]$.

(Note that this problem arises in attempting to implement a single-input–single-output filter having $z$-transform $W$ on a digital computer using only integer arithmetic.)

**12.** Consider the matrix Riccati equation

$$\dot{Z} = B + AZ - ZD - ZCZ,$$

where $Z = m \times n$, $A = m \times m$, $B = m \times n$, $C = n \times m$, $D = n \times n$ are real matrices. Also, consider the linear system

$$\dot{X} = AX + BY,$$
$$\dot{Y} = CX + DY, \tag{2.11}$$

where $X = m \times n$, $Y = n \times n$ are matrix functions, $A$, $B$, $C$, $D$ as before. Let $F(t)$ be the fundamental matrix for (*) such that $F(0) = I$. We can regard $F(t)$ as a curve in $\mathrm{GL}(n + m, R)$, the general linear group. Let the subspace of $R^{n+m}$ spanned by the columns of the matrix $\left[\begin{smallmatrix} X \\ Y \end{smallmatrix}\right]$ be denoted by $[[X|Y]]$. Prove the following:

(a) If $U = \{g\left[\begin{smallmatrix} Q \\ I \end{smallmatrix}\right] : g \in \mathrm{GL}(n + m, R)\}$, then $\left[\begin{smallmatrix} X \\ Y \end{smallmatrix}\right] \in U$ if and only if the column rank of $\left[\begin{smallmatrix} X \\ Y \end{smallmatrix}\right]$ equals $n$;

(b)  Let $G_{n,m}$ denote the Grassman space of $n$-dimensional subspaces in $R^{n+m}$. Then the map

$$\pi: \quad U \to G_{n,m}$$

$$\left[\tfrac{X}{Y}\right] \mapsto [[X|Y]]$$

is well defined and the action

$$\psi: \quad GL(m+n, R) \times G_{n,m} \to G_{n,m}$$

$$(g, [[X|Y]]) \mapsto \pi g \left[\tfrac{X}{Y}\right]$$

is transitive;

(c)  If $\phi(t, [[X|Y]])$ is the solution to the Riccati equation with $\phi(0, [[X|Y]]) = [[X|Y]]$, then

$$\phi(t, [[X|Y]]) = \psi(F(t), [[X|Y]])$$

(i.e., the Riccati equation is a flow on $G_{n,m}$).

(d)  If $Z(0) = Z_0$, $X(0) = X_0$, $Y(0) = Y_0$, then the solution of the Riccati equation is given by

$$Z(t) = X(t)Y^{-1}(t),$$

whenever $Y(t)$ is nonsingular. If we define $V = \{\left[\tfrac{X}{Y}\right]: \det Y \neq 0\}$ and let $\eta: \pi(V) \to M(m, n) = m \times n$ matrices

$$[[X|Y]] \mapsto XY^{-1},$$

then $\eta$ is a coordinate chart on $\pi(V)$. Further, the solution of the Riccati equation is

$$Z(t) = \eta \circ \phi(t, [[Z_0|I]])$$

as long as $\phi(t, [[Z_0|I]])$ remains in $V$.

**13.**  Let $M$ be a smooth manifold and let $V: M \to TM$ be a vector field that is different from zero only on a compact subset $K$ of $M$. Show that there exists a one-parameter group of diffeomorphisms $g_t: M \to M$, such that $v$ is the flow field, i.e.,

$$\frac{d}{dt}(g_t x) = v(g_t x).$$

**14.**  Let $\Sigma_{n,m,p} = (F, G, H)$ be the set of all constant linear systems of finite dimension $n$, with $m$ inputs and $p$ outputs and let $\Sigma^c \subset \Sigma_{n,m,p}$ be the set of completely reachable systems. Show that $\Sigma^c$ is a Zariski open subset of $\Sigma_{n,m,p}$.

**NOTES AND REFERENCES**

**Section 2.II**    The basic algebraic concepts discussed here are available in numerous standard sources, including

G. Birkhoff and S. MacLane, "A Survey of Modern Algebra," 3rd ed., Macmillan, New York, 1965.

N. Jacobson, "Lectures in Abstract Algebra. Vol. I. Basic Concepts," Van Nostrand, Princeton, New Jersey, 1951.

S. Lang, "Algebra," Addison-Wesley, Reading, Massachusetts, 1965.

I. N. Herstein, "Topics in Algebra," Blaisdell, New York, 1964.

B. L. Van der Waerden, "Algebra," Vols. 1 and 2, Ungar, New York, 1970.

For results on linear algebra, and especially matrix theory, the following are strongly recommended:

R. Bellman, "Introduction to Matrix Analysis," 2nd Ed., McGraw-Hill, New York, 1970.

F. Gantmacher, "Matrix Theory," Chelsea, New York, 1969.

M. Marcus and H. Minc, "A Survey of Matrix Theory and Matrix Inequalities," Prindle, Weber & Schmidt, Boston, 1964.

N. Efimov and E. Rozendorn, "Linear Algebra and Multidimensional Geometry," Mir, Moscow, 1975. [English]

For additional developments on the idea of controllability subspaces, see

W. M. Wonham, "Linear Multivariate Control: A Geometric Approach," in Lecture Notes in Econ. and Math. Systems, Vol. 101, Springer, Berlin, 1974.

**Section 2.III**    An extremely readable and gentle introduction to the ideas underlying differentiable manifolds is the classic work

L. Auslander and R. Mackenzie, "Introduction to Differentiable Manifolds," McGraw-Hill, New York, 1963.

See also

R. Bishop and R. Crittenden, "Geometry of Manifolds," Academic Press, New York, 1964.

I. M. Singer and J. Thorpe, "Lecture Notes on Elementary Topology and Geometry," Scott, Foresman and Co., Glenview, Illinois, 1976.

A treatment oriented more toward the study of differential equations and dynamic systems is found in

V. I. Arnol'd, "Ordinary Differential Equations," MIT Press, Cambridge, Massachusetts, 1973.

R. Abraham and J. Marsden, "Foundations of Mechanics," 2nd Ed., Addison-Wesley, Reading, Massachusetts, 1978.

A more detailed view of the electrical circuit example is given in

T. Matsumoto, On several geometric aspects of nonlinear networks, *J. Franklin Inst.* **301** (1976), 203–225.

**Section 2.IV**   An excellent introduction to the uses of elementary algebraic geometry in the study of linear systems is

R. Hermann, "Linear Systems Theory and Introductory Algebraic Geometry," *in* Interdisciplinary Mathematics, Vol. 8, Math. Sci. Press, Brookline, Massachusetts, 1974.

An introduction to basic aspects of algebraic geometry accessible to undergraduates is

W. E. Jenner, "Rudiments of Algebraic Geometry," Oxford Univ. Press, New York, 1963.

Classically oriented works for specialists include

I. R. Shafarevich, "Basic Algebraic Geometry," Springer, Berlin, 1974.
W. V. D. Hodge and D. Pedoe, "Methods of Algebraic Geometry," Vols. 1 and 2, Cambridge Univ. Press, Cambridge, 1968.

A system-theoretic view of the relationship between discrete-time polynomial systems and commutative algebras is

E. Sontag, "Polynomial Response Maps," Lecture Notes in Control and Information Sciences, Vol. 13, Springer, Berlin, 1979.

The work on polynomial systems described in the text is from

J. Bailieul, Controllability and observability of polynomial dynamic systems, *Nonlinear Analysis-TMA* **5** (1981), 543–552.

**Section 2.V**   The treatment of Grassmann varieties and their relationship to matrix Riccati equations follows that in

R. Hermann, "Algebraic Topics in Systems Theory," *in* Interdisciplinary Mathematics, Vol. 8, Math. Sci. Press, Brookline, Massachusetts, 1973.

See also the books on algebraic geometry cited earlier.

# 3

# A Modern View
# of Linear System Theory

## I. INTRODUCTION

Certainly, one of the central aims of system theory is the creation of a general theory of nonlinear processes, which mirrors that currently available for linear processes. This is not to say that the last word has been written on linear theory, as a number of interesting and important questions are still outstanding; however, it is fair to say that the major questions surrounding the basic concepts of reachability, observability, canonical realizations, stability, and optimality are fairly well understood and the principal outstanding issues are of a more technical than foundational nature.

In this chapter, we present a brief summary of the theory of linear systems using the language and mathematical methods outlined in Chapters 1 and 2. Our objective is to review not only the terminology and key results of the linear theory, but also to indicate the power and scope of the algebraic and geometrical methods in providing a clear, concise, elegant, and comprehensive framework within which to study the problems of linear systems. The simple, natural expressions of the fundamental results of linear system theory in algebraic and geometric terms strongly suggest the use of this language in extending and generalizing results to the nonlinear case.

Since it is assumed that the reader has some background in elementary linear system theory, we shall not provide too much by way of introductory definitions here. Should the reader feel uncomfortable with this assumption, consultation of Casti (1977) on linear systems will provide the necessary background material. In fact, it is an illuminating and instructive exercise to compare the *standard* statements of the basic theorems of linear system theory given in terms of vectors and matrices, to their more abstract versions presented here.

## II. MATHEMATICAL DESCRIPTION OF A LINEAR SYSTEM

We adopt the following standard definition of a linear system:

**Definition 3.1**   A *discrete-time, constant, linear, m-input, p-output dynamical system* $\Sigma$ *over a field* $k$ is a composite concept $(F, G, H)$, where

$$F: \quad X \rightarrow X,$$

$$G: \quad k^m \rightarrow X,$$

$$H: \quad X \rightarrow k^p,$$

are abstract $k$-homomorphisms, with $X$ an abstract vector space over $k$. The *dimension* of $\Sigma$ is, by definition, dim $X$. Naturally, once we fix a basis in $X$, the $k$-homomorphisms $F, G, H$ can be identified with their corresponding matrix representations.

The dynamical interpretation of $\Sigma$ is given by the equations

$$x(t + 1) = Fx(t) + Gu(t),$$

$$y(t) = Hx(t),$$

with $t \in Z$, $x(\cdot) \in X$, $u(\cdot) \in k^m$, and $y(\cdot) \in k^p$.

Definition 3.1 describes what is usually termed the *internal* model of a system $\Sigma$. We now define the corresponding *external*, or input–output, model.

**Definition 3.2**   A *linear, zero-state, input–output map over* $k$ is a map $f$: $\Omega \rightarrow \Gamma$ such that

(a)   $\Omega = \{$all $k$-vector-sequences $\omega$: $Z \rightarrow k^m$, such that $\omega(t) = 0$ for all $t < t^- \leq 0$ and all $t > 0$, where $t^-$ is some finite integer$\}$,

(b)   $\Gamma = \{$all $k$-vector-sequences $\gamma$: $Z \rightarrow k^p$ such that $\gamma(t) = 0$ for all $t \geq 0\}$,

(c)   $\Omega$ and $\Gamma$ are $k$-vector-spaces with $f$ a $k$-homomorphism.

(d) $f$ is translation invariant in the sense that the following diagram commutes:

$$
\begin{array}{ccc}
\Omega & \xrightarrow{\ f\ } & \Gamma \\
\sigma_\Omega \downarrow & & \downarrow \sigma_\Gamma \\
\Omega & \xrightarrow[\ f\ ]{} & \Gamma
\end{array}
$$

where $\sigma_\Omega$ and $\sigma_\Gamma$ are shift operators defined by

$$\sigma_\Omega = (0, \ldots, \omega(-1), \omega(0); 0, \ldots) \mapsto (0, \ldots, \omega(0), 0; 0, \ldots),$$

$$\sigma_\Gamma = (0, \ldots, 0; \gamma(1), \gamma(2), \ldots) \mapsto (0, \ldots, 0; \gamma(2), \gamma(3), \ldots).$$

REMARK 1    We may interpret the shift operators $\sigma_\Omega$ and $\sigma_\Gamma$ as

$$\sigma_\Omega = \text{shift left and append a zero,}$$

$$\sigma_\Gamma = \text{shift left and discard first symbol.}$$

REMARK 2    The sequences $[f(e_i)]_j = j$th component of the vector $f(e_i)$, with $e_i = i$th unit vector, i.e.,

$$
[e_i]_k = \begin{cases} 1, & i = k, \\ 0, & i \neq k, \end{cases} \quad i = 1, 2, \ldots, m,
$$

will provide the same information as the impulse-response map of a continuous-time, constant linear system. Knowledge of these sequences suffices to determine the zero-state input–output behavior of a constant linear system.

In our standard notation we have $e_i \in \Omega$ corresponding to the sequence

$$
\omega_k(t) = \begin{cases} \delta_{ik}, & t = 0, \\ 0, & t \neq 0. \end{cases}
$$

The fundamental problem of linear system theory is to construct (*realize*) a canonical linear dynamical system $\Sigma$, whose input–output map $f_\Sigma$ agrees with a given input–output map $f$. Regarding $(F, G, H)$ as matrices, for a moment, Definitions 3.1 and 3.2 immediately imply that $\Sigma$ realizes $f$ if and only if

$$[f(e_i)]_j = ([HG]_{ji}, [HFG]_{ji}, [HF^2G]_{ji}, \ldots).$$

## III. THE MODULE STRUCTURE OF $\Omega$. $\Gamma$, AND $X$

Our main objective now is to establish the following

***Fundamental Theorem of Linear System Theory***    *The natural state set $X_f$ associated with a discrete-time, linear, constant input–output map $f$ over $k$*

*admits the structure of a finitely generated module over the ring $k[z]$ (poly-nomials in the indeterminate $z$ with coefficients in $k$).*

To prove the theorem, we shall introduce a number of definitions and constructions, which will ultimately enable us to verify that the state set $X_f$ (as defined below) satisfies the axioms for a finitely generated module over $k[z]$. It is most convenient to introduce the various canonical constructions in a sequence of steps.

STEP 1    $\Omega \approx k^m[z]$, regarding $k^m[z]$ as a *k-vector-space*. The explicit form of the isomorphism is

$$\omega \approx \sum_{t \in Z} \omega(t)z^{-t} \in k^m[z].$$

Note that by Definition 3.2(a), this sum is always finite, and $t \leq 0$ by the convention adopted in the definition.

STEP 2    $\Omega \approx k^m[z]$, regarding $k^m[z]$ as a *$k[z]$-module*. In fact, $\Omega$ is a *free* $k[z]$-module with the $m$ generators $\{e_1, e_2, \ldots, e_m\}$, where

$$e_i = \begin{bmatrix} 0 \\ 0 \\ \vdots \\ 0 \\ 1 \\ 0 \\ \vdots \\ 0 \end{bmatrix} \leftarrow \text{ith position.}$$

This claim is easily validated by defining the action of $k[z]$ on $\Omega$ through scalar multiplication as

$$\cdot : \quad k[z] \times \Omega \to \Omega,$$

$$(\pi, \omega) \mapsto \pi \cdot \omega,$$

with

$$\pi \cdot \omega = \begin{bmatrix} \pi\omega_1 \\ \pi\omega_2 \\ \vdots \\ \pi\omega_m \end{bmatrix}, \qquad \omega_j \in k[z], \quad j = 1, 2, \ldots, m.$$

Here $\pi\omega_j$ is the usual product of one polynomial in $k[z]$ by another.

STEP 3    On $\Omega$ the action of the shift operator $\sigma_\Omega$ is represented by multipli-cation by $z$. Thus, *dynamical action* is transformed into the *algebraic* operation of multiplication.

STEP 4    $\Gamma$ is isomophic to the $k$-vector-subspace of $k^p[[z^{-1}]]$ (formal power series in $z^{-1}$) consisting of all formal power series with no constant term. The explicit isomorphism is

$$\gamma \approx \sum_{t\in Z} \gamma(t)z^{-t} \in k^p[[z^{-1}]].$$

In general, the sum is infinite and is to be interpreted strictly algebraically with no question of convergence. The isomorphism is completed by noting that $\gamma(0) = 0$.

STEP 5    $\Gamma$ has the structure of a $k[z]$-module by defining scalar multiplication as

$$\cdot \;:\; k[z] \times \Gamma \to \Gamma,$$

$$(\pi, \gamma) \mapsto \pi \cdot \gamma = \pi(\sigma_\Gamma)\gamma,$$

This product is equivalent to the rule: multiply $\gamma$ by $\pi$ in the usual way and then delete all terms containing no negative powers of $z$.

We have now seen that $\Omega$ and $\Gamma$ admit natural $k[z]$-module structures. It is now necessary to connect these structures up with the input–output map $f$. To this end we have

**Definition 3.3**    Given two inputs $\omega$, $\omega' \in \Omega$, we say that $\omega$ is *Nerode equivalent* to $\omega'$, written $\omega \equiv_f \omega'$ if and only if

$$f(\omega \circ v) = f(\omega' \circ v) \qquad \text{for all} \quad v \in \Omega.$$

Here $\circ$ denotes the operation of concatenation in $\Omega$, i.e.,

$$\circ \;:\; \Omega \times \Omega \to \Omega,$$

$$(\omega, v) \mapsto \sigma_\Omega^{|v|}\omega \vee v,$$

where $|v| = $ length of $v$ and $\vee$ is the *join* operation

$$\omega \vee \omega' = (0, \ldots, \omega(-t), \ldots, \omega(-1), \omega'(-t), \ldots, \omega'(-1); 0, \ldots).$$

It is easily verified that $\equiv_f$ defines an equivalence relation on $\Omega$.

**Definition 3.4**    The set of equivalence classes under $\equiv_f$, denoted $X_f = \{(\omega)_f : \omega \in \Omega\}$ is the *state set* of the input–output map $f$.

We now return to the problem of relating the module structure on $\Omega$ and $\Gamma$ to the map $f$ and its state set $X_f$.

**Proposition 3.1**    *The Nerode equivalence classes $X_f$ of $f$ are isomorphic to the $k[z]$ quotient module $\Omega/\ker f$.*

PROOF    By the relation

$$\omega \circ v = z^{|v|}\omega + v$$

and the $k$-linearity of $f$, we have

$$f(\omega \circ v) = f(\omega' \circ v) \qquad \text{for all} \quad v \in \Omega$$

if and only if

$$f(z^r \cdot \omega) = f(z^r \cdot \omega') \qquad \text{for all} \quad r \geq 0 \text{ in } Z.$$

There is no intrinsic reason for selecting the input space $\Omega$ to relate to $X_f$. By duality we could just as easily have chosen the output set $\Gamma$, as indicated in the problems at the end of the chapter.

The preceding development shows that the state set of the input–output map $f$ can be given the structure of a $k[z]$-module. Let us now consider the corresponding question for the state set $X_\Sigma$ of a dynamical system given in *internal* form.

**Proposition 3.2**   *The state set $X_\Sigma$ of the system $\Sigma = (F, G, -)$ admits a $k[z]$-module structure.*

PROOF   $X = k^n$ is already a $k$-vector-space. To make it into a $k[z]$-module, we define scalar multiplication as

$$\cdot : \quad k[z] \times k^n \to k^n,$$

$$(\pi, x) \mapsto \pi(F)x.$$

(Here $\pi(F)$ is just the polynomial $\pi(\cdot)$ evaluated at the matrix $F$).

Let us now restate some basic facts of system theory in the above module-theoretic language.

**Proposition 3.3**   *In the system $\Sigma = (F, G, H)$ with state module $X$, the map $F: X_\Sigma \to X_\Sigma$ is given by $x \mapsto z \cdot x$.*

PROOF   The result follows immediately from Proposition 3.2, if $X = X_\Sigma$. If $X = X_f$, then

$$x(1) = Fx(0) + G\omega(0) = F[\xi]_f + G\omega(0)$$

assuming $x(0)$ results from the input $\xi$. This implies that $x(1)$ results from the input $z \cdot \xi + \omega(0)$. Hence

$$x(1) = [z \cdot \xi + \omega(0)]_f$$

$$= z \cdot [\xi]_f + [\omega(0)]_f$$

$$= z \cdot [\xi]_f + G\omega(0)$$

which establishes the result.

We can now restate the usual criterion for reachability in more elegant fashion.

**Proposition 3.4**   *The system* $\Sigma = (F, G, -)$ *is completely reachable if and only if the columns of* $G$ *generate the* $k[z]$-*module* $X_\Sigma$.

PROOF    Assume any $x \in X_\Sigma$ can be written as

$$x = \sum_{j=1}^{m} \pi_j g_j, \qquad \pi_j \in k[z], \quad G = [g_1, g_2, \ldots, g_m].$$

By Proposition 3.3, this is the same as saying

$$x = \sum_{j=1}^{m} \pi_j(F) g_j$$

which is equivalent to complete reachability by the usual criterion involving the matrix

$$\mathscr{C} = [G, FG, F^2 G, \ldots, F^{n-1} G].$$

It is an easy exercise in application of the basic definitions to show that the external system with state module $X_f$ is both completely reachable and completely observable. Let us now show how to obtain a module-theoretic definition of complete observability for the internal system $\Sigma = (F, -, H)$.

Consider the $k$-homomorphism $H: X_\Sigma \to Y = k^p$. Let us extend $H$ to a $k[z]$-homomorphism $\bar{H}$ as

$$\bar{H}:  \quad X_\Sigma \to \Gamma,$$

$$x \mapsto (Hx, H(z \cdot x), H(z^2 \cdot x), \ldots).$$

From the standard definition of an observable state, we see that no nonzero element of the quotient module $X_\Sigma/\ker \bar{H}$ is unobservable. Thus, we have

**Proposition 3.5**   *The system* $\Sigma = (F, -, H)$ *is completely observable if and only if the quotient module* $X_\Sigma/\ker \bar{H}$ *is isomorphic with* $X_\Sigma$.

The above reachability–observability results suggest two important modules:

(i)   the submodule of $X_\Sigma$ generated by $G$, i.e., $k[z]G$;
(ii)  the quotient module $X_\Sigma/\ker \bar{H}$, characterizing the observable states of $\Sigma$.

If we are interested in states which are *both* reachable and observable the obvious thing to do is factor the unobservable states out of the submodule of reachable states. This new quotient module $X_\Sigma^0 = k[z]G/\ker \bar{H}$ is called the *canonical state set* for the system $\Sigma = (F, G, H)$. If we have $X_\Sigma^0 \approx X_\Sigma$, then we say that $X_\Sigma$ is *canonical* relative to $G, H$.

This terminology now allows us to address the question of modeling input–output data by an internal system $\Sigma$. The first main result is

***Correspondence Theorem***    *There is a bijective correspondence between the set of $k[z]$-homomorphisms $f: \Omega \to \Gamma$ and the set of canonical systems $\Sigma$, modulo a basis change in $X_\Sigma$.*

In other words, every input–output map $f$ has associated with it an internal model $\Sigma$, which is unique up to a coordinate change in the state space $X_\Sigma$.

## IV. SOME SYSTEM-THEORETIC CONSEQUENCES

The above module theory framework has exhibited a number of basic system-theoretic facts in clearer and sharper detail. However, there are a number of less obvious results which can also be obtained deriving mainly from the fact that $k[z]$ is a principal ideal domain. Here we sketch a few of the most interesting developments, leaving others to the Exercises and Problems section at the end of the chapter.

Let us begin by recalling the notion of a torsion module.

***Definition 3.5***    A module $M$ over a commutative ring $R$ is said to be a *torsion module* if for every $m \in M$, there exists an $r \in R$ such that $r \cdot m = 0$. If this is not the case, then $M$ is called a *free* module.

***Definition 3.6***    If $L \subset M$, the annihilator $A_L$ of $L$ is the set

$$A_L = \{r \in R : r \cdot l = 0 \text{ for all } l \in L\}.$$

REMARKS    (1) $A_L$ is an ideal in $R$. (2) $M$ a torsion module does *not* imply $A_L \neq 0$.

Definitions 3.5 and 3.6 allow us to prove the following important system-theoretic fact:

***Theorem 3.1***    $\Sigma$ *is finite-dimensional if and only if $X_\Sigma$ is a torsion $k[z]$-module.* (Recall that dim $\Sigma < \infty$ means dim $X_\Sigma < \infty$ regarded as a $k$-vector-space.)

PROOF    Let $X_\Sigma$ be finitely generated by the $q$ elements $x_1, \ldots, x_q \in X_\Sigma$. Thus,

$$A_{X_\Sigma} = A_{x_1} \cap A_{x_2} \cap \cdots \cap A_{x_q}.$$

Since $k[z]$ is a principal ideal domain, each $A_{x_j}$ is a principal ideal, say $\gamma_j k[z]$, $\gamma_j \in k[z]$. If $X_\Sigma$ is a torsion module, deg $\gamma_j = n_j > 0$ for all $j = 1$, $2, \ldots, q$. Hence, we can replace the expression

$$x = \sum_{j=1}^{q} \pi_j \cdot x_j, \qquad \pi_j \in k[z]$$

by

$$x = \sum_{j=1}^{q} [\pi_j (\text{mod } \gamma_j)] \cdot x_j,$$

which shows that $X_\Sigma$ as a *k-module* is generated by the finite set

$$x_1, z \cdot x_1, \ldots, z^{n_1-1} \cdot x_1, x_2, z \cdot x_2, \ldots, z^{n_2-1} \cdot x_2, \ldots, x_q, \ldots, z^{n_q-1} \cdot x_q,$$

i.e., $\Sigma$ is finite dimensional.

On the other hand, assume $\dim \Sigma < \infty$. Let $\Psi_F$ be the minimal polynomial of the map $F : x \mapsto z \cdot x$. Since $X_\Sigma$ is finite dimensional as a *k-module*, $\deg \Psi_F > 0$. This means that $\Psi_F$ annihilates every $x \in X_\Sigma$, so that $X_\Sigma$ is a torsion $k[z]$-module.

Since these results have established the Fundamental Theorem, namely, that the natural state set of $\Sigma$ (either $X_f$ or $X_\Sigma$) admits the structure of a finitely generated $k[z]$-module, we can apply the following central result of algebra to linear dynamical systems.

**Invariant Factor Theorem for Modules**   *Every finitely generated module M with n generators over a principal ideal domain R is isomorphic to*

$$R/\Psi_1 R \oplus R/\Psi_2 R \oplus \cdots \oplus R/\Psi_r R \oplus R^s$$

*where the $R/\Psi_i R$ are quotient rings of R regarded as modules over R, the $\Psi_i$ are uniquely determined by M up to units in R, $\Psi_i | \Psi_{i-1}$, $R^s$ denotes the free R-module with s generators and $r + s \leq n$.*

Note that $M$ is a torsion module if and only if $s = 0$. Thus, $\dim \Sigma < \infty$ if and only if $s = 0$.

We defer a direct system-theoretic translation of the Invariant Factor Theorem to Section V. For the moment, let us push the abstract algebra a bit further and consider the important case when $M$ is *cyclic*, i.e., generated by a single element. For the special case of interest for linear system theory $R = k[z]$. Let the state module $X$ be generated by the element $g$. If $\Psi_g$ is the *minimal polynomial* of $g$, we can prove the important result.

***Lemma 3.1***   *The state module $X \approx k[z]/\Psi_g k[z]$.*

For ease of notation, we write $\Psi_g = \Psi$. Since $X$ is cyclic, $R$ is commutative, and $\Psi_g$ annihilates all $x \in X$.

Let us recall that the elements of $k[z]/\Psi k[z]$ are the residue classes of the polynomial $\pi (\text{mod } \Psi)$, i.e., the remainder after dividing $\pi$ by $\Psi$, $\pi \in k[z]$. If we write these classes as $[\pi]$, the notation $\tilde{\pi}$ will refer to the standard representative from $[\pi]$, i.e., a polynomial of least degree in $[\pi]$. The element $\tilde{\pi}$ is uniquely determined by the conditions that $\tilde{\pi} \in [\pi]$ and $\deg \tilde{\pi} < \deg \Psi$.

It is now easy to establish the result that $k[z]/\Psi k[z]$ is isomorphic to the *k*-vector-space $\{\tilde{\pi} \in k[z] : \deg \tilde{\pi} < n = \deg \Psi\}$. This leads to the interesting

***Proposition 3.6***   *If $X_\Sigma$ is cyclic with minimal polynomial $\Psi$, then $\dim \Sigma = \deg \Psi$.*

Since the Invariant Factor Theorem exhibits the $k[z]$-module $X$ as the direct sum of cyclic $k[z]$-modules, we can compute the dim $\Sigma$ exactly from

**Proposition 3.7**   *If $X_f$ is a torsion module with invariant factors $\Psi_1, \Psi_2, \ldots, \Psi_r$, then*

$$\dim \Sigma = \deg \Psi_1 + \deg \Psi_2 + \cdots + \deg \Psi_r.$$

The dynamical behavior of a cyclic $X_f$ is described by the map, inputs $\rightarrow$ states, which we write as

$$\omega \mapsto [\omega] = \omega \bmod \Psi_f = \tilde{\omega}.$$

Intuitively, $X_f$ is a pattern recognition device in that an input $\omega$ is presented to $X_f$ and stored as the remainder after division by $\Psi_f$. The stored pattern $\tilde{\omega}$ may have no *obvious* relation to $\omega$ since $\Psi_f$ may be quite complicated as the following examples due to R. Kalman show. Nonetheless, the operation of the system is quite simple in the algebraic sense.

**Example 1**   $\Psi_f(z) = z^k$. Then $[\omega]_f = \tilde{\omega} = \omega_0 + \cdots + \omega_{k-1} z^{k-1}$. This system *remembers* the last $k$ input values.

**Example 2**   $\Psi_f(z) = z - 1$. Thus, $z = 1 \bmod \Psi_f$. Hence, $[\omega]_f = \tilde{\omega} = \omega_0 + \omega_1 + \cdots + \omega_r$, $r = \deg \omega$. This system *integrates* the input $\omega$.

**Example 3**   $\Psi_f(z) = z^k - \alpha$. Here we have $z^{kl}\omega = \alpha^l \omega \bmod \Psi_f$. This system is sensitive to inputs of period $k$ in that such patterns are reinforced, whereas nonperiodic patterns are averaged out. However, past inputs can be enhanced or deemphasized by selecting $\alpha > 1$ or $\alpha < 1$.

Another type of problem which can be dealt with algebraically is the following controllability question:

**Example 4**   Find an input $\omega$ which transfers a given state $x$ to 0. Assume that $X$ is a cyclic $k[z]$-module with generator $g$ and annihilator $\Psi$. Then we can write

$$x = \xi \cdot g = \tilde{\xi} \cdot g \qquad \text{if} \quad \xi = \tilde{\xi} \bmod \Psi.$$

Thus, the problem is to find an input $\omega$ such that

$$x \cdot \omega = (z^{1+d}\xi + \omega) \cdot g = 0,$$

where $d$ is an integer such that $d \geq \deg \omega$. Since $g \neq 0$, it is clear that $\omega$ must satisfy

$$z^{1+d}\xi + \omega = 0 \bmod \Psi, \qquad d \geq \deg \omega.$$

Unfortunately, deg $\omega$ enters nonlinearly here in the exponent; however, since the equation must hold only mod $\Psi$, we can choose $d$ arbitrarily, subject only to the condition that $d \geq n - 1$. Then a solution to the problem is

$$\omega = -z^{1+d}\xi + v\Psi,$$

where $v \in k[z]$ is chosen so that deg $\omega = d$. Note, however, that such an $\omega$ *may not* be the $\omega$ of minimal degree transferring $x \to 0$. If we want the solution of minimal degree which transfers $x \to 0$, we must take

$$\deg \omega = p \qquad \text{iff} \quad \deg z^{\widehat{p+1}}\xi = p, \qquad p \leq n.$$

A number of other important system-theoretic facts such as the control canonical form and the pole-shifting theorem shall be deferred to a later section. Let us now examine the classical concept of a transfer function in the light of the foregoing algebraic set-up.

## V.  TRANSFER FUNCTIONS

The machinery introduced in the earlier sections allows us to introduce the classical transfer function as a natural algebraic object, independent of the heuristic notion involving Laplace transforms of inputs and outputs.

If we consider an arbitrary $k[z]$-homomorphism $f: \Omega \to \Gamma$ we have that $f$ is *equivalent* to the set $\{f(e_i): i = 1, 2, \ldots, m, e_i = i\text{th unit vector}\}$, since

$$f(\omega) = \sum_{j=1}^{m} \omega_j \cdot f(e_j) \in \Gamma.$$

By our earlier definition of the $k[z]$-module $\Gamma$, each $f(e_j)$ is a formal power series in $z^{-1}$ with no constant term. Our approach is to represent these formal power series by ratios of polynomials. These ratios are what we shall call *transfer functions*. Elements $f(\omega)$ will then appear as the product of a polynomial times a ratio of polynomials. The relevant rules of calculation will then constitute a totally algebraic version of the so-called Heaviside *calculus*.

We begin with a $k[z]$-torsion-module $X_f = \Omega/\ker f$, with $\psi =$ minimal polynomial of $X_f$. Then

$$\psi \cdot f(e_j) = f(\psi \cdot e_j) = \eta([\psi \cdot e_j]) = \eta(\psi \cdot [e_j]) = 0. \tag{3.1}$$

(Here $\cdot$ denotes the special module product in $\Gamma$, while no dot will represent the *ordinary* product of a vector of polynomials by the single polynomial $\psi$). Thus, calculation (3.1) implies that the ordinary product

$$\psi f(e_j) = \theta_j \in k^p[z], \qquad j = 1, 2, \ldots, m,$$

i.e., $\psi$ *cancels* out the output $f(e_j)$, leaving the $p$-vector of ordinary polynomials $\theta_j$. Now let us *define*

$$f(e_j) = \theta_j/\psi. \tag{3.2}$$

It is easily checked that the formal division of $\theta_j$ by $\psi$ into ascending powers of $z^{-1}$ has the coefficient of $z^0$ as zero. The construction (3.2) leads to the basic

**Representation Theorem**   *Let $f: \Omega \to \Gamma$ be any $k[z]$-homomorphism with annihilating polynomial $\psi$. Then $f$ is uniquely determined by its $p \times m$ transfer function matrix $W(z)$, whose columns are the p-vector rational functions $f(e_j) = \theta_j/\psi$, in the indeterminate $z$, $j = 1, \ldots, m$. Conversely, any matrix $W(z)$ with proper rational elements induces a unique $k[z]$-homomorphism $f_W$ by the rule*

$$f_W: \quad \Omega \to \Gamma : e_j \mapsto \theta_j/\psi_W,$$

*where $\psi_W$ is the least common denominator of $W$. The element $\psi_W$ is the annihilating polynomial of the $k[z]$-module $X_W$ induced by $f_W$.*

This theorem shows that $W$ and $f$ are equivalent objects. Thus, to compute $f(\omega)$ for a given $\omega \in \Omega$, we can proceed as follows:

1. Compute the ordinary vector-matrix product $W(z)\omega$.
2. Expand the results in powers of $z^{-1}$ and throw away all terms involving nonnegative powers of $z$; the result is $f(\omega)$.

We have already seen the invariant factor theorem for modules in Section IV. The corresponding classical result for polynomial matrices is

**Invariant Factor Theorem for Polynomial Matrices**   *Let $P$ be a $p \times m$ matrix with elements in a principal ideal domain $R$. Then*

$$P = A\Lambda B,$$

*where $A$ and $B$ are matrices of sizes $p \times p$, $m \times m$, respectively, with elements in $R$ and $\det A$, $\det B$ are units in $R$. The matrix*

$$\Lambda = \mathrm{diag}(\lambda_1, \lambda_2, \ldots, \lambda_q, 0, \cdots, 0), \qquad \lambda_i \in R$$

*is unique (up to units in $R$) with $\lambda_i|\lambda_{i+1}$, $\tau = 1, 2, \ldots, q - 1$, $q = \mathrm{rank}\, P$. The elements $\lambda_i$ are called the invariant factors of $P$.*

As should be expected there is a direct relation between the elements $\psi_i$ of the module-theoretic invariant factor theorem and the elements $\lambda_i$ of the classical polynomial matrix version. In fact, they are equal as the following shows:

**Theorem 3.2**   *The invariant factors of a finitely generated torsion $k[z]$-module $X$ with annihilating polynomial $\psi$ and generators $\{g_1, g_2, \ldots, g_m\}$, are* *identical to those of the polynomial matrix $\psi W(z)$, where $W(z)$ is the transfer function matrix associated with $X$ by the rule*

$$W(z) = H(zI - F)^{-1}G,$$

*where*

$$F\colon \quad X \to X\colon \quad x \mapsto z \cdot x,$$

$$G\colon \quad k^m \to X\colon \quad (\alpha_1, \ldots, \alpha_m) \mapsto \sum_{k=1}^{m} \alpha_k g_k, \quad \alpha_i \in k,$$

$$H\colon \quad X \to k^p\colon \quad g_k \mapsto e_k.$$

Now let $X_W$ be the $k[z]$-module induced by $W(z)$ as in the Representation Theorem. Our question is: how are the invariant factors $\{\psi_i\}$ associated with $X_W$ related to the invariant factors of $W(z)$? The answer is provided by

**Theorem 3.3**   *Let $\{\lambda_1, \lambda_2, \ldots, \lambda_q\}$ be the invariant factors of $\psi W$ and let $(\lambda_i, \psi) = \theta_i, \tau = 1, 2, \ldots, q$. Then the invariant factors of $X_W$ are*

$$\psi_1 = \psi,$$

$$\psi_2 = \psi/\theta_2,$$

$$\psi_3 = \psi/\theta_3,$$

$$\vdots$$

$$\psi_r = \psi/\theta_r,$$

*where $r$ equals the smallest integer such that $\psi | \lambda_i$ for $i = r + 1, \ldots, q = \mathrm{rank}\ \psi W$.*

Viewed another way, we have

$$\lambda_i/\psi = (\lambda_i/\theta_i)/(\psi/\theta_i), \qquad \theta_i = (\lambda_i, \omega)$$

since the invariant factors of $W$ must be equal to those of $X_W$ (by the bijective correspondence $W \leftrightarrow X_W$). Thus, we see that

$\psi_i = $ denominator of $\lambda_i/\psi$ after cancellation of all common factors.

The invariant factor theorems enable us to address the question of when a system $\Sigma_1$ can be *simulated* by a system $\Sigma_2$, i.e., when the desired external behavior of $\Sigma_1$ can be reproduced by altering the dynamical behavior of $\Sigma_2$ through feedback-free coding of its inputs and outputs involving delay. In other words, we want $\Sigma_2$ to act like a machine with transfer function $W_1$ by recoding its inputs and outputs. To make this problem precise, we have

**Definition 3.7**   $\Sigma_1 | \Sigma_2$ (i.e., $\Sigma_1$ can be *simulated* by $\Sigma_2$) if and only if $X_{\Sigma_1} | X_{\Sigma_2}$, i.e., if and only if $X_{\Sigma_1}$ is isomorphic to a submodule of $X_{\Sigma_2}$ (or isomorphic to a quotient module of $X_{\Sigma_2}$).

The main result governing the issue of whether $\Sigma_1 | \Sigma_2$, is the classical theorem

**Theorem 3.4** *Let R be a principal ideal domain and X, Y R-modules. Then $Y | X$ if and only if*

$$\psi_i(Y) | \psi_i(X), \qquad i = 1, 2, \ldots, r(Y) \le r(X).$$

The above criterion settles the basic simulation question in terms of the invariant factors of the respective state modules $X_{\Sigma_1}$, $X_{\Sigma_2}$. Since $X_\Sigma \approx W$, it is to be expected that a similar test involving the invariant factors of $W_{\Sigma_1}(z)$, $W_{\Sigma_2}(z)$ holds. To formalize this notion, we state

**Definition 3.8** Let $W_1$ and $W_2$ be transfer functions matrices. Then $W_1 | W_2$, i.e., $W_1$ *divides* $W_2$ if and only if there exist matrices $V$, $Z$ over $k[z]$ such that

$$W_1 = V W_2 Z.$$

Now we can state

**Theorem 3.5** $W_1 | W_2$ *if and only if* $\psi_i(W_1) | \psi_i(W_2)$, $i = 1, 2, \ldots, r$.

Putting Theorems 3.4 and 3.5 together, we arrive at the

**Prime Decomposition Theorem for Linear Systems** *The following conditions are equivalent:*

1. $W_1 | W_2$,
2. $\psi_i(W_1) | \psi_i(W_2)$ *for all i,*
3. $\Sigma_1 | \Sigma_2$.

REMARK 1    The results enable us to say that the dynamical behavior of $\Sigma_2$ can be arbitrarily altered by feedback-free coding of its inputs and outputs if and only if the invariant factors of the desired external behavior $W_{\Sigma_1}$ are divisors of the invariant factors of the external behavior $W_{\Sigma_2}$ of the given system $\Sigma_2$. Thus, we may regard the invariant factors as the basic building-blocks of linear systems in that they cannot be simulated from smaller units by feedback-free coding. We shall make this notion mathematically precise and explicit in Section VI.

REMARK 2    To see how the *coding* operation needed to make $\Sigma_2$ simulate $\Sigma_1$ works, consider the following procedure: The original input $\omega_2$ is replaced by $\omega_1 = B(z)\omega_2$. Similarly, the original output $\gamma_2$ is replaced by $\gamma_1 = A(z)\gamma_2$. Now $\Sigma_2$ will act like a system $\Sigma_1$ with a transfer function $W_1(z) = AW_2B$. However, this equation will still be satisfied if $A$ and $B$ are replaced by $\tilde{A}$, $\tilde{B}$ (i.e., $A$, $B$ mod $\psi_{W_2}$). Thus, the coding operations $A$ and $B$ can be carried out physically using only a delay of $d = \deg \psi_{W_2}$ units, i.e., it is necessary only to store the last $d$ inputs and outputs.

## VI. REALIZATION OF TRANSFER FUNCTIONS

Given a proper rational matrix $W(z)$ whose entries have least common denominator $\psi$, the matrix $\psi W$ is clearly a polynomial matrix which, by the invariant factor theorem, can be represented as

$$\psi W = A\Lambda B,$$

where $\det A$, $\det B$ are units in $k[z]$, with $\Lambda$ a diagonal matrix containing the invariant factors $\lambda_1, \lambda_2, \ldots, \lambda_r$. If we replace each polynomial $\pi$ in the above representation by its canonical representative $\tilde{\pi}$ in the class $\pi \bmod \psi$, we have the alternate representation

$$\psi W = PLQ \bmod \psi, \qquad (3.3)$$

where $\det P$, $\det Q$ are units in $k[z]/k[z]\psi$ and $L$ is a diagonal matrix, unique up to units in $k[z]/k[z]\psi$. The canonical realization problem for transfer functions is to determine a system $\Sigma_W = (F, G, H)$ such that

(i)   $W(z) = H(zI - F)^{-1}G$,
(ii)  $\dim \Sigma_W = \dim X_W$.

In this section, we develop an explicit procedure for computing such a realization from a given $W$.

Let us begin with the following easy result.

***Lemma 3.2***   *Let $F$ be the companion matrix*

$$F = \begin{bmatrix} 0 & 1 & 0 & \cdots & 0 \\ 0 & 0 & 1 & & 0 \\ \vdots & & & & \vdots \\ 0 & 0 & 0 & & 1 \\ -\alpha_n & -\alpha_{n-1} & -\alpha_{n-2} & \cdots & -\alpha_1 \end{bmatrix}$$

*with characteristic polynomial*

$$\psi_F(z) = z^n + \alpha_1 z^{n-1} + \cdots + \alpha_n.$$

*Then*

$$\psi_F(z)(zI - F)^{-1} = v(z)w'(z) \bmod \psi_F,$$

*where*

$$v(z) = \begin{bmatrix} 1 \\ z \\ \vdots \\ z^{n-1} \end{bmatrix}, \qquad w(z) = \begin{bmatrix} z^{n-1} + \alpha_1 z^{n-2} + \cdots + \alpha_{n-1} \\ \vdots \\ z + \alpha_1 \\ 1 \end{bmatrix}.$$

The proof is immediate by a direct calculation.

The canonical realization of $W(z)$ now proceeds according to the following steps:

**Realization Algorithm for $W(z)$**

1. Compute the invariant factors $\{\psi_i\}$ of $W(z)$.
2. Calculate the representation (3.3) for $\psi W(z)$ and write $L = \text{diag}(l_1, l_2, \ldots)$, $p_i = i$th column of $P$, $q_i' = i$th row of $Q$, $\mu_i = (l_i, \psi)$.
3. For each invariant factor $\psi_i$ of $W$, let $F_i$ = companion matrix of $\psi_i$, i.e., $\psi_{F_i} = \psi_i$. Let $v_i(z)$, $w_i(z)$ be the associated polynomial vectors from Lemma 3.2.
4. Solve the pair of equations

$$H_i v_i = (l_i/\mu_i)p_i \bmod \psi_i, \qquad i = 1, 2, \ldots, q,$$
$$w_i' G_i = q_i' \bmod \psi_i. \tag{3.4}$$

The mod $\psi_i$ operation allows us to assume that the elements on the right side of Eqs. (3.4) have $\deg < \deg \psi_i$; hence, the equations for $H_i$ and $G_i$ have *unique* solutions.

5. Write the realization as

$$F = \text{diag}(F_1, F_2, \ldots, F_q),$$

$$G = \begin{bmatrix} G_1 \\ G_2 \\ \vdots \\ G_q \end{bmatrix}, \qquad H = [H_1, H_2, \ldots, H_q].$$

The general structure of a linear system is formalized by the following realization theorem.

**Theorem 3.6** *Every proper rational transfer function matrix $W$ may be realized as the direct sum of the systems*

$$\Sigma_i = (F_i, G_i, H_i),$$

*where $F_i$ is a cyclic matrix with characteristic polynomial $\psi_i$ and $G_i$ and $H_i$ are computed as in the Realization Algorithm.*

Schematically, this realization looks as in Fig. 3.1. We note that the figure makes clear the high degree of internal connectivity in a *canonical* realization of $W$. Figure 3.1 should be contrasted with Fig. 3.2, in which a conventional realization of $W$ is displayed. Such a realization results from an arbitrary choice of connections and is *almost never* canonical.

The solution to the realization problem via the invariant factor theorem provides complete information concerning the structure of a canonical realization. However, the cost of using such a method is high since computation of the invariant factors is both time consuming and complex. Some

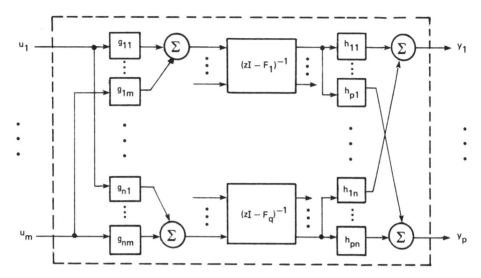

**FIG. 3.1**    General diagram of a linear system.

alternate approaches are considered in the problems at the end of the chapter. In Section VII, we shall consider the

**Question.**    If we do not want to know the invariant factors, but only the matrices $F$, $G$, $H$ of a canonical realization, can we find a simpler algorithm than that provided by the invariant factor theorem?

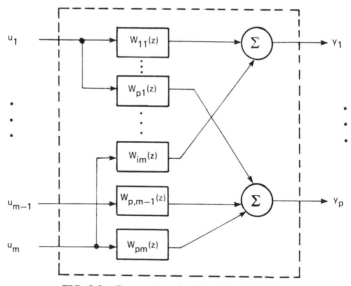

**FIG. 3.2**    Conventional realization of $W(z)$

## VII. THE CONSTRUCTION
## OF CANONICAL REALIZATIONS

Abstractly, we may consider the realization problem as a factorization of the input–output map $f: \Omega \to \Gamma$ through the state space $X$ (see Fig. 3.3). Here we define a realization to be *canonical* if and only if the map $g$ is *onto*, while $h$ is 1–1. Realizations always exist since, for example, we could take $X = \Omega$, $g =$ identity on $\Omega$, $h = f$. Of course, this realization is both trivial and useless, as well as noncanonical. The module machinery has already shown how to construct a canonical realization from a transfer matrix, *provided* we are willing to compute the invariant factors of $W$. In this section, we pursue the problem of actual construction of a canonical realization from two directions:

1. streamlining the algorithm for construction of $\Sigma$ from $W$ *without* first computing invariant factors;
2. direct construction of $\Sigma$ from the *behavior* sequence $B = \{A_1, A_2, \dots\}$ induced by the map $f$ as

$$f(\omega)(1) = \sum_{t \le 0} A_{-t+1}\omega(t),$$

where the $A_k$ are $p \times m$ matrices over the field $k$. Clearly if $\Sigma = (F, G, H)$ realizes $f$, then we have

$$f(\omega)(1) = \sum_{t \le 0} HF^{-t}G\omega(t)$$

so a realization of $B$ is equivalent to finding a $\Sigma$ such that

$$A_{k+1} = HF^kG, \qquad k = 0, 1, 2, \dots .$$

We have already seen (via the Correspondence Theorem) that any two canonical realizations must be related via a basis change in the state space $X$. Part of the justification for regarding an observable and reachable realization as being a *natural* requirement is the following easy result.

**Theorem 3.7**   *The* dim $\Sigma$ *is minimal over the class of all realizations of* $f$ *if and only if* $\Sigma$ *is a canonical realization of* $f$.

PROOF   Let $\hat{\Sigma}$ be any realization and let $\Sigma$ be a canonical realization. Then $f = \hat{h} \circ \hat{g}$ and therefore $\hat{h}(\hat{X}) \supset$ range $f$. But $X \approx$ range $f$, since $f$ may be

**FIG. 3.3**   Factorization of the map $f$.

factored canonically as $\Omega \twoheadrightarrow$ range $f \rightarrow \Gamma$, where the second map is the natural injection. So

$$\dim \hat{\Sigma} \doteq \dim \hat{X} \geq \dim \text{range } f = \dim X \doteq \dim \Sigma.$$

For equality to hold in the middle expression, we must have $\hat{h}(\hat{X}) \approx$ range $f$, i.e., $\hat{h}$ is 1–1. Moreover, range $\hat{g} \approx \hat{X}$ (since otherwise $f \neq h \circ g$), which implies $\hat{g}$ is onto. Thus, $\dim \hat{X}$ a minimum implies that the factorization is canonical.

To streamline the realization algorithm given earlier, we begin with a *noncanonical*, but easily obtained realization of the transfer function matrix $W(z)$. Let us write

$$\psi W(z) = z^{q-1} R_0 + z^{q-2} R_1 + \cdots + R_{q-1},$$

where

$$\psi(z) = z^q + \psi_1 z^{q-1} + \cdots + \psi_q$$

is the monic least common denominator of all elements $w_{ij}(z)$ of $W(z)$. The $p \times m$ matrices $\{R_i\}$ are, of course, constant. Then it is easily verified that a realization of $W(z)$ is

$$F = \begin{bmatrix} 0 & I_m & 0 & \cdots & 0 \\ 0 & 0 & I_m & & 0 \\ \vdots & & & & \\ -\psi_q I_m & -\psi_{q-1} I_m & & \cdots & -\psi_1 I_m \end{bmatrix}, \quad G = \begin{bmatrix} 0 \\ 0 \\ \vdots \\ 0 \\ I_m \end{bmatrix},$$

$$H = [R_{q-1} R_{q-2} \cdots R_0],$$

where $I_m = m \times m$ identity matrix. It is easy to check that the system $\Sigma = (F, G, H)$ realizes $W(z)$ and is even completely reachable. The problem is that, in general, the above realization is far from completely observable, hence, it is not canonical (unless $m = 1$ and $W(z)$ is irreducible).

To *reduce* the $\Sigma$ to a canonical realization, we make the simplifying assumption that the denominators of the elements $w_{ij}(z)$ of $W(z)$ have only simple zeroes $z_1, z_2, \ldots, z_s$. Define the matrix

$$K_i = \lim_{z \to z_i} (z - z_i) W(z), \qquad i = 1, 2, \ldots, s$$

and let $r_i = \text{rank } K_i$. By definition of rank, there exist $(p \times r_i)$ and $(r_i \times m)$ matrices $L_i$ and $M_i$, respectively, such that

$$K_i = L_i M_i.$$

Now we can state the easy result

**Theorem 3.8**   *A canonical realization of* $W(z)$ *is given by*

$$\hat{F} = \text{diag}(z_1 I_{r_1}, z_2 I_{r_2}, \ldots, z_s I_{r_s}),$$

$$\hat{G} = \begin{bmatrix} M_1 \\ M_2 \\ \vdots \\ M_s \end{bmatrix}, \qquad \hat{H}[L_1, L_2, \ldots, L_s].$$

PROOF   A direct computation shows that $\hat{\Sigma} = (\hat{F}, \hat{G}, \hat{H})$ is such that

$$H(zI - F)^{-1}G = \sum_{i+1}^{s} K_i/(z - z_i) = W(z)$$

by the assumption on the zeroes of the denominator of $w_{ij}(z)$.

To prove that $\hat{\Sigma}$ is canonical, we must show that it is reachable and observable. The reachability matrix is

$$\mathscr{C} = \begin{bmatrix} M_1 & z_1 M_1 & z_1^2 M_1 & \cdots & z_1^{n-1} M_1 \\ M_2 & z_2 M_2 & z_2^2 M_2 & & z_2^{n-1} M_2 \\ \vdots & & & & \\ M_s & z_s M_s & z_s^2 M_s & \cdots & z_s^{n-1} M_s \end{bmatrix},$$

where $n = r_1 + r_2 + \cdots + r_s$. Since rank $M_i = r_i$ and the $z_i$ are distinct, rank $\mathscr{C} = n$ implying $\hat{\Sigma}$ is reachable. The observability condition is proved similarly.

**Example**   Consider the transfer matrix

$$W(z) = \frac{1}{\psi(z)} \begin{bmatrix} (z^2 + 6) & (z^2 + z + 4) \\ (2z^2 - 7z - 2) & (z^2 - 5z - 2) \end{bmatrix},$$

$$\psi(z) = z^3 + 2z^2 - z - 2.$$

The elements of $W$ all have the same denominator $\psi(z)$, which has the simple roots $z_1 = 1, z_2 = -1, z_3 = -2$. Computing the matrix $K_1$, we have

$$K_1 = \lim_{z \to 1} (z - 1)W(z) = \begin{bmatrix} \frac{7}{6} & 1 \\ -\frac{7}{6} & -1 \end{bmatrix}$$

so that rank $K_1 = r_1 = 1$. Furthermore, $K_1$ can be factored as

$$K_1 = L_1 M_1 = \begin{bmatrix} 1 \\ -1 \end{bmatrix} \begin{bmatrix} \frac{7}{6} & 1 \end{bmatrix}.$$

Similarly, we find $r_2 = 1, r_3 = 1$, with

$$K_2 = L_2 M_2 = \begin{bmatrix} 1 \\ 1 \end{bmatrix} [-\tfrac{7}{2} \ \ -2],$$

$$K_3 = L_3 M_3 = \begin{bmatrix} 1 \\ 2 \end{bmatrix} [\tfrac{10}{3} \ \ 2].$$

Hence, a canonical realization of $W(z)$ is

$$F = \text{diag}(1, -1, -2), \qquad G = \begin{bmatrix} \tfrac{7}{6} & 1 \\ -\tfrac{7}{2} & -2 \\ \tfrac{10}{3} & 2 \end{bmatrix}, \qquad H = \begin{bmatrix} 1 & 1 & 1 \\ -1 & 1 & 2 \end{bmatrix}.$$

We have already pointed out that the $k[z]$-homomorphism $f \colon \Omega \to \Gamma$ induces a behavior sequence $B = \{A_1, A_2, A_3, \ldots\}$. On the other hand, if we are given a transfer matrix $W(z)$ (which, as we know from Section VI is equivalent to $f$), we can expand $W(z)$ about $z = \infty$ to get

$$W(z) = L_1 z^{-1} + L_2 z^{-2} + L_3 z^{-3} + \cdots,$$

where $\{L_i\}$ are $p \times m$ constant matrices. Since $f$ and $W$ must generate the same input–output behavior, we must have

$$A_i \equiv L_i, \qquad i = 1, 2, \ldots.$$

Thus, any procedure for generating a canonical realization for $W(z)$ must be capable of generating a similar realization for $B$ *and conversely*. We have already seen how to canonically realize $W$, so let us turn to the realization of $B$.

**Definition 3.9**  A dynamical system $\Sigma = (F, G, H)$ *realizes* the infinite matrix sequence $B = \{A_1, A_2, \ldots\}$ if and only if

$$A_{k+1} = HF^k G, \qquad k = 0, 1, 2, \ldots.$$

The mathematical *gadget* we need to deal with the realization of $B$ is the (infinite) *Hankel* matrix associated with $B$, denoted $\mathscr{H}(B)$. Explicitly

$$\mathscr{H}(B) = \begin{bmatrix} A_1 & A_2 & A_3 & \cdots \\ A_2 & A_3 & A_4 & \\ A_3 & A_4 & A_5 & \\ \vdots & & & \ddots \end{bmatrix}.$$

We let $\mathscr{H}_{\mu,\nu}$ denote the $\mu \times \nu$ block submatrix of $\mathscr{H}$ appearing in the upper left-hand corner of $\mathscr{H}$. Basically, the utility of the Hankel matrix $\mathscr{H}$ in realization theory comes from its role as a matrix representation of the map

$f: \Omega \to \Gamma$, when $\omega \in \Omega$ is regarded as an infinite column vector with elements $(\omega_1(0), \ldots, \omega_m(0), \omega_1(1), \ldots)$.

Realizations of $B$ and the properties of $\mathscr{H}(B)$ are related through

**Theorem 3.9**   *Let $\Sigma$ be any realization of $B$. Then*

$$\text{rank } \mathscr{H}_{\mu,\nu}(B) \leq \dim \Sigma \qquad \text{for all } \mu, \nu \geq 1.$$

**Corollary**   *The sequence $B$ has a finite-dimensional realization if and only if* rank $\mathscr{H}_{\mu,\nu}(B)$ *is constant for $\mu, \nu$ sufficiently large.*

PROOF   To avoid an empty (but formally correct) argument, assume $\dim \Sigma = n < \infty$. Define from $\Sigma$ the block matrices

$$\mathscr{C}_\nu = [G, FG, \ldots, F^{\nu-1}G],$$

$$\theta_\mu = [H', H'F', \ldots, H'(F')^{\mu-1}].$$

Then

$$\theta'_\mu \mathscr{C}_\nu = \mathscr{H}_{\mu,\nu}(B).$$

Since rank $\mathscr{C}_\nu$ and rank $\theta_\mu \leq n = \dim \Sigma$, the theorem reduces to the standard matrix fact

$$\text{rank}(AB) \leq \min\{\text{rank } A, \text{rank } B\}.$$

Now let us turn our attention to proving the *if* part of the corollary, thereby producing an effective algorithm (Ho's Algorithm) for canonically realizing $B$. For this we require

**Definition 3.10**   The infinite Hankel matrix $\mathscr{H}(B)$ has *finite length* $\lambda = (\lambda', \lambda'')$ if and only if one of the following two equivalent conditions holds:

$$\lambda' = \min\{l: \text{rank } \mathscr{H}_{l,\nu} = \text{rank } \mathscr{H}_{l+k,\nu} \text{ for all } k, \nu = 1, 2, \ldots\} < \infty,$$

$$\lambda'' = \min\{m: \text{rank } \mathscr{H}_{\mu,m} = \text{rank } \mathscr{H}_{\mu,m+k} \text{ for all } k, \mu = 1, 2, \ldots\} < \infty.$$

We call $\lambda'$ the *row length* of $\mathscr{H}$ and $\lambda''$ the *column length* of $\mathscr{H}$. The last ingredient we need is the notion of a *shift* of the sequence $B$.

**Definition 3.11**   The (left) *shift operator* $\sigma_B$ on an infinite sequence $B$ is given by

$$\sigma_B^k: \quad (A_1, A_2, \ldots) \mapsto (A_{1+k}, A_{2+k}, \ldots).$$

The corresponding shift operator on Hankel matrices is then

$$\sigma_H^k: \quad \mathscr{H}(B) \mapsto \mathscr{H}(\sigma_B^k B).$$

Since we have seen earlier that the shift operator is the algebraic equivalent of the dynamics $F$, it should come as no surprise that $\sigma_B$ will play a central role in realizing the sequence $B$. The connection between $\mathcal{H}$ having finite length and the shift operator $\sigma_B$ is that finite length is equivalent to $\sigma_B$ having finite-dimensional left- and right-matrix representations, i.e., there exist finite block matrices $S$ and $Z$ such that

$$\sigma_H^k \mathcal{H}_{l',l''}(B) = S\mathcal{H}_{l',l''}(B), = \mathcal{H}_{l',l''}(B)Z.$$

We are finally in a position to state the

**Ho Realization Algorithm**    *Consider any infinite sequence $B$ of finite length with associated Hankel matrix $\mathcal{H}$. The following steps will produce a canonical realization of $B$.*

   1. *Determine $\lambda'$, $\lambda''$.*
   2. *Compute $n = \text{rank } \mathcal{H}_{\lambda',\lambda''}$.*
   3. *Determine nonsingular matrices $P$ and $Q$ of sizes $p\lambda' \times p\lambda'$ and $m\lambda'' \times m\lambda''$, respectively, such that*

$$P\mathcal{H}_{\lambda',\lambda''}Q = \begin{bmatrix} I_n & 0 \\ 0 & 0 \end{bmatrix}.$$

(Note that $P$ and $Q$ are determined as part of the process of determining the number $n$.)
   4. *Write the realization $\Sigma = (F, G, H)$ as*

$$F = \mathcal{K}_n P[\sigma_H \mathcal{H}_{\lambda',\lambda''}]Q\mathcal{K}^n,$$

$$G = \mathcal{K}_n P\mathcal{H}_{\lambda',\lambda''}\mathcal{K}^m,$$

$$H = \mathcal{K}_p \mathcal{H}_{\lambda',\lambda''}Q\mathcal{K}^n,$$

*where $\mathcal{K}_p$, $\mathcal{K}^m$ are idempotent editing matrices having the effect*: retain first $p$ rows *and* retain first $m$ columns, *respectively.*

    The most serious *apparent* drawback to the employment of the Ho Algorithm is the need to verify the assumption that $B$ is of finite length. If additional information is given in advance concerning $B$, then this requirement can sometimes be seen by inspection to hold, e.g., $A_k = 0$ for all $k$ greater than some fixed $N$ or $A_k$ equal to coefficients of the expansion of a rational matrix function. However, even in the general case the finite length difficulty is more apparent than real as the next result demonstrates.

**Rank Condition Theorem**    *Let $B$ be any infinite behavior sequence with corresponding Hankel matrix $\mathcal{H}$. Suppose there exist integers $r$ and $s$ such that*

$$\text{rank } \mathcal{H}_{r,s}(B) = \text{rank } \mathcal{H}_{r+1,s}(B) = \text{rank } \mathcal{H}_{r,s+1}(B). \qquad (3.5)$$

*Then there exists a unique extension $\hat{B}$ of $B$ of order $r + s$ such that $\lambda'_B \leq r$*

*and $\lambda_B'' \leq s$. Moreover, applying the Ho Algorithm with $\lambda' = r$ and $\lambda'' = s$ produces a canonical realization of $\hat{B}$.*

So, we see that a canonical realization of some extension of $B$ is always possible as soon as the rank condition (3.5) is satisfied. Furthermore, (3.5) can be used as a practical criterion for constructing a canonical realization for some $B$ known to be of finite length, but without being given $\lambda'$ and $\lambda''$.

If the Ho Algorithm is applied without any information concerning the condition (3.5), then the system $\Sigma$ produced will always realize *some* extension of $B$, at least of order 1. Details of how to determine the maximal order of this extension, at least for scalar behavior sequences, are given in the chapter references.

### Example:   The Pell Numbers

To illustrate use of the Ho Algorithm and the Rank Condition Theorem, let us construct a canonical realization of the sequence of Pell numbers

$$B = \{1, 2, 5, 12, 29, 70, \ldots\}.$$

The second-order difference equation generating $B$ is

$$A_{n+2} = 2A_{n+1} + A_n,$$

which suggests that the entire sequence $B$ can be generated by a two-dimensional canonical model $\Sigma$. We now establish this result by the Ho Algorithm. Consider the matrix $\mathscr{H}_{11} = [A_1] = [1]$. It is easy to see that

$$\text{rank } \mathscr{H}_{11} = 1 = \text{rank } \mathscr{H}_{21} = \text{rank}\begin{bmatrix} 1 \\ 2 \end{bmatrix} = \text{rank } \mathscr{H}_{12} = \text{rank } [1\ 2].$$

So, the sequence $\{A_1\}$ can be canonically realized by a one-dimensional $\Sigma$. Applying Ho's procedure immediately yields

$$P = [1], \quad Q = [1]$$

and

$$\Sigma_1: \quad F = [2], \quad G = [1], \quad H = [1].$$

The system $\Sigma_1$ extends the sequence $\{1\}$ to $\{1, 2, 4\}$, which does not agree with $\{A_1, A_2, A_3\}$. So, to realize $\{A_1, A_2, A_3\}$, we must examine more data.

Consider next the Hankel array $\mathscr{H}_{22} = \begin{bmatrix} 1 & 2 \\ 2 & 5 \end{bmatrix}$, obtained from the sequence $\{A_1, A_2, A_3\}$. We easily see that

$$\text{rank } \mathscr{H}_{22} = 2 = \text{rank } \mathscr{H}_{23} = \text{rank}\begin{bmatrix} 1 & 2 & 5 \\ 2 & 5 & 12 \end{bmatrix} = \text{rank } \mathscr{H}_{32} = \text{rank}\begin{bmatrix} 1 & 2 \\ 2 & 5 \\ 5 & 12 \end{bmatrix}.$$

So, we can canonically realize $\{A_1, A_2, A_3\}$ with a 2-dimensional realization. Factoring $\mathcal{H}_{22}$ by the Ho Algorithm, we have $P\mathcal{H}_{22}Q = \begin{bmatrix} 1 & 0 \\ 0 & 1 \end{bmatrix}$, where

$$P = \begin{bmatrix} 1 & 0 \\ 2 & -1 \end{bmatrix}, \qquad Q = \begin{bmatrix} 1 & 2 \\ 0 & -1 \end{bmatrix}.$$

The remaining steps of the algorithm yield

$$\Sigma_2: \quad F = \begin{bmatrix} 2 & -1 \\ -1 & 0 \end{bmatrix}, \quad G = \begin{bmatrix} 1 \\ 0 \end{bmatrix}, \quad H = [1 \ 0].$$

After a few calculations, we can verify that $\Sigma_2$ produces the original sequence of Pell numbers $B$. This can also be seen by examining the ranks of the matrices $\mathcal{H}_{rr}$, $r > 2$. Of course, without knowledge of the recurrence relation for the $\{A_i\}$, we could never *empirically* check the Rank Condition Theorem for *all* $A_i$, since this would entail the examination of an infinite amount of data. This leads to the remaining interesting

**Question.** What can be said if the assumptions of the Rank Condition Theorem are not satisfied for a *finite* amount of data $A_1, A_2, \ldots, A_N$, and any $r$, $s$ satisfying $r + s = N$?

This *partial realization* problem is addressed in Section VIII.

## VIII. PARTIAL REALIZATIONS

The basic flaw in the foregoing modeling theory à lá the Ho Algorithm is the underlying assumption that the behavior sequence $B$ has a finite-dimensional realization. But, suppose we are given an input–output map $f$ and associated sequence $B = \{A_1, A_2, \ldots\}$, but that we know or assume nothing about the finite dimensionality of the map $f$. But, suppose we pick numbers $\lambda'$, $\lambda''$ arbitrarily and compute a dynamical system according to the Ho Algorithm.

**Question.** What are the properties of such a $\Sigma$?
**Question.** Is $\Sigma$ canonical?
**Question.** Does $\Sigma$ realize a part of $B$?

The answer to these questions is provided by the

***Partial Realization Theorem*** *Let $N$, $N'$ be integers such that*

$$\text{rank } \mathcal{H}_{N',N} = \text{rank } \mathcal{H}_{N'+1,N} = \text{rank } \mathcal{H}_{N',N+1} \tag{3.6}$$

*and let $N_0 = N + N'$. Then a system $\Sigma$ given by the Ho Algorithm with $\lambda = N$, $\lambda' = N'$ is a canonical partial realization of order $N_0$, i.e., it realizes* *the sequence $B_{N_0} = \{A_1, A_2, \ldots, A_{N_0}\}$. Furthermore, if the above rank condition does not hold for $N$, $N'$, then every partial realization of $f$ has dimension greater than rank $\mathscr{H}_{N,N}$.*

REMARK 1    For partial realizations, *minimal* implies *canonical*, but not conversely. In fact, *minimal* realizations are not necessarily unique.

REMARK 2    In general, there is no way to say whether or not a partial realization of $f$ is useful or not. For example, consider the transfer function matrix

$$W(z) = W_1(z) + z^{-h} W_2(z),$$

with $h$ much larger than the degree of the common denominator of $W_1$. The effect of the second term will be absent from $\mathscr{H}_{rr}$, for all $r \geq \deg \psi_{W_1} \ll h$. Thus, we get a minimal realization $\Sigma_1$ of $W_1$ by the Ho method and, since

$$W(z) - W_{\Sigma_1}(z) = W(z) - W_1(z) = z^{-h} W_2(z),$$

it is clear that the minimal realization of the remainder has dimension equal to dim $z^{-h} W_2(z)$.

The interesting aspects of the partial realization problem arise when the rank condition (3.6) is not satisfied. Thus, we have the partial sequence

$$B_M = \{A_1, A_2, \ldots, A_M\}$$

and our problem is to *extend* this sequence (we hope, uniquely) to an infinite sequence which can be described via the compact triple $\Sigma = (F, G, H)$. Let us define

$n_1(M) =$ the number of linearly independent rows in the block row
$\quad [A_1, \ldots, A_M]$;

$n_2(M) =$ the number of linearly independent rows in the block row
$\quad [A_2, \ldots, A_M]$, which are also linearly independent of the
$\quad$ rows in the block row $[A_1, \ldots, A_{M-1}]$. $\qquad (3.7)$

$\vdots$

$n_M(M) =$ the number of linearly independent rows in $A_M$ which are
$\quad$ also linearly independent of the rows of the matrices
$\quad A_1, A_2, \ldots, A_{M-1}$.

Define

$$\hat{n}(M) = n_1(M) + n_2(M) + \cdots + n_M(M).$$

It can be shown that the dimension of the minimal realization of any extension of $B_M$ is always $\geq \hat{n}(M)$.

Similarly, we can obtain *lower bounds* for the values of $N, N'$ for which the rank conditions can be satisfied for any extension of $B_M$ as follows:

$N'(M) =$ the first integer such that every row of the block row $[A_{N'+1}, \ldots, A_M]$ is linearly dependent on the rows of $\mathscr{H}_{N', M-N'}$;                    (3.8)

$N(M) =$ the first integer such that every column of the block column

$$\begin{bmatrix} A_{N+1} \\ \vdots \\ A_M \end{bmatrix}$$

is linearly dependent on the columns of $\mathscr{H}_{M-N,N}$.

The surprising and happy fact is that all of these lower bounds can actually be obtained as the following result illustrates.

***Main Extension Theorem*** *Let $B_M$ be a fixed partial sequence with the integers $\hat{n}(M)$, $N(M)$, $N'(M)$ as defined in Eqs. (3.7) and (3.8). Then*

(i)  *$\hat{n}(M) = \dim \Sigma_M$, where $\Sigma_M = (F_M, G_M, H_M)$ is the minimal realization of any extension of $B_M$.*

(ii)  *$N(M)$, $N'(M)$ are the smallest integers such that the rank condition (3.6) holds for some extension of $B_M$;*

(iii)  *$N(M)$, $N'(M)$ are the smallest integers such that the rank condition (3.6) holds for all minimal realizations;*

(iv)  *there is a minimal extension of order $M' = N + N'$ for which the rank condition (3.6) holds. The realization of this extension can be carried out (nonuniquely) by the Ho Algorithm;*

(v)  *every extension of $B_M$ which is fixed up to $M'$ is uniquely determined thereafter.*

Only recently was the partial realization problem completely and definitively settled for scalar behavior sequences. Since the details would take us too far off the main course of this chapter, we do not present them here and refer only to the chapter notes and bibliography.

## IX. POLE-SHIFTING AND STABILITY

Given the dynamical system $\Sigma$,

$$\dot{x} = Fx + Gu, \qquad x(0) = c,$$

one of the oldest system-theoretic questions is whether $\Sigma$ is asymptotically stable, i.e., if $c \neq 0$, does $x(t) \to 0$ as $t \to \infty$. Clearly, if the characteristic values of $F$ lie in the left half-plane, then $\Sigma$ is stable with no control needed. Furthermore, if $F$ has some unstable roots, then the classical Pole-Shifting Theorem tells us that if the pair $(F, G)$ is reachable, we may choose a feedback control $u(t) = -Kx(t)$, such that $F - GK$ has prescribed characteristic roots.

The module-theoretic machinery we developed allows us to extend the Pole-Shifting Theorem to the case of an arbitrary field $k$. For a single-input system, the statement of the result is

***Pole-Shifting Theorem (single-input version)***  *Let $k$ be an arbitrary field with $X$ a cyclic $k[z]$-module with generator $g$ and minimal polynomial $\chi(z) = z^n + \alpha_1 z^{n-1} + \cdots + \alpha_n$, $\deg \chi = n$. Then there is a bijection between $n$th degree polynomials $\pi(z) = z^n + \beta_1 z^{n-1} + \cdots + \beta_n \in k[z]$ and $k$-homomorphisms $l: k^n \to k^n: \chi^{(j)} \cdot g \mapsto l_j \cdot g \ (j = 1, \ldots, n)$, such that $\pi$ is the minimal polynomial for the new module structure induced on $X$ by the map $z_*$: $x \mapsto z \cdot g - l(x)$. (Here the elements $\chi^{(j)}$ are defined by*

$$e_n = g = z \cdot g = \chi^{(1)}(z) \cdot g,$$

$$e_{n-1} = z \cdot g + \alpha_1 \cdot g = \chi^{(2)}(z) \cdot g,$$

$$\vdots$$

$$e_1 = z^{n-1} \cdot g + \alpha_1 z^{n-2} \cdot g + \cdots + \alpha_{n-1} \cdot g = \chi^{(n)}(z) \cdot g.$$

REMARK 1   Having $X$ cyclic with generator $g$ means, of course, that the underlying system $\Sigma$ is completely reachable.

REMARK 2   The map $l$ defines a *control law* for $\Sigma$. The passage from $z$ to $z_*$ is the module-theoretic version of the passage from open-loop to closed-loop control.

REMARK 3   Extension of the result to multiple-input systems is possible, at the expense of considerable additional algebraic machinery. The references should be consulted for details.

REMARK 4   The choice of control $l_j = \beta_j - \alpha_j$ induces the correspondence $\pi \leftrightarrow l$, which is the stated bijection of the theorem.

## X.  SOME GEOMETRIC ASPECTS
## OF LINEAR SYSTEMS

Our approach to the study of linear systems has been resolutely algebraic. There are several justifications for taking such a path:

(i)  The algebraic machinery enables us to unify the time-domain (state variable) and frequency-domain (transfer function) views of linear systems.

(ii)  algebra is congenial for computation. Since digital computers cannot, in general, represent real numbers, the methods and spirit of analysis (i.e., limiting operations) cannot be directly carried over to computational algorithms. On the other hand, algebra deals with mathematical abstractions which are closely related to computer organization and programming.

(iii)  the main emphasis in algebra is upon the construction of new mathematical objects from given objects in a natural (i.e., canonical) way. This is exactly what system theory is all about; namely, the determination of *good* models from given data.

Notwithstanding these strong arguments for adoption of an algebraic outlook, there are a number of additional insights to be gained about linear systems by also examining them with *geometric* tools. As always, no single approach can be expected to be uniformly most powerful and, as we shall see, some of the most interesting and powerful methods of modern geometry have direct bearing on important structural aspects of linear systems. Furthermore, the geometric methods, just as the algebraic, hold promise for providing a suitable foundation on which to launch a concerted attack on many nonlinear processes. In the next few sections we shall see that holomorphic vector bundles, Grassmann manifolds, and almost-onto maps may all be effectively employed to study the *global* structure of linear dynamical systems. Some extensions to the nonlinear case will be seen throughout the remaining chapters.

Let us begin our study by introducing the notion of a *vector bundle* for the system $\Sigma$ given by its transfer matrix $W(z) = H(zI - F)^{-1}G$. In fact, there are at least three such bundles which are of interest for system theorists. First of all, we add the *point at infinity* to $\mathbb{C}$ to compactify the complex numbers, obtaining in the usual way the Riemann sphere $S^2 = \mathbb{C} \cup \{\infty\}$. Now rewrite the transfer matrix $W(z)$ as

$$z\hat{x} = F\hat{x} + G\hat{u},$$
$$\hat{y} = H\hat{x}, \tag{3.9}$$

where $\hat{x}$, $\hat{u}$, $\hat{y}$ are, of course, the transformed variables. Since we will be interested in the point $z = \infty$, we can substitute $z = 1/\tau$ and let $\tau \to 0$ enabling us to rewrite the relations (3.9) as

$$\hat{x} = \tau(F\hat{x} + G\hat{u}),$$
$$\hat{y} = H\hat{x},$$

or, as $\tau \to 0$, $\hat{x} = 0$, $\hat{y} = 0$.

Define the three sets

$E = \{(z, \hat{x}, \hat{u}, \hat{y}): (3.9) \text{ is satisfied for } z \in \mathbb{C}\}$

$\quad = \{(\infty, 0, \hat{u}, 0) \text{ if } z = \infty\},$

$E' = \{(z, \hat{u}, \hat{y}): \text{for each } z \in \mathbb{C}, \text{ there } exists \ \hat{x} \in X \text{ such that } (3.9) \text{ is satisfied}\}$

$\quad = \{(\infty, \hat{u}, 0) \text{ if } z = \infty\},$

$E'' = \{(z, \hat{x}, \hat{u}): \text{if } z \in \mathbb{C}, (3.9) \text{ is satisfied}\}$

$\quad = \{(\infty, 0, \hat{u}) \text{ if } z = \infty\}.$

Since $E \subset S^2 \times X \times U \times Y$, $E' \subset S^2 \times U \times Y$, $E'' \subset S^2 \times X \times U$, the *bundles* $E, E', E''$ can be given various topological structures as needed. Also, in all three cases we define *projections* onto the first factor, e.g., $\pi: E \to S^2$, $(z, \hat{x}, \hat{u}, \hat{y}) \mapsto z$. Note that the *fibers* of these maps $\pi^{-1}(z), \pi'^{-1}(z), \pi''^{-1}(z)$ are *vector spaces*. For instance, $\pi^{-1}(\bar{z}) = E(\bar{z}) = \{(\hat{x}, \hat{u}, \hat{y}):(3.9) \text{ is satisfied at } z = \bar{z}\}$. $E(\bar{z})$ is a subspace of $X \oplus U \oplus Y$, which we may identify with $X \times U \times Y$.

The property that the map $\pi: E \to S^2$, with fibers as vector spaces means that the spaces $E, E', E''$ with maps $\pi, \pi', \pi''$ are *vector bundles*. Note also that the $z$-dependent solutions of (3.9), essentially the transfer matrix $W(z)$, form *cross sections* of these bundles.

We now utilize the notion of a Grassmann space to define a *canonical* or *standard* vector bundle $\hat{E}$. Let $V$ be a vector space and let $G(V)$ denote its associated Grassmann space. A point of $\hat{E}$ is a pair $(\gamma, v), \gamma \in G(V), v \in \gamma$. The projection $\hat{\pi}: \hat{E} \to G(V)$ is given by $\hat{\pi}(\gamma, v) = \gamma$. Thus, the fibers of $\hat{E}$ above the point $\gamma$ in the base is just $\gamma$ itself *regarded as a vector space*.

The last elementary concept we need is the notion of a *pull-back* of the canonical bundle via a map $\phi$. Let $\phi: X \to G(V)$ be a map of any space $X$ into $G(V)$. We can define a vector bundle $\tilde{E}$ with base $X$ by letting a point of $\tilde{E}$ be a pair $(x, v), x \in X, v \in \phi(x)$. We map $\tilde{E}$ into $\hat{E}$ as

$$\psi: \tilde{E} \to \hat{E}, \qquad (x, v) \mapsto (\phi(x), v).$$

Diagramatically, we have

$$
\begin{array}{ccc}
\tilde{E} & \xrightarrow{\ \psi\ } & \hat{E} \\
\ \downarrow{\scriptstyle \tilde{\pi}} & & \ \downarrow{\scriptstyle \hat{\pi}} \\
X & \xrightarrow[\ \phi\ ]{} & G(V)
\end{array}
$$

and the above definitions show that our diagram of maps is commutative. The vector bundle $\tilde{E}$ is said to be the *pull-back* of the canonical bundle via the map $\phi$.

The point of introducing $\phi$ is to have a way of *replacing* the vector bundle $\tilde{E}$ by the map $\phi$ from the base space of $\tilde{E}$ to a *standard space* $G(V)$. It turns out that the topological and algebraic properties of such maps $\phi$ are of considerable importance in the study of invariants of vector bundles.

Now let us show how this machinery may be employed to deal with some standard linear system questions. Consider the system (3.9) and let $V = X \times U, W = X$. Define the map $\gamma : S^2 \to G(V)$ by the rule $\gamma(z) = \{(x, u) : (F - zI)x + Gu = 0\}$. Then we have that the vector bundle $E''$ introduced above is a pull-back of the canonical bundle $\hat{E}$ via the map $\gamma$. The following result can now be established.

**Theorem 3.10**    *If the system* (3.9) *is reachable then dim* $\gamma(z) = $ dim $U$ *for all* $z \in S^2$, *i.e., the bundle* $E''$ *is nonsingular.*

This result is important since it establishes a direct connection between a basic system property—reachability and a bundle property—nonsingularity. We shall use this same idea now to show that reachability *and* observability together (i.e., (3.9) canonical) imply another interesting bundle-theoretic property.

Consider the two bundles $E'$ and $E''$ with the fibers denoted $E'(z)$ and $E''(z)$, i.e.,

$$E'(z) = \{(u, y) : \text{there exists an } x \text{ such that (3.9) is satisfied}\},$$

$$E''(z) = \{(x, u) : zx = Fx + Gu\}.$$

(Here we omit the $\hat{\phantom{x}}$ symbol for ease of notation.) Now let $h : E'' \to E'$ be the linear bundle map given by $h(x, u) = (u, Hx), (x, u) \in E''(z)$. We now have the

**Bundle Isomorphism Theorem**    *If* (3.9) *is canonical, i.e., reachable and observable, then* $h : E'' \to E'$ *is a bundle isomorphism.*

PROOF    By construction the map $h$ is onto $E'$. We must only show that it is 1–1 on $E''$.

First, since (3.9) is reachable, $E''$ is nonsingular, i.e., all of its fibers $E''(z)$ have the same dimension. Let $(x, u) \in E''(z)$ be such that $h(x, u) = 0$, i.e., $u = Hx = 0$. Then, $zx = Fx$, implying $x$ is a characteristic vector of $F$. Also,

$$HFx = zHx = 0,$$
$$HF^2x = 0, \ldots.$$

Observability now implies that $x = 0$, showing that $h$ is 1–1, hence, an isomorphism.

Another way of looking at this result is to introduce the *pencil of matrices* $A(z) = [F - zI, G]$. Clearly, $E''(z) = \ker A(z)$. The bundle $E''$ is called the *kernel bundle* of $A(z)$ on $S^2$. The theorem then says that the map $h$ from the kernel bundle of the *internal* description of the system is isomorphic to the bundle $E'$ generated from the *external* description if and only if (3.9) is canonical.

## XI. FEEDBACK, THE McMILLAN DEGREE, AND KRONECKER INDICES

So far, we have spoken about a single system $\Sigma$ characterized by its transfer matrix $W(z)$. Now let us consider the question of when two systems $\Sigma = (F, G, H), \Sigma' = (F', G', H')$ are *equivalent* (i.e., transformable one to the other) under the following group of transformations:

(i)   *state* coordinate changes $T: (F, G, H) \mapsto (TFT^{-1}, TG, HT^{-1})$,
(ii)  *input* coordinate changes $V: (F, G, H) \mapsto (F, GV^{-1}, H)$,
(iii) *output* coordinate changes $U: (F, G, H) \mapsto (F, G, UH)$,
(iv)  *state feedback* $L: (F, G, H) \mapsto (F - GL, G, H)$.

A little bit of algebra quickly shows that under the *feedback group*, the respective transfer matrices of the systems $\Sigma, \Sigma'$ are related as

$$W'(z) = VW(z)U(I - LVW(z)U)^{-1}.$$

The important point to note is that the transformation $W \to W'$ is a *fractional linear transformation*, suggesting that the natural setting in which to study feedback is a Grassmann manifold, since as we saw in Chapter 2, the Grassmann manifolds are the homogeneous spaces of the group of fractional linear transformations. For each $W(z)$ we shall construct a map

$$\phi_W: \quad S^2 \to G^m(\mathbb{C}^{m+p}),$$

where $G^m(\mathbb{C}^{m+p})$ is the Grassmann manifold of $m$-dimensional subspaces of the $(m + p)$-dimensional complex space. We shall see that $\Sigma$ and $\Sigma'$ are then feedback equivalent if and only if $\phi_W$ and $\phi_{W'}$ are transformable into each other under $GL(p + m, \mathbb{C})$ acting on $G^m(\mathbb{C}^{m+p})$. Such an approach also enables us to define an algebraic invariant of the map $\phi_{W'}$ which turns out to be the classical McMillan degree of $W(z)$, enabling us to characterize systems in the same equivalence class.

In another direction, since we have already seen that $G^m(\mathbb{C}^{m+p})$ has a canonical vector bundle structure, we can use $\phi_W$ to construct a new bundle, the pull-back, on $S^2$. We shall also see that feedback equivalent systems determine isomorphic vector bundles. Furthermore, since a complete classification of holomorphic vector bundles on $S^2$ is known (via the work of Grothendeick), we obtain a complete set of feedback invariants which correspond to the well-known Kronecker invariants of $\Sigma$. Let us now proceed to construct $\phi_W$.

For each $z \in \mathbb{C}$, define

$$\phi_W(z) = \{(W(z)u, u): u \in \mathbb{C}^m\};$$

$\phi_W$ is defined everywhere except at the poles of $W(z)$. Using the (not entirely trivial) fact that there exist polynomial matrices $N(z)$, $D(z)$ such that $W(z) = N(z)D^{-1}(z)$, we can extend $\phi_W(z)$ to all $\mathbb{C}$ by defining

$$\phi_W(z) = \{(N(z)u, D(z)u): u \in \mathbb{C}^m\}.$$

By setting $\phi_W(\infty) = \{(0, u): u \in \mathbb{C}^m\}$, it can be shown that $\phi_W$ is defined everywhere on $S^2$ and takes values in $G^m(\mathbb{C}^{m+p})$ (since $\phi_W(z)$ is a subspace of $\mathbb{C}^m \times \mathbb{C}^p$), i.e., $\mathbb{C}$.

At this point, it is instructive to examine the effect of a feedback law $L$ on the transfer matrix $W(z)$ and the consequent action through $\phi_W(z)$ in $G^m(\mathbb{C}^{m+p})$. A small calculation shows that a feedback law $L$ transforms

$$W(z) \to W(z)[I + LW(z)]^{-1}.$$

Now consider the matrix $A = \begin{bmatrix} I & 0 \\ L & I \end{bmatrix}$ acting on $\phi_W(z)$. We have

$$A(\phi_W(z)) = \{(W(z)u, (LW(z) + I)u): u \in \mathbb{C}^m\}.$$

Putting these computations together, we see that

$$A(\phi_W(z)) = \phi_{W'}(z)$$

with $W' = W(I + LW)^{-1}$, whenever $(I + LW)^{-1}$ exists. Thus, feedback is determined by a *linear* action on a Grassmann manifold. It can be shown that the other coordinate changes in the feedback group can also be realized by corresponding linear actions, as well.

To *geometrically* define the McMillan degree of $W(z)$, let $r = \binom{p+m}{p}$ and $P_{r-1}(\mathbb{C})$ be the projective space for which $\mathbb{C}^r$ is the space of homogeneous coordinates. The transfer matrix $W(z)$ determines a rational map $S^2 \to P_{r-1}(\mathbb{C})$ and the McMillan degree $\delta$ of $W(z)$ is equal to the number of intersections of $\phi(P_1(\mathbb{C}))$ with a certain hyperplane $\mathcal{N}$ in $P_{r-1}(\mathbb{C})$. Without going into more detail, it is difficult to describe $\mathcal{N}$, but the important point is that the *algebraic* quantity $\delta(W)$, usually defined as $\delta(W) = \deg[\det D(z)]$, can be defined in purely geometric terms, as well. As is well known, $\delta(W) = \dim \Sigma$. Relative to the problem of feedback equivalence, we can state that $\Sigma$ and $\Sigma'$ are feedback equivalent if and only if $\delta(W) = \delta(W')$.

Now let us return for a moment to vector bundles. We have already seen that the vector bundles associated with a transfer matrix $W(z)$ and its canonical model $\Sigma$ are isomorphic. Now what about the case when we have two input systems $\Sigma = (F, G, -)$, $\Sigma' = (F', G', -)$ (here we neglect the output) which are feedback equivalent, i.e.,

$$F' = T(F + GL)T^{-1}, \qquad G' = TGV.$$

What is the connection between feedback equivalence and the properties of the vector bundles corresponding to $\Sigma$ and $\Sigma'$? This question is answered by

**Theorem 3.11** *The input systems $\Sigma$ and $\Sigma'$ are feedback equivalent if and only if their corresponding bundles are isomorphic.*

We have assigned a holomorphic vector bundle $E'$ with base $S^2$ with each transfer matrix $W(z)$ as

$$E' = \{(z, u, y): y = W(z)u, u \in \mathbb{C}^m, y \in \mathbb{C}^p\}.$$

This is just the pullback of $\phi_W(z)$. By general results, every such bundle is isomorphic to a direct sum of line bundles and the isomorphism classes are in 1–1 correspondence with sets of positive integers $k_1 \geq k_2 \geq \cdots \geq k_r$, where $k_i$ = degree of the $i$th line bundle in the decomposition. It can be proved that the McMillan degree of the $i$th line bundle equals $k_i$, which in turn equals the classical $i$th Kronecker index of the matrix pencil $[F - zI, G]$. Thus, the set $\{k_i\}$ forms a complete system of *arithmetic* invariants for the feedback group.

## PROBLEMS AND EXERCISES

**1.** Show that the state set $X_f$ defined as $\Omega/\ker$ f is isomorphic to the set $\hat{X}_f = f(\Omega)$ and, consequently, that the module-theoretic description of $\Sigma$ from the text could be developed using $\hat{X}_f$ instead of $X_f$.

In $X_f$, state transitions are defined by

$$F: \quad [\omega]_f \rightarrow [z \cdot \omega]_f = z \cdot [\omega]_f.$$

How would they be defined in $\hat{X}_f$?

**2.** Consider the action of $GL(n, k)$ on pairs $(F, G): (F, G) \rightarrow (gFg^{-1}, gG) = (\hat{F}, \hat{G})$, $g \in GL(n, k)$, $k$ an arbitrary field. The *stabilizer* of $(F, G)$ in $GL(n, k)$ is $\{g \in Gl(n, k): (F, G) = (\hat{F}, \hat{G})\}$. Show that if $(F, G)$ is completely reachable, then the stabilizer = identity. Show that the converse is false by constructing a counterexample. (Hint: consider the field $Z/2$.)

**3.** Consider the following pattern discrimination problem: we want to construct a linear system that will recognize an input $\phi$ as $\phi \bmod \psi \neq 0$ and will recognize a different input $\theta$ as $\theta \bmod \psi = 0 \bmod \psi$. Show that a solution $\psi$ exists if and only if $\theta$ is not a factor of $\phi$.

**4.** Let $\Sigma = (F, G, H)$ and define the $k$-linear *dual* of $\Sigma$ as $\Sigma^* = (F', H', G')$, where $'$ denotes matrix transpose. Show that the state set $X_{\Sigma^*}$ of $\Sigma^*$ can be given the structure of a $k[z^{-1}]$-module in the following fashion:

(i)   regarded as a vector space, $X_{\Sigma^*}$ is the dual of $X$ regarded as a $k$-vector space;

(ii)   define the scalar product in $X^*$ as $(z^{-1} \cdot x^*)(x) = x^*(Fx)$. The states of $X_{\Sigma^*}$ are called the *costates* of $\Sigma$.

Now show that $\Sigma = (F, -, H)$ is completely observable if and only if $H'$ generates $X_{\Sigma^*}$ and prove the Duality Principle that the observable *co*states of $\Sigma$ are the reachable states of $\Sigma^*$.

**5.**   Consider a behavior sequence $B = \{a_1, a_2, a_3, \ldots\}$, where the $\{a_i\}$ are *scalars*. Show that the rank criterion

$$\text{rank } \mathscr{H}_{r+1,m} = \text{rank } \mathscr{H}_{rm} = \text{rank } \mathscr{H}_{r,m+1}$$

is satisfied infinitely often for the principal submatrices of the Hankel matrix $\mathscr{H}$ of $B$.

**6.**   Let $GL(n, k)$ act on pairs $(F, G)$ in the usual state coordinate transformation fashion, i.e., $(F, G) \to (TFT^{-1}, TG)$. Define the matrix

$$R(F, G) = (G, FG, F^2G, \ldots, F^{n-1}G, F^nG)$$

and assume that $(F, G)$ is completely reachable. Extend the action of $GL(n, k)$ to $R(F, G)$ in the obvious way. Order and number the columns of $R(F, G)$ as $01, 02, \ldots, 0m; 11, \ldots, nm$ and define a multi-index $v$ to be *nice* if the elements $v$ have the property that if $jl \in v$, then all indices $j'l, 0 \le j' \le j$ are also in $v$. A *successor* $\sigma$ of $v$ is a multiindex such that $\sigma = v - jl + pq$, where $p$ is such that $p'q \in v$ for all $0 \le p' < p$.

Prove that there exists at least one nice $v$ such that det $R(F, G)_v \ne 0$ and, conversely, that if det $R(F, G)_v = 0$ for all nice $v$, then $(F, G)$ is not reachable.

Next show that the orbits of $(F, G)$ under $GL(n, k)$ form a quasi-projective variety $V$ and that the nice neighborhood det $R(F, G)_v$ cover $V$. Further, each neighborhood is isomorphic to $k^{nm}$. (Hint: consider the Plücker map $\phi : (F, G) \to (\text{det } R(F, G)_\rho)$, where $\rho$ is nice or a successor. For details of this construction, see R. Kalman, Algebraic geometric description of the class of linear systems of constant dimension, in *Eighth Princeton Conf. on Info. Sci. and Systems*, March 1974.)

**7.**   Let $K, L, M$ be modules over a fixed ring $R$. The sequence

$$0 \to K \xrightarrow{\delta} L \xrightarrow{\epsilon} M \xrightarrow{i} 0$$

is called *exact* if (i) $\epsilon$ is onto, (ii) $\delta$ is 1–1, and (iii) $M \approx L/K$.

Let $f : \Omega \to \Gamma$ be an external description of $\Sigma$ and let $K = \ker f, L = \Omega$. Show that if the sequence is exact, then $M$ is the canonical state set $X_f$ of $\Sigma$.

What interpretation can be given to the homology modules $H_0 = \ker i/\operatorname{im} \epsilon = M/\operatorname{im} \Omega$ and $H_1 = \ker \epsilon/\operatorname{im} \delta$?

**8.** Consider the following diagram of maps

$$
\begin{array}{ccc}
X_f & \xrightarrow{\ w\ } & Z_f \\
{\scriptstyle g}\nearrow & & \searrow{\scriptstyle h} \\
\Omega & \xrightarrow[\ f\ ]{} & \Gamma
\end{array}
$$

where $f: \omega \mapsto y(z^{-1})$, $g: \omega \mapsto [\omega]_f$, $h: y(\cdot) \mapsto y(z^{-1})$, with $g$ being onto and $h$ 1–1. Here $X_f$ is the canonical state module, which is assumed to be torsion. Let $\chi(z)$ be the characteristic polynomial of $X_f$. Show that if $w$ is an isomorphism, that is, $f$ is canonically factored as $f = h \circ w \circ g$, then $Z_f$ is a submodule of $\Gamma$ having generators $q_i(z)/\chi(z)$, where $q_i(z)$ is the image in $\Gamma$ of the generator $g_i$ of $\Omega$. In other words, $X_f$ and $Z_f$ are equivalent objects thereby demonstrating the existence of *transfer functions* and their equivalence to a state-variable model for a system $\Sigma$.

**9.** Consider the two polynomials

$$
f(z) = z^n + f_1 z^{n-1} + f_2 z^{n-2} + \cdots + f_n,
$$
$$
g(z) = g_1 z^{n-1} + g_2 z^{n-2} + \cdots + g_n,
$$

and the associated matrices

$$
F = \begin{bmatrix} 0 & 0 & \cdots & 0 & -f_n \\ 1 & 0 & & 0 & -f_{n-1} \\ 0 & 1 & & 0 & -f_{n-2} \\ \vdots & & & & \vdots \\ 0 & 0 & \cdots & 1 & -f_1 \end{bmatrix}, \qquad G = \begin{bmatrix} g_n \\ \vdots \\ g_1 \end{bmatrix}.
$$

If $\mathscr{C}$ represents the usual controllability matrix

$$
\mathscr{C} = [G | FG | \cdots | F^{n-1}G]
$$

and $(f, g)$ is the monic polynomial which is the greatest common factor of $f$ and $g$, show that

(a) $\mathscr{C} = g(F)$;

(b) $\lambda_i(g(F)) = g(\phi_i)$, where $\phi_i = i$th root of $f$;

(c) $\deg(f, g) = n - \operatorname{rank} \mathscr{C}$;

(d) $(f, g) = g/h$, where $h(z)$ is the minimal polynomial of $G$ relative to $F$, i.e.,

$$
F^{n-r}G + h_1 F^{n-r-1}G + \cdots + h_{n-r}G = 0,
$$

with $r$ minimal.

**10.** Let $k$ be a Noetherian integral domain with identity and let $K$ be its quotient field. Show that a given behavior sequence $B = \{A_1, A_2, \ldots\}$ over $k$ has a finite-dimensional realization over $k$ if and only if $B$ has a finite-dimensional realization over $K$. In other words, it is not necessary to go outside the domain of *numbers* expressing the data to construct a model of the data.

(a)  Show that under the feedback group, this system has the canonical form

$$F_* = F, \qquad G_* = G, \qquad H_* = \begin{bmatrix} 0 & 0 & \alpha_{13} \\ \alpha_{13}\alpha_{21} - \alpha_{11} & \alpha_{23}\alpha_{13}\alpha_{22} - \alpha_{12}\alpha_{23} & \alpha_{23} \end{bmatrix},$$

where $\alpha_{ij}$ are invariants of the group action.

(b)  Show that decoupling is possible only if one of the following conditions holds:

$$\alpha_{12}\alpha_{23} \neq \alpha_{22}\alpha_{13} \qquad \text{unless either} \quad \alpha_{12} = \alpha_{13} = 0 \quad \text{or} \tag{i}$$
$$\alpha_{22} = \alpha_{23} = 0,$$

$$\alpha_{11}\alpha_{23} \neq 0 \qquad \text{if } \alpha_{12} = \alpha_{13} = 0; \tag{ii}$$

$$\alpha_{21}\alpha_{13} \neq 0 \qquad \text{if } \alpha_{22} = \alpha_{23} = 0. \tag{iii}$$

**11.**  Let $(F, G)$ be completely reachable with $\hat{m} = \text{rank } G$. Further, let $k_1 \geq \cdots \geq k_{\hat{m}}$ be the *ordered* control invariants of $(F, G)$ and let $\psi_1, \ldots, \psi_r$ be arbitrary monic polynomials subject to

(i)   $\psi_i | \psi_{i-1}, i = 1, 2, \ldots, r - 1; r \leq \hat{m}$,
(ii)  $\deg \psi_1 \geq k_1, \deg \psi_1 + \deg \psi_2 \geq k_1 + k_2, \ldots$.

Show that there exists a matrix $L$ such that $F - GL$ has the invariant factors $\psi_1, \psi_2, \ldots, \psi_r$. In other words, the structure of the system $x = Fx + Gu$ can be altered arbitrarily by linear feedback, subject to the above *lower* bound on the size of the cyclic blocks given by the control invariants. (Remark: The control, or Kronecker, invariants $\{k_i\}$ are defined as follows: write the elements of $[G|FG|\cdots|F^{n-1}G]$ as

$$\{g_1, g_2, \ldots, g_m, Fg_1, Fg_2, \ldots, Fg_m, F^2g_1, \ldots, F^{n-1}g_m\}.$$

Then $k_i$ is defined as the smallest positive integer such that $F^{k_i}g_i$ is linearly dependent upon the elements *preceding* it in the above list.)

**12.**  Given a system $\Sigma = (F, G, H)$, subject to the action of the feedback group, the *decoupling* problem involves whether or not there is an element in the orbit of a fixed $(F, G, H)$ for which the transfer function is diagonal, with nonzero diagonal elements. Assume that the fixed system is given by $\Sigma$:

$$F = \begin{bmatrix} 0 & 1 & 0 \\ 0 & 0 & 0 \\ 0 & 0 & 0 \end{bmatrix}, \qquad G = \begin{bmatrix} 0 & 0 \\ 1 & 0 \\ 0 & 1 \end{bmatrix}, \qquad H = \begin{bmatrix} h_{11} & h_{12} & h_{13} \\ h_{21} & h_{22} & h_{23} \end{bmatrix}.$$

**13.** The natural state space of a finite-dimensional linear system is either the torsion quotient module $\Omega/\ker f$ or the torsion submodule $f(\Omega)$.

(a) Show that a quotient module of $\Omega$ is a finitely generated torsion $k[z]$-module if and only if it is of the form $\Omega/D\Omega$, where $D$ is a nonsingular $m \times m$ polynomial matrix, i.e., it is of the form $\mathrm{Coker}(D)$.

(b) Let $Z \subset \Gamma$. Show that $Z$ is a finitely generated torsion $k[z]$-submodule of $\Gamma$ if and only if $Z = \ker(D)$ for some nonsingular $p \times p$ polynomial matrix $D$. (This result enables us to test whether a given quotient or submodule could form the natural state set of a finite-dimensional linear system.)

**14.** Let $\Sigma = \{(F, G) : F = n \times n,\ G = n \times m \text{ real matrices}\}$ and let the feedback group $\mathscr{F}$ act on $\Sigma$ as in the text. Choose $\sigma \in \Sigma$ and let $\mathscr{F}(\sigma)$ denote its orbit. Show that the tangent space to $\mathscr{F}(\sigma)$ at $\sigma$ (when identified with a linear subspace of $\Sigma$ using the vector space structure of $\Sigma$) is given by

$$\{([T, F] - GK, TG) : T \in L(R^n, R^n),\ K \in L(R^n, R^m)\},$$

where $[\cdot, \cdot]$ denotes the usual Lie product in $R^n$, i.e., the matrix commutator.

Using this result, show that the projection $\pi$ of the orbit onto $L(R^n, R^n)$ is given by $\pi[g\sigma] = T(F - GK)T^{-1}$, where $\sigma \in \Sigma$, $g \in \mathscr{F}$. Consequently, prove that $\pi(\mathscr{F}(\sigma))$ contains a Zariski open subset of $L(R^n, R^n)$.

**15.** Let $\sigma_1 = (F_1, G_1), \sigma_2 = (F_2, G_2)$ be two systems over an algebraically closed field $k$. We say $\sigma_1$ is *state-space equivalent* to $\sigma_2$ if there exists a coordinate change $T \in GL(n, k)$ such that $F_2 = TF_1T^{-1}$, $G_2 = TG_1$. Show that $\sigma_1$ is state space equivalent to $\sigma_2$ if and only if

(i) $\chi_{F_1}(z) = \chi_{F_2}(z)$;
(ii) $\mathrm{rank}(F_1 \otimes I - I \otimes F_1)$
    $= \mathrm{rank}(F_2 \otimes I - I \otimes F_2) = \mathrm{rank}(F_1 \otimes I - I \otimes F_2)$;
(iii) $\dim g(\sigma_1) = \dim g(\sigma_2)$;
(iv) $\dim O(\hat{\sigma}_1) = \dim O(\hat{\sigma}_2)$,

where $\chi_F(z)$ is the characteristic polynomial of $F$, $\otimes$ *denotes the Kronecker product*, $g(\sigma)$ is the $F$ submodule of $k^n$ generated by $GL(n, k)$, and $O(\hat{\sigma})$ is the orbit under $GL(n, k)$ of the parallel sum of $\sigma$ with itself. (This theorem gives a decision procedure for establishing whether *any* two systems are state-space equivalent. If we restrict attention to the subset of reachable and observable systems then, of course, $\sigma_1 \sim \sigma_2$ if and only if they have the same transfer function.)

## NOTES AND REFERENCES

**Section 3.II**   There are a number of excellent volumes on elementary linear system theory which provide all the necessary background for the advanced material presented here. For the most part, we follow the treatment in

J. Casti, "Dynamical Systems and Their Applications: Linear Theory," Academic Press, New York, 1977.

See also

R. Brockett, "Finite-Dimensional Linear Systems," Wiley, New York, 1970.
T. Fortmann and C. Hitz, "An Introduction to Linear Control Systems," Dekker, New York, 1977.
H. H. Rosenbrock, "State-Space and Multivariable Theory" Wiley, London, 1970.

**Section 3.III**   The definitive statement of the module-theoretic treatment of linear systems is presented in

R. Kalman, R. Falb, and M. Arbib, "Topics in Mathematical System Theory," McGraw-Hill, New York, 1969.

The material synthesized in this volume is based on the earlier works of R. E. Kalman, the most important being

R. Kalman, Algebraic structure of linear dynamical systems, *Proc. Nat. Acad. Sci. U.S.A.* **54** (1965), 1503–1508.
R. Kalman, Algebraic aspects of the theory of dynamical systems *in* "Differential Equations and Dynamical Systems" (J. Hale and J. LaSalle, eds.), Academic Press, New York, 1967.
R. Kalman, "Lectures on Controllability and Observability," Centro Internazionale Matematico Estivo Summer Course 1968, Cremonese, Rome.

**Section 3.IV**   For additional examples of how a linear system can be used as a pattern recognition device, especially in the context of brain modeling, see

R. Kalman, On the mathematics of model building, *in* "Neutral Networks" (E. Caianiello, ed.), Springer, New York, 1968.

**Section 3.V**   The historical use of transfer functions to describe a linear system stems from work in electrical circuit design. To some extent this is unfortunate, since a number of issues extraneous to the *mathematical* relationship between transfer functions and linear systems were obscured for several decades. For instance, the usual discussions of transfer functions rely upon various convergence arguments for the contour integral defining the Laplace transform, conveying the erroneous impression that only stable systems can be studied by transform means. The algebraic treatment arising from the module-theoretic view shows that no questions of convergence enter at all. The mathematical basis for transfer functions is the existence of a $k[z]$-module structure on $\Omega$ for which the input–output map $f$ is a homomorphism. This is purely algebraic fact. Additionally, the module machinery allows us to treat both continuous and discrete-time processes using the same formalism. Thus, both the Laplace transform and the *z-transform* methods are unified in the algebraic treatment.

For some classically oriented views on transform methods, see

I. Horovitz and U. Shaked, The superiority of transfer function over state variable methods in linear, time-invariant feedback systems designs, *IEEE Trans. Automat. Control* **AC-20** (1975), 84–97.
L. Zadeh and C. Desoer, "Linear Systems Theory," McGraw-Hill, New York, 1963.
J. Rubio, "The Theory of Linear Systems," Academic Press, New York, 1971.
M. Smyth, "Linear Engineering Systems," Pergamon, New York, 1972.

**Section 3.VI**  Two seminal semiclassical papers which led directly to the algebraic treatment of transfer function realization are

R. Kalman, Mathematical description of linear dynamical systems, *SIAM J. Control* **1** (1963), 152–192.
R. Kalman, Irreducible realizations and the degree of a rational matrix, *SIAM J. Control Optim.* **13** (1965), 520–544.

Both of these papers contain a wealth of concrete examples of the abstract realization procedures presented in the text.

The Invariant Factor Theorem can be proved in many different ways at several levels of algebraic generality. For instance, see

F. Gantmacher, "Matrix Theory," Vol. 1, Chelsea, New York, 1959.
A. Albert, "Fundamental Concepts of Higher Algebra," Univ. of Chicago Press, Chicago, 1965.
N. Jacobson, "Lectures in Abstract Algebra. Vol. 2. Linear Algebra," Van Nostrand, New York, 1953.

**Section 3.VII**  There are numerous formally different, but equivalent, methods for realizing a given transfer matrix. For example, see

H. Rosenbrock, Computations of minimal representations of a rational transfer function matrix, *Proc. IEEE* **115** (1968), 325–327.
D. Mayne, A computational procedure for the minimal realization of transfer function matrices, *Proc. IEEE*, **115** (1968), 1368–1383.
E. Gilbert, Controllability and observability in multivariable systems, *SIAM J. Control* **1** (1963), 120–151.

The first effective procedure for carrying out the realization procedure for input–output data given in *Markov* form is

B. L. Ho and R. Kalman, Effective construction of linear state variable models from input–output functions, *Regelungstechnik* **14** (1966), 545–548.

Other procedures improving upon aspects of Ho's method are presented in

L. Silverman, Realization of linear dynamical systems, *IEEE Trans. Automat. Control* **AC-16** (1971), 554–567.

J. Rissanen, Recursive identification of linear systems, *SIAM J. Control. Optim.* **9** (1971), 420–430.

J. Willems, "Minimal Realization in State Space Form From Input–Output Data," Mathematics Institute Report, Univ. of Groningen, Groningen, The Netherlands, May, 1973.

R. Guidorzi, Canonical structures in the identification of multivariable systems, *Automatica* **11** (1975), 361–374.

For processes governed by partial differential or differential-delay equations, the state space is infinite dimensional, in general. For the realization of such systems, see

J. Baras, R. Brockett, and P. Fuhrmann, State-space models for infinite-dimensional systems, *IEEE Trans. Automat. Control* **AC-19** (1974), 693–700.

J. Baras and R. Brockett, H²-functions and infinite-dimensional realization theory, *SIAM J. Control Optim.* **13** (1975), 221–241.

**Section 3.VIII**   The idea of partial realization is actually equivalent to the classical idea of Padé approximation, which concerns the problem of finding for a given Laurent series $\sum a_i z^{-i}$, a strictly proper rational function $f$ with denominator of minimal degree whose Laurent expansion in $z^{-1}$ agrees with the given series through the first $r$ terms, for some specified *finite* $r$. The first systematic account of the partial realization problem is given in

R. Kalman, On partial realizations of a linear input–output map, in "Guillemin Anniversary Volume" (N. deClaris and R. Kalman, eds.), Holt, Rinehart & Winston, New York, 1968.

A definitive sharpening of these results is

R. Kalman, On partial realizations, transfer functions, and canonical forms, *Acta Polytech. Scand. Math.* **31** (1979), 9–32.

**Section 3.IX**   According to popular legend, the Pole-Shifting Theorem was first proved around 1959 by J. Bertram and later by R. Bass. The first published proof for multi-input systems seems to be

W. M. Wonham, On pole assignment in multi-input controllable linear systems, *IEEE Trans. Automat. Control*, **AC-12** (1967), 660–665.

We say that $\Sigma = (F,G)$ is *coefficient assignable* if given any monic polynomial $p(z)$, there exists a $m \times n$ matrix $K$ such that $\det(zI - F + GK) = p(z)$. Over a field, coefficient assignability is equivalent to pole assignability; however, over a general ring $R$, coefficient assignability is a much stronger property. For an example over a general ring showing that complete reachability is not enough to ensure coefficient assignability for multi-input systems, see

R. Bumby and E. Sontag, Reachability does not imply coefficient assignability, *Notice Amer. Math. Soc.*, 1978.

**Section 3.X**   The ideas of this section have been extensively pursued and expounded by R. Hermann in a continuing series of books and research articles

R. Hermann, "Interdisciplinary Mathematics," Vols. 8, 9, 11, 13, 20, 21, Math. Sci. Press, Brookline, Massachusetts, 1974–1980.

Probably the most complete and accessible work on algebraic geometry and its uses in linear system analyses is

A. Tannenbaum, "Invariance and System Theory: Algebraic and Geometric Aspects," *in* Lecture Notes in Mathematics, Vol. 849, Springer, Berlin, 1981.

See also the works

R. Hermann and C. Martin, Applications of algebraic geometry to systems theory, Part I, *IEEE Trans. Automat. Control* **AC-22** (1977), 19–25.

R. Brockett, Some geometric questions in the theory of linear systems, *IEEE Trans. Automat. Control* **AC-21** (1976), 449–464.

C. Byrnes and N. Hurt, On the module of linear dynamical systems, *Advan. in Math. Suppl. Stud.* **4** (1979), 83–122.

C. Byrnes and P. Falb, Applications of algebraic geometry in systems theory, *Amer. J. Math.* **101** (1979), 337–363.

C. Byrnes and C. Martin (eds.), "Algebraic and Geometric Methods in Linear System Theory," Lectures in Applied Math. Vol. 18, Amer. Math. Soc., Providence, Rhode Island, 1980.

**Section 3.XI**   The feedback group and the Kronecker indices seems to have first been introduced into linear system theory by Brunovsky in

P. Brunovsky, A classification of linear controllable systems, *Kybernetika* **3** (1970), 176–188.

See also,

R. Kalman, Kronecker invariants and feedback, *in* "Ordinary Differential Equations" (L. Weiss, ed.), Academic Press, New York, 1971.

The relationship between the Kronecker indices and the McMillan degree of a transfer matrix is spelled out in detail in

C. Martin and R. Hermann, "Applications of algebraic geometry to systems theory: The McMillan degree and Kronecker indices of transfer functions as topological and holomorphic invariants, *SIAM J. Control Optim.* **16** (1978), 743–755.

Related results arc

R. Brockett, Lie algebras and rational functions: some control-theoretic questions, *in* "Proc. Queens' Symposium on Lie Theory and Its Applications" (W. Rossmann, ed.), Queens University, Kingston, Ontario, 1978.

R. Brockett and C. Byrnes, Multivariable Nyquist criteria, root loci, and pole placement: A geometric viewpoint, *IEEE Trans. Automat. Control* **AC-26** (1981), 271–284.

M. Hazelwinkel, Moduli and canonical forms for linear dynamical systems. III. The algebraic–geometric case, *in* "Geometric Control Theory" (C. Martin and R. Hermann, eds.), Math. Sci. Press, Brookline, Massachusetts, 1977.

# 4

# Reachability and Controllability

## I. INTRODUCTION

Given a dynamical system $\Sigma$ currently in a known state $x_0$, what states can $\Sigma$ attain at some future time $T$ under the action of inputs chosen from a specified set $\Omega$? Roughly speaking, this is a statement of the problem of *reachability*. A variation of this problem occurs when we desire to transfer $\Sigma$ from $x_0$ to a given equilibrium state (usually the origin). We then speak of a problem of *controllability*. As is evident, the essence of the reachability–controllability question is to decide what can be done with $\Sigma$ considering the control resources available. To transform the intuitive content of the reachability problem into a meaningful mathematical statement, a number of points in the problem statement need clarification.

The above problem statement contains a number of vague aspects which must be formalized. Among the major unclear points are

   (i)   Is the future time $T$ fixed in advance or can $T$ be any positive number (including $\infty$)?

   (ii)   What is the structure of the elements in the set $\Omega$? For instance, must the inputs be bounded, nonnegative, periodic, etc.?

   (iii)   What is the structure of the system state space $X$? Are there physically reachable states which must be excluded from the attainable set due to other problem considerations?

110

Let us assume for the moment that these questions have been settled and consider the dynamical system

$$\dot{x} = \sum_{i=1}^{m} u_i(t) f_i(x), \qquad x(0) = x_0 \in R^n \qquad (4.1)$$

with the vector functions $f_i(\cdot)$ smooth enough to define a unique solution for any admissible inputs.

**Question.** Under what conditions does there exist a smooth $p$-dimensional manifold $M \subset R^n$, $p \leq n$, such that the $\{f_i(x)\}$ span the tangent space of $M$ at each point?

The obvious connection between this question and the problem of reachability is that if such an $M$ exists, then the state $x$ can move anywhere within $M$ but not out of it.

The existence of such a manifold $M$ hinges upon application of the following special input:

$$u_1(s) = \begin{cases} 1, & 0 \leq s < t, \\ -1, & 2t \leq s < 3t, \\ 0, & \text{otherwise,} \end{cases}$$

$$u_2(s) = \begin{cases} 1, & t \leq s < 2t, \\ -1, & 3t \leq s < 4t, \\ 0, & \text{otherwise,} \end{cases}$$

$$u_i(s) = 0, \qquad i = 3, 4, \ldots, m.$$

Basically, we are following the curves $\dot{x} = f_1(x)$, $\dot{x} = f_2(x)$, $\dot{x} = -f_1(x)$, $\dot{x} = -f_2(x)$ for $t$ units of time each. Employing the second-order expansion

$$x(t) = x_0 + t f_i(x_0) + \left(\frac{t^2}{2}\right)\left(\frac{\partial f_i}{\partial x}\right) f_i(x_0) + O(t^3),$$

the system state $x(4t)$ can be seen to be

$$\exp(-t f_2) \exp(-t f_1) \exp(t f_2) \exp(t f_1) x_0$$
$$= x_0 + (t^2/2)[f_1, f_2] x_0 + O(t^3),$$

where

$$[f_1, f_2] = \left(\frac{\partial f_2}{\partial x}\right) f_1 - \left(\frac{\partial f_1}{\partial x}\right) f_2,$$

the Lie bracket of the vector fields $f_1$ and $f_2$. Thus, if $[f_1, f_2]$ is not a linear combination of $f_1, f_2, \ldots, f_m$, then $[f_1, f_2]$ represents a new direction in which the state can move and the problem of finding a manifold $M$ whose tangent space is spanned by $\{f_i\}$ is not solvable. This simple example shows the central role of the Lie bracket operation in deciding the question of reachability.

The above calculations strongly suggest that not only is $(\exp tf_1)x_0$ and $(\exp tf_2)x_0$ in the reachable set from $x_0$, but also $(\exp t[f_1, f_2])x_0$. It is reasonable now to conjecture that $(\exp tf)x_0$ is also in the reachable set from $x_0$ if $f$ can be expressed as a bracketed combination of $\{f_i\}$, i.e., $f$ is contained in the Lie algebra $\{f_i\}_{LA}$. We let diff($M$) be the group of diffeomorphisms of $M$ and denote $\{\exp\{f_i\}\}_G$ as the smallest subgroup of diff($M$) which contains $\exp tf$ for $f \in \{f_i\}$. Then any $x \in M$ of the form $x = \{\exp\{f_i\}\}_G x_0$ can be reached from $x_0$ using piecewise constant controls. A major system-theoretic question now is whether the two sets $\{\exp\{f_i\}\}_G x_0$ and $\{exp\{f_i\}_{LA}\}_G x_0$ differ. Intuitively, the second set seems larger. However, as we shall see below, an old theorem of Chow shows that, under mild hypotheses, they are really equal. Thus, for systems of the form (4.1), Chow's theorem essentially disposes of the reachability question. Part of our aim in this chapter is to see how far the basic ideas developed for (4.1) can be extended for more general systems of the form

$$\dot{x} = g(x) + \sum_{i=1}^{m} u_i(t) f_i(x) \tag{4.2}$$

involving the drift term $g(x)$.


## II. BASIC DEFINITIONS AND PROBLEM STATEMENT

Consider the nonlinear system

$$\dot{x} = f(x, u), \qquad x(0) = x_0, \tag{$\Sigma$}$$

$$y(t) = h(x),$$

where $u \in \Omega$, an admissible set of $R^m$-valued input functions, $y \in \Gamma$, a set of $R^p$-valued output functions and $x \in M$, a $C^\infty$-connected manifold of dimension $n$. To simplify our notation, it is assumed that $M$ admits globally defined coordinates $x = (x_1, x_2, \ldots, x_n)$, allowing us to identify the points of $M$ with their coordinate representations and to write our control system in the usual engineering form $\Sigma$. Furthermore, we assume that $f(\cdot)$ and $h(\cdot)$ are $C^\infty$ functions of their arguments and that $\Sigma$ is *complete*, i.e., for every bounded measureable control $u(t)$ and every $x_0 \in M$, there exists a solution of $\dot{x} = f(x, u)$ satisfying $x(0) = x_0$ and $x(t) \in M$ for all real $t$.

***Definition 4.1*** Given a point $x^* \in M$, we say that $x^*$ is *reachable* from $x_0$ at $T$ if there exists a bounded measurable input $u \in \Omega$, such that the trajectory of $\Sigma$ satisfies $x(0) = x_0$, $x(T) = x^*$, $x(t) \in M$, $0 \leq t \leq T$. The set of states reachable from $x_0$ is denoted by

$$\mathcal{R}(x_0) = \bigcup_{0 \leq T \leq \infty} \{x: x \text{ reachable from } x_0 \text{ at time } T\}.$$

We say that $\Sigma$ is *reachable at* $x_0$ if $\mathcal{R}(x_0) = M$ and *reachable* if $\mathcal{R}(x) = M$ for all $x \in M$.

The problem with Definition 4.1 is that when $f(x, u)$ is nonlinear, it may be necessary to travel either a long distance or a long time to reach points near $x_0$. Thus, the property of reachability from $x_0$ may not always be of practical use. These unpleasant possibilities force us to introduce a *local* version of reachability.

***Definition 4.2*** The system $\Sigma$ is *locally reachable at* $x_0$ if for every neighborhood $U$ of $x_0$, $\mathcal{R}(x_0) \cap U$ is also a neighborhood of $x_0$ with the trajectory from $x_0$ to $\mathcal{R}(x_0) \cap U$ lying entirely within $U$. The system $\Sigma$ is *locally reachable* if it is locally reachable for each $x \in M$.

Unfortunately, the reachability concept given in Definitions 4.1 and 4.2 is not symmetric: $x^*$ may be reachable from $x_0$ but not conversely (in contrast with the case of constant linear systems). To remedy this situation, we need a weaker notion of reachability.

***Definition 4.3*** Two states $x^*$ and $\bar{x}$ are *weakly reachable* from each other if and only if there exist states $x^0, x^1, \ldots, x^k \in M$ such that $x^0 = x^*$, $x^k = \bar{x}$ and either $x^i$ is reachable from $x^{i-1}$ or $x^{i-1}$ is reachable from $x^i$, $i = 1, 2, \ldots, k$. The system $\Sigma$ is called *weakly reachable* if it is weakly reachable from every $x \in M$. It should be noted that weak reachability is a global concept, so we can define a local version of it just as was done in Definition 4.2 for reachability.

The implications that exist between the various reachability concepts are shown in the following diagram.

$$\text{locally reachable} \Rightarrow \text{reachable}$$
$$\Downarrow$$
$$\text{locally weakly reachable} \Rightarrow \text{weakly reachable.}$$

For constant linear systems it can be shown that all four reachability concepts coincide. The problem is to decide which concept is the right one to focus attention on if we wish to generalize the convenient algebraic test familiar from the linear theory (i.e., $\Sigma$ reachable $\Leftrightarrow$ rank $[G, FG, \ldots, F^{n-1}G] = n$). As we show below, the relevant concept in this connection turns out to be local weak reachability.

In Chapter 2 we introduced the Lie bracket of two vector fields $p(x)$ and $q(x)$ on $M$ as

$$[p, q](x) = \left(\frac{\partial q}{\partial x}\right)p - \left(\frac{\partial p}{\partial x}\right)q\Bigg|_x.$$

The set of all $C^\infty$ vector fields on $M$ is an infinite-dimensional vector space denoted by $X(M)$ and becomes a Lie algebra under multiplication defined by the Lie bracket operation.

Each *constant* control $u \in \Omega$ defines a vector field $f(x, u) \in X(M)$. We let $F_0$ denote the subset of all such vector fields, i.e., $F_0$ is the set of all vector fields generated from $f(x, \cdot)$ through the use of constant inputs. Let $F$ denote the smallest subalgebra of $X(M)$ containing $F_0$. Elements of $F$ are linear combinations of elements of the form

$$[f^1[f^2 \cdots [f^i, f^{i+1}] \cdots]],$$

where $f^i \doteq f(x, u^i)$ for some constant $u^i \in \Omega$. We let $T(x)$ be the space of tangent vectors spanned by the vector fields of $F$ at the point $x \in M$.

**Definition 4.4**  The system $\Sigma$ is said to satisfy the *reachability rank condition at* $x_0$ if the dimension of $T(x_0)$ is $n$. If this is true for every $x \in M$, then $\Sigma$ satisfies the *reachability rank condition*.

In principle, the reachability rank condition is a computable test involving formation of the elements of $F$ and checking to see if there are $n$ linearly independent elements evaluated at the given point $x$. Or, conversely, proving that the structure of the elements of $F$ is such that no matter how many brackets of brackets of brackets, etc., we take, $n$ linearly independent vectors will not appear. In the linear case, the Cayley–Hamilton theorem assures us that we need check only a finite number $N$ of elements from $F$ and that $N$ can be specified in *advance*. In the general nonlinear situation, it is strictly caveat emptor and we shall have to impose additional hypotheses on the elements of $X(M)$ to cut the computation down to practically computable levels.

We note in passing that dim $T(x_0)$ is always either 0 or 1 if $F_0$ contains only one element. However, as soon as we have two or more vectors in $F_0$, dim $T(x_0)$ can be very large. For instance, in $R^n$, the system defined by the two vector fields

$$V_1 = \begin{bmatrix} 1 \\ 0 \\ \vdots \\ 0 \end{bmatrix}, \qquad V_2 = \begin{bmatrix} x_1 \\ x_1^2 \\ x_1^3 \\ \vdots \\ x_1^n \end{bmatrix}$$

has dim $T(0) = n$ because

$$[v_1[v_1[v_1 \cdots [v_1, v_2]] \cdots] = r!e_r,$$

$$\underbrace{\qquad\qquad\qquad\qquad\qquad}_{r \text{ times}}$$

where $e_r = r$th unit vector in the canonical basis of $R^n$.

For some of our results, it is convenient to adopt a variant of the notation introduced above. Consider the collection of symbols of the form

$$\{(t_1, f^1)(t_2, f^2) \cdots (t_p, f^p): p \text{ a nonnegative integer, } f^i \in X(M), t_i \in R\}.$$

We take concatenation as the law of composition for such symbols and adopt the two simplification rules:

(i)   if $f^i = f^{i+1}$, then replace $(t_i, f^i)(t_{i+1}, f^{i+1})$ by $(t_i + t_{i+1}, f^i)$;
(ii)   suppress terms of the form $(0, f)$.

The set of all irreducible sequences is called the *control group* associated with $X(M)$ and denoted $G(X)$. The group action is defined by

$$(t_1, f^1)(t_2, f^2) \cdots (t_p, f^p)x = (\exp t_1 f^1)(\exp t_2 f^2) \cdots (\exp t_p f^p)x,$$

where $(\exp t_i f^i)x^*$ is the solution curve (flow) at $t = t_i$ of the equation $\dot{x} = f(x, u^i), x(0) = x^*$.

If the initial point is $x \in M$, the *orbit* $G(X) \cdot x$ of $x$ is the set

$$G(X) \cdot x = \{(\exp t_1 f^1)(\exp t_2 f^2) \cdots (\exp t_p f^p)x:$$

$$f^i \in X(M), t_i \in R, p \geq 0\}. \tag{4.3}$$

The positive orbit $G^+(X)x$ is the set (4.3) when $t_i \in R^+$, while the orbit at time $t$, $G_t(X)x$, is $G(X)x$ with the additional condition $\sum_{i=1}^{p} t_i = t$.

The essential reachability questions that we now want to answer are:

1.  What is the structure of $G(X)x$?
2.  What is the structure of $G^+(X)x$?

By an answer, we understand a *computable* algorithm which, in terms of the given data $\Omega$, $x_0$, $T$, and $f(\cdot, \cdot)$, enables us to settle the question. As we shall see, most of the essential aspects of questions 1 and 2 are solved except for:

(i)   When is $G^+(X)x$ or $G_t(X)x$ closed?
(ii)   When is $G^+(X)x = M$?

Unfortunately, for control purposes questions (i) and (ii) are the two most relevant ones. However, good partial results are available and a complete answer to (i) and (ii) can be given for some classes of systems.

**Example:  A Switching Circuit**

To illustrate the above point of view, consider the elementary switching circuit in Fig. 4.1. Here we assume that the capacitances $C_1$ and $C_2$ and the inductances $L_1$ and $L_2$ equal 1. If we denote the voltages across each capacitor as $V_1$ and $V_2$, with the current being $i$, we have

$$
\begin{array}{ccc}
\text{switch in left} & \left\{ \begin{array}{ll} \dfrac{dV_1}{dt} = -i, & \dfrac{dV_1}{dt} = 0 \\[2ex] \dfrac{dV_2}{dt} = 0, & \dfrac{dV_2}{dt} = -i, \\[2ex] \dfrac{di}{dt} = V_1 & \dfrac{di}{dt} = V_2 \end{array} \right\} & \text{switch in right} \\
\text{position} & & \text{position.}
\end{array}
$$

Thus, no matter what we are doing with the switch, the position vector $(V_1, V_2, i)$ is orthogonal to the velocity. Consequently, the dynamical motion of the system is restricted to lie on a sphere $S$ whose radius equals the norm of the initial state $(V_1^0, V_2^0, i^0)$. (We remark that this result hinges on $L_i = C_i$, $i = 1, 2$, i.e., $\Sigma$ is a conservative system. We shall see later that this situation is typical for Hamiltonian dynamical systems.)

As noted a moment ago, in some cases the reachability rank condition may be difficult to verify due to a lack of a nonlinear version of the Cayley–Hamilton theorem. In theory we could compute bracket after bracket in the Lie algebra $F$ with no assurance that the next bracket would not yield a vector field linearly independent of those previously computed.

To rule out this type of behavior, we introduce the notion of an involutive system of vector fields.

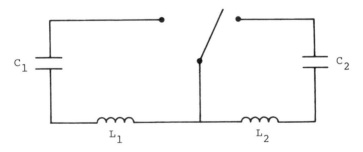

**FIG. 4.1**  LC switching circuit.

**Definition 4.5**   A set of vector fields $\{f^i\}_{i=1}^r$ is called *involutive* if there exist functions $\gamma_{ijk}(x)$ such that

$$[f^i, f^j](x) = \sum_{k=1}^{r} \gamma_{ijk}(x) f^k(x).$$

The property of being involutive is a necessary condition to be able to *integrate* the vector fields, $f^1, \ldots, f^r$ to obtain a solution manifold for the differential equation $\dot{x} = f(x)$. In a moment we shall see that under mild regularity assumptions, it is also sufficient to assert the existence of maximal solutions.

## III. SOLUTION MANIFOLDS
## FOR DYNAMICAL SYSTEMS

Before tackling the reachability problem, we make a brief digression to consider the structure of the manifold $G(X)x$. The basic theorem telling us about the geometric character of $G(X)x$ is the following result of Frobenius and Chow.

**Theorem 4.1**   (Frobenius–Chow)   *Let* $\{f^i\}_{i=1}^r$ *be an involutive collection of vector fields which are* $C^\infty$ *on a* $C^\infty$ *manifold* $M$, *with* dim span$\{f^i\}$ *constant for all* $x \in M$. *Then given any* $x_0 \in M$ *there exists a maximal submanifold* $N \subset M$ *containing* $x_0$ *such that* $\{f^i\}$ *spans the tangent space of* $N$ *at each point of* $N$.

REMARK 1   If $M$ is analytic, the requirement that the dim span$\{f^i\}$ be equal to a constant is automatically satisfied.

REMARK 2   If $X = \{f^i\}$ and if dim span$\{f^i\} = r$, then $N = G(X)x$ and we have dim $N = r$.

**Example**   To illustrate the Frobenius–Chow theorem, consider the analytic vector fields in $M = R^3$,

$$f^1(x) = \begin{bmatrix} 0 \\ x_2 \\ -x_3 \end{bmatrix}, \qquad f^2(x) = \begin{bmatrix} -x_3 \\ 0 \\ x_1 \end{bmatrix}, \qquad f^3(x) = \begin{bmatrix} x_2 \\ -x_1 \\ 0 \end{bmatrix}.$$

It is easy to verify that this collection is involutive and if we consider any $x_0 \in R^3$, it is possible to integrate the vector fields $\{f^i\}$ through that point. For instance, if $x_0 = \frac{1}{3}(\sqrt{3}, \sqrt{3}, \sqrt{3})$, then $N = \{x: \|x\| = 1\}$ is the corresponding solution manifold. In fact, in this example the vectors $f^1, f^2, f^3$ are tangent to the spherical shell $N$ at each point.

If we allow both negative and positive time, the problem of complete reachability for the involutive system of vector fields $\{f^i\}$ may be restated: does the maximal submanifold $N = M$? To answer this question, a more explicit characterization of $N$ is needed.

Recall that for a given vector field $f$ on $M$ and for each real $t$, $\exp tf$ defines a map $M \to M$, whose action is determined by the flow of the differential equation $\dot{x} = f(x)$ on $M$. The characterization of $N$ needed to decide the reachability question is now given by the following result of Chow.

***Theorem 4.2*** (Chow)   *Let $\{f^i\}_{i=1}^r$ be a collection of vector fields such that $\{f^i\}_{LA}$ is $C^\infty$ on a $C^\infty$-manifold $M$ with* dim span $\{f^i\}_{LA}$ *equal to a constant on $M$. Then given any $x_0 \in M$, there exists a maximal submanifold $N \subset M$ containing $x_0$ such that*

$$N = \{\exp\{f^i\}\}_G x_0 = \{\exp\{f^i\}_{LA}\}_G x_0.$$

REMARK 1   If $M$ and $\{f^i\}$ are analytic, the requirement on dim span$\{f^i\}_{LA}$ is automatically satisfied, as in the Frobenius–Chow theorem.

REMARK 2   The surprising part of Chow's theorem is that the set of vector fields $\exp\{f^i\}_{LA}\}_G$ appears to be much larger than $\{\exp\{f^i\}\}_G$. Consequently, we would expect to be able to *reach* more points of $M$ using the first set. However, Chow's result shows that, in fact, the two sets $\{\exp\{f^i\}\}_G x_0$ and $\{\exp\{f^i\}_{LA}\}_G x_0$ are actually the same.

Since Chow's theorem does not distinguish between positive and negative time, the submanifold $N$ may include points which can only be reached by passing backward along one of the vector fields $\{f^i\}_{LA}$. Thus, the set $G^+(\{f^i\}_{LA})x$ will, in general, only be a proper subset of $N$.

For the dynamical system  $\dot{x} = f(x)$, $x(0) = x_0$, the problem of *local reachability* involves conditions such that $(\exp tf)x_0 \in$ interior $\mathcal{R}(t, x_0)$. For this we need some assurance that $G^+(X)x_0$ has a nonempty interior, where $X = \{f^i\}_{LA}$. Fortunately, the reachability rank condition provides the basis for a computable test, as the following result shows.

***Theorem 4.3***   *Let $M = R^n$ and assume that the set $X$ has rank $n$ at $x_0$. Then*

(i)   *in every neighborhood of $x_0$ the set $G^+(X)x_0$ has interior points;*

(ii)   *the set $G(X)x_0$ is a neighborhood of $x_0$.*

PROOF   Assume the rank $X = n$ at $x_0$. Then at least one vector in $X$ is not zero at $x_0$. Let $f^1 \neq 0$. For $\epsilon$ sufficiently small, the set

$$S^1 = \{(\exp t_1 f^1)x_0 : 0 < t_1 < \epsilon\}$$

is a smooth submanifold of $R^n$. There exists a point $z_1 = (\exp \gamma_1 f^1)x_0$ in

$S^1$ and a vector $f^2 \in X$ such that $f^1|_{z_1}$ and $f^2|_{z_1}$ are linearly independent for, if not, all the vectors of $X$ are tangent to $S^1$, which would imply rank $X = 1$.
For $\epsilon_2$ sufficiently small, the set

$$S^2 = \{(\exp t_2 f^2)(\exp t_1 f^1)x_0 : \theta_1 - \epsilon_2 < t_1 \ll \theta_1 + \epsilon_2, 0 \ll t_2 \ll \epsilon_2\}$$

is a submanifold of $R^n$. If $n > 2$, there exists a point $z_2 = (\exp \delta_2 f^2)$ $(\exp \delta_1 f^1)x_0$ in $S^2$ and a vector $f^3$ such that $f^3|_{z_2}$, $f^2|_{z_2}$, $f^1|_{z_2}$ are independent for the same reasons as before. Continuing in this fashion, we define $S^3, S^4, \ldots$, up to $S^n$, which is an open subset of $R^n$ and is contained in $G^+(X)x_0$ by construction. Since $\epsilon_1, \epsilon_2, \ldots, \epsilon_n$ can be chosen arbitrarily small, the proof works in any neighborhood of $x_0$.

***Corollary*** *If* rank $X = n$ *at* $x_0 \in M$, *then the interior points of* $G^+(X)x_0$ *are dense in* $G^+(X)x_0$, *i.e.,*

$$G^+(X)x_0 \subset \overline{\text{Int}\ G^+(X)x_0}.$$

In view of the central role played by the reachability rank condition, it is of some importance to have an idea as to how frequently we can expect it to be satisfied. In other words, given a collection of smooth vector fields $X$ on a smooth manifold $M$, will the rank condition *usually* be satisfied for all $x \in M$? Happily, the answer is that the rank condition is *generic*, as our next result shows.

***Theorem 4.4*** *In the set* $X(M)$ *of all smooth vector fields on* $M$, *the set of those smooth families which satisfy the reachability rank condition for all* $x \in M$ *contains an open, dense subset, i.e., the rank condition is generic.*

PROOF   See chapter references.

REMARK 1   The topology on $X(M)$ in Theorem 4.4 is the usual Whitney $C^\infty$-topology.

REMARK 2   For a generic system $V$, we have that $G(V)x = M$ for all $x \in M$. In other words, the system is completely reachable using positive *and* negative time.

To illustrate certain important aspects of the preceding results, we present a few examples.

***Example 1*** Let $M = R^2$ and let the family of vector fields $X$ consist of $f^1(x) = \begin{bmatrix} 1 \\ 0 \end{bmatrix}$, $f^2(x) = \begin{bmatrix} 0 \\ 1 \end{bmatrix}$. Thus, the reachability rank condition is satisfied and we can apply Theorem 4.3 to conclude that for any $x_0 \in R^2$, the set $G^+(F_0)x_0$ contains interior points, and $G(F_0)x_0$ is a neighborhood of $x_0$ (see Fig. 4.2). (We recall that $F_0$ is a set of constant vector fields.) We note

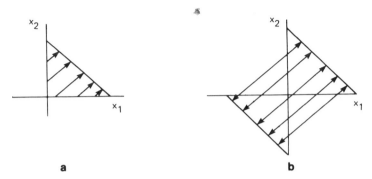

**a**                                      **b**

**FIG. 4.2**   The reachable sets for example 1 (a) $G^+(F_0)x_0$, (b) $G(F_0)x_0$.

that only by allowing negative time can we ensure being able to reach a full neighborhood of $x_0$.

***Example 2***   Again let $M = R^2$, with $X$ being

$$f^1(x) = \begin{bmatrix} 1 - x_2^2 \\ 1 \end{bmatrix}, \qquad f^2(x) = \begin{bmatrix} 1 - x_2^2 \\ -1 \end{bmatrix}.$$

In this case the rank condition is satisfied by $f^1$ and $f^2$ if $x_2 \neq \pm 1$, i.e., for almost every $x \in M$. However, the set $G^+(X)x$ looks something like that depicted in Fig. 4.3, for $x_0 = 0$. The point is that the set $G^+(X)x$ has an interior but is not closed.

If we assume that the vector fields and $M$ are analytic rather than just smooth ($C^\infty$), then it is reasonable to expect global results from knowledge of the *coefficients* at a point $x \in M$. It turns out that this is actually the case as we shall display during the course of our treatment of controlled dynamical processes in succeeding sections.

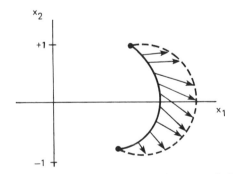

**FIG. 4.3**   The positive time set for Example 2.

## IV. SOME GENERAL RESULTS

Before considering detailed reachability results for specific classes of nonlinear systems, we pause for a moment to discuss some fairly general results for smooth and analytic systems. These results are not only of considerable interest in their own right, but they also provide the basis for some of our later results on linear-analytic and bilinear systems.

We consider the system $\Sigma$

$$\dot{x} = f(x, u), \qquad x(0) = x_0$$

defined on a smooth $(C^\infty)$ manifold $M$, with the conditions on $u$ as given in Section I. Our first result shows the connection between the rank condition at $x_0$ and reachability.

**Theorem 4.5**  *If $\Sigma$ satisfies the reachability rank condition at $x_0$, then $\Sigma$ is locally weakly reachable at $x_0$.*

PROOF  Choose a neighborhood $U$ of $x_0$ so that $\Sigma$ satisfies the rank condition for all $x \in U$. Define the sequence $V^{j-1}$ of submanifolds of $M$ as

$$V^{j-1} = \{(\exp(s_{j-1})f^{j-1})(\exp(s_{j-2})f^{j-2}) \cdots (\exp s_1 f^1)x_0 : (s_1, s_2, \ldots, s_{j-i})$$

is some open subset of the positive orthant in $R^{j-i}\}$.

Clearly $V^{j-1} \subset \mathcal{R}(\infty, x_0) \cap U$. If $j \leq n$, we construct $V^j$ by using an input $u^j \in \Omega$ and $x^{j-1} \in V^{j-1}$. This can always be done for, if not, then $F$ restricted to $V^{j-1}$ is a subalgebra of $X(V^{j-1})$, which implies $\dim F(x) \leq j - 1 < n$ on $V^{j-1} \leq U$, contradicting the rank condition.

Thus, for every neighborhood $U$ of $x_0$, the interior of $\mathcal{R}(t, x_0) \neq \{\theta\}$. Now choose a control $u(t)$, $t_0 \leq t \leq t_1$, such that the trajectory $x(t)$ satisfies $x(t_0) = x_0$, $x(t_1) = x^1 \in \operatorname{int} \mathcal{R}(t_1, x_0)$ and $x(t) \in U$ for $t_0 \leq t \leq t_1$. Then the flow of the vector field $f(x, u(t))$ is a diffeomorphism of a neighborhood $V$ of $x^1$ onto a neighborhood of $x_0$. Further, we can choose $V \subset \mathcal{R}(t, x_0)$ small enough so that the flow from $t_0$ is contained in the weakly reachable set from $x_0$, completing the proof. Thus, for smooth systems the rank condition is sufficient to guarantee local weak reachability. The converse is not quite true but we do have

**Theorem 4.6**  *If $\Sigma$ is locally weakly reachable, then the reachability rank condition is satisfied on an open, dense subset of $M$, i.e., the rank condition is satisfied generically on $M$.*

PROOF  For any system, the reachability rank condition is satisfied on an open subset of $M$, possible empty.

Suppose there exists an open subset $U$ of $M$, where $\dim F(x) < n$. Let $\dim F(x) = k < n$ for all $x \in U$. For an $x_0 \in U$, let $\hat{U}$ denote the maximal

integral submanifold of $F(x)$ in $U$ guaranteed by Frobenius' theorem. Then
$\mathcal{R}(x_0) \subseteq \hat{U}$ and by putting Theorems 4.3 and 4.5 together, we have that $\Sigma$
is locally weakly reachable if and only if for every $x \in M$ and every neighbor-
hood $U$ of $x$, int $\mathcal{R}(x) \neq \emptyset$. Thus, if dim $F(x_0) = k < n$, $\Sigma$ is not locally
weakly reachable at $x_0$, contradicting the hypothesis. Hence, the rank con-
dition is satisfied on a dense subset of $M$.

The preceding results can be substantially strengthened if we demand that
the manifold $M$ and the vector field $F$ be analytic, rather than just $C^\infty$. In
this analytic case we can establish

**Theorem 4.7** *If the system $\Sigma$ is analytic, then the following conditions are
equivalent*:

   (i)  $\Sigma$ *is weakly reachable*;
   (ii) $\Sigma$ *is locally weakly reachable*;
   (iii) *the reachability rank condition is satisfied for all $x \in M$.*

PROOF    See chapter references.

**Example 1**    The simplest illustration of the use of Theorems 4.5–4.7 is to
recapture the standard result of the linear theory. In this case we have

$$\dot{x} = Fx + Gu$$

implying $F_0 = \{Fx + Gu : u \in \Omega, \Omega$ are piecewise constant functions$\}$. Thus,
the Lie algebra $\{f^i\}_{LA}$ is generated by the vector fields $\{Fx, g_1, g_2, \ldots, g_m\}$,
where $g_i = i$th column of $G$, regarded as a constant vector field. Here, of
course, the manifold $M = R^n$ and so the system $\Sigma$ is analytic. Computing
the brackets yields

$$[Fx, g_j] = -Fg_j, \qquad [g_i, g_j] = 0,$$
$$[Fx, [Fx, g_j]] = F^2 g_j, \qquad [g_i, [Fx, g_j]] = 0, \ldots.$$

The Cayley–Hamilton theorem implies that $F$ is spanned by the vector field
$Fx$ and the constant vector fields $\{F^i g_j : i = 0, 1, \ldots, n-1; j = 1, 2, \ldots, m\}$.
Thus, the rank condition reduces to the standard condition that the matrix
$\mathscr{C} = [G|FG|\cdots|F^{n-1}G]$ have rank $n$. Hence, by Theorem 4.7, $\Sigma$ is locally
weakly reachable if and only if rank $\mathscr{C} = n$. But, for linear systems all notions
of reachability are equivalent which establishes the result.

**Example 2**    (Urban Migration)    In a certain simplified model of urban
population migration involving the population composition of established
neighborhoods, the following dynamical system arises:

$$\dot{x}_1 = -\frac{\alpha x_1 x_2}{x_1 + x_2} - x_1 u, \qquad x_1(0) = N,$$
$$\dot{x}_2 = \beta[N - x_1 - x_2], \qquad x_2(0) = 0.$$

Here $x_1$ and $x_2$ represent the population of whites and blacks in the neighborhood, respectively, $\alpha$ and $\beta$ are proportionality constants, and $N$ is the total housing stock available. The control function $u(t)$ represents the net emigration–immigration factor for whites seeking better housing. The question of interest for us is whether the original all-white neighborhood can be converted to one which is racially mixed (at some specified level) solely by manipulating the white emigration rate. It is fairly evident that if the emigration rate $u(t)$ is unrestricted, then this should be the case. On the other hand, if $u(t) \geq 0$, then the neighborhood should eventually shift from all white to all black. Let us see how to obtain these results from Theorems 4.5–4.7.

We first rewrite the original system as

$$\dot{x} = p(x) + u(t)g(x) \doteq f(x, u),$$

where $x = (x_1, x_2)$, $x_0 = (N, 0)'$ and

$$p(x) = \begin{bmatrix} -\dfrac{\alpha x_1 x_2}{x_1 + x_2} \\ \beta(N - x_1 - x_2) \end{bmatrix}, \qquad g(x) = \begin{bmatrix} -x_1 \\ 0 \end{bmatrix}.$$

To check the reachability rank condition at $x_0$, we must construct $\{p(x), g(x)\}_{LA}|_{x_0}$. We have

$$p(x_0) = \begin{bmatrix} 0 \\ 0 \end{bmatrix}, \qquad g(x_0) = \begin{bmatrix} -N \\ 0 \end{bmatrix}, \qquad [p, g](x_0) = \begin{bmatrix} 0 \\ \beta N \end{bmatrix}.$$

Since the physical constraints of the situation require $u(t) \geq 0$, the only vector fields we need consider for reachability are those corresponding to $u = 0$ and $u = \gamma > 0$. Thus, $f^1(x_0) = f(x_0, 0)$, $f^2(x_0) = f(x_0, \gamma)$. Since $f(x, u) = p(x) + ug(x)$, we see that $\{f^1(x_0), f^2(x_0)\}_{LA} = \{\binom{0}{0}, \binom{-N}{0}, \binom{0}{-\beta\gamma N}\}$ which has rank 2. So, the rank condition fails and, since $\Sigma$ is analytic (because $x_1 + x_2 > 0$), we see that the system is locally reachable by Theorem 4.7 (Fig. 4.4). Note, however, that the reachable set does have a nonempty interior. This can be established by appeal to Theorem 4.3(i) with the vector fields $X = \{p(x), g(x)\}$, since $\{p(x), g(x)\}_{LA}$ has rank 2 at $x_0$.

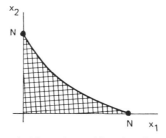

**FIG. 4.4**   The reachable set in positive time for urban migration.

## V. LINEAR-ANALYTIC SYSTEMS

The urban migration example introduces an extremely important class of nonlinear processes in which the control enters linearly, the so-called *linear-analytic* systems. The general form of such a system is

$$\dot{x} = p(x) + \sum_{i=1}^{M} u_i(t)g^i(x), \qquad x(0) = x_0, \tag{4.4}$$

where $p(\cdot)$ and $g^i(\cdot)$ are smooth (or analytic) functions of $x \in M$, $(u_1, u_2, \ldots, u_m) \in R^m$. We shall let $\Omega$ be locally bounded measurable functions on $[0, \infty]$ and, to distinguish interesting subcases, we adopt the notation

$$\Omega_U = \{u(t): u(t) \text{ takes arbitrary values in } R^m\}$$

$$= \textit{unrestricted controls,}$$

$$\Omega_R = \{u(t): |u_i(t)| \leq 1\}$$

$$= \textit{restricted controls,}$$

$$\Omega_B = \{u(t): u_i(t) = \pm 1\}$$

$$= \textit{bang-bang controls.}$$

To indicate the reachable set under each of the foregoing control sets, we write $\mathcal{R}_U(t, x_0)$, $\mathcal{R}_R(t, x_0)$, or $\mathcal{R}_B(t, x_0)$, respectively.

First let us examine the interior of the reachable set for the control sets above. Fortunately, the reachability rank condition can be used as a convenient test for the interior to be nonempty as the following result shows.

***Theorem 4.8***  *If* $\dim\{p, g^1, g^2, \ldots, g^m\}_{LA} = \dim M$ *at a point* $x_0 \in M$, *then for every* $t > 0$ *the interior points of* $\mathcal{R}_\alpha(t, x_0)$ *are dense in* $\mathcal{R}_\alpha(t, x_0)$, *where* $\alpha$ *can be any one of the symbols, U, R, B.*

PROOF   This result follows immediately from the corollary to Theorem 4.3 as soon as we recognize that the rank of the family $\{p(x) + \sum_{i=1}^{m} u_i g^i : u \in \Omega_B\}$ at $x_0$ equals $\dim\{p, g^1, g^2, \ldots, g^m\}_{LA}$ at $x_0$.

REMARK   The condition of the theorem is also necessary in the analytic case.

The reachability question is easily disposed of in the homogeneous case when we have no drift term, i.e., $p(x) \equiv 0$.

***Theorem 4.9***   *Assume* $p(x) \equiv 0$. *Then if the* $\dim\{g^1, g^2, \ldots, g^m\}_{LA} = \dim M$ *for all* $x \in M$, *we have*

(i)   $\mathcal{R}_R(\infty, x_0) = \mathcal{R}_B(\infty, x_0) = M$ *for all* $x_0 \in M$;
(ii)  $\mathcal{R}_U(t, x_0) = M$ *for all* $x_0 \in M$, $t > 0$.

PROOF   In this case we can *reverse time* since the trajectory corresponding to some constant control $u$ can be followed backward using the control $(-u)$ and the result follows immediately from Theorem 4.3.

REMARK   As above, the rank condition on $\{g^i\}_{LA}$ is also necessary in the analytic case.

Now let us consider the effect of the *drift* term $p(x)$. Assume that $\dim\{g^i\}_{LA} = \dim M$ for all $x \in M$. If we take a point $y \in M$, we know by the last theorem that any neighborhood of $y$ is reachable from $x_0$ at an arbitrary time $t > 0$ using $\bar{u} \in \Omega_U$. During a *short* time the introduction of the drift term $p(x)$ should introduce only a *small* error in our being able to reach $y$ from $x_0$. It is now plausible to conjecture that a control *near* $\bar{u}$ will enable us to reach $y$ exactly in some greater time. This argument can be formalized using fixed-point ideas. We state the final result as

**Theorem 4.10**   *Consider the linear-analytic system* (4.4) *and let* $\dim\{g^i\} = \dim M$ *for all* $x \in M$. *Then for every* $x_0 \in M$ *we have* $\mathcal{R}_U(\infty, x_0) = M$.

PROOF   See C. Lobry, Section 4.II Notes and References.

As we have noted earlier, the basic problem with the drift term $p(x)$ is that it is possible that some points in $M$ might be reachable only by passing backward along the vector field $p(x)$, i.e., by using negative time. What we need are necessary and sufficient conditions for $(\exp t_p)(x_0) \in \operatorname{int} \mathcal{R}(t, x_0)$ for all $t > 0$. The basic results in this direction are summarized in

**Theorem 4.11**

(i)   $\operatorname{int} \cup_{0 \leq t \leq T} \mathcal{R}(t, x_0) \neq 0$ *for all* $T > 0$ *if and only if* $\dim\{p, g^i\}_{LA}(x_0) = \dim M$.

(ii)   $\operatorname{int} \mathcal{R}(t, x_0) \neq \{0\}$ *for all* $t > 0$ *if and only if* $\dim\{p, g^i\}_{LA}(x_0) = \dim M$.

(iii)   $(\exp t_p)x_0 \in \operatorname{int} \mathcal{R}(t, x_0)$ *for all* $t > 0$ *if* $\dim\{p, g^i\}_{LA}(x_0) = \dim M$.

PROOF   See C. Lobry, Section 4.II Notes and references.

REMARK   If $\dim M = 2$, then the rank condition in part (iii) is also necessary.

**Example**   Let $M = \{x \in R^3 : x_3 > 0\}$ and consider the system

$$\begin{bmatrix} \dot{x}_1 \\ \dot{x}_2 \\ \dot{x}_3 \end{bmatrix} = \begin{bmatrix} x_2 \\ -\dfrac{\sin x_1}{x_3} - \dfrac{2ux_2}{x_3} \\ u \end{bmatrix} = p(x) + ug(x),$$

where

$$p(x) = \begin{bmatrix} x_2 \\ -\dfrac{\sin x_1}{x_3} \\ 0 \end{bmatrix}, \qquad g(x) = \begin{bmatrix} 0 \\ -\dfrac{2x_2}{x_3} \\ 1 \end{bmatrix}.$$

Upon computing the bracket $[p, g](x)$, we have

$$[p, g] = \begin{bmatrix} -\dfrac{2x_2}{x_3} \\[2mm] \dfrac{\sin x_1}{x_3^2} \\[2mm] 0 \end{bmatrix}.$$

Thus, it is easy to verify that $\dim\{p, g\}_{\text{LA}} = 3$, for all $x \in M$ unless $x_2^0$ or $x_1^0 = \pm n\pi$. Thus, the rank condition is satisfied for all $x_0$ such that $x_2^0 \neq 0$, $x_1^0 \neq \pm n\pi$.

## VI. THE ROLE OF THE STATE MANIFOLD $M$

Before considering more specialized subclasses of nonlinear dynamics, it is instructive to examine the effect of the topological structure of $M$ on the question of reachability. In the results cited so far, $M$ has been assumed to be an arbitrary differentiable (or analytic) manifold. To indicate some of the advantages and (disadvantages) associated with the imposition of additional structure upon $M$, we consider the following examples.

**Example 1**   Let the system $\Sigma$ be given by the dynamics

$$\dot{x}_1 = \tfrac{1}{2}(1 + f(x_1, x_2)) + \tfrac{1}{2}(1 - f(x_1, x_2))u,$$

$$\dot{x}_1 = \tfrac{1}{2}g(x_1, x_2) - \tfrac{1}{2}g(x_1, x_2)u,$$

with $(x_1, x_2) \in R^2$, i.e., $M = R^2$, $g$, and $f$ analytic on $M$.

First, note that the control $u = +1$ leads to the vector field $f^1 = \binom{1}{0}$, while the control $u = -1$ yields $f^2 = \left[\begin{smallmatrix} f(x_1, x_2) \\ g(x_1, x_2) \end{smallmatrix}\right]$. Thus, this class of systems is parameterized by the set of vector fields in the plane. If we restrict ourselves to nonvanishing vector fields, i.e., $f(x_1, x_2)^2 + g(x_1, x_2)^2 > 0$, it turns out that the two sets

$$M^+ = \{x: g(x_1, x_2) = 0, f(x_1, x_2) > 0\},$$

$$M^- = \{x: g(x_1, x_2) = 0, f(x_1, x_2) < 0\},$$

play an important role in the reachability analysis. In fact, we can prove: *if the system $\Sigma$ is reachable, then the set $M^-$ is nonempty.*

What is of interest about this result is that it is false if we change the structure of $M$. For example, if $M$ is a two-dimensional torus, then the necessary condition fails. Furthermore, more complicated examples can be given to show that knowledge of $M^{\pm}$ is not sufficient, in general, to determine reachability.

Now that we have seen how a change in the structure of $M$ can complicate the reachability problem, let us consider how changes of a different type can simplify and sharpen our earlier results.

***Example 2***   Let $M = $ Lie group $G$. In this case the Lie algebra of vector fields $\{p, g^i\}_{LA}$ determines a Lie subgroup $S$ of $M$. The question of reachability now reduces to whether $\mathcal{R}(\infty, e)$ is a subgroup, where $e$ is the identity of the Lie group $G$.

The reachability question is easily settled if $G$ is compact by the following result. *If $G$ is compact, then (4.4) is arbitrary-interval completely reachable* (i.e., $\mathcal{R}_\alpha(T, g) = G$, for all $T > 0$, $g \in G$, $\alpha = U$, $R$, or $B$) *if and only if* $\{p(x), g^i(x)\}_{LA}$ *is the Lie algebra of $G$ for all* $x \in G$.

As a special case, we can consider $M = GL(n, R)$, the Lie group of invertible, real $n \times n$ matrices. Here the Lie bracket of the vector fields $X \to A^i X$, $X \to A^j X$ is the vector field $X \to (A^i A^j - A^j A^i)X = [A^i, A^j]X$, i.e., $[A^i, A^j]$ is a *commutator* of $A^i$ and $A^j$. Applying the above general result, we see that the matrix system

$$\frac{dX}{dt} = \left[ P + \sum_{i=1}^{m} u_i(t)G^i \right] X, \qquad X \in GL(n, R)$$

is completely reachable from the identity $e = I$, if and only if

$$\{P, G^1, G^2, \ldots G^m\}_{LA} = GL(n, R) = M.$$

We shall have more detailed results on this special class of bilinear systems in Section VII.

## VII.  BILINEAR SYSTEMS

In the class of linear-analytic systems, certainly the most complete reachability results are available for the so-called *bilinear* systems, which take the form

$$\dot{x} = Fx + Gu + \sum_{i=1}^{m} N_i u_i(t),$$

where $F$ and $N_i$ are $n \times n$ real matrices and $G$ is an $n \times m$ real matrix.

There are a number of theoretical and practical motivations for the study of bilinear processes, not the least of which is that the systems can be parameterized by matrices leading to the conjecture that by *souping-up* the linear results, we could also settle the important reachability questions for bilinear systems with simple algebraic tests as in the linear case. The partial validation of this conjecture will be an important part of our story throughout this chapter.

Without loss of generality, we consider the *homogeneous-in-the-state* system

$$\dot{x} = \left(F + \sum_{i=1}^{m} N_i u_i(t)\right)x, \qquad x(0) = x_0 \neq 0. \tag{4.5}$$

(*Remark*: The case when $G \neq 0$ can be reduced to the above case by adding extra components to the state and/or control and constraining them to be equal to 1). As noted in Example 2 of Section VI, we can express the state of our system as $x(t) = X(t)x_0$, where $X(t) \in GL(n, R)$. Thus, to study reachability we may confine our attention to the matrix system

$$\dot{X} = [F + \Sigma N_i u_i(t)]X, \qquad X(0) = I.$$

Here the state manifold is $M = GL(n, R)$, a Lie group. We have already seen that the reachability properties of this system are determined by the Lie algebra of the elements $\{F, N_1, N_2, \ldots, N_m\}$. The following theorem sharpens our earlier result.

**Theorem 4.12**   Let $\pounds = \{F, N_1, \ldots, N_m\}_{\text{LA}}$ *and let*

$$GL(n, R)(\pounds) = \{\Gamma \in GL(n, R): \Gamma = e^{A_1}e^{A_2}\cdots e^{A_m}, A_i \in \pounds$$

$$i = 1, \ldots, m; m = 1, 2, \ldots\}$$

*be compact. Then*

(i)   $\cup_{t>0} \mathscr{R}(t, I) = GL(n, R)(\pounds),$
(ii)   *there exists a* $0 < T < \infty$ *such that*

$$\mathscr{R}(T, I) = \bigcup_{t \geq 0} \mathscr{R}(t, I) = GL(n, R)(\pounds).$$

PROOF   The proof uses the fact that $M$ compact means that $\mathscr{R}_\alpha(\infty, I)$ is a subgroup of $M$ for $\alpha = U$, $R$, or $B$. The remaining details can be found in Notes and References.

In short, this result tells us that the reachable set from $I$ is $GL(n, R)(\pounds)$ and that points that can be reached at all will be reached in some finite time $T$.

REMARK   In the strictly bilinear case when $F = 0$, the compactness assumption on $GL(n, R)(\pounds)$ can be dropped.

REMARK   If $F = 0$, the system is completely reachable on $R^n - \{0\}$ if and only if dim $\pounds = n$.

**Example**   Consider the homogeneous bilinear system

$$\dot{x}_1 = x_1, \qquad\qquad x_1(0) = x_1^0,$$

$$\dot{x}_2 = (x_1 + x_2)(1 + u), \qquad x_2(0) = x_2^0.$$

Clearly, this system is not reachable. Let us employ Theorem 4.12 to establish this fact directly.

The relevant matrices for this system are

$$F = \begin{bmatrix} 1 & 0 \\ 1 & 1 \end{bmatrix}, \qquad N = \begin{bmatrix} 0 & 0 \\ 1 & 1 \end{bmatrix}.$$

Computing the Lie brackets for $\pounds$ we have

$$[F, N] = \begin{bmatrix} 0 & 0 \\ -1 & 1 \end{bmatrix}, \qquad [F, [F, N]] = \begin{bmatrix} -1 & 0 \\ 0 & 0 \end{bmatrix}$$

$$[N, [F, N]] = \begin{bmatrix} 0 & 0 \\ 0 & 1 \end{bmatrix}, \dots$$

It is easy to see that every element of $\pounds$ has the form $\begin{bmatrix} x & 0 \\ x & x \end{bmatrix}$, where $x$ denotes some nonzero entry. Thus, $\pounds$ can never generate $GL(2, R)$. Consequently, our system is not completely reachable.

An alternate approach to the study of the inhomogeneous bilinear system (4.5) $(G \neq 0)$ is to examine its equilibrium points. For brevity, let us write $\sum_{i=1}^{m} N_i x u_i \doteq Nxu$. Then if $\bar{u}$ is a constant control such that $|u_i| \leq 1$, the equilibrium point(s) $x^*(\bar{u})$ satisfy the equation

$$Fx + Nx\bar{u} + G\bar{u} = 0.$$

Solving for $x$, we find

$$x^*(\bar{u}) = -(F + N'\bar{u})^{-1} G\bar{u}, \qquad (4.6)$$

assuming that $G\bar{u}$ is not in the range of $F + N'\bar{u}$ whenever $F + N'\bar{u}$ is singular. As $\bar{u}$ ranges over the unit $m$-cube $H$, expression (4.6) describes the equilibrium set.

Theorem 4.13 provides sufficient conditions for the bilinear system (4.5) to be completely controllable to the origin.

**Theorem 4.13**  *The bilinear system* (4.5) *is completely controllable (using piecewise-continuous inputs) if*

(a)  *there exist constant controls* $u^+$ *and* $u^-$ *in* $H$ *such that* $\operatorname{Re} \lambda_i(F + N'u^+) > 0$, $\operatorname{Re} \lambda_i(F + N'u^-) < 0$, *with* $x^*(u^+)$ *and* $x^*(u^-)$ *contained in a connected subset of the equilibrium set;*

(b)  *for each* $x^*(\bar{u})$, *there exists a* $v \in R^m$ *such that the pair* $\{F + N'\bar{u}, (Nx^*(\bar{u}) + G)v\}$ *is controllable in the usual sense.*

PROOF    See R. Mohler, Section 4.VII Notes and References.

Important properties of the reachable set for a compact control set are that it be convex and closed, regardless of the initial state. These properties are important for understanding the time-optimal control problem and for generating computational algorithms for determining optimal controls. For bilinear systems the reachable set is usually not convex (or even closed) unless $\Omega$ is both compact and convex.

In the general case $\dot{x} = f(x) + g(x, u)$, and if $g(x, u)$ has the property that at each $x$, $g(x, \Omega)$ is a closed convex set, then Filippov's theorem asserts that $\mathscr{R}(t, x_0)$ is closed for all $t$ and $x_0$. If, in addition, $f(\gamma x_1 + (1 - \gamma)x_2) = \gamma f(x_1) + (1 - \gamma)f(x_2)$ and $\gamma g(x_1, \Omega) + (1 - \gamma)g(x_2, \Omega) \in g(\gamma x_1 + (1 - \gamma)x_2, \Omega)$ then $\mathscr{R}(t, x_0)$ is convex.

In the special case when rank $N_i = 1$, we can give much more specific results on the structure of $\mathscr{R}(t, x_0)$. Let us write $N_i = b_i c_i'$, where $b_i$ and $c_i$ are $n$-dimensional vectors. The first result involves the case of small $t$.

**Theorem 4.14**   *Let $x_0$ be given and assume $c_i' x_0 \neq 0$, $i = 1, 2, \ldots, m$. Then there exists a $T > 0$ such that for each $t$, $0 \le t \le T$, $\mathscr{R}_R(t, x_0)$ is convex.*

PROOF   See R. Brockett, Section 4.VII Notes and References.

To *globalize* this result to the case $T = \infty$, additional hypotheses on the structure of $F$, $b_i$, and $c_i$ are needed. One such set of conditions is suggested by the well-known matrix-theoretic fact that if the off-diagonal entries of a matrix A are nonnegative and the vector $c$ has nonnegative entries, then the solution of the linear differential equation $\dot{x} = Ax$, $x(0) = c$ has $x_i(t) \ge 0$ for all $t \ge 0$. Since the nonnegative vectors in $R^n$ form a convex set, the obvious application to bilinear systems is

**Theorem 4.15**   *Suppose each entry of $c_i$ is nonnegative and that the matrix $F + \sum_{i=1}^{m} u_i(t) b_i c_i'$ has nonnegative off-diagonal entries for all $t > 0$ and all $u \in \Omega_R$. Then $\mathscr{R}_R(t, x_0)$ is convex for all $t > 0$.*

PROOF   Apply this matrix result to the bilinear system with $x_0 = 0$.


**VIII. POLYNOMIAL SYSTEMS**

Intermediate between the linear-analytic systems and the bilinear systems are polynomial systems of the form

$$\dot{x} = f(x) + u(t)g(x), \tag{4.6}$$

where $f(\cdot)$, $g(\cdot)$ are polynomial functions of their arguments and for simplicity, we assume $u(\cdot)$ is a scalar piecewise-smooth control. The extension to vector controls is immediate at the expense of a more elaborate notation. The polynomial structure of $f$ and $g$ suggest that some of the concepts from algebraic geometry introduced in Chapter 2 will play a useful role in determining properties of the reachable set for (4.6). We refer to Chapter 2 for the notation we will use. In addition, we need two new concepts.

Let $f(\cdot)$, $g(\cdot) \in k[s]$, where $k = R$ or $\mathbb{C}$. If $F(s)$ is a column vector with entries in $k[s]$, the *Lie derivative* of $f$ with respect to $F$, $L_F(f(s))$, is defined as

$$L_F(f(s)) \doteq d_s f(F(s)) = \sum_{i=1}^{n} \frac{\partial f}{\partial s_i}(s) F_i(s).$$

Next, given a set $Q \subseteq k[s]$ and a set $P$ whose elements are column vectors of polynomials, define

$I(Q; P) =$ the smallest polynomial ideal in $k[s]$ containing $Q$ and closed
  under Lie differentiation with respect to elements from $P$.

The ideal $I(Q; P)$ provides the key ingredient for the following important result.

**Theorem 4.16**   *Let $V$ be an algebraic set in $k^n$. If $\mathcal{R}(\infty, x_0) \subseteq V$ for each $x_0 \in V$, then $I(\mathcal{V}(V); \{f, g\}) = \mathcal{V}(V)$. If for any ideal $\mathcal{V}$ defining $V$ we have $I(\mathcal{V}; \{f, g\}) = \mathcal{V}$, then $\mathcal{R}(\infty, x_0) \subseteq V$ for all $x_0 \in V$.*

PROOF   By the arguments given in Chapter 2, it suffices to prove the result for the case $f(x) = Ax^{[p]}$, $g(x) = Bx^{[q]}$. Furthermore, it is enough to prove that $\mathcal{R}(\infty, x_0) \subseteq V$ if and only if for each $h \in \mathcal{V}(V)$, we also have $d_s h(As^{[p]}) \in \mathcal{V}(V)$ and $d_s h(Bs^{[q]}) \in \mathcal{V}(V)$.

Suppose that for each $x_0 \in V$, $\mathcal{R}(\infty, x_0) \subseteq V$. Let $h \in \mathcal{V}(V)$. Then $h(x(t)) \equiv 0$ for all trajectories initiating at any $x_0 \in V$. Differentiating both sides of this identity gives

$$d_{x(t)} h(Ax(t)^{[p]} + u(t)Bx(t)^{[q]}) \equiv 0.$$

Since this must hold for all possible $u(\cdot)$, we conclude that

$$d_{x(t)} h(Ax(t)^{[p]}) \equiv 0, \qquad d_{x(t)} h(Bx(t)^{[q]}) \equiv 0$$

along $x(t)$. Since these identities must hold for all $x_0 \in V$, $d_s h(As^{[p]})$ and $d_s h(Bs^{[q]})$ vanish identically on $V$.

Now suppose that whenever a polynomial $h$ vanishes on $V$, we have $d_s h(As^{[p]}) \equiv 0$ and $d_s h(Bs^{[q]}) \equiv 0$ on $V$. By the Hilbert Basis Theorem, $\mathcal{V}(V)$ is finitely generated by, say, $\{h_1, h_2, \ldots, h_r\}$. Let $x(t)$ be an arbitrary but fixed trajectory of (4.6) with initial point $x_0 \in V$. For each $i = 1, 2, \ldots, r$, let $y_i(t) = h_i(x(t))$. Since $h_1, \ldots, h_r$ generate $\mathcal{V}(V)$ and since by hypothesis $d_s h_i(As^{[p]} + u(t)Bs^{[q]}) \in \mathcal{V}(V)$ for each $i$, there are polynomials $g_{ij}(t, s) \in k[s_1, \ldots, s_n]$ such that

$$d_s h_i(As^{[p]} + u(t)Bs^{[q]}) = \sum_{l=1}^{r} g_{il}(t, s) h_i(s).$$

We define the matrix $H(t) \doteq [g_{ij}(t, x(t))]$. Now we form the vector $y(t) = (y_1(t), \ldots, y_r(t))'$. Then $y(t) \in k^r$ and $\dot{y}(t) = H(t)y(t)$, $y(0) = 0$. Thus, $h_i(x(t)) = 0$

for $t \geq 0$, implying $x(t) \in V$. Since the trajectory $x(t)$ was arbitrary, we see that if $x_0 \in V$, $\mathcal{R}(\infty, x_0) \subseteq V$.

REMARK   It is important to note that the statement $\mathcal{R}(\infty, x_0) \subseteq V$ for each $x_0 \in V$ does not imply $I(\mathcal{V}; \{f, g\}) = \mathcal{V}$ for an *arbitrary* $\mathcal{V}$ defining $V$. It holds only if $\mathcal{V}$ is the *smallest* defining ideal. For example, let $\mathcal{V} \subseteq k[s_1, s_2]$ be generated by the polynomials

$$\phi_1(s_1, s_2) = s_1^2, \qquad \phi_2(s_1, s_2) = s_2,$$

and let

$$f(s_1, s_2) = \begin{pmatrix} 0 \\ s_1 \end{pmatrix}, \qquad g(s_1, s_2) = \begin{pmatrix} 0 \\ 0 \end{pmatrix}.$$

Then $V(\mathcal{V}) = \{\begin{pmatrix} 0 \\ 0 \end{pmatrix}\}$ and it is easy to verify that $\mathcal{R}(\infty, x_0) \subseteq V$ for each $x_0 \in V$. Nevertheless, $I(\mathcal{V}; \{f, g\}) = \mathcal{V}(V)$, which properly contains $\mathcal{V}$.

We can now employ the foregoing result to test whether or not a given algebraic set $V$ contains points reachable from $x_0$. More importantly, we also now have the basis for a procedure to actually construct $\mathcal{R}(\infty, x_0)$: first, find an ideal $\mathcal{V}$ such that $I(\mathcal{V}; \{f, g\}) = \mathcal{V}$. Next construct the algebraic set $V = \{x \in k^n : \phi(x) = 0, \phi \in \mathcal{V}\}$. Then we must have $\mathcal{R}(\infty, x_0) \subseteq V$. In general, the containment will be proper. At present, conditions for equality are unknown for general polynomial $f$ and $g$, but it has been conjectured that the set $V$, together with some algebraic *inequalities*, will characterize $\mathcal{R}(\infty, x_0)$ exactly. In other words, $\mathcal{R}(\infty, x_0)$ is a *semi-algebraic* set.

A very useful consequence of Theorem 4.16 is a computable algebraic criterion for int $\mathcal{R}(t, x_0) \neq \phi$ for all $t > 0$ for the polynomial system

$$\dot{x} = Ax^{[p]} + bu, \qquad x(0) = x_0,$$

where $x^{[p]}$ is the weighted $p$-form defined in Chapter 2. If we write $f(x) = Ax^{[p]}$, then the $p$th differential $d^p f$ defines a symmetric $p$-linear mapping of

$$\underbrace{k^n \times k^n \times \cdots \times k^n}_{p\text{-times}} \to k.$$

Consider now a set of vectors $\mathcal{B}$ generated as follows:

(i)   let $b \in \mathcal{B}$
(ii)   if $v_1, v_2, \ldots, v_p \in \mathcal{B}$, then let the vector $d^p f(v_1, v_2, \ldots, v_p)$ be added to $\mathcal{B}$.
Define the *order* of an element $v_{p+1} \in \mathcal{B}$ as

$$\text{order } v_{p+1} \doteq 1 + \sum_{i=1}^{p} \text{order } v_i.$$

By definition, order $b = 1$. The connection between the set $\mathcal{B}$ and $\mathcal{R}(t, x_0)$ is the following result.

**Theorem 4.17**  *The system* $\dot{x} = Ax^{[p]} + bu$, $x(0) = x_0$ *has* int $\mathscr{R}(t, x_0) \neq \phi$ *if and only if the elements of $\mathscr{B}$ of order less than or equal to $1 + p + p^2 + \cdots + p^{n-1}$ generate $k^n$.*

PROOF  See Notes and References.

Theorem 4.17 improves upon the result of Theorem 4.11 in that the number of elements needed to check the dimensionality condition is finite and computable *in advance*. Thus, Theorem 4.17 is a generalization of the standard result for constant linear systems, where the finiteness condition is a consequence of the Cayley–Hamilton theorem. Thus, the result of Theorem 4.17 might be thought of as an extension of the Cayley–Hamilton theorem for $p$-linear maps.

## IX. DISCRETE-TIME SYSTEMS

To this point, our results have all been given in terms of continuous-time dynamical systems. This has been due to the heavy emphasis upon tools from differential geometry (Frobenius' theorem, Chow's theorem, Lie derivatives, etc.), which we have employed. However, if we argue by analogy with the linear case it seems reasonable to suppose that certain technical difficulties can be side-stepped if we would consider *discrete-time* systems of the form

$$x(k + 1) = f(x(k), u(k)), \quad x(0) = x_0.$$

In particular, the results of Chapter 3 show that a purely algebraic theory of linear systems can be developed in the discrete-time setting. In this section we shall examine some of the reachability results available for discrete-time bilinear systems.

At first we consider the reachability properties of the system

$$x(k + 1) = \left[ F + \sum_{i=1}^{m} u_i(k)N_i \right] x(k) + Gu(k), \qquad x(0) = 0.$$

The state space is taken to be $M = R^n$. Let us introduce the notation

$\langle F, N_1, N_2, \ldots, N_m \rangle (G) \doteq$ the smallest subspace of $R^n$ invariant under $F, N_1, \ldots, N_m$ containing range $G$.

The following lemma enables us to construct $\langle F, N_1, \ldots, N_m \rangle (G)$.

**Lemma 4.1**  *Define the matrix sequence $\{P_i\}$ as $P_1 = G$, $P_{i+1} = [FP_i | N_1 P_i | \cdots | N_m P_i]$. Let $\hat{P}_j = [P_1 | P_2 | \cdots | P_j]$. Then*

$$\langle F, N_1, \ldots, N_m \rangle (G) = \text{range } \hat{P}_n.$$

PROOF   Easy exercise in linear algebra.

The connection between Lemma 4.1 and reachability is

**Theorem 4.18**   *For the discrete-time bilinear system with* $G \neq 0$, *the states reachable from the origin span the subspace of* $R^n$ *given by*

$$H_m \doteq \langle F, N_1, N_2, \ldots, N_m \rangle(G) = \text{range } \hat{P}_n.$$

PROOF   To begin with, a basis $\{x_1, x_2, \ldots, x_r\}$ of $H_m$ is reachable from the origin. Thus, $(F + \sum_{i=1}^m N_i u_i) x_j + Gu \in H_m$ for all $u \in R^m$, $j = 1$, $2$, ..., $r$. Furthermore, $Gu \in H_m$ since $x(k + 1) \in H_m$ if $x(k) \in H_m$. Hence, $(F + \sum_{i=1}^m N_i u_i) H_m \subseteq H_m$ for all $u \in R^m$. It now follows that $H_m$ contains range $G$ and is invariant under $F, N_1, \ldots, N_m$. Therefore, $H_m \supseteq \langle F, N_1, N_2, \ldots, N_m \rangle(G)$, because the latter, by definition, is the smallest subspace with these properties. We must now show the opposite inclusion.

Using the fact that range $G \subseteq H_m$ and $(F + \sum_{i=1}^m N_i u_i) H_m \subseteq H_m$, we note that any subspace of $R^n$ invariant with respect to $F, N_1, N_2, \ldots, N_m$ and containing range $G$ is such that at any of its points we can move only to an $x(k + 1)$ which also belongs to this subspace. This implies that $\langle F, N_1, N_2, \ldots, N_m \rangle(G)$, the smallest such subspace, contains all trajectories starting at the origin, i.e., $\langle F, N_1, N_2, \ldots, N_m \rangle(G) \supset H_m$, completing the theorem.

Now consider the single-input homogeneous system

$$x(k + 1) = [F + Nu(k)]x(k), \qquad x(0) = x_0 \qquad (4.7)$$

with state space $M = R^n - \{0\}$. Let us define the $n \times L$ matrix

$$\mathscr{C}_L(x) = [F^{L-1}Nx | \cdots | F^{L-i-1}NF^i x | \cdots | NF^{L-1}x].$$

The next result gives an easy sufficient condition for complete reachability of (4.6).

**Theorem 4.19**   *If there exists a positive integer* $L$ *in the range* $1 \leq L \leq n$, *such that*

(i)   $P^{-1}FP$ *is orthogonal for some real* $P$,

(ii)   $\text{rank } \mathscr{C}_L(x) = n$ *for all* $x \in M$, *then* (4.7) *is completely reachable from any* $x_0$ *using controls such that* $|u(k)| < \delta$ *for any* $\delta > 0$.

PROOF   The key steps are to establish from (ii) that $\mathscr{R}(t, x_0)$ is open. Then we show that a subsequence of $\{F^i\}_{i=1}^\infty$ converges to the identity. Thus, from $x_0$ we can reach a neighborhood of $x_0$ and these neighborhoods can be chained together to reach any given point from $x_0$ in a finite number of steps.

REMARK   $\text{rank } \mathscr{C}_n^2(x) = \text{rank } \mathscr{C}_L(x)$ for all $L \geq n^2$ and for all $x \in M$ by the Cayley–Hamilton theorem. Hence condition (ii) holds for $L$ no greater than $n^2$, if it holds at all.

REMARK    The following conditions are equivalent to (i):

1. $|\det F| = 1$ and $\{F^i\}_{i=1}^{\infty}$ is bounded in $R^{n^2}$;
2. $F$ is diagonalizable with $|\lambda_i(F)| = 1$;
3. For some $Q > 0$, $F'QF = Q$.

**Example**    Consider the system matrices

$$F = \begin{bmatrix} 1 & 0 \\ -1 & -1 \end{bmatrix}, \qquad N = \begin{bmatrix} 1 & 4 \\ 3 & -2 \end{bmatrix}, \qquad x_0 = \begin{bmatrix} a \\ b \end{bmatrix}.$$

Since $F^2 = I$, rank $\mathscr{C}_4(x) = \text{rank}\begin{bmatrix} a+4b & -3a-4b \\ -4a-2b & a+2b \end{bmatrix}$. Thus, rank $\mathscr{C}_4(x) < 2$ if and only if $x \in S$, where

$$S = \left\{ \begin{pmatrix} a \\ b \end{pmatrix} \in M : a = 0 \right\}.$$

Thus $S$ divides $M$ into two separate reachable regions: the open left half-plane and the open right half-plane. That is, any two states in these half-planes can be connected by a control sequence with all $|u(k)| < \delta$ for any $\delta > 0$.

## X. INPUT CONSTRUCTION

The preceding results provide the needed tools for deciding whether a given state is reachable from $x_0$ but fail to explicitly specify how to construct an input which will accomplish a feasible transfer. Let us now consider this *construction* question in more detail.

Assume we wish to transfer $\Sigma$ to the origin and that we have measured the system to be in state $q$ at time $t = t_1$. The local reachability question can be considered to be the determination of an input which would drive the trajectory of $\Sigma$ in the *direction* $-q$.

To be more explicit, consider the scalar input linear-analytic system

$$\dot{x} = p(x) + u(t)g(x) \qquad (4.8)$$

with bounded controls $|u(t)| \le 1$. Further, assume that

$$\dim\{p, g\}_{\text{LA}}(0) = n$$

so that $\Sigma$ is locally weakly reachable in a neighborhood of the origin. The problem in the construction of our control law is that the directions which are *instantaneously* possible are $p(q) + \mu g(q)$, $-1 \le \mu \le 1$, and $-q$ need not be among these directions. For notational simplicity, let us write $(adp, g) = [p, q]$, $(ad^{k+1}p, g) = [p, (ad^kp, g)]$. Now we write $q$ as

$$q = \sum_{i=1}^{n} \alpha_i(ad^{i-1}p, g)(0).$$

Then if we can generate the directions $\pm(ad^j p, g)(0)$ via compositions of solutions of (4.8) with controls $|u| \leq 1$, it follows that we can generate the direction $-q$.

To illustrate how to employ the above idea, let $n = 3$ and define

$$q(\epsilon)x = q_2^{e_3}(|\alpha_3|\epsilon) \circ q_1^{e_2}(|\alpha_2|\epsilon) \circ q_0^{e_1}(|\alpha_1|\epsilon)x, \tag{4.9}$$

where

$$e_j = \begin{cases} + & \text{if } \alpha_j < 0, \\ - & \text{if } \alpha_j > 0, \end{cases}$$

and

$$q_0^{\pm}(s)x = \exp(s(p \pm g))x,$$

$$q_1^{\pm}(s)x = \exp\sqrt{s}(p \pm g) \circ \exp\sqrt{s}(p \pm g)x$$

$$= \exp(2\sqrt{s}p \pm \sqrt{s}[p, g] + O(s))x,$$

$$q_2^{\pm}(s)x = \exp(2s^{1/4}p \pm s(ad^2 p, g) + O(s))x.$$

These flows are chosen so that if $p(0) = 0$ and

$$|p(x)| \leq c|x|, \qquad \text{then} \qquad \left.\frac{dq^{\pm}}{ds}(s)x\right|_{s=0} = \pm(ad^j p, g)(x).$$

Thus, if $x = \sum_{i=1}^{3} \alpha_i(ad^{i-1}p, g)(0)$, then

$$q(s)x - x = (s + s^{1/2} + (s/2)^{1/4})p(x)$$

$$- s\sum_{i=1}^{3} \alpha_i(ad^{i-1}p, g)(x) + O(s). \tag{4.10}$$

Hence, if $x$ is near 0 and $s \ll 1$, $q(s)x - x = sx + O(s)$ and formula (4.10) shows how to choose a control over the interval $[0, \sum_{i=1}^{3} |\alpha_i|s]$ to move the state essentially in the direction $-x$, i.e., toward the origin.

Let us now summarize the steps in the input construction procedure:

1. measure the current state $x$;
2. express $x = \sum_{i=1}^{3} \alpha_i(ad^{i-1}p, g)(x)$;
3. use (4.10) to determine an *open-loop* input $u(t, x)$ over the interval $0 \leq t \leq \sum_{i=1}^{3} |\alpha_i|s$;
4. remeasure the new state and repeat steps 1–3.

REMARK    Even though the measured state $x$ is used to compute the input, the control law is still open loop since no state over the interval $0 \leq t \leq \sum_{i=1}^{3} |\alpha_i|s$ is measured.

The formulae (4.10) for generating $\pm(ad^k p, g)(x)$ are but one of many possible schemes. The question (as yet unanswered) arises as to whether a different scheme can be derived in which the terms $O(s)$ are actually *insignificant* when compared to $\pm s(ad^k p, g)$ for large $k$. In the formulae (4.10), the term $O(s)$ in $q_k^{\pm}(s)x$ is of the form $(s^{1+1/2k})w$ for some vector $w$ in $\{(ad^i p, g): i = 0, 1, \ldots\}_{LA}$. Numerically, this is *not* insignificant when compared to $\pm s(ad^k p, g)$ for $k$ large.

## XI. CONTROL CANONICAL FORM AND SYSTEM INVARIANTS

One of the most important tools of linear system theory for the study of control is the so-called *control canonical form*, in which the single-input system

$$\dot{x} = Fx + gu,$$

is reduced via linear coordinate changes in the state and control spaces to

$$\dot{\bar{x}} = \bar{F}\bar{x} + \bar{g}\bar{u},$$

where

$$\bar{F} = \begin{bmatrix} 0 & 1 & 0 & \cdots & 0 \\ 0 & 0 & 1 & & 0 \\ \vdots & & & & \vdots \\ 0 & 0 & 0 & & 1 \\ -\alpha_n & -\alpha_{n-1} & -\alpha_{n-2} & \cdots & -\alpha_1 \end{bmatrix}, \quad \bar{g} = \begin{bmatrix} 0 \\ 0 \\ \vdots \\ 0 \\ 1 \end{bmatrix},$$

where $\alpha_i$ are the coefficients of the characteristic polynomial of $F$. Extension of this result to multi-input systems is also well known and involves the computation of certain arithmetic invariants of the action of the group of coordinate changes. Details of this construction and its employment in various situations is covered in the author's earlier book cited in Notes and References. Here we wish to consider the extension of the control canonical form to nonlinear processes.

For simplicity, consider the single-input linear analytic system

$$\dot{x} = f(x) + u(t)g(x). \tag{$\Sigma$}$$

We wish to investigate the existence of smooth transformations $\{T_1, T_2, \ldots, T_{n+1}\}$ such that

$$x_i \mapsto T_i(x_1, \ldots, x_n) \doteq y_i, \quad i = 1, 2, \ldots, n,$$

$$u \mapsto T_{n+1}(x_1, \ldots, x_n, u) \doteq v,$$

in such a way that the system $\Sigma$ is transformed into the standard *linear* system

$$\dot{y}_1 = y_2,$$
$$\dot{y}_2 = y_3,$$
$$\vdots$$
$$\dot{y}_{n-1} = y_n,$$
$$\dot{y}_n = v.$$

To make $T = \{T_1, \ldots, T_{n+1}\}$ into a legitimate coordinate transformation, we require that

1. $T_i(0) = 0$;
2. $T_1, \ldots, T_n$ have a nonsingular Jacobian on $R^n$;
3. $T_{n+1}$ can be inverted for $u$ for all $x \in R^n$.

We begin our search for $T$ by starting locally. It can be shown that necessary and sufficient conditions for the existence of $T$ locally are

(i)  the set $\{g, [f, g], \ldots, (ad^{n-1}f, g)\}$ are linearly independent in some neighborhood $U$ of the origin;
(ii)  the set $\{g, [f, g], \ldots, (ad^{n-2}f, g)\}$ is involutive in $U$. Under these conditions, $T$ must satisfy the relations

$$\langle dT_i, g \rangle = 0, \qquad\qquad i = 1, 2, \ldots, n-1,$$
$$\langle dT_i, f \rangle = L_f(T_i) = T_{i+1}, \qquad i = 1, 2, \ldots, n-1, \qquad (4.11)$$
$$\langle dT_n, f + ug \rangle = L_{f+ug}(T_n) = T_{n+1},$$

where if $f$ is a smooth vector field and $h$ a smooth function,

$$L_f(h) = \langle dh, f \rangle = \frac{\partial h}{\partial x_1} f_1 + \cdots + \frac{\partial h}{\partial x_n} f_n.$$

Thus, to find $T$ satisfying the requisite conditions to transform $\Sigma$ to linear canonical form, we must find a transformation $T_1$ such that $T_1(0) = 0$ and

$$\langle dT_1, (ad^k f, g) \rangle = 0, \qquad k = 0, 1, \ldots, n-2,$$
$$\langle dT_1, (ad^{n-1}f, g) \rangle \neq 0.$$

The remaining $T_i$ can then be obtained recursively from relations (4.11).

The procedure for finding $T_1$ is as follows. Introduce parameters $t_1$, $t_2, \ldots, t_{n-1}$. For all $t_1 \in R$, solve the equation

$$\frac{dx}{dt_1} = (ad^{n-1}f, g), \qquad x(0) = 0.$$

Then for all $t_2$, solve

$$\frac{dx}{dt_2} = (ad^{n-2}f, g), \qquad x(t_1, 0) = x(t_1).$$

Continue in this way solving

$$\frac{dx}{dt_3} = (ad^{n-3}f, g), \qquad x(t_1, t_2, 0) = x(t_1, t_2)$$

until

$$\frac{dx}{dt_n} = g, \qquad x(t_1, t_2, \ldots, t_{n-1}, 0) = x(t_1, \ldots, t_{n-1}).$$

In this fashion we construct a function

$$(t_1, t_2, \ldots, t_n) \mapsto (x_1(t_1, t_2, \ldots, t_n), x_2(t_1, t_2, \ldots, t_n), \ldots, x_n(t_1, \ldots, t_n)),$$

which has the Jacobian matrix

$$J = \left[ \frac{\partial x_i}{\partial t_j} \right], \qquad i, j = 1, 2, \ldots, n. \tag{4.12}$$

Matrix $J$ is nonsingular at the origin, so the inverse function theorem ensures that we can solve for $t_1, t_2, \ldots, t_n$ in terms of $x_1, x_2, \ldots, x_n$ locally. Using the involutive hypothesis (ii), Frobenius' theorem ensures that if we fix $t_1$ and let $t_2, \ldots, t_n$ vary, we obtain an integral manifold of $g$, $[f, g], \ldots,$ $(ad^{n-2}f, g)$. Thus, the natural choice is to take $T_1 = t_1(x_1, \ldots, x_n)$.

***Example***  Consider the system

$$\dot{x}_1 = \tfrac{1}{2}x_1^2 + e^{x_2} + x_2,$$
$$\dot{x}_2 = x_1^2 + u.$$

Thus,

$$f(x) = \begin{bmatrix} \tfrac{1}{2}x_1^2 + e^{x_2} + x_2 \\ x_1^2 \end{bmatrix}, \qquad g(x) = \begin{bmatrix} 0 \\ 1 \end{bmatrix}.$$

We have

$$[f, g] = \begin{bmatrix} -(e^{x_2} + 1) \\ 0 \end{bmatrix},$$

which is linearly independent of $g$ on $R^2$. The involutive assumption is trivally satisfied.

First, we solve

$$\frac{dx_1}{dt_1} = -(e^{x_2} + 1), \qquad x_1(0) = 0,$$

$$\frac{dx_2}{dt_1} = 0, \qquad\qquad x_2(0) = 0.$$

This yields

$$x_1(t_1) = -2t_1, \qquad x_2(t_1) = 0.$$

Next, we find

$$\frac{dx_1}{dt_2} = 0, \qquad x_1(t_1, 0) = -2t_1,$$

$$\frac{dx_2}{dt_2} = 1, \qquad x_2(t_1, 0) = 0.$$

This gives

$$x_1 = -2t_1, \qquad x_2 = t_2.$$

Hence, the transformation $T_1$ is

$$T_1 = t_1 = -\tfrac{1}{2}x_1.$$

Employing the earlier recursive relations for $T_2$ and $T_3$, we find

$$T_2(x_1, x_2) = -\tfrac{1}{2}(\tfrac{1}{2}x_1^2 + e^{x_2} + x_2),$$
$$T_3(x_1, x_2, u) = -\tfrac{1}{2}x_1(\tfrac{1}{2}x_1^2 + e^{x_2} + x_2) - \tfrac{1}{2}(e^{x_2} + 1)(x_1^2 + u).$$

In the preceding local development, the only possible obstacle to extending the local construction of the $T_i$ to all of $R^n$ is contained in the Jacobian matrix $J$. The basic result which guarantees global existence of $T$ is

**Theorem 4.20**    Let $H: R^n \to R^n$ be a differentiable map, with Jacobian $J(x)$. If there exists a constant $\epsilon > 0$ such that the leading principal minors of $J$ satisfy

$$|\Delta_1| \geq \epsilon, \qquad \left|\frac{\Delta_2}{\Delta_1}\right| \geq \epsilon, \dots, \left|\frac{\Delta_n}{\Delta_{n-1}}\right| \geq \epsilon, \qquad (4.13)$$

for all $x \in R^n$, then $H$ is $1$–$1$ on $R^n$.

Application of Theorem 4.20 to the matrix $J$ given in Eq. (4.12) shows that the transformation $T$ exists globally if the *ratio* condition (4.13) holds. For instance, in the example we have

$$J = \begin{bmatrix} -2 & 0 \\ 0 & 1 \end{bmatrix},$$

so that the ratio test holds with $\epsilon = \frac{1}{2}$.

## PROBLEMS AND EXERCISES

**1.** (a)  Consider the system

$$\dot{x} = f(x) + g(x)u, \qquad x(0) = x_0 \in M, \tag{$\Sigma$}$$

where $M$ is a connected real-analytic two-dimensional manifold. Let $f$ and $g$ be real-analytic vector fields on $M$, that are linearly independent at some point $x \in M$, and let $u$ be a real scalar input. Further, suppose that every nontrivial integral curve of $g$ has a point $p$ where $f$ and $g$ are linearly dependent, with $g(p) \neq 0$, and that $[f, g]$ and $g$ are linearly independent at $p$. Show that $\Sigma$ is controllable from any $x_0$ such that $\dim\{f, g\}_{\mathrm{LA}} = 2$ at $x_0$. (Note that this is a global controllability result for two-dimensional systems.)
  (b)  Apply this result to the systems

$$f(x) = \begin{pmatrix} 4 \\ x_2 \end{pmatrix}, \qquad g(x) = \begin{pmatrix} x_2 \\ 1 \end{pmatrix}$$

and

$$f(x) = \begin{pmatrix} x_2 \\ x_1 \end{pmatrix}, \qquad g(x) = \begin{pmatrix} x_1 \\ 4x_2 \end{pmatrix}.$$

**2.**  Under the same assumptions as Problem 1, but with $M$ simply connected, show that $\Sigma$ is not controllable if there exists an integral curve of $g$ that disconnects $M$ and which does not intersect the set of points where $f$ and $g$ are linearly dependent. Does this result apply to the system

$$f(x) = \begin{pmatrix} -2x_2^2 \\ 1 \end{pmatrix}, \qquad g(x) = \begin{pmatrix} x_2^2 \\ 1 \end{pmatrix}?$$

**3.**  Consider the matrix system

$$\frac{dX}{dt} = FX + u(t)GX, \qquad X(0) = I,$$

where

$$F = \begin{bmatrix} 1 & 0 & 0 \\ 0 & 0 & 1 \\ 0 & 0 & 0 \end{bmatrix}, \qquad G = \begin{bmatrix} 0 & 0 & 0 \\ 0 & 1 & 0 \\ 0 & 0 & 0 \end{bmatrix}.$$

Let $u(t)$ be a piecewise constant scalar input, $t \geq 0$. Show that $\mathcal{R}(t, I)$ is a subset of $3 \times 3$ matrices having nonnegative elements.

**4.**  Consider the system

$$\frac{dx}{dt} = f(x) + u_1 g_1(x) + u_2 g_2(x), \qquad x \in R^3,$$

where

$$f(x) = \begin{pmatrix} 0 \\ x_1 x_2 \\ x_2 \end{pmatrix}, \qquad g_1(x) = \begin{pmatrix} 0 \\ x_1 \\ 0 \end{pmatrix}, \qquad g_2(x) = \begin{pmatrix} 1 \\ 0 \\ x_1 \end{pmatrix}.$$

Show that $\mathcal{R}(t, x_0) = R^3, t > 0$.

**5.**  Consider the system

$$\dot{x} = f(x) + \sum_{i=1}^{m} u_i(t) g_i(x), \qquad x(0) = x_0 \in M. \tag{$\Sigma$}$$

Assume that $\{g_1, \dots, g_m\}$ are involutive and that every integral submanifold $N$ of $g_1, \dots, g_m$ in $M$ contains a point $x$ where $f$ is tangent to $N$. Let $x$ be a critical point for $f$ and let $h_1, \dots, h_k$ be a basis near $x$ for the Lie algebra generated by $g_1, \dots, g_m$. Further, define $\hat{f} = f - \sum_{i=1}^{k} c_i h_i$, $c_i$ scalars, and assume there exist integers $i_1, i_2, \dots, i_m$ such that the space spanned by $\{g_i(x), (\mathrm{ad}\hat{f}, g_i)(x), \dots, (\mathrm{ad}^{i_1}\hat{f}, g_i)(x), \dots, (\mathrm{ad}^{i_m}\hat{f}, g_m)(x)\}$ has dimension $n$. Show that under these conditions $(\Sigma)$ is globally controllable.

**6.**  Consider the system

$$\dot{x} = f(x) + u(t) g(x), \qquad x(0) = x_0. \tag{$\Sigma$}$$

(a)  Show that the composition $\exp(tf) \circ y(t, u)$ is a solution of $(\Sigma)$ if and only if $y$ satisfies the auxilary equation

$$\dot{y}(t) = u(t) \sum_{j=0}^{\infty} \frac{(-t)^j}{j!} (\mathrm{ad}^j f, g)(y), \qquad y(0) = x_0, \tag{$*$}$$

(b)  Let $L$ be the Lie algebra generated by $\{\mathrm{ad}^j f, g): j = 0, 1, \dots\}$. We say $L$ is decomposable at $x_0$ if when $\dim L(x_0) = m$, there exist $m$ vector fields $v_1, \dots, v_m \in L$ such that the solution of $(*)$ can be written as

$$y(t, u) = (\exp F_1(t, u) v_1 \circ \cdots \circ \exp F_m(t, u) v_m)(x_0).$$

Show that the functions $F_i(t, u)$ are solutions of a reduced equation of the form

$$\dot{x} = u(t) G(t, x), \qquad x(0) = 0, \tag{$\dagger$}$$

where the $i$th component $G_i = G_i(t, x_1, \dots, x_{i-1})$. In other words, determination of the $F_i(t, u)$ reduces the solution of $\Sigma$ to that of $(\dagger)$, via $(*)$:

(c) Show that if $L$ is nilpotent, then $L$ is decomposable at each $x \in M$.

7.  (a)  Consider the homogenous polynomial system

$$\dot{x} = Ax^{[p]} + \sum_{i=1}^{m} u_i(t)B_i x^{[q_i]}, \qquad x(0) = x_0.$$

Show that the reachable set from $x_0$, $\cup_{t \geq 0} \mathcal{R}(t, x_0)$ is contained in an algebraic set $V$ for each $x_0 \in k^n$ if and only if for each $f \in \mathcal{V}(V)$, we also have

$$d_s f(As^{[p]}) \in \mathcal{V}(V) \qquad \text{and} \qquad d_s f(B_i s^{[q_i]}) \in \mathcal{V}(V).$$

(b)  Suppose there is a nonzero $\binom{n+r-1}{r}$-vector $v \in \ker(A'_{[r]}) \cap \ker(B'_{i[r]})$. Show that for each $x_0 \in k^n$, the reachable set from $x_0$ is contained in $\{x \in k^n : v'x^{[r]} = c\}$, where $c = v'x_0^{[r]}$.

8.  Consider the system

$$\dot{X} = \hat{F}X + \sum_{i=1}^{m} u_i(t)\hat{G}_i X(t) + \sum_{i=1}^{r} v_i(t)\hat{H}_i X(t),$$

where

$$\hat{F} = \begin{bmatrix} F & 0 \\ 0 & 0 \end{bmatrix}, \qquad \hat{G}_i = \begin{bmatrix} 0 & 0 \\ 0 & G_i \end{bmatrix}, \qquad \hat{H}_i = \begin{bmatrix} 0 & H_i \\ 0 & 0 \end{bmatrix};$$

$G_i$, $H_i$ are square matrices. Show that the reachable set is

$$\mathcal{R}(t; I) = \exp Ft\{\exp\{Ad_F, \hat{G}_i, \hat{H}_i\}_F\}_{\mathcal{J}},$$

where $Ad_A\{B, C\}$ is the smallest Lie algebra containing $\{B, C\}$ and closed under Lie bracketing with $A$, and $\mathcal{J}$ denotes the Lie group formed from this algebra.

9.  Consider the system

$$\dot{x} = f(x) + u(t)g(x), \qquad x(0) = x_0.$$

Let $L = \{f, g\}_{LA}$ and let $L_0$ be the smallest subalgebra of $L$ containing $g$ and closed under Lie bracketing with $f$. Suppose that for all $h \in L_0$, we have

$$[h, g] = \alpha_h g$$

for some scalar $\alpha$. Show that

$$\mathcal{R}(t, x_0) = \{\exp L_0\}_{\mathcal{J}} \exp tfx_0.$$

10.  Let the system

$$\dot{x} = Fx + Gu + h(x, u, t), \qquad x(0) = x_0,$$

be such that

(i)  $h$ is continuous in all arguments;

(ii) $h$ is periodic in $t$, with period $T > 0$ for each fixed $x$, $u$;

(iii) $(F, G)$ is reachable.

Show that for each $\alpha$, $\beta \in R^m$, $x_0$, $x^* \in R^n$ and $0 < t_1 < T$, there exists a control $u \in C[0, T]$ such that

(a) $u(0) = u(T) = \alpha, u(t_1) = \beta$;

(b) $x(t_1) = x^*$,

i.e., that the system is globally reachable.

**11.** The control system

$$\dot{x} = f(x) + \sum_{i=1}^{m} u_i(t)g_i(x), \qquad x \in R^n,$$

is called *odd* if $f(-x) = -f(x)$. Show that if $f$ and $g_i$ are analytic, then the set $\mathcal{R}(T, 0)$ is a neighborhood of the origin for every $T > 0$ if and only if $\dim\{f, g_i\}_{LA} = n$.

**12.** Consider the real-analytic system

$$\dot{x} = f(x) + \sum_{i=1}^{n-1} u_i(t)g_i(x), \qquad x(0) = x_0 \in M,$$

where $M$ is a connected real-analytic manifold. Let $L_A$ and $L'_A$ denote the Lie algebras generated by $\{f, g_i\}$ and $\{g_i\}$, respectively. Show that if $\dim L_A(x_0) = n$ and that $f, g_1, \ldots, g_{n-1}$ are linearly independent at some point of $M$, then the set $\mathcal{R}(x_0)$ is the smallest open subset of $M$ satisfying

(i) $x_0 \in \bar{\mathcal{R}}(x_0)$;

(ii) $\partial \bar{\mathcal{R}}(x_0)$ contains the integral manifolds of $L'_A$ which intersect it;

(iii) $f$ points in the direction of $\bar{\mathcal{R}}(x_0)$ on $\partial \mathcal{R}(x_0)$.

**13.** Show that the reachable set for the bilinear system

$$\dot{x} = \left( F + \sum_{i=1}^{m} u_i(t)G_i \right) x, \qquad x(0) = x_0$$

is a *subspace* if and only if there exists a nonsingular matrix $P$ such that

$$PFP^{-1} = \begin{bmatrix} F_{11} & 0 \\ F_{21} & F_{22} \end{bmatrix}, \qquad PG_iP^{-1} = \begin{bmatrix} G_{11}^i & 0 \\ G_{21}^i & G_{22}^i \end{bmatrix}, \qquad P^{-1}x_0 = \begin{bmatrix} 0 \\ \bar{x}_0 \end{bmatrix},$$

where the "0" blocks all have the same size.

**14.** Controllability in a sphere. Suppose the system

$$\dot{x} = \left( F + \sum_{i=1}^{m} u_i(t)G_i \right) x, \qquad x(0) = x_0,$$

is such that $F, G_1, \ldots, G_m$ are all skew-symmetric matrices ensuring that $\|x(t)\| = \|x_0\|$ for all $t$. Show that any point of the sphere $\{x: \|x\| = \|x_0\|\}$ is reachable from $x_0$ if and only if the matrix Lie algebra generated by $F, G_1, \ldots, G_m$ is

(i)    $SO(n)$ for $n = 0$ mod 2;
(ii)   $SO(n)$ or the real part of $SU(n/2)$ or $U(n)$ for $n = 1$ mod 2;
(iii)  the real part of $Sp(n/2)$ for $n = 1$ mod 4;
(iv)  $G_2$ if $n = 6$;
(v)   $Sp(8)$ if $n = 7$;
(vi)  $Sp(16)$ if $n = 15$.

**15.**  Consider the bilinear system

$$\dot{x} = Fx + \sum_{i=1}^{m} u_i(t)g_i, \qquad x(0) = x_0.$$

Assume $u(t)$ is differentiable and that $u(t) > 0$. Prove that the reachable set at time $T > 0$ is given by

$$\mathcal{R}(x_0, T) = \{x: x = e^{FT}x_0 + K\{e^{Ft}G: 0 \le t \le T\}\},$$

where $K\{e^{At}B: 0 \le t \le T\}$ denotes the interior of the smallest convex cone with vertex zero containing the vectors $e^{Ft}g_i, 0 \le t \le T$.

**16.**  Let the inhomogeneous bilinear system

$$\dot{x} = Fx + Gu + \sum_{i=1}^{m} N_i x u_i(t), \qquad x(0) = x_0,$$

be given, where $F, N_i$ are $n \times n$ real matrices, $G$ is $n \times m$. Show that this system is completely controllable if the sequence of vectors $\{S_0^1, \ldots, S_0^m, S_1^1, \ldots, S_{n-1}^1, \ldots, S_{n-1}^m\}$ spans $R^n$, where

$$S_k^i = F^k g_i + (ad_F^k N_i)x_0, \qquad k = 0, 1, \ldots, n-1, \quad i = 1, 2, \ldots, m,$$

$$ad_F^k N_i = [F, ad_F^{k-1}N_i], \qquad ad_F^0 N_i = N_i,$$

and $g_i$ is the $i$th column of $G$.

**17.**  Consider the discrete-time system

$$x_{k+1} = g[u_k] \circ f[x_k], \qquad x_k \in X, \quad u_k \in U,$$

where the state and input spaces are finite groups with $\circ$ the group operation in $X$ and the maps $f, g$ are group homomorphisms. We say that the system is *controllable from* $x_1 \in X$ if for any $x_2 \in X$, there is a sequence $\{u_i\}$ in $U$

such that the system moves from $x_1$ to $x_2$ under this input. Let $e \in X$ be the identity of the group $X$. Show that

(i) the system is controllable if and only if it is controllable from $e$;
(ii) the set of reachable states from $e$ is given by

$$\mathscr{R}(e) = g(U) \circ fg(U) \circ \cdots \circ f^{n-1}g(U);$$

(iii) $\mathscr{R}(e)$ is a subgroup of $X$ if $X$ is abelian.

**18.** (a)   Show that the system

$$\dot{x} = f(x) + u(t)g(x), \qquad x \in R^3$$

with

$$f(x) = \begin{pmatrix} \sin x_2 \\ \sin x_3 \\ 0 \end{pmatrix}, \qquad g(x) = \begin{pmatrix} 0 \\ 0 \\ 1 \end{pmatrix}$$

can be transformed into a canonical linear system in the neighborhood

$$U = \{x \in R^3 : -\pi/2 < x_2, x_3 < \pi/2\}$$

but not globally.

(b)   Prove that a transformation $T = (T_1, T_2, T_3, T_4)$ accomplishing this reduction is given by

$$T_1 = x_1, \qquad T_2 = x_2,$$

$$T_3 = \cos x_2 \sin x_3, \qquad T_4 = -\sin x_2 \sin^2 x_3 + (\cos x_2 \cos x_3)u.$$

## NOTES AND REFERENCES

**Section 4.I**   For a more complete exposition of Chow's theorem in the context of control theory, see the articles

R. Brockett, Nonlinear systems and differential geometry, *Proc. IEEE* **64** (1976), 61–72.
J. Casti, Recent developments and future perspectives in nonlinear system theory, *SIAM Rev.* **24** (1982), 301–331.

**Section 4.II**   Our definitions of reachability follow the pattern given in

R. Hermann and A. Krener, Nonlinear controllability and observability, *IEEE Trans. Automat. Control* **AC-22** (1977), 720–740.

See also the article

C. Lobry, Controllability of nonlinear control dynamical systems *in* "Control Theory and Topics in Functional Analysis," Vol. 1, Int'l. Atomic Energy Agency, Vienna, 1976.

**Section 4.III**   The proofs of Theorems 4.3, 4.4, follow those in the Lobry article cited above.

A good reference for many of the ideas of this section is the book

D. Mayne and R. Brockett, eds., "Geometric Methods in Systems Theory," Reidel, Dordrecht, 1973.

**Section 4.IV** Most of the results of this section follow those given in the Hermann–Krener paper cited in Section 4.2.

The example on urban migration is taken from

J. Casti, Topological methods for social and behavioral systems, *Internat. J. Gen. Systems* **4** (1982), 187–210.

**Section 4.V** In addition to the Brockett, Lobry, and Hermann–Krener articles cited above, reachability results for linear-analytic systems are also given in

G. W. Haynes and H. Hermes, Nonlinear controllability via lie theory, *SIAM J. Control Optim.* **8** (1970), 450–460.

R. Hirschorn, Global controllability of nonlinear systems, *SIAM J. Control Optim.* **14** (1976), 700–711.

H. Sussman and V. Jurdevic, Controllability of nonlinear systems, *J. Differential Equations* **12** (1972), 95–116.

H. Hermes, On local and global controllability, *SIAM J. Optim. Control* **12** (1974), 252–261.

**Section 4.VI** This material is covered in more detail in the article by Lobry cited under Section 4.2.

**Section 4.VII** A *meta-theorem* for bilinear systems is *that whatever can be proved for linear systems can be extended to bilinear systems using the same mathematical apparatus.* The results of this section bear out this contention. Some good general references on bilinear processes are

C. Bruni, G. Di Pillo, and G. Koch, Bilinear systems: An appealing class of "nearly linear" systems in theory and application, *IEEE Trans. Automat. Control* **AC19** (1974), 334–348.

R. Mohler and W. Kolodziej, An overview of bilinear system theory and applications, *IEEE Trans. Systems Man Cybernet.* **SMC10** (1980), 683–688.

R. Mohler, "Bilinear Control Processes," Academic Press, New York, 1973.

R. Mohler and A. Ruberti, eds., Theory and Application of Variable Structure Systems, Academic Press, New York, 1972.

There is a certain sense in which all sufficiently smooth nonlinear systems can be regarded as bilinear processes. Under certain smoothness and causality conditions, Sussman has shown that if $F$ is a bounded input–output map, then for every $\epsilon > 0$, there is a bilinear system whose input–output map $\phi$ is $\epsilon$-close to $F$ in the sup norm. For more results in this direction, see

H. Sussman, Semigroup representations, bilinear approximations of input–output maps and generalized inputs, *in* "Mathematical System Theory" (G. Marchesini and S. Mitter, eds.), Springer, New York, 1976.

J. Lo, Global bilinearization of systems with control appearing linearly, *SIAM J. Optim. Control* **13** (1975), 875–885.

A. Krener, Bilinear and nonlinear realizations of input–output maps, *SIAM J. Optim. Control* **13** (1975), 827–834.

For results on the reachable set for bilinear processes, we follow

R. Brockett, On the reachable set for bilinear systems, *in* "Variable Structure Systems with Applications to Economics and Biology" (A. Rubertic and R. Mohler, eds.), pp. 54–63, Springer, New York, 1975.

W. Boothby, Some comments on positive orthant controllability of bilinear systems, *SIAM Control J.*, **20** (1982), 634–644.

J. Gauthier and G. Bonnard, Controllability of bilinear systems, *SIAM Control J.*, **20** (1982), 377–384.

A. Frazho, Abstract bilinear systems: the forward shift approach, *Math. Sys. Th.*, **14** (1981), 83–94.

A. Frazho, A shift operator approach to bilinear systems theory, *SIAM Control J.*, **18** (1980), 640–658.

H. Sira-Ramirez, On the convex hull of reachable sets for bilinear systems, *Proc. 1980 Joint Auto. Control Conf.*, IEEE, San Francisco, p. 742.

**Section 4.VIII**    The results of this section are treated in much greater detail in the pioneering papers

J. Baillieul, The geometry of homogeneous polynomial dynamical systems, *Nonlinear Anal. TMA* **4** (1980), 879–900.

J. Baillieul, Controllability and observability of polynomial dynamical systems, *Nonlinear Anal. TMA* **5** (1981), 543–552.

See also

E. Sontag and Y. Rouchaleau, On discrete-time polynomial systems, *Nonlinear Anal. TMA* **1** (1976), 55–64.

W. Postev, An overview of polynomic system theory, *Proc. IEEE* **64** (1976), 18–23.

**Section 4.IX**    The reachability results for bilinear processes are from

A. Isidori and A. Ruberti, Realization theory of bilinear systems, *in* "Geometric Methods in System Theory" (D. Mayne and R. Brockett, eds.), Reidel, Dordrecht, 1973.

A. Ruberti, A. Isidori, and P. d'Alessandro, "Theory of Bilinear Dynamical Systems," Lecture notes from a course at CISM, Udine, Italy, 1972, Springer, Vienna, 1972.

**Section 4.X**    In general, the construction of an input sequence locally transforming $x_0$ to $x^*$ can be achieved by using the elements of the Lie algebra generated by $\{f^i\}(x_0)$, where $f^i(x) = f(x, u^i)$, $u^i$ a constant. The more sophisticated approach developed in this section is from

H. Hermes, On the synthesis of a stabilizing feedback control via lie-algebraic methods, *SIAM J. Control Optim.* **18** (1980), 352–361.

**Section 4.XI**   For a discussion of how to extend the Kronecker invariants of linear system theory to nonlinear process, see

R. Brockett, Feedback invariants for nonlinear systems, *in* "Proceedings, IFAC Congress, Helsinki," 1978.

The approach of this section follows

L. Hurt and R. Su, Global mapping of nonlinear systems, *in* "Proceedings, 1981 Joint Auto. Control Conference," IEEE, New York.

Related results are found in

R. Su, On the linear equivalents of nonlinear systems, *Systems and Control Lett.*, in press.
A. Krener, On the equivalence of control systems and the linearization of nonlinear systems, *SIAM J. Control Optim.* **11** (1973), 670–676.

# 5
# Observability, Realization, and Estimation

## I. MEASUREMENTS AND STATE DETERMINATION

Just as all aspects of controllability are concerned with the way in which we can interact with a system $\Sigma$ by means of *inputs*, problems of observability focus upon the manner in which interaction can occur through measured *outputs*. Roughly speaking, the central question of observability has to do with how much information about the internal state of $\Sigma$ is contained in the observed output.

Observability is a fundamental system property for a variety of reasons, among them:

(i)  The problem of regulator construction relies for its success upon being able to *feed back* good estimates of the state, which must be obtained via various procedures based on observability arguments.

(ii)  Observability is one of the main components in realization theory, where it forms one of the two system properties characterizing canonical models.

(iii)  Problems of parameter identification are closely related to questions of observability.

(iv)  For state regulation, the optimal control law will be stable only if the unstable states are *observed* by the criterion.

(v)  If the state dynamics and output are contaminated by noise, the optimal estimation of the system state by the so-called Kalman filter proceeds via an effective observer construction, with parameters optimized on the basis of available statistical data.

To speak more precisely about the question of state reconstruction, it is necessary to specify the conditions under which the experiments with $\Sigma$ are to be carried out. This leads to several versions of the observability problem which, generally speaking, coincide only for the case of linear systems. Some of the possible observability notions are

(a)  *Normal observability.* This is the term we reserve for the standard multiple-experiment initial-state situation. Here $\Sigma$ is observable if any two initial states can be distinguished by *some* input–output experiment. Since the input to be applied depends on the state to be identified, practical determination of an initial state relies on being able to somehow reset the system back to this (unknown) initial state, or alternately having many copies of $\Sigma$ all in the same initial state.

(b)  *Single-experiment observability.* In this case there exists a *single* input (over some finite-time interval) which by itself permits the determination of the initial state through the measured output. This is certainly a much more desirable situation than in normal observability and, happily, it can be shown that (a) is equivalent to (b) for linear systems where, in fact, *any* long enough input distinguishes *any* pair of states. Actually, this result holds more generally for any system whose output is the sum of a function of the initial state alone and a function of the input alone.

(c)  *Final-state determinability.* Here we are concerned with being able to determine the state of $\Sigma$ *after* the input is applied. $\Sigma$ is final-state determinable if there exists *some* input $u$ which permits determination of the state after $u$ is applied. Thus, if two states produce the same output sequence under $u$, then these states are necessarily sent to the same state under $u$. It is clear that (b) $\Rightarrow$ (c).

(d)  *Generic final-state determinability.* In contrast with (c), now we require that final states can be determined with *no* experimentation. Thus, ideally we would have the situation in which *any* input, (of long enough duration) permits final-state determination. This can be shown to be too restrictive so the condition is weakened to the requirement that *almost any* input permits determination of the final state. Surprisingly, it will be shown later that (a) $\Rightarrow$ (d) for polynomial systems, which means that just observing the *generic* input–output behavior of a canonical polynomial model is enough to be able to determine the final state.

## II. SOME BASIC DEFINITIONS

We consider as always the system $\Sigma$ given in the form

$$\dot{x} = f(x, u),$$
$$y(t) = h(x), \qquad x(0) = x_0, \tag{$\Sigma$}$$

with $x \in M$, $u \in \Omega$ and $f$ and $h$ smooth (or analytic) functions. The pair of initial states $x_0$, $x_0$ are said to be *indistinguishable* if for every $u \in \Omega$, we have $y_0(t) = y'(t)$ for $0 \le t \le T$, where $y_0$, $y$ are the outputs associated with the two initial states and $T > 0$ is an arbitrary, but fixed, real number. The relation of indistinguishability is an equivalence relation on $M$. If the equivalence class of each $x_0 \in M$ consists of $x_0$ alone, then we say that $\Sigma$ is *observable*. (This is the concept of normal observability discussed in Section I(a)).

Notice that normal observability is a global concept, as it might be necessary to travel a considerable distance or take $T$ large to distinguish between the points of $M$. Thus, just as for reachability, it is convenient to introduce a stronger localized version of observability.

*Definition 5.1*   We say that $\Sigma$ is *locally observable at* $x_0$ if for every open neighborhood $U$ of $x_0$ we have that the set of points indistinguishable from $x_0$ in $U$ via trajectories in $U$ is $x_0$ itself. $\Sigma$ is *locally observable* if it is so for all $x_0 \in M$.

On the other hand, it may also prove useful to weaken the notion of observability in those instances where it is sufficient to distinguish $x_0$ from its neighbors. In this direction we have

*Definition 5.2*   $\Sigma$ is said to be *locally weakly observable at* $x_0$ if there exists an open neighborhood $U$ of $x_0$ such that for every open neighborhood $V \subset U$, we have the set of points in $V$ indistinguishable from $x_0$ is $x_0$ itself. Basically, $\Sigma$ is locally weakly observable if it is possible to instantaneously distinguish $x_0$ from its neighbors for all $x_0$.

Just as for reachability, the advantage of local weak observability is that it lends itself to a simple algebraic test. In analogy with the reachability case, we have the following implications:

$$
\begin{array}{ccc}
\Sigma \quad \text{locally observable} & \Rightarrow & \Sigma \quad \text{observable} \\
\Downarrow & & \Downarrow \\
\Sigma \quad \text{locally weakly observable} & \Rightarrow & \Sigma \quad \text{weakly observable.}
\end{array}
$$

To speak of local observability we need the idea of Lie differentiation, a multidimensional generalization of the directional derivative.

**Definition 5.3**  Let $h \in X(M)$ be a smooth vector field on $M$ and let $\phi \in C^\infty(M)$. Then the *Lie derivative* of $\phi$ in the direction $h$ is given by

$$L_h(\phi)(x) = \frac{\partial \phi}{\partial x}(x)h(x).$$

Note that since $\partial \phi / \partial x$ is a row vector, $L_h(\phi)$ is also a row vector-valued function.

Now let $\mathscr{G}_0$ denote the subset of $C^\infty(M)$ consisting of the functions $h_1(x)$, $h_2(x), \ldots, h_p(x)$, i.e., the components of the observation vector function $h(x)$. Further, let $\mathscr{G}$ be the smallest vector space generated by $\mathscr{G}_0$ and elements obtained from $\mathscr{G}_0$ by Lie differentiation in the direction of elements from $\mathscr{F}_0$ (we recall that $\mathscr{F}_0$ is the set of all vector fields generated from $f(x, .)$ using constant controls). A typical element of $\mathscr{G}$ is a finite linear combination of elements of the form

$$L_{f^i}(\cdots (L_{f^k}(h_i)) \cdots),$$

where $f^i(x) = f(x, u^i)$ for $u^i \in \Omega$, a constant input. It is easily verified that $\mathscr{G}$ is closed under Lie differentiation by elements of $\mathscr{F}$ also.

Next we define $X^*(M)$ to be the real vector space of one-forms on $M$, i.e., the set of all finite $C^\infty(M)$ linear combinations of gradients of elements from $C^\infty(M)$. Further, let

$$d\mathscr{G}_0 = \{d\phi : \phi \in \mathscr{G}_0\},$$

$$d\mathscr{G} = \{d\phi : \phi \in \mathscr{G}\}.$$

From the well-known identity

$$L_q(d\phi) = dL_q(\phi),$$

it follows that $d\mathscr{G}$ is the smallest linear space of one-forms containing $d\mathscr{G}_0$ which is closed under Lie differentiation by elements of $\mathscr{F}$. The elements of $d\mathscr{G}$ are finite linear combinations of elements of the form

$$dL_{f^i}(\cdots (L_{f^k}(h_i)) \cdots) = L_{f^i}(\cdots (L_{f^k}(dh_i)) \cdots).$$

Let $d\mathscr{G}(x)$ denote the space of vectors obtained by evaluating the elements of $d\mathscr{G}$ at $x$.

**Definition 5.4**  The system $\Sigma$ is said to satisfy the *observability rank condition* at $x_0$ if dim $d\mathscr{G}(x_0) = n$. If dim $d\mathscr{G}(x) = n$ for all $x \in M$, then $\Sigma$ is said to satisfy the observability rank condition.

The observability rank condition is important as it provides the basis for an *algebraically* computable test for local weak observability.

## III. BASIC OBSERVABILITY RESULTS

The first line of attack on any nonlinear problem is to investigate the possibility of applying the linear theory to a local linearization of the system $\Sigma$ in neighborhood of a reference trajectory. Let $(x_0(t), u_0(t))$ be a state-input reference pair. Then the linearized version of $\Sigma$, call it $\Sigma_L$, about $(x_0(t), u_0(t))$ is

$$\dot{z}(t) = F(t)z(t) + G(t)v(t),$$

$$w(t) = H(t)z(t),$$

$$(\Sigma_L)$$

where $z(t) = x(t) - x_0(t)$, $v(t) = u(t) - u_0(t)$, $w(t) = y(t) - y_0(t)$, and

$$F(t) = \left.\frac{\partial f(x, u)}{\partial x}\right|_{(x_0, u_0)}, \qquad G(t) = \left.\frac{\partial f}{\partial u}\right|_{(x_0, u_0)},$$

$$H(t) = \left.\frac{\partial h}{\partial x}\right|_{(x_0, u_0)}.$$

For sake of exposition, let us now assume $u_0 = x_0 = 0$. We must settle the

*Question.   Under what circumstances is it true that the complete observability of $\Sigma_L$ implies $\Sigma$ is locally completely observable?*

To answer this question, we have

***Theorem 5.1***   Assume $f(0, 0) = 0$, $h(0) = 0$, and that $\Sigma_L$ is completely observable. Then $\Sigma$ is locally completely observable.

The proof of this result is standard and can be found in the sources cited in Notes and references.

Thus, Theorem 5.1 shows that complete observability of $\Sigma_L$ is a *sufficient* condition for the *local* complete observability of the nonlinear process $\Sigma$. However, this result is far from necessary as the following example demonstrates:

$$\dot{x}_1 = x_2 + u(t),$$

$$\dot{x}_2 = -x_1,$$

$$y(t) = x_1^2.$$

The linear approximation $\Sigma_L$ is not observable in a neighborhood of the $x_1 = 0$ axis for any input $u(t)$. However, the output of the nonlinear system distinguishes all initial states (including those on the $x_1 = 0$ axis) through suitable nonzero inputs $u(t)$. The above example also illustrates the important point made earlier that, for nonlinear observability, the input $u(t)$ is important. Unlike the linear case, where it suffices to assume $u(t)$ identically zero, for nonlinear process the observability of $\Sigma$ depends on the input in an essential manner. We shall make this dependence explicit in the results cited throughout this chapter.

Now let us return to the nonlinear process $\Sigma$ under the assumption given in Section II. Our goal is to provide an *algebraic* test for the property of local weak observability. The basic result in this direction is the following theorem, originally due to Hermann and Krener, which utilizes the observability rank criterion in a direct extension of the rank condition from linear theory to establish local weak observability conditions for smooth nonlinear processes.

**Theorem 5.2**   *If $\Sigma$ satisfies the observability rank condition at $x_0$, then $\Sigma$ is locally weakly observable at $x_0$.*

PROOF   If the dim $d\mathcal{G}(x_0) = n$, then there exist $n$ functions $\phi_1$, $\phi_2$, ..., $\phi_n \in \mathcal{G}$ such that $d\phi_1(x_0), \ldots, d\phi_n(x_0)$ are linearly independent. Define a map

$$\Phi: \qquad x \to (\phi_1(x), \ldots, \phi_n(x))'.$$

The Jacobian of $\Phi$ at $x_0$ is nonsingular, so $\Phi$ restricted to some open neighborhood $U$ of $x_0$ is 1–1. If $V \subseteq U$ is an open neighborhood of $x_0$, then the set of points indistinguishable from $x_0$ by trajectories in $V$ consists of $x_0$ itself. Thus, $\Sigma$ is locally weakly reachable at $x_0$.

The converse of this theorem is almost true as the following theorem illustrates.

**Theorem 5.3**   *If $\Sigma$ is locally weakly observable then the observability rank condition is satisfied generically.*

PROOF   See Notes and References.

In Chapter 4 we have seen that for analytic systems weak reachability, local weak and the reachability rank condition are equivalent. The same result holds for observability of analytic systems if $\Sigma$ is also weakly reachable as the following theorem demonstrates.

**Theorem 5.4**   *Let $\Sigma$ be a weakly reachable analytic system. Then $\Sigma$ is weakly observable if and only if the observability rank condition is satisfied.*

PROOF   (Outline)   Since $\Sigma$ is weakly reachable, $\Sigma$ satisfies the reachability rank condition. Using the techniques of Chapter 4 and the analyticity of $\Sigma$, we must show that dim $d\mathcal{G}(x) = $ const. This involves showing that if $x_0$ and $x_1$ are weakly reachable, then dim $d\mathcal{G}(x_0) = $ dim $d\mathcal{G}(x_1)$, implying that dim $d\mathcal{G}(x) = $ const.

**Example 1:   Bilinear dynamics, linear observations**

Consider the bilinear process

$$\dot{x} = Fx + \sum_{i=1}^{m} u_i N_i x, \qquad x(0) = x_0, \tag{5.1}$$

with linear observations

$$y = Hx, \qquad y \in R^p.$$

Here $M = R^n$, $F$, $N_i$ are constant matrices of appropriate sizes. In this case

$$\mathscr{G} = \left\{ \frac{\partial}{\partial x}(H_i x) Px : i = 1, 2, \ldots, p, \; Px \in \mathscr{F} \right\},$$

where $H_i$ is the $i$th row of $H$, $\mathscr{F}$ is the Lie algebra generated by $f^i(x)$ as defined in Chapter 4. The algebra $d\mathscr{G}$ is given by

$$d\mathscr{G} = \left\{ \frac{\partial}{\partial x}(H_i x) P : i = 1, 2, \ldots, p; \; Px \in \mathscr{F} \right\}.$$

Thus the bilinear system with linear outputs is locally weakly observable at $x_0$ if and only if dim $d\mathscr{G}(x_0) = n$.

The abstract characterization of the observability of the bilinear dynamics above can be made more explicit by means of the following result.

**Theorem 5.5**   *The set of all unobservable (i.e., indistinguishable) states of the bilinear system (5.1) is the largest subspace $\theta$ of $R^n$ contained in the kernel of $H$, and which is invariant under $F, N_1, N_2, \ldots, N_m$.*

PROOF   It is easy to see that the set of unobservable states $\theta$ is a subspace of $R^n$. From the well-known fact that for any differential equation $\dot{z} = f(z, t)$, if $y(t) \in \theta$, then $\dot{y}(t) \in \theta$, we see that

$$\left( F + \sum_{i=1}^{m} N_i u_i \right) \theta \subseteq \theta \qquad \text{for all } u_i \in R^m.$$

Moreover, from the observation equation $y = Hx$, we have

$$\theta \subseteq \ker H.$$

Therefore, $\theta$ is invariant under $F, N_1, \ldots, N_m$ and is contained in ker $H$.

The reverse inclusion is straightforward and is left to the reader.

Theorem 5.5 suggests the following computational algorithm for calculating the subspace $\theta$:

(i)   let $U_1 = \text{range } H'$;
(ii)   calculate the subspace $U_{i+1} = U_i + N_1' U_i + \cdots + N_m' U_i$;

(iii)   find the integer $k^*$ such that $U_{k^*} = U_{k^*-1}$ and set $Z = $ range $U_{k^*}$;
(iv)   $\theta = Z^{\perp}$, the orthogonal complement of $Z$.

## Example 2:   Linear Systems

To see that the observability rank condition of Theorem 5.4 indeed generalizes the usual rank condition for the observability of linear systems, consider the dynamics

$$\dot{x} = Fx + Gu,$$

and observation

$$y = Hx.$$

In this case, the space of vector fields $\mathscr{F}$ is generated by the elements

$$\{Fx, F^i g_j, \, i = 1, 2, \ldots, n-1 ; j = 1, 2, \ldots, m\}.$$

If we let $h_j$ denote the $j$th row of $H$, then the relevant Lie derivatives are

$$L_{Fx}(h_j F^i)(x) = h_j F^{i+1} x,$$
$$L_{Fig_j}(h_k F^l)(x) = h_k F^{i+l} g_j,$$
$$L_{Fx}(h_j F^l g_k) = 0.$$

Thus, by the Cayley–Hamilton theorem $\mathscr{G}$ is generated by the set

$$\{h_i F^k, h_i F^k g_j : i = 1, 2, \ldots, p; j = 1, 2, \ldots, m; k = 0, 1, \ldots, n-1\}$$

and $d\mathscr{G}(x)$ is generated by

$$\theta = \{h_i F^k : i = 1, 2, \ldots, p; k = 0, 1, \ldots, n-1\}.$$

Since $d\mathscr{G}(x)$ is independent of $x$, it is of constant dimension and the observability rank condition reduces to the requirement that $\theta$ consist of $n$ linearly independent elements.

The algebraic criterion for observability given by Theorem 5.4 is local in character, i.e., it tells us whether all states in some sufficiently small neighborhood of $x_0$ are observable, but gives no information on how small is *sufficiently* small. To obtain a *global* criterion, we introduce the quantities

$$H_k(x(t)) = (h_0(x), h_1(x), \ldots, h_{k-1}(x)),$$

where

$$h_0(x) = y(t),$$

$$h_k(x) = \frac{\partial h_{k-1}}{\partial x}(x) f(x, 0), \qquad k = 1, 2, \ldots, n,$$

where $h(\cdot)$ and $f(\cdot, \cdot)$ are the observation function and dynamics of the system $\Sigma$, resp.

Let $X_0$ denote the set of initial states. Then the system $\Sigma$ will certainly be observable if the map

$$\mathcal{H} : X_0 \to H_n(X_0)$$

is injective, i.e., if $\mathcal{H}$ is 1–1. In general, though, the injectivity of $\mathcal{H}$ is not necessary. The following version of the inverse function theorem gives conditions under which $\mathcal{H}$ is *globally* invertible.

**Theorem 5.6**   *Let $J(x)$ be the Jacobian map of $\mathcal{H}$ at x. If there exists an $\epsilon > 0$ such that*

$$|\Delta_1| \geq \epsilon, \qquad \left|\frac{\Delta_2}{\Delta_1}\right| \geq \epsilon, \ldots, \left|\frac{\Delta_n}{\Delta_{n-1}}\right| \geq \epsilon,$$

*for all $x \in X_0$, where $\Delta_i = $ ith leading minor of J, then $\mathcal{H}$ is 1–1 on $X_0$.*

**Example**   Assume we have the system

$$\dot{x}_1 = \tfrac{1}{2}x_1^2 + e^{x_2} + x_2,$$

$$\dot{x}_2 = x_1^2,$$

$$y(t) = x_1(t).$$

Then

$$H_2(x) = \begin{pmatrix} x_1 \\ \tfrac{1}{2}x_1^2 + e^{x_2} + 1 \end{pmatrix}$$

and

$$J(x) = \begin{bmatrix} 1 & 0 \\ x_1 & e^{x_2} + 1 \end{bmatrix}.$$

Thus, $\Delta_1 = 1$, $\Delta_2 = e^{x_2} + 1$, so that the conditions of Theorem 5.6 are satisfied for $\epsilon = 1$ and the system is globally observable.

The extent to which the above sufficient condition for global observability is also necessary depends upon the degree of smoothness in the system dynamics $f$ and the observation function $h$. For analytic and polynomial systems, Theorem 5.7 provides necessary and sufficient conditions for global observability.

**Theorem 5.7**   (a)   *Let $f$ and $h$ be analytic functions on $R^n$. Then $\Sigma$ is globally completely observable if and only if the functions $H_k(x)$ are 1–1, $k = 1, 2, \ldots$;*
    (b)   *Let $f$ and $h$ be polynomial on $R^n$. Then the system $\Sigma$ is globally com-*

*pletely observable if and only if the j*th *observability mapping* $H_j(x)$ *is one-to-one for some* $j \geq 1$.

PROOF    See Notes and References.

REMARK    The first part of Theorem 5.7 states that for $\Sigma$, an infinite amount of derivative data $d^k y/dt^k(0)$ is necessary to uniquely determine the initial state of $\Sigma$. However, part (b) shows that for polynomial systems, observability can be decided by examining only a *finite* amount of data (the fact that only a finite number of observability mappings $H_j(x)$ need be tested follows from the Hilbert Basis Theorem).

## IV. POLYNOMIAL SYSTEMS

The key element in being able to make effective use of the abstract results detailed above for studying observability properties of $\Sigma$ is *finiteness*, i.e., being able to provide an a priori finite bound for the number of calculations needed to obtain the result of a given test. As we have seen, such a finiteness property is *not* available, in general, and it is only by the imposition of considerable structure upon the dynamics and observation equation of $\Sigma$ that it can be made to appear. As noted in Theorem 5.7, even the seemingly severe restriction of analyticity is, generally speaking, not strong enough and further restrictions must be added.

It appears that the only broad class of interesting systems for which finite observability tests can be exhibited are those systems that display *polynomial* behavior in the dynamics $f$ and observations $h$. Contained within the confines of such systems are our familiar linear and bilinear processes, as well as more general processes involving polynomial behavior. In this section, we shall confine our attentions to homogeneous polynomial systems of the form

$$\dot{x} = Fx^{[p]} + u(t)Gx^{[q]}, \qquad x(0) = x_0,$$

$$y(t) = Hx^{[r]},$$

(5.2)

where $x \in R^n$, $y \in R$, and $F, G, H$ are real matrics of appropriate sizes. As in Chapter 4, the symbol $x^{[p]}$ denotes a $z$-tuple of weighted $p$-forms in the components of $x$, with $z = \binom{n+p-1}{p}$. That is,

$$x^{[p]} = (x_1^p, \alpha_1 x_1^{p-1} x_2, \alpha_2 x_2^{p-1} x_3, \ldots, x_n^p)',$$

where the entries are ordered lexicographically, and the weights are chosen so that

$$\|x^{[p]}\| = \|x\|^p.$$

Hence, a typical entry has the form $\alpha x_1^{p_1} x_2^{p_2}, \ldots, x_n^{p_n}$, $\Sigma p_i = p$ and $\alpha = \sqrt{p!/(p_1! p_2! \cdots p_n!)}$. By definition, $x^{[0]}$ is the scalar 1 for all $n$-tuples $x$.

We shall first develop a test for determining when two initial states $x_0$, $x_0'$ are indistinguishable if the system input $u(t) \equiv 0$. Define

$A(x)$ = the set of all initial states which cannot be distinguished from $x$ using the zero input and observing $y(t)$ on any interval $[0, T]$.

It is straightforward to verify that the relation $x_0$ indistinguishable from $x_0'$ is an equivalence relation denoted $x_0 \sim_A x_0'$.

For ease of exposition, we introduce the notation

$$f(x) = Fx^{[p]}, \qquad g(x) = Gx^{[q]}, \qquad h(x) = Hx^{[r]},$$

and for any piecewise smooth input $u(\cdot)$, we let $\gamma_t^u(x_0)$ denote the flow determined by the differential equation (5.2).

Next, define the set of polynomials

$$\mathcal{F} = \{L_f^k(h): k = 0, 1, 2, \ldots\},$$

where, as before, $L_f^k(h)$ denotes the $k$th Lie derivative of $h$ in the direction $f$. The relationship between the set $A(x_0)$ and the set $\mathcal{F}$ is given by

**Theorem 5.8**   $A(x_0) = A(x_0')$ *if and only if* $\phi(x_0) = \phi(x_0')$ *for all* $\phi \in \mathcal{F}$.

PROOF   Suppose $A(x_0) = A(x_0')$. Then $h(\gamma_t^0(x_0)) \equiv h(\gamma_t^0(x_0'))$ on $[0, \delta]$ for all $\delta > 0$. Differentiating both sides $k$ times yields $L_f^k h(\gamma_t^0(x_0)) \equiv L_f^k h(\gamma_t^0(x_0'))$. Hence, $L_f^k h(x_0) = L_f^k h(x_0')$ for $k = 0, 1, \ldots$, which proves the *only if* portion of the theorem.

Now suppose that $\phi(x_0) = \phi(x_0')$ for all $\phi \in \mathcal{F}$. Let $\delta > 0$ be given. We must show that $h(\gamma_t^0(x_0)) = h(\gamma_t^0(x_0'))$ for each $t \in [0, \delta]$. Since $h(\gamma_t^0(x_0))$ and $h(\gamma_t^0(x_0'))$ are analytic, we can expand about $t = 0$ obtaining

$$h(\gamma_t^0(x_0)) = h(x_0) + L_f h(x_0)t + \tfrac{1}{2}L_f^2 h(x_0)t^2 + \cdots,$$

$$h(\gamma_t^0(x_0')) = h(x_0') + L_f h(x_0')t + \tfrac{1}{2}L_f^2 h(x_0')t^2 + \cdots.$$

By hypothesis the Taylor coefficients are equal, so $h(\gamma_t^0(x_0)) = h(\gamma_t^0(x_0'))$ on their common interval of convergence. The theorem is then proven using a direct analytic continuation argument.

Theorem 5.8 shows that a decision procedure for the equivalence relation $\sim_A$ can be formed by means of evaluation of polynomials from the set $\mathcal{F}$: two states $x_0$, $x_0'$ are indistinguishable using zero-input if and only if all polynomials in $\mathcal{F}$ yield the same values when evaluated on $x_0$ and $x_0'$.

Unfortunately, Theorem 5.8 does not rule out the possibility that some *nonzero* input $u(t)$ may be able to separate $x_0$, $x_0'$ that are equivalent under $\sim_A$. To deal with this case, it is useful to define a new set

$B(x)$ = the set of all initial states which for *any* piecewise smooth input $u$ are indistinguishable from $x$.

Again, we note that indistinguishability in this *B-sense* is also an equivalent relation, denoted $\sim_B$. The relation $\sim_B$ is finer than $\sim_A$ in the sense that $B(x) \subseteq A(x)$ and, in general, this inclusion is strict. However, in the special case of linear systems ($p = r = 1$, $q = 0$), the two coincide.

Next, we recursively define the set of polynomials

$$\mathscr{G}_0 = \{h\}, \qquad \mathscr{G}_k = \{L_f(\phi), L_g(\phi): \phi \in \mathscr{G}_{k-1}\}.$$

Let $\mathscr{G} = \cup_{k\geq 0}\, \mathscr{G}_k$. (Note that these sets are the same as the sets $\mathscr{G}, \mathscr{G}_0$ defined in Section II for the general multi-output case.) Then Theorem 5.4 can be restated in terms of the sets $B(x)$ and $\mathscr{G}$.

**Theorem 5.9**   $B(x_0) = B(x_0')$, if and only if $\phi(x_0) = \phi(x_0')$ for all $\phi \in \mathscr{G}$.

**Example**   Consider the system

$$\dot{x}_1 = x_2 + u(t)$$
$$\dot{x}_2 = -x_1$$
$$y(t) = x_1^2(t).$$

Under the input $u(t) \equiv 0$, the motion of the system for any $x_0 \neq 0$ is restricted to a circle centered at the origin. We can calculate the first few elements of the set $\mathscr{F}$ as

$$h(s_1, s_2) = s_1^2, \qquad L_f(h(s_1, s_2)) = 2s_1 s_2,$$
$$L_f^2(h(s_1, s_2)) = 2(s_2^2 - s_1^2), \qquad L_f^3(h(s_1, s_2)) = -8s_1 s_2.$$

It is clear that $\mathscr{F}$ consists of various multiples of $s_1^2$, $s_1 s_2$ and $s_2^2 - s_1^2$. It then follows from Theorem 5.8 that $A(x) = \{x, -x\}$ for each $x \in R^2$. On the other hand,

$$L_g(h(s_1, s_2)) = 2s_1, \qquad L_f L_g(h(s_1, s_2)) = 2s_2$$

are elements of $\mathscr{G}$. Hence $B(x) = \{x\}$ for all $x \in R^2$.

This example shows that certain states are distinguishable by using a nonzero input that are not distinguishable by observing only the output of the free motion of the system.

Theorems 5.8 and 5.9 can also be used to address the question of whether the system is in its equilibrium, or rest position $x_0 = 0$. In other words, by examination of the system output, we would like to determine if $x_0 = 0$. Depending on whether the input $u(t)$ is identically zero, the answer to this question revolves about our ability to develop a useful characterization of the set $A(0)$ (or $B(0)$).

Let us define

$$\mathcal{G}_k = \bigcup_{j=0}^{k} \{\phi \in \mathcal{G}_j : \deg \phi \geq 1\}, \qquad \hat{\mathcal{G}} = \bigcup_{k \geq 0} \hat{\mathcal{G}}_k.$$

Since both $\mathcal{F}$ and $\hat{\mathcal{G}}$ are sets of polynomials, they each determine algebraic sets $V(\mathcal{F})$, $V(\hat{\mathcal{G}})$, the zero sets. Using these sets, it is easy to prove

**Theorem 5.10**    (i) $A(0) = V(\mathcal{F})$, (ii) $B(0) \subseteq V(\hat{\mathcal{G}})$.

PROOF   Let $x \in A(0)$. Then by Theorem 5.8, $\phi(x) = \phi(0) = 0$ for all $\phi \in \mathcal{F}$. Hence $x \in V(\mathcal{F})$. On the other hand, if $x \in V(\mathcal{F})$, then $\phi(x) = 0$ for all $\phi \in \mathcal{F}$. Hence, $\phi(x) = \phi(0)$ for all $\phi \in \mathcal{F}$ and it follow from Theorem 5.8 that $x \in A(0)$. Part (ii) is established in a similar fashion using Theorem 5.9.

The main problem now becomes deciding when $A(0) = \{0\}$ (or when $B(0) = \{0\}$). In view of Theorem 5.10, this will be the case if $V(\mathcal{F}) = \{0\}$. We may find $V(\mathcal{F})$ explicitly by solving a set of simultaneous homogeneous algebraic equations $\phi(x) = 0$ for $\phi \in \mathcal{F}_k$, where $\mathcal{F}_k = \{h, L_f(h), \ldots, L_f^k(h)\}$ is some finite basis for the polynomial ideal generated by $\mathcal{F}$ (the existence of a *finite* $k$ is a consequence of the Hilbert Basis Theorem). In particular, $V(\mathcal{F}) = \{0\}$ if and only if the *resultant* of the corresponding system of algebraic equations does not vanish. This is a finitely verifiable condition for $A(0) = \{0\}$.

## V. REALIZATION THEORY

The specification of the realization problem for linear systems is simplified by the fact that it is easy to parameterize the input, output, and state spaces via a globally defined coordinate system. This fact enables us to reduce the problem of construction of a canonical model from input–output data to a problem of linear algebra involving matrices. In the nonlinear case no such global coordinate system exists, in general, and it is necessary to take considerable care in defining what we mean by the problem *data*. We can no longer regard the input–output data as being represented by an object as simple as an infinite sequence of matrices or, equivalently, a matrix transfer function. So, the first step in the construction of an effective nonlinear realization procedure is to develop a generalization of the transfer matrix suitable for describing the input–output behavior of a reasonably broad class of nonlinear processes.

If we consider the nonlinear system

$$\dot{x} = f(x, u), \qquad x(0) = x_0,$$

$$y = h(x),$$

(Σ)

then it is natural to attempt to represent the output in terms of the input as a series expansion

$$y(t) = w_0(t) + \int_0^t w_1(t, s)u(s)\, ds$$

$$+ \int_0^t \int_0^{s_1} w_2(t, s_1, s_2)u(s_2)u(s_1)\, ds_2\, ds_1 + \cdots.$$

(5.3)

Formally, the *Volterra series* expansion (5.3) is a generalization of the linear variation of constants formula

$$y(t) = He^{Ft}x_0 + \int_0^t He^{F(t-s)}Gu(s)\, ds.$$

Arguing by analogy with the linear case, the realization problem for non-linear systems may be expressed as: *given the sequence of Volterra kernels* $\omega = \{w_0, w_1, w_2, \ldots\}$, *find a canonical model* $N = (f, h)$ *whose input–output behavior generates* $\omega$.

Without further hypotheses on the analytic behavior of $f, h$, together with a suitable definition of *canonical model*, the realization problem as stated is much too ambitious and, in general, unsolvable. So, let us initially consider conditions under which the Volterra series exists and is unique. Further, we restrict attention to the class of linear-analytic systems, i.e., $f(x, u) = f(x) + u(t)g(x)$, where $f(\cdot)$, $g(\cdot)$, and $h(\cdot)$ are analytic vector fields. The basic result for Volterra series expansions is

**Theorem 5.11** *If $f$, $g$, and $h$ are analytic vector fields and if $\dot{x} = f(x)$ has a solution on $[0, T]$ with $x(0) = x_0$, then the input–output behavior of $(\Sigma)$ has a unique Volterra series representation on $[0, T]$.*

In the case of a bilinear system where $f(x) = Fx$, $g(x) = Gx$, $h(x) = x$, $u(\cdot)$ is a scalar control, the Volterra kernels can be explicitly computed as

$$w_n(t, s_1, \ldots, s_n) = e^{Ft}e^{-Fs_1}Ge^{Fs_1}e^{-Fs_2}Ge^{Fs_2}\cdots e^{-Fs_n}Ge^{Fs_n}x_0.$$

It can be shown that for bilinear systems the Volterra series converges *globally* for all locally bounded $u$.

The global convergence of the Volterra series for bilinear processes suggests an approach to the construction of a Volterra expansion in the general case. First, expand all functions into their Taylor series, forming a sequence

of bilinear approximations of increasing accuracy. We then compute the
Volterra series for each bilinear approximation. However, the simple system

$$\dot{x} = u^2 x, \qquad x(0) = 1, \qquad h(x) = x,$$

shows that, in general, no Volterra expansion exists which is valid for all
$u$ such that $\|u\|$ is sufficiently small. Further details on the above bilinear
approximation technique can be found in the Notes and References.

Now let us turn to the definition of a canonical model for a nonlinear
process. As noted earlier, in the linear case we say a model is canonical if it is
both reachable (controllable) and observable (constructible). Such a model
is also minimal in the sense that the state space has smallest possible dimension (as a vector space) over all such realizations. To preserve this minimality
property, we make

**Definition 5.5**   A system $N$ is called *locally weakly minimal* if it is locally
weakly controllable and locally weakly observable.

The relevance of Definition 5.5 to the realization problem is seen from the
following result.

**Theorem 5.12**   *Let $N$, $\hat{N}$ be two nonlinear systems with input sets $\Omega = \hat{\Omega}$,
and state manifolds $M$ and $\hat{M}$ of dimensions $m$, $\hat{m}$, respectively. Suppose $(N, x_0)$
and $(\hat{N}, \hat{x}_0)$ realize the same input–output map. Then if $\hat{N}$ is locally weakly
minimal, $\hat{m} \leq m$.* Thus, we see that two locally weakly minimal realization of
the same input–output map must be of the same state dimension which is
minimal over all possible realizations.

REMARK   Two locally weakly minimal realizations need not be diffeomorphic, in contrast with the linear case. This is seen from the two systems

$$N: \quad \dot{x} = u, \qquad y_1 = \cos x, \qquad y_2 = \sin x,$$

$$\hat{N}: \quad \dot{\theta} = u, \qquad y_1 = \cos \theta, \qquad y_2 = \sin \theta,$$

with $\Omega = \hat{\Omega} = R$, $M = R$, $\hat{M} = S^1$, the unit circle, $y \in R^2$, $x_0 = 0$, $\theta_0 = 0$.
Here $N$ and $\hat{N}$ realize the same input–output map. Furthermore, both
systems are locally weakly controllable and observable.

The above result leaves open the question if two canonical realizations are
isomorphic, i.e., given two nonlinear systems $N$ and $\hat{N}$, with state manifolds
$M$ and $\hat{M}$,

$$\dot{x} = f(x, y),$$
$$y = h(x),$$

$$\tag{N}$$

$$\dot{z} = \hat{f}(z, u),$$
$$y = \hat{h}(z),$$

$$\tag{$\hat{N}$}$$

when does there exist a diffeomorphism $\phi: M \to \hat{M}$ such that $x = \phi(z)$, $z = \phi^{-1}(x)$, or, equivalently,

$$\frac{\partial \phi}{\partial z} f(\phi(z), u) = \hat{f}(\cdot, u),$$

$$h(\phi(z)) = \hat{h}(\cdot).$$

The answer to this question is provided by the following restatement of a result of Sussman.

**Theorem 5.13**   Let there be given a mapping $G_{x_0, u}$ which to each input $u(t)$, $0 \le t \le T$, assigns a curve $y(t)$ and assume that there exists a finite-dimensional analytic complete system

$$\dot{x} = f(x, u), \qquad x(0) = x_0,$$

$$y = h(x), \qquad x \in M,$$

which realizes the map $G_{x_0, u}$. Then $G_{x_0, u}$ can also be realized by a system which is weakly controllable and observable. Furthermore, any two such realizations are isomorphic.

REMARK    In all the results above, as well as those to follow, the conditions of analyticity and completeness of the defining vector fields is crucial. The reason is clear: analyticity forces a certain type of *rigidity* upon the system, i.e., the global behavior of the system is determined by its behavior in an arbitrarily small open set. Completeness is also a natural condition since without this property the system is not totally specified, as it is then necessary to speak about the type of behavior exhibited in the neighborhood of the vector field singularity. Fortunately, analyticity and completeness are properties possessed by any class of systems defined by sets of algebraic equations having a reasonable amount of homogeneity. For instance, linear systems and bilinear systems are included in this class, together with any other type of system which is both finite dimensional, *algebraic*, and bounded.

Now let us turn to some realization results for specific classes of nonlinear systems. For ease of notation, we consider only single-input, single-output systems, citing references for the more general case.

## A. Bilinear Systems

Given a sequence of Volterra kernels $\{w_i\}_{i=0}^{\infty}$, the first question is to determine conditions under which the sequence may be realized by a bilinear system. For this we need the concept of a factorizable sequence of kernels.

**Definition 5.6**   A sequence of kernels $\{w_i\}_{i=2}^{\infty}$ is said to be *factorizable* if there exist three matrix functions $F(\cdot)$, $G(\cdot)$, $H(t, \cdot)$ of sizes $n \times n$, $n \times 1$,

$1 \times n$, respectively, such that

$$w_i(t, s_1, \ldots, s_i) = H(t, s_1)F(s_2 - s_1) \cdots F(s_{i-1} - s_{i-2})G(s_i - s_{i-1}),$$

$$s_1 \leq s_2 \leq \cdots \leq s_i.$$

The set $\{F, G, H\}$ is called the *factorization* of $\{w_i\}$ and the number $n$ is its *dimension*. A factorization $\{F_0, G_0, H_0\}$ of minimal dimension is called a *minimal* factorization.

We can now characterize those Volterra kernels which can be realized by a bilinear system.

**Theorem 5.14**   *The sequence of Volterra kernels $\{w_i\}_{i=1}^{\infty}$ is realizable by a bilinear system if and only if $w_1$ has a proper rational Laplace transform and $\{w_i\}_{i=2}^{\infty}$ is factorizable by functions $F$, $G$, $H$ with proper rational Laplace transforms.*

Let us assume that a given sequence of kernels $\{w_i\}$ is bilinearly realizable. We then face the question of the construction of a minimal realization and its properties. The main result in this regard is

**Theorem 5.15**   *For a sequence of bilinearly realizable kernels $\{w_i\}$, the minimal realizations are such that*

(i)   *the state space dimension $n_0$ is given by the dimension of the linear system whose impulse response matrix is*

$$W(s) = \left[ \begin{array}{c|c} w_1(t, s) & H_0(t, s) \\ \hline G_0(s) & F_0(s) \end{array} \right];$$

(ii)   *any two minimal realizations*

$$\dot{x} = Ax + Bu + Nxu,$$

$$y = Cx,$$

$$\dot{z} = \hat{A}z + \hat{B}u + \hat{N}zu,$$

$$y = \hat{C}z,$$

*are related by a linear transformation of their state spaces, i.e., there exists an $n_0 \times n_0$ matrix $T$ such that*

$$\hat{A} = TAT^{-1}, \qquad \hat{B} = TB, \qquad \hat{N} = TNT^{-1}, \qquad \hat{C} = CT^{-1}.$$

Theorem 5.15 provides the basic information needed to actually construct the matrices $A$, $B$, $C$, $N$ of a minimal realization. Since $W(s)$ is the impulse response of a linear system of dimension $n_0$, there must exist three matrices $P$, $Q$, $R$ of sizes $n_0 \times n_0$, $n_0 \times (n + 1)$, $(n + 1) \times n_0$ such that

$$W(s) = Re^{Ps}Q.$$

By partitioning $Q$ and $R$ as

$$R = \begin{pmatrix} R_1 \\ R_2 \end{pmatrix}, \qquad Q = (Q_1 \quad Q_2),$$

where $R_1$ is $1 \times n_0$ and $Q_1$ is $n_0 \times 1$, we obtain

$$w_1(t, s) = R_1 e^{Ps} Q_1, \qquad H_0(t, s) = R_1 e^{Ps} Q_2,$$
$$G_0(s) = R_2 e^{Ps} Q_1, \qquad F_0(s) = R_2 e^{Ps} Q_2.$$

We now define the matrices of our minimal realization as

$$A = P, \qquad B = Q_1, \qquad C = R_1, \qquad N = Q_2 R_2.$$

Thus, the surprising conclusion is that the realization procedure for bilinear systems can be carried out using essentially the same techniques as those employed in the linear case once the minimal factorization $\{F_0, G_0, H_0\}$ has been found.

## B.  Linear-Analytic Systems

The general question of when a given Volterra series $\{w_i\}_{i=0}^{\infty}$ admits realization by a finite-dimensional linear-analytic system $\{f, g, h\}$ of the form

$$\dot{x} = f(x) + u g(x),$$
$$x = h(x),$$

has no easily computable answer, although some difficult to test conditions have been given. On the other hand, if the Volterra series is finite then the results are quite easy to check and reasonably complete. For their statement, we make

***Definition 5.7***  A Volterra kernal $w(t, s_1, \ldots, s_r)$ is called *separable* if it can be expressed as a finite sum

$$w(t, s_1, \ldots, s_r) = \sum_{i=1}^{m} \gamma_i^1(t) \gamma_i^2(s_1) \cdots \gamma_i^r(s_r).$$

It is called *differentiably separable* if each $\gamma_i$ is differentiable and is *stationary* if

$$w(t, s_1, \ldots, s_r) = w(0, s_1 - t, s_2 - t, \ldots, s_r - t).$$

The main theorem characterizing the realization of finite Volterra series by a linear-analytic system is

***Theorem 5.16***  *A finite Volterra series is realizable by a (stationary) linear-analytic system if and only if each term in the series is individually realizable*

*by a (stationary) linear-analytic system. Furthermore, this will be the case if
and only if the kernels are (stationary and differentiably) separable.*

This result leaves open the question of actual computation of the vector
fields $\{f, g, h\}$ defining the linear-analytic realization of a finite Volterra
series. However, this problem is formally bypassed by the following result.

**Theorem 5.17**  *A finite Volterra series has a (stationary) linear-analytic
realization if and only if it has a (stationary) bilinear realization.*

From Theorem 5.17 it is tempting to conclude that there is no necessity
to study linear-analytic systems when given a finite Volterra series, since we
can always realize the data with a bilinear model. Unfortunately, the situation is not quite this simple since the dimension of the canonical bilinear
realization will usually be somewhat greater than that of the corresponding
linear-analytic model. To illustrate this point, consider the finite Volterra
series

$$w_0(t) = 0, \qquad w_1(t, s_1) = \exp(t - s_1), \qquad w_2(t, s_1, s_2) = 0,$$

$$w_3(t, s_1, s_2, s_3) = \tfrac{1}{3}\exp[3(t - s_1)]\exp[2(s_1 - s_2)]\exp[(s_2 - s_3)],$$

$$w_i = 0, \qquad i \geq 4.$$

This series is realized by the three-dimensional bilinear model

$$\dot{x} = Fx + Gu + Nxu,$$

$$y(t) = x(t),$$

where

$$F = \begin{bmatrix} 1 & 0 & \frac{1}{6} \\ 0 & 2 & 0 \\ 0 & 0 & 3 \end{bmatrix}, \qquad N = \begin{bmatrix} 0 & 0 & 0 \\ 2 & 0 & 0 \\ 0 & 3 & 0 \end{bmatrix}, \qquad G = \begin{bmatrix} 1 \\ 0 \\ 0 \end{bmatrix}.$$

However, the same set of kernels is also realized by the one-dimensional
linear-analytic system

$$\dot{x} = \sin x + u(t), \qquad x(0) = 0,$$

$$y(t) = x(t).$$

Another interesting example is $\dot{x} = u$, $y = x^n$, which requires an $n$th order
bilinear realization.

## C. Polynomial Systems

If the system input–output map is of polynomial type, i.e., each term in the
Volterra series is a polynomial function of its arguments, then an elegant

realization theory for such maps has been developed by Sontag in the *discrete-time* case. Since presentation of the details would entail too large an excursion into algebraic geometry, we loosely summarize the main results referring to the Notes and References for a more complete account.

For simplicity, we restrict our account to *bounded* polynomial input–output maps $f$, which means that there exists an integer $\alpha$ such that the degree of each term in the Volterra series for $f$ is uniformly bounded by $\alpha$. The main realization result for bounded polynomial input–output maps is

**Theorem 5.18**  *If a bounded input–output map is at all realizable by a polynomial system, then it is realizable by an observable state-affine system of the form*

$$x(t + 1) = F(u(t))x(t) + G(u(t)), \qquad x(0) = 0,$$

$$y(t) = Hx(t),$$

*where $F(\cdot)$ and $G(\cdot)$ are polynomial matrices, $H$ is a linear map and the system state space is $R^n$.*

An observable state-affine realization is termed *span-canonical* if the subspace of reachable states is all of $R^n$. Then it can be shown that a span-canonical realization of a given bounded finitely realizable $f$ always exists and any two such realizations are related by a state coordinate change. Furthermore, a realization is span-canonical if and only if its dimension $n$ is minimal among all state-affine realizations of the same input–output map.

### D.  "Almost"-Linear Systems

By imposing special types of nonlinearities upon a standard linear system, it is possible to employ techniques similar to the usual linear methods for realization of input–output maps. In this regard we note the *factorable* Volterra systems, having the internal form

$$\dot{x} = Fx + gu(t),$$

$$y(t) = \prod_{i=1}^{k} c_i x_i(t).$$

Here the nonlinearities enter only through the system output. Utilizing tensor products, it can be shown that the input–output behavior of such a process can be described by a so-called Volterra transfer function $H(s_1, \ldots, s_k)$. Since a factorable Volterra system consists of $k$ linear subsystems connected in parallel, with the outputs multiplied, the realization problem reduces to determining the transfer functions $H_1(s), \ldots, H_k(s)$ of each subsystem from

$H(s_1, \ldots, s_k)$. If the $H_i(s)$ are known, then standard linear theory provides the overall system realization.

## VI. NONLINEAR FILTERING AND ESTIMATION

Consider the system

$$dx(t) = f(x, u, w, \alpha)dt, \qquad x(0) = x_0, \qquad (\Sigma)$$

$$dy(t) = h(x, v)dt,$$

where $x \in R^n$, $u \in R^m$, $y \in R^p$ are as before, with $v(t)$, $w(t)$ being stochastic processes with known statistics, $\alpha \in R^l$ a vector of system parameters. Here we interpret the dynamics for $x$ and $y$ as stochastic differential equations.

Assume that we are given observations of the input and output of the system over some time interval $0 \leq t \leq T$. Then two distinct problems arise, depending upon the presence or absence of the noise processes $v$ and $w$:

### Problem I:  The Identification Problem

In this case, we assume $v \equiv w \equiv 0$, i.e., the system uncertainties and measurement noise are absent and the only task is to identify the unknown system parameters $\alpha$.

Formally, this problem may be reduce to the standard observability set-up described above by introducing the auxiliary state variables $x_i = \alpha_{i-n}$, $i = n + 1, \ldots, n + l$, with the dynamics $\dot{x}_i = 0$. Identification of the last $l$ components of the initial state using the observed input–output data then constitutes a solution of the problem. The theorems given earlier provide the basis for deciding when this can be done.

Somewhat more interesting is the case in which the noise processes $v$ and $w$ are nonzero. This situation leads to

### Problem II:  The Filtering Problem

Given the system input–output behavior $(u(t), y(t))$ over the interval $0 \leq t \leq T$, and given the statistical properties of the stochastic processes $v$ and $w$, estimate the current system state $\hat{x}(T)$ in the *best possible* fashion. In the literature, *best possible* has many different interpretations: least-squares, minimum variance, minmax, and so on, depending upon tastes and interests. In the special case of linear systems with Gaussian noise processes, all of the standard concepts of *best* turn out to be equivalent but, as usual, for nonlinear processes this is not the case.

Since there is an extensive literature devoted to the filtering problem, here we shall confine our attention to only the most basic result and to some recent extensions that make use of the Lie algebraic ideas developed in the earlier chapters.

We consider the Ito stochastic differential system

$$dx(t) = f(x(t))dt + G(x(t))dw(t),$$

$$dz(t) = h(x(t))dt + R^{1/2}(t)dv(t),$$

where $w$ and $v$ are independent unit variance vector Wiener processes, $f$ and $h$ are vector-valued functions, while $G$ is a matrix function. The symmetric matrix $R > 0$. Assume we are given the observations $Z(t) = \{z(s): 0 \le s \le t\}$. The optimal (minimum variance) estimate of $x(t)$ is the conditional mean $\hat{x}(t)$, i.e.,

$$\hat{x}(t) \doteq E[x(t)|Z(t)].$$

The fundamental theorem of filtering theory provides the equations that $\hat{x}(t)$ must satisfy.

**Theorem 5.19**   *The conditional mean $\hat{x}(t)$ satisfies the Ito stochastic differential equation*

$$d\hat{x}(t) = [\hat{f}(x(t)) - (\widehat{x(t)h'} - \hat{x}(t)\hat{h}')R^{-1}(t)\hat{h}]dt$$

$$+ (\widehat{x(t)h'} - \hat{x}(t)\hat{h}')R^{-1}(t)dz(t),$$

*where ^ denotes conditional expectation given $Z.(t)$, $h$ denotes $h(x(t))$, and $h'$ denotes the transpose of $h$.*

*Furthermore, the conditional probability density $p(t, x)$ of $x(t)$ given $Z(t)$ satisfies the stochastic partial differential equation*

$$dp(t, x) = \pounds p(t, x)dt + (h(x) - \hat{h}(x))'R^{-1}(t)(dz(t) - \hat{h}(x)dt)p(t, x),$$

*where the forward diffusion operator*

$$\pounds(g) = -\sum_{i=1}^{n} \frac{\partial(f_i g)}{\partial x_i} + \frac{1}{2}\sum_{i=1}^{n}\sum_{j=1}^{n} \frac{\partial^2((GG')_{ij}g)}{\partial x_i \partial x_j}.$$

The proof of this theorem is available in any of the standard references on stochastic filtering.

Note that the equation for $\hat{x}$ is not recursive and, in general, involves an infinite-dimensional computation. Aside from the case of linear dynamics, linear observations and Gaussian noises, in which case the Kalman filter is optimal, there are few known cases for which the optimal estimator is finite-dimensional.

In recent years, the theory of Lie algebras has been shown to play an important role in allowing us to compute some statistics about the conditional density using a finite-dimensional estimator. These Lie algebraic results give some insight into certain nonlinear estimation problems and some assistance in searching for finite-dimensional estimators. However, to actually construct a finite-dimensional filter, other techniques will also have to be employed.

To see how the Lie algebraic ideas enter into the filtering problem, instead of studying the partial differential equation for the conditional density $p(t, x)$, we consider the Zakai equation for an unnormalized conditional density $\rho(t, x)$,

$$d\rho(t, x) = \pounds\rho(t, x)dt + h(x)\rho(t, x)dz(t),$$

where the relation between $p(t, x)$ and $\rho(t, x)$ is

$$p(t, x) = \rho(t, x)\Big/\int \rho(t, x)dx.$$

The Zakai equation is far simpler than the equation for $p(t, x)$; indeed, regarding $z$ as an input, it is a bilinear equation in $\rho$. In view of our earlier connections between bilinear processes and Lie algebras, it is this fact that strongly suggests that Lie algebraic techniques may be brought to bear in this situation.

Now let us *assume* that some statistic of the conditional distribution of $x$ given $z$ can be calculated with a finite-dimensional recursive estimator of the form

$$dy(t) = a(y)dt + b(y)dz(t),$$

$$E[c(x(t))|Z(t)] = q(y(t)),$$

where $y$ evolves on a finite-dimensional manifold, and $a$, $b$, and $q$ are analytic. Note that the statistic $q(y)$ could also be computed from $\rho(t, x)$ by

$$E[c(x(t))|Z(t)] = \frac{\int c(x)\rho(t, x)dx}{\int \rho(t, x)dx}.$$

For sake of computational convenience, we write the Ito equations for $\rho$ and $y$ in the Stratonovich form

$$d\rho(t, x) = [\pounds - \tfrac{1}{2}h^2(x)]\rho(t, x)dt + h(x)\rho(t, x)dz(t),$$

$$dy(t) = \bar{a}(y)dt + b(y)dz(t),$$

where the $i$th component of the vector $\bar{a}(y)$ is

$$\bar{a}_i(y) = a_i(y) - \frac{1}{2}\sum_{j=1}^{n} b_j(y)\frac{\partial b_i(y)}{\partial y_j}.$$

Thus, we now have *two* systems for computing the statistic $q(y)$:

(i)  via the bilinear *infinite-dimensional* equation for $\rho(t, x)$;
(ii)  via the nonlinear *finite-dimensional* equation for $y$. The question to be addressed is: under what conditions is the Lie algebra generated by $\bar{a}$ and

$b$ (under the commutator $[\bar{a}, b] = (\partial b/\partial y)\bar{a} - (\partial\bar{a}/\partial y)b$) a homomorphic image (quotient) of the Lie algebra $L(\Sigma)$ generated by $A_0 = \pounds - \frac{1}{2}h^2(x)$ and $B_0 = h(x)$ (under the commutator $[A_0, B_0] = A_0B_0 - B_0A_0$)? On the other hand, any homomorphic image of $L(\Sigma)$ into a Lie algebra generated by $p + 1$ complete vector fields $\bar{a}, b_1, b_2, \ldots, b_p$ on a finite-dimensional manifold allows us to compute *some* information about the conditional density with a finite-dimensional estimator of the foregoing type.

Unfortunately, it is not yet clear to what degree of generality such arguments are valid. What *is* clear is that there is a strong relationship between the structure of $L(\Sigma)$ and the existence of finite-dimensional filters. If $L(\Sigma)$ is itself finite-dimensional, a finite-dimensional estimator can, in some cases, be constructed by integrating the Lie algebra representation. In fact, if $L(\Sigma)$ or any of its quotients is finite dimensional, then by Ado's theorem this Lie algebra has a faithful finite-dimensional representation. Thus, it can be realized with *linear* vector fields on a finite-dimensional manifold, which may result in a *bilinear* filter computing some nonzero statistic. However, actually computing the mapping of $\rho(t, x)$ to $q(y)$ (i.e., deciding *which* statistic the filter computes) is a difficult task. Also, just a Lie algebra homomorphism from $L(\Sigma)$ to a Lie algebra of vector fields is not enough. In addition, we need compatibility conditions in terms of the natural representations of the Lie algebras operating on the space of functions on the manifolds involved. Even if $L(\Sigma)$ or its quotients are *infinite* dimensional, it is still possible that these Lie algebras can be realized by *nonlinear* vector fields on a *finite*-dimensional manifold. General conditions under which this can be done is an unsolved problem. However, for certain classes of Lie algebras it can be shown that such a finite-dimensional realization is not possible. The so-called Weyl algebras $W_n$ consisting of the algebra of all polynomial differential operators in $n$ variables is a case in point. Neither $W_n$ nor any quotient of $W_n$ can be realized by vector fields with either $C^\infty$ or formal power series coefficients on a finite-dimensional manifold. Thus, for such problems no statistic of the conditional density can be computed with a finite-dimensional recursive filter. We close this section by giving an example of a problem for which the Lie algebraic techniques do succeed in providing a recursive finite-dimensional nonlinear estimator.

Consider the system with state equations

$$dx_1(t) = dw(t),$$

$$dx_2(t) = x_1^2(t)dt,$$

and observations

$$dz(t) = x_1(t)dt + dv(t),$$

where $v$ and $w$ are unit variance Wiener processes, $\{x_1(0), x_2(0), v, w\}$ are independent and $x(0)$ is Gaussian. The estimate $\hat{x}_1(t)$ can, of course, be calculated with the Kalman filter, but the computation of $\hat{x}_2(t)$ requires a non-linear estimator.

For our system, the Zakai equation (in Stratonovich form) is

$$dp(t, x) = \left( -x_1^2 \frac{\partial}{\partial x_2} + \frac{1}{2} \frac{\partial^2}{\partial x_1^2} - \frac{1}{2} x_1^2 \right) p(t, x)dt + x_1 p(t, x)dz(t),$$

so that the Lie algebra $L(\Sigma)$ is generated by

$$A_0 = -x_1^2 \frac{\partial}{\partial x_2} + \frac{1}{2} \frac{\partial^2}{\partial x_1^2} - \frac{1}{2} x_1^2,$$

$$B_0 = x_1.$$

The following result can be established concerning the structure of $L(\Sigma)$:

**Theorem 5.20**   (i)   *The Lie algebra $L(\Sigma)$ generated by $A_0$ and $B_0$ has as basis the elements $A_0$, $B_i = x_1(\partial^i/\partial x_2^i)$, $C_i = \partial/\partial x_1(\partial^i/\partial x_2^i)$, $D_i = \partial^i/\partial x_2^i$, $i = 0, 1, 2, \ldots$.*
(ii)   *The commutation relations are*

$$[A_0, B_i] = C_i,$$

$$[A_0, C_i] = B_i + 2B_{i+1},$$

$$[A_0, D_j] = [B_i, D_j] = [C_i, D_j] = [B_i, B_j] = [C_i, C_j] = 0,$$

$$[B_i, C_j] = -D_{i+j}, \cdot \text{ all } i, j.$$

(iii)   *The center of $L(\Sigma)$ is $D_i$, $i = 0, 1, 2, \ldots$.*
(iv)   *For any ideal $I$, $L(\Sigma)/I$ is finite dimensional.*
(v)   *Let $I_j$ be the ideal generated by $B_j$, with basis $\{B_i, C_i, D_i; i \geq j\}$. Then $I_0 \supset I_1 \supset \cdots$, and $\cap_j I_j = \{0\}$. Thus, the canonical map $\pi: L(\Sigma) \to \oplus_j L(\Sigma)/I_j$ is injective.*
(vi)   *$L(\Sigma)$ is the semidirect sum of $A_0$ and the nilpotent ideal $I_0$; hence $L(\Sigma)$ is solvable.*

Since there are an infinite number of finite-dimensional quotients (homomorphic images of $L(\Sigma)$), our earlier remarks strongly suggest that many statistics of the conditional distribution can be computed with finite-dimensional estimators. We shall consider, for example, the quotient $L(\Sigma)/I_4$, which is realized by the estimator which computes $\hat{x}_1$ and $\hat{x}_2^i = E[x_2^i(t)|Z(t)]$, $i = 1, 2, 3$.

Let us introduce the state $[x_1, \xi, \theta, \phi]$. Then the Kalman filter for the linear system with states $[x_1, \xi, \theta, \phi]$ and observations $z$ computes $[\hat{x}_1, \hat{\xi}, \hat{\theta}, \hat{\phi}]$ via the usual estimation equation. Since the conditional density of $x_1$, given $z$ is Gaussian, we can compute the higher conditional moments of $x_2$ in terms of the lower moments. The filter which accomplishes this is given by

$$d\hat{X} = a_0 dt + b_0 dz,$$

where
$$\hat{X} = [\hat{x}_1, \hat{\xi}, \hat{x}_2, \hat{\theta}, \hat{x}_2^2, \hat{\phi}, \hat{x}_2^3, t]',$$

$$a_0 = \begin{bmatrix} -\hat{x}_1 P \\ \hat{x}_1(1 - P_{12}) - \hat{\xi}P^{-1} \\ \hat{x}_1^2 - 2\hat{x}_1\hat{\xi}P + P - PP_{12} \\ \hat{x}_1(P_{12} - P_{13}) + \hat{\xi}P(1 - P_{12}) - \hat{\theta}P^{-1} \\ 2\hat{x}_1^2\hat{x}_2 + 2\hat{x}_2 P + 8\hat{x}_1\hat{\xi}P + 4PP_{12} - 4\hat{x}_1\hat{\xi}\hat{x}_2 P \\ - 8\hat{x}_1\hat{\theta}P - 2\hat{x}_2 PP_{12} - 4\hat{\xi}^2 P^2 - 4PP_{13} \\ \hat{x}_1(P_{13} - P_{14}) + \hat{\xi}P(P_{12} - P_{13}) + \hat{\theta}(P - PP_{12}) - \hat{\phi}P^{-1} \\ 3\hat{x}_1^2\hat{x}_2^2 + 3\hat{x}_2^2 P + 24\hat{x}_1\hat{\xi}\hat{x}_2 P + 48\hat{x}_1\hat{\theta}P + 24\hat{\xi}^2 P^2 \\ + 12\hat{x}_2 PP_{12} + 24PP_{13} - 3\hat{x}_2^2 PP_{12} - 48\hat{\xi}\hat{\theta}P^2 - 12\hat{x}_2 PP_{13} \\ 1 \end{bmatrix},$$

$$b_0 = \begin{bmatrix} P \\ P_{12} \\ 2\hat{\xi}P \\ P_{13} \\ 4\hat{\xi}\hat{x}_2 P + 8\hat{\theta}P \\ P_{14} \\ 6\hat{\xi}\hat{x}_2^2 P + 24\hat{\theta}\hat{x}_2 P + 48\hat{\phi}P \\ 0 \end{bmatrix}, \qquad \hat{X}(0) = \begin{bmatrix} Ex_1(0) \\ 0 \\ Ex_2(0) \\ 0 \\ Ex_2^2(0) \\ 0 \\ Ex_2^3(0) \\ 0 \end{bmatrix}.$$

The nonrandom conditional covariance equations are

$$\frac{dP}{dt} = 1 - P^2,$$

$$\frac{dP_{12}}{dt} = P - (P + P^{-1})P_{12},$$

$$\frac{dP_{13}}{dt} = 2PP_{12} - PP_{12}^2 - (P + P^{-1})P_{13},$$

$$\frac{dP_{14}}{dt} = 2PP_{13} + PP_{12}^2 - 2PP_{12}P_{13} - (P + P^{-1})P_{14},$$

$$P(0) = \text{cov}(x_1(0)) \neq 0, \qquad P_{12}(0) = P_{13}(0) = P_{14}(0) = 0.$$

The quantity $[P, P_{12}, P_{13}, P_{14}]$ is the first row of the Kalman filter co-variance matrix.

The filter just presented can be viewed as a cascade of linear filters. As noted, $[\hat{x}_1, \hat{\xi}, \hat{\theta}, \hat{\phi}, t]$ satisfies a linear equation; some of these states then "feedforward" and can be regarded as parameters in a linear equation for $\hat{x}_2$;

the states $\hat{x}_1$, $\hat{\xi}$, $\hat{\theta}$, $\hat{x}_2$, $t$ then feedforward as parameters into a linear system for $\hat{x}_2^2$ and so on.

To study the structure of the estimation problem in the terms discussed above, we must study the Lie algebra generated by $a_0$ and $b_0$. Call this algebra $F$. We have

**Theorem 5.21**  (i)   *The Lie algebra $F$ has basis elements $a_0$, $b_i$, $c_i$, $i = 0, 1, 2, 3$; $d_i$, $i = 1, 2, 3$, where $a_0$, $b_0$ are as above, and*

$$c_0 = [1\ 0\ 0\ 0\ 0\ 0\ 0\ 0]', \qquad c_1 = [0\ P^{-1}\ 0\ 0\ 0\ 0\ 0\ 0]',$$

$$c_2 = [0\ 0\ 0\ P^{-1}\ 0\ 0\ 0\ 0]', \qquad c_3 = [0\ 0\ 0\ 0\ 0\ P^{-1}\ 0\ 0]',$$

$$b_1 = \begin{bmatrix} 0 \\ 1 \\ 2\hat{x}_1 \\ P_{12} \\ 4\hat{x}_1\hat{x}_2 + 8\hat{\xi}P \\ P_{13} \\ 6\hat{x}_1\hat{x}_2^2 + 24\hat{\xi}\hat{x}_2 P + 48\hat{\theta}P \\ 0 \end{bmatrix}, \qquad b_2 = \begin{bmatrix} 0 \\ 0 \\ 0 \\ 1 \\ 8\hat{x}_1 \\ P_{12} \\ 24\hat{x}_1\hat{x}_2 + 48\hat{\xi}P \\ 0 \end{bmatrix},$$

$$b_3 = \begin{bmatrix} 0 \\ 0 \\ 0 \\ 0 \\ 0 \\ 1 \\ 48\hat{x}_1 \\ 0 \end{bmatrix}, \qquad d_1 = \begin{bmatrix} 0 \\ 0 \\ 1 \\ 0 \\ 2\hat{x}_2 \\ 0 \\ 3\hat{x}_2^2 \\ 0 \end{bmatrix}, \qquad d_2 = \begin{bmatrix} 0 \\ 0 \\ 0 \\ 0 \\ 1 \\ 0 \\ 3\hat{x}_2 \\ 0 \end{bmatrix}, \qquad d_3 = \begin{bmatrix} 0 \\ 0 \\ 0 \\ 0 \\ 0 \\ 0 \\ 1 \\ 0 \end{bmatrix}.$$

(ii)   *The commutation relations are*

$$[a_0, b_i] = c_i, \qquad\qquad i = 0, 1, 2, 3,$$

$$[a_0, c_i] = b_i - b_{i+1}, \qquad i = 0, 1, 2,$$

$$[a_0, c_3] = b_3,$$

$$[b_i, c_j] = \begin{cases} -2d_{i+j}, & i + j = 1, \\ -8d_{i+j}, & i + j = 2, \\ -48d_{i+j}, & i + j = 3, \\ 0 & \text{other} \end{cases}$$

$$[a_0, d_j] = [b_i, d_j] = [c_i, d_j] = 0.$$

(iii)  *Let $\bar{I}_4$ be the ideal in $L(\Sigma)$ having basis $B_i$, $C_i$, $D_i$, $i \geq 4$ and $D_0$. Then $F$ is isomorphic to $L(\Sigma)/\bar{I}_4$.*

(iv)  *The isomorphism $\psi$ between $L(\Sigma)/\bar{I}_4$ and $F$ is given by*

$$\psi(A_0) = a_0; \qquad \psi(B_i) = (\tfrac{1}{2})^i b_i,$$

$$\psi(C_i) = (-\tfrac{1}{2})^i c_i, \qquad i = 0, 1, 2, 3.$$

$$\psi(D_i) = (-1)^i (i!) d_i, \qquad i = 1, 2, 3;$$

$$\psi(E) = 0, \qquad E \in \bar{I}_4.$$

(v)  *$F$ is the semidirect sum of $a_0$ and the nilpotent ideal generated by $b_0$.*

REMARK    One of the conditions for the existence of a Lie algebra homomorphism from $L$ to the Lie algebra of the finite-dimensional estimator is that the estimator be a *minimal* realization, in some sense. If we consider the output of the above estimator to be $\hat{x}_2^3$ and consider the estimator as a realization of the input–output map from $z$ to $\hat{x}_2^3$, then it can be verified from our earlier machinery that the realization is locally weakly controllable and locally weakly observable. This implies that there is no other realization having lower dimension. It is in this sense that the *states* $\hat{\xi}$, $\hat{\theta}$, $\hat{\phi}$ are necessary for the computation of $\hat{x}_2^3$.

## PROBLEMS AND EXERCISES

**1.**  (a)  Consider the input–output description of a homogeneous, stationary single-input–single-output system of degree $n$

$$y(t) = \int_0^\infty \cdots \int_0^\infty h(t_1, \ldots, t_n) u(t - t_1) \cdots u(t - t_n) dt_1 \cdots dt_n,$$

where $h$ is $0$ outside the regions $t_i \geq 0$. Let

$$H(s_1, s_2, \ldots, s_n) = \int_0^\infty \cdots \int_0^\infty h(t_1, \ldots, t_n) e^{-s_1 t_1} \cdots e^{-s_n t_n} dt_1 \cdots dt_n$$

be the *transfer function* of the kernel $h$. Write

$$H(s_1, s_2, \ldots, s_n) = P(s_1, \ldots, s_n)/Q(s_1, \ldots, s_n),$$

where $P$ and $Q$ are polynomials in the $s_i$. Call $H$ *strictly proper* if $\deg Q > \deg P$ in $s_j$ for each $j = 1, 2, \ldots, n$ and call $H$ *reduced* if $P$ and $Q$ have no common factors. Finally, call $H$ *recognizable* if $Q(s_1, \ldots, s_n)$ can be written as $Q(s_1, \ldots, s_n) = Q_1(s_1) Q_2(s_2) \cdots Q_n(s_n)$, where $Q_i(s_i)$ is a polynomial in $s_i$.

Prove the following realization result. The transfer matrix $H$ can be realized by a finite-dimensional bilinear system

$$\dot{x} = Fx + Gxu + gu,$$

$$y = hx(t), \qquad x(0) = 0,$$

if and only if the reduced form of $H$ is strictly proper and recognizable.

(b)   Show that if the poles of $H(s_1, s_2, \ldots, s_n)$ all lie in the left half-plane, then the system is bounded-input–bounded-output stable.

**2.**   (a)   Let $\xi$ be a smooth vector field on a smooth manifold $M$ having the property that $\xi$ has only a finite number of equilibrium points and a finite number of closed orbits of period $\leq T$. Let $h: M \to R$ be a smooth observation function. We say that the system $(\xi, h)$ is *P-observable* if and only if for each pair $(x, y) \in M \times M$, $x \neq y$, there exists a finite set of points $P = \{t_i\}_{i=1}^N$ such that $h \circ \phi_{t_i}(y) \neq h \circ \phi_{t_i}(y)$, where $\phi_t(\cdot)$ is the flow on $M$ induced by the vector field $\xi$.

(a)   Show that if dim $M = n$, then the set of observation functions $h$ such that $(\xi, h)$ is $P$-observable is open and dense in $C^\infty(M, R)$ if $P$ contains at least $(2n + 1)$ sample points, i.e., $N \geq 2n + 1$.

(Thus, for a given vector field $\xi$, almost any measuring device $h$ will suffice to observe $\xi$ provided at least $2n + 1$ samples of $\xi$ are taken).

(b)   Prove that if a fixed measurement function $h$ is given together with a $T > 0$, then the set of smooth vector fields $\xi$ such that $(\xi, h)$ is $P$-observable is open and dense in the set of smooth vector fields on $M$ if $N \geq 2n + 1$.

(In other words, a given measurement system can identify almost any vector field if at least $2n + 1$ measurements are taken.)

(c)   Show by counterexamples that, in general, the bound on the number of points in the sample program cannot be improved in either case (a) or (b).

**3.**   Consider the discrete-time system

$$x_{t+1} = f(x_t),$$

$$y_t = h(x_t),$$

where $f: M \to M$ is an analytic map, $h: M \to N$ an analytic output map, $M, N$ analytic manifolds with dim $M = n$. We say that the system is *strongly locally observable* at $x \in M$ if there exists a neighborhood $U$ of $x$ such that for any $\bar{x} \in U$, $h(f^k(\bar{x})) = h(f^k(x))$, $k = 0, 1, 2, \ldots, n - 1$ implies $\bar{x} = x$. Define the map $\theta: M \to N^n$ by

$$\theta(x) \doteq (h(x), h(f(x)), \ldots, h(f^{n-1}(x))).$$

We say that the system satisfies the *observability rank condition* at $x$ if rank $\theta(x) = n$.

Prove the following assertions:

(i)  if the system satisfies the observability rank condition at $x$, then it is strongly locally observable at $x$;

(ii)  if the system is strongly locally observable at each $x \in M$, then the observability rank condition is satisfied on an open, dense submanifold of $M$.

(Note that these results extend Theorems 5.2 and 5.3 to discrete-time systems.)

**4.**  Consider the system

$$\dot{x} = f(x), \qquad x \in R^n$$

$$y = h(x),$$

where $f \in C^n(R^n, R^n)$, $h \in C^n(R^n, R)$, $n \geq 2$. Assume that $\dim\{x \in R^n : f(x) = 0\} \geq 2$. Show that in this case, the pair $(f, h)$ will be unobservable for any $h \in C^n(R^n, R)$.

**5.**  (a)  Show that the system

$$\dot{x}_1 = -x_1 - x_1^3 - x_2^3,$$

$$\dot{x}_2 = -x_2 + x_1 x_2^2$$

is not completely observable with any linear scalar observation function $h(x_1, x_2) = \alpha_1 x_1 + \alpha_2 x_2$, but is globally observable for any polynomial observation function $h(x_1)$ such that $h'(0) \neq 0$.

(b)  Show that the system

$$\dot{x}_1 = x_1 + e^{-2t} x_2 \sin x_2,$$

$$\dot{x}_2 = x_2 + e^{-2t} x_1 \sin x_1,$$

$$y(t) = x_1 + x_2^3$$

is globally observable.

**6.**  Consider the system $\Pi_K$

$$\dot{x} = Fx(t) + gu(t),$$

$$y(t) = \gamma \prod_{i=1}^{K} h_i x_i(t), \qquad \gamma \text{ an arbitrary scalar,}$$

where

$$x(t) = \begin{bmatrix} x_1(t) \\ x_2(t) \\ \vdots \\ x_K(t) \end{bmatrix}, \qquad F = \begin{bmatrix} F_1 & & & \\ & F_2 & & \\ & & \ddots & \\ & & & F_K \end{bmatrix}, \qquad g = \begin{bmatrix} g_1 \\ g_2 \\ \vdots \\ g_K \end{bmatrix},$$

with dim $x_i = n_i$, $\sum_{j=1}^K n_j = n$. Let $\Lambda_i$ denote the vector whose entries are the distinct characteristic values of $F_i$ and define the Kronecker sum of two such vectors by

$$\Lambda_1 \oplus \Lambda_2 = (\lambda_{11} + \lambda_{21}, \lambda_{11} + \lambda_{22}, \ldots, \lambda_{11} + \lambda_{2,p_2}, \ldots,$$

$$\lambda_{1,p_1} + \lambda_{21}, \lambda_{1,p_1} + \lambda_{22}, \ldots, \lambda_{1,p_1} + \lambda_{2,p_2}), \qquad p_i \leq n_i.$$

Prove that the system $\prod_K$ is completely observable (as a linear system) if and only if $\Lambda_1 \oplus \Lambda_2 \oplus \cdots \oplus \Lambda_K$ has distinct entries and at most one of the subsystems has multiple characteristic values.

(We remark that $\prod_K$ represents a collection of $K$ independent linear systems, coupled by multiplication of their outputs.)

7.  Define $\otimes$ as the usual Kronecker product and set

$$x^\otimes(t) = x_1(t) \otimes x_2(t) \otimes \cdots \otimes x_K(t),$$

$$F^\otimes = F_1 \otimes I_{n_2} \otimes \cdots \otimes I_{n_K} + I_{n_1} \otimes F_2 \otimes I_{n_3} \otimes \cdots \otimes I_{n_K}$$

$$+ \cdots + I_{n_1} \otimes \cdots \otimes I_{nK} - 1 \otimes F_K,$$

$$n^\otimes = \prod_{i=1}^K n_i, \qquad h^\otimes = h_1 \otimes h_2 \otimes \cdots \otimes h_K.$$

Show that the transfer function for $\prod_K$ is given by

$$W(s) = \gamma h^\otimes (sI_{n\otimes} - F^\otimes)^{-1} g^\otimes,$$

where $g^\otimes = (g_1 \otimes g_2 \otimes \cdots \otimes g_K)'$.

8.  (a)  Show that the system

$$\dot{x}_1 = u, \qquad\qquad x_1(0) = 0,$$

$$\dot{x}_2 = x_1 + x_1^2 + u, \qquad x_2(0) = 0, \qquad\qquad (\text{I})$$

$$y = x_1^2 + x_2,$$

and the system

$$\dot{z}_1 = u, \qquad\qquad z_1(0) = 0,$$

$$\dot{z}_2 = z_1 + u, \qquad\qquad z_2(0) = 0,$$

$$\dot{z}_3 = z_1^2, \qquad\qquad z_3(0) = 0, \qquad\qquad (\text{II})$$

$$y = z_1^2 + z_2 + z_3,$$

have the same input–output behavior, but that (I) is reachable and observable, while (II) is reachable but not observable, hence not canonical.

(b)  Show that the Volterra kernels for (I) are given by

$$w_1(t, \tau_1) = (t - \tau_1 + 1), \qquad w_2(t, \tau_1, \tau_2) = 2(t - \tau_1 + 1),$$

i.e., its Volterra series is finite of degree 2,

$$y(t) = 2 \int_0^t \int_0^{\tau_1} (t - \tau_1 + 1)u(\tau_1)u(\tau_2)d\tau_1 d\tau_2 + \int_0^t (t - \tau_1 + 1)u(\tau_1)d\tau_1.$$

**9.**  Consider the discrete-time polynomial system

$$x_1(t + 1) = x_2(t),$$
$$x_2(t + 1) = x_1(t),$$
$$x_3(t + 1) = x_3(t),$$
$$x_4(t + 1) = x_1(t)u_1^2(t) + x_2(t)u_2^2(t) + x_3(t),$$
$$y(t) = x_4(t) = h(x(t)),$$

where $u(t) \in U = R^2$. Show that the system is *algebraically observable*, i.e., each coordinate function $x_i: X \rightarrow R$ is a polynomial function of the polynomial functions $h$ and its compositions with the coordinate projections. Show that this result fails if $U$ is the circle $u_1^2 + u_2^2 = 1$ and that in this case the indistinguishable pairs of states are those on the lines parallel to $\{x_4 = 0, x_1 - x_2 = 0, x_2 + x_3 = 0\}$.

**10.**  The following equation is often used to describe rainfall runoff from a water basin system:

$$K_2\ddot{Q} + K_1NQ^{N-1}\dot{Q} + Q = u(t),$$

where $Q(t)$ is the direct runoff at time $t$ and $u(t)$ is the excess rainfall, with $K_1, K_2, N$ constants characterizing the basin. This system can be rewritten as

$$\dot{x}_1 = x_2,$$
$$\dot{x}_2 = -x_3x_4x_5x_1^{x_5-1}x_2 - x_4x_1 + x_4u,$$
$$\dot{x}_3 = 0,$$
$$\dot{x}_4 = 0,$$
$$\dot{x}_5 = 0,$$
$$y(t) = x_1(t),$$

where we have let

$$x_1 = Q, \qquad x_2 = \dot{Q}, \qquad x_3 = K_1, \qquad x_4 = 1/K_2, \qquad x_5 = N.$$

From what initial states $x(0)$ can the parameters $K_1$, $K_2$, $N$ be identified using a finite record $y(t)$, $0 \le t \le T < \infty$?

**11.** Let $\mathscr{C}$ be a matrix group and assume that the set of points $R$ reachable from the identity for the system

$$\dot{X}(t) = [F + (\sum u_i(t)G_i)]X, \qquad X(0) = X_0,$$

$$y(t) = \mathscr{C}X(t)$$

is a group. Show that the set of initial states that are indistinguishable from the identity is

$$\mathscr{P} = \{P: APA^{-1} \in \mathscr{C} \text{ for all } A \in R\}$$

and that $\mathscr{P}$ is a normal subgroup of $\mathscr{P}R$ and a subgroup of $\mathscr{C}$.

**12.** Consider the system

$$\dot{x} = f(x),$$

$$y(t) = h(x),$$

where $f \in C^{k-1}(R^n)$, $h \in C^k(R^n)$. Define the observability mapping $H_k$: $R^n \to R^k$ by

$$H_k(x) = \begin{bmatrix} h_0(x) \\ h_1(x) \\ \vdots \\ h_{k-1}(x) \end{bmatrix},$$

where

$$h_0(x) = y(t),$$

$$h_1(x) = \frac{\partial h_0(x)}{\partial x} f(x) = \frac{d}{dt} y(t),$$

$$h_2(x) = \frac{\partial h_1(x)}{\partial x} f(x) = \frac{d^2}{dt^2} y(t),$$

$$\vdots \qquad\qquad \vdots$$

$$h_{k-1}(x) = \frac{\partial h_{k-2}(x)}{\partial x} f(x) = \frac{d^{k-1}}{dt} y(t).$$

(a)  Show that the system is observable if $H_k(x)$ is 1–1 on $R^n$.

(b)  If $f$ and $h$ are polynomials on $R^n$, show that the system is observable if and only if there exists an integer $j \ge 1$ such that $H_j(x)$ is 1–1 on $R^n$.

(c)   Consider the special case when

$$f(x) = Fx + g, \qquad h(x) = p_m(x),$$

where $F = n \times n$, $g = n \times 1$, and $p_m(x)$ is a polynomial of degree $m$. Show that the integer $j$ of part (b) satisfies the bound

$$j \le \sum_{i=0}^{m} (n + i - 1)!/(i!(n - 1)!).$$

(d)   If $f(x) = Fx$ and $h(x) = (x, c) + (x, Dx)$, where $F = n \times n$, $c = n \times 1$, $D =$ symmetric $n \times n$, show that the system is observable if and only if

$$\text{rank } \frac{\partial H_j}{\partial x} = n \qquad \text{for all } x \in R^n,$$

where $j = n(n - 3)/2$. Furthermore, in this case show that if the system is observable, then the pair $(F, c)$ is also observable in the usual linear system sense.

**13.**   Consider the linear-analytic system

$$\dot{x} = f(x) + \sum_{i=1}^{m} u_i g_i(x), \qquad x(0) = x_0,$$

$$y = h(x),$$

where $x \in R^n$, $u_i \in R^m$, $y \in R^p$, $f, g_i, h$ analytic.

(a)   Prove that if the equation $\dot{x} = f(x)$, $x(0) = x_0$, has a solution on $[0, T]$, then the input–output map for the system has a unique Volterra expansion.

(b)   Let $\psi_1, \psi_2$ be input–output maps that have Volterra expansions of length $k$. If $\psi_1 = \psi_2 + O(\|u\|^k)$, then $w_m^1 = w_m^2$, $1 \le m \le k$, where $w_m^i$ is the $m$th Volterra kernel of $\psi_i$, $i = 1, 2$.

**14.**   Given the nonautonomous nonlinear system

$$\dot{x} = f(x, t), \qquad x(t_0) = x_0$$

$$y = h(x, t),$$

$f, h \in C^1$, define

$$F(t) = \frac{\partial f}{\partial x}\bigg|_{x = x(t; x_0)}, \qquad H(t) = \frac{\partial h}{\partial x}\bigg|_{x = x(t; x_0)},$$

$$M(x_0) \doteq M(x_0; t_0, t_1) = \int_0^{t_1} \phi'(s, t_0) H'(s) H(s) \phi(s, t_0) ds,$$

where $\phi(t, s)$ is the transition matrix of $F(t)$. Let $S$ be a set of initial states.

(a)  Prove that the system is *unobservable* in $S$ if and only if for every $x_0$, $x_0^* \in S$, with $\delta x_0 = x_0 - x_0^* \neq 0$, there exists a $\theta$, $0 < \theta < 1$, such that for all $t \in [t_0, t_1]$.

(i)  $M(\bar{x}_0)\delta x_0 = 0$,
(ii)  $h(x(t; x_0^*), t) - h(x(t; x_0), t) = \partial h(x(t; x_0)/\partial x_0, t)\big|_{\substack{\delta x_0 \\ x_0 = \bar{x}_0}}$, where $\bar{x}_0 = x_0 + \theta\delta x_0$.

(b)  If $M(x_0) > 0$ for all $x_0 \in S$ and $S$ is convex, then the system is completely observable.

(c)  Assume that the observation process is corrupted by a zero-mean white Gaussian noise $n(t)$ with a unitary spectral density function, i.e., we observe

$$z(t) = y(t) + n(t).$$

Show that for $S$ convex, if there exists an unbiased estimator for each $x_0 \in S$ based on $z(t)$, $t_0 \leq t \leq t_1$, with finite error covariance matrix $P$, then the system is completely observable. (Hint: Show that $M(x_0)$ is the Fisher information matrix for the linear system $(F(t), H(t))$ and apply the linear estimation theory results).

(d)  Show that the converse to part (c) is false by the counterexample $S = [1, \infty]$, $\dot{x} = 0$, $z(t) = y(t) + n(t)$, $y(t) = [\frac{1}{2}\log x(t)]^{1/2}$, i.e., this system is observable, but there exists no unbiased estimator of $x_0$ at 1 with finite variance.

**15.**  The following system describes the rotation of a rigid body steered by a pair of opposing gas jets and whose rotation about a fixed axis can be observed.

$$\dot{x}_1 = a_1 x_2 x_3 + b_1 u(t),$$
$$\dot{x}_2 = a_2 x_1 x_3 + b_2 u(t),$$
$$\dot{x}_3 = a_3 x_1 x_2 + b_3 u(t),$$
$$y(t) = c_1 x_1 + c_2 x_2 + c_3 x_3,$$
$$a_1 + a_2 + a_3 + a_1 a_2 a_3 = 0,$$
$$c_1^2 + c_2^2 + c_3^2 = 1, \qquad -1 \leq a_i \leq 1.$$

Here $x_i(t)$ is the angular velocity about the $i$th principal axis of inertia, where the principal moments of inertia, $I_1$, $I_2$, $I_3$ are given in terms of the $a_i$ by

$$a_1 = (I_2 - I_3)/I_1, \qquad a_2 = (I_3 - I_1)/I_2, \qquad a_3 = (I_1 - I_2)/I_3.$$

The output $y(t)$ is the component of angular velocity about the axis $(c_1, c_2, c_3)$ (with respect to the principal axis coordinate system).

Suppose $u(t) \equiv 0$ and that $y(t)$ is observed on $[0, T]$. Show that any initial state $x_0 \neq 0$ is distinguishable from the origin if and only if $a_1 a_2 a_3 c_1 c_2 c_3 \neq 0$. Furthermore, show that this condition is also necessary and sufficient for all but finitely many initial states to be distinguishable from any given $x_0$.

**16.**  Consider the bilinear system

$$\frac{dx}{dt} = Fx + uGx.$$

Show that the Volterra series for the system is finite if and only if the smallest associative algebra containing $\{G, ad_F^k G\}$, $k = 0, 1, \ldots$, is nilpotent, where $ad_F^k(\cdot) = [F, [F, \cdot], \ldots]]$. (Recall that a Lie algebra $A$ is nilpotent if $[T, [T, M]] = 0$ for $T, M \in A$).

**17.**  Consider the signal observation model

$$dx = f(x)dt + g(x)db(t), \qquad x(0) = x_0,$$

$$dy = h(x)dt + dw(t), \qquad y(0) = 0,$$

where $x \in R^n$, $b \in R^m$, $y \in R^p$ with $b$, $w$ independent, standard Brownian motions. The *estimation algebra* $\Lambda$ for this process is the Lie algebra generated by the operators

$$\pounds_0 = \pounds^* - \tfrac{1}{2} \sum_{i=1}^{p} h_i^2,$$

and $h_i$, $i = 1, 2, \ldots, p$, where

$$\pounds^* \phi = \frac{1}{2} \sum_{i,j=1}^{n} \frac{\partial^2}{\partial x_i \partial x_j} (gg')_{ij} \phi - \sum_{i=1}^{n} \frac{\partial}{\partial x_i} f_i(x) \phi.$$

(Here when we say a function of $h$ belongs to $\Lambda$, we mean the operator *multiplication by $h(x)$*). Assume $f, h \in C^\infty(U)$, where $U$ is an open, connected region in $R^n$, $m \geq n$, $g(x) = G =$ const. $n \times m$ matrix of rank $r$.

(a)  Show that if dim $\Lambda < \infty$ and if a function $h \in \Lambda$, then $h$ must be a polynomial of degree $\leq 2$.

(b)  In the special case $n = m = p = 1$, $g = 1$, show that dim $\Lambda < \infty$ only if

(i)  $h(x) = \alpha x$,

$$f' + f^2 = ax^2 + bx + c$$

or

(ii)  $h(x) = \alpha x^2 + \beta x$, $\alpha \neq 0$ and

$$f' + f^2 = -h^2 + a(2\alpha x + \beta)^2 + b + c(2\alpha x + \beta)^{-2}$$

or

$$f' + f^2 = -h^2 + ax^2 + bx + c.$$

**18.** Let $W_n$ denote the associative algebra: $R\langle x_1, x_2, \ldots, x_n; d/dx_1, \ldots, d/dx_n\rangle$ of all partial differential operators in $\partial/\partial x_1, \ldots, \partial/\partial x_n$ with polynomial coefficients, $n = 1, 2, \ldots$. A basis for $W_n$ (as a vector space over $R$) consists of the monomials

$$x^\alpha \frac{\partial^\beta}{\partial x^\beta} \doteq x_1^{\alpha_1} \cdots x_n^{\alpha_n} \frac{\partial^{\beta_1}}{\partial x_1^{\beta_1}} \cdots \frac{\partial^{\beta_n}}{\partial x_n^{\beta_n}}, \qquad \alpha_i, \beta_j \in Z \cup \{0\}.$$

(a)   Let $M$ be a finite-dimensional smooth manifold. Show that there are no nonzero homomorphisms of the Lie algebra $W_n \rightarrow V(M)$, where $V(M)$ are smooth vector fields on $M$, $n = 1, 2, \ldots$. Consequently, if $W_n$ is the estimation algebra of a given system, there are no nonzero statistics of this system that can be computed by a finite-dimensional filter.

(b)   Show that the cubic sensor

$$dx = db,$$

$$dy = x^3 dt + dw,$$

has $W_1$ as its estimation algebra.

**19.**   Show that the stochastic linear system

$$dx = db,$$

$$dy = xdt + dw$$

has a four-dimensional estimation algebra generated by the elements

$$\left\{ \frac{1}{2} \frac{d^2}{dx^2} - \frac{1}{2} x^2, x, \frac{d}{dx}, 1 \right\}.$$

(This is called the *oscillator* algebra.)

**20.**   Consider the linear system with noise-corrupted coefficients

$$dx = a(t)xdt + \beta db_1,$$

$$da = db_2,$$

$$dy = xdt + dw,$$

$b_1, b_2, w$ independent Brownian motions. Show that the estimation algebra for this problem is $W_2$. Hence, no statistic is computable by a finite-dimensional filter.

## NOTES AND REFERENCES

**Section 5.I**   An excellent account of the various types of observability for nonlinear processes and their interconnections is found in

E. Sontag, On the observability of polynomial systems. I. Finite-time problems, *SIAM J. Control Optim.* **17** (1979), 139–151.

In the theory of finite automata, observability is called *diagnosing* and in fact, most of the proofs of system observability closely follow those in automata theory, with a new type of finiteness (algebraic, linear, analytic, …) replacing set-theoretic finiteness. For an account of the automata results, see

A. Gill, "Introduction to the Theory of Finite-State Machines," McGraw-Hill, New York, 1962.
S. Eilenberg, "Automata, Languages and Machines," Part A, Academic Press, New York, 1974.

**Section 5.II**   The basic definitions follow the paper

R. Hermann and A. Krener, Nonlinear controllability and observability, *IEEE Trans. Automat. Control* **AC-22** (1977), 728–740.

For a discussion of some of the potential drawbacks to our notion of observability, see the introduction to the paper

A. J. Van der Schaft, Observability and controllability for smooth nonlinear systems, *SIAM J. Control Optim.* **20** (1982), 338–354.

**Section 5.III**   Extensive discussion and proofs of Theorems 5.2–5.4 are given in the Hermann and Krener paper cited under Section 5.1.

Results on observability for bilinear systems are given in

A. Ruberti, A. Isidori, and P. d'Alessandro, "Theory of Bilinear Dynamical Systems," CISM Lectures No. 158, Springer, Vienna, 1972.

Theorem 5.6 is from the paper

E. Griffith and K. S. P. Kumar, On the observability of nonlinear systems, *J. Math. Anal. Appl.* **35** (1971), 135–147.

For the proof of Theorem 5.7 see

Y. Inouye, On the observability of autonomous nonlinear systems, *J. Math. Anal. Appl.* **60** (1977), 236–247.

**Section 5.IV**   Most of the material of this section follows the very important work of Baillieul, first reported in

J. Baillieul, Controllability and observability of polynomial dynamical systems, *Nonlinear Anal.* **5** (1981), 543–552.

See also

E. Sontag, "Polynomial Response Maps," Lecture Notes in Control, Vol. 13, Springer, Berlin, 1979.
W. A. Porter, An overview of polynomic system theory, *Proc. IEEE* **64** (1976), 18–23.

The importance of polynomial systems in the general scheme of things is derived from the fact that, in some suitable norm, virtually every sufficiently smooth system can be arbitrarily closely approximated by a polynomial process. Even stronger, in some cases the tools of singularity theory (see Chapter 6), can be used to find coordinate systems in which this approximation is *exact*, sometimes even globally. This idea is the basis underlying the standard forms of catastrophe theory and has not been as actively pursued as its importance warrants in control and system theory.

**Section 5.V**    General results on the existence and uniqueness of Volterra kernels are given in

C. Lesiak and A. Krener, The existence and uniqueness of volterra series for nonlinear systems, *IEEE Trans. Automat. Control* **AC-23** (1978), 1090–1095.

State-space isomorphism results can be found in, for example,

H. Sussman, Minimal realization of nonlinear systems, *in* "Geometric Methods in System Theory" (D. Mayne and R. Brockett, eds.), Reidel, Dordrecht, 1973.

and in the Hermann and Krener paper cited under Section 5.2.

Bilinear approximation techniques are considered in

R. Brockett, Nonlinear systems and differential geometry, *Proc. IEEE* **64** (1976), 61–72.

For the realization algorithms for bilinear systems, see

P. d'Alessandro, A. Isidori, and A. Ruberti, Realization and structure theory of bilinear systems, *SIAM J. Control Optim.* **12** (1974), 517–535.

A. Isidori, Direct construction of minimal bilinear realizations from nonlinear input–output maps, *IEEE Trans. Automat. Control* **AC-18** (1973), 626–631.

E. Fornasini and G. Marchesini, Algebraic realization theory of bilinear discrete-time input–output maps, *J. Franklin Inst.* **301** (1976), 143–159.

The circumstances under which a Volterra series is finite is covered in

R. Brockett, Volterra series and geometric control theory, *Automatica* **12** (1976), 167–176.

P. Crouch, Finite Volterra series, *in* "Geometric Control Theory" (C. Martin and R. Hermann, eds.), Math. Sci. Press, Brookline, Massachusetts, 1977.

For polynomial systems, see the Sontag book and Porter article under Section 5.4.

Factorable Volterra systems, like the *almost linear* system of the text, are studied in

I. Harper and W. Rugh, Structural features of factorable Volterra systems, *IEEE Trans. Automat. Control* **AC-21** (1976), 822–832.

**Section 5.VI**    By far, the best single source for the current state of nonlinear filtering and estimation theory is

M. Hazelwinkel and J. Willems, eds., "Stochastic Systems: The Mathematics of Filtering and Identification and Applications," Reidel, Dordrecht, 1981.

See also the papers

S. A. Billings, Identification of nonlinear systems—A survey, *IEE Proc.* 127 (1980), 272–285.
S. Y. Fakhouri, Identification of the Volterra kernels of nonlinear systems, *IEE Proc.* **127** (1980), 296–304.

The example given the text is from the work

M. Hazewinkel, Chang-Huan Liu, and S. Marcus, Some examples of Lie algebraic structure in nonlinear estimation, *in* "Proceedings, Joint Auto. Control Conf.," San Francisco, 1980.

Of special interest is the paper

R. Brockett, Nonlinear systems and nonlinear estimation theory, *in* "Stochastic Systems: The Mathematics of Filtering and Identification and Application" (M. Hazenwinkel and J. Willems, eds.), Reidel, Dordrecht, 1981.

This paper presents a comprehensive view of the Lie algebraic approach to nonlinear filtering from a tutorial standpoint. See also the paper

M. Hazewinkel and S. Marcus, On Lie algebras and finite-dimensional filtering, *Stochastics*, in press.

# 6

# Stability Theory: Singularities, Bifurcations, and Catastrophes

## I. CONCEPTS OF STABILITY

Intuitively, the idea of an object being stable involves the notion of some property of the object being preserved, in some sense, in the face of external forces or perturbations acting upon the object. This basic idea takes on two quite different forms when translated into system-theoretic terms.

The first case arises if we consider the dynamical behavior of a *single* system. In this situation, we are usually concerned with whether the system will return to some normal mode of behavior (e.g., an equilibrium position) if the outside forces move the system state away from its normal position. Auxiliary issues surrounding the speed and manner in which the return to the normal position is achieved, the classes of disturbances for which the system returns to normal, and so on form the *bread-and-butter* issues comprising such stability studies. The general circle of mathematical questions arising in the study of stability of a single system is usually termed *Lyapunov stability*, in recognition of the pioneering work undertaken by Lyapunov in the last century to make these notions mathematically operational.

The second major class of stability questions comes up when we consider

190

*families* of systems, rather than just a single process. In such situations, our concern shifts to the foundational question of whether a particular property, such as hyperbolicity of orbits, is displayed by all (or, at least, almost all) members of the family. In this case, the perturbations consist of a movement from one member of the family to another, i.e., the passage from one system to another *nearby* system, and we are interested in what properties are preserved as we move through the family and, in particular, we are interested in those distinguished members of the family for which a property is *lost* (or acquired). Generally speaking, the loss of a property constitutes a *bifurcation* which, by virtue of the change in properties, implies a behavioral change. We shall make all of these notions precise in later sections, but for now let us consider a few illustrative examples of the foregoing ideas.

***Example 1***   Consider the *single* two-dimensional system

$$\dot{x}_1 = 2x_1[(1 - x_1^2 - x_2^2)/(x_1 + 1)^2 + x_2^2] + x_1 x_2,$$
$$\dot{x}_2 = \tfrac{1}{2}(1 - x_1^2 - x_2^2) - [4x_1^2 x_2/(x_1 + 1)^2 + x_2^2].$$

This system has an equilibrium at the point $x^* = (1, 0)$. We are interested in those initial states $x \neq x^*$, for which the system trajectory will be such that $x(t) \to x^*$, as $t \to \infty$. The collection of initial points $x(0)$ such that $\lim_{t \to \infty} x(t; x(0)) = x^*$ is called the *domain of attraction* of the state $x^*$. Using the methods outlined later in the chapter, it can be shown that the domain of attraction of the equilibrium $x^* = (1, 0)$ consists of the entire right half-plane, i.e., the boundary of the domain of attraction is the $x_2$ axis. Thus, any disturbance away from $x^*$ which does not force the system state across the $x_2$ axis will preserve the property of the asymptotic behavior of the system being a return to $x^*$. This example clearly illustrates the point that it is meaningless to speak of the stability of a system without specifying the class of disturbances. In this case, the system is stable relative to perturbations that do not force the state across the $x_2$ axis, but *unstable* relative to perturbations that do.

***Example 2***   Consider the equation for the damped harmonic oscillator

$$\ddot{x} + a\dot{x} + x = 0, \qquad a \geq 0,$$
$$x(0) = x_0 \neq 0, \qquad \dot{x}(0) = 0 \tag{$\Sigma_a$}$$

This is a *family* $\Sigma_a$ of systems parameterized by the damping factor $a$. Our concern will be with the preservation of the property of asymptotic stability of the origin as we pass from one member of the family to another by variation of the damping factor.

It is an easy exercise to show that the system trajectories are

$$x_a(t) = c_1(a)e^{\lambda_1(a)t} + c_2(a)e^{\lambda_2(a)t},$$

where

$$c_1(a) = \frac{-x_0\lambda_2(a)}{\lambda_1(a) - \lambda_2(a)}, \qquad c_2(a) = \frac{x_0\lambda_1(a)}{\lambda_1(a) - \lambda_2(a)},$$

$$\lambda_{1,2}(a) = \frac{-a \pm \sqrt{a^2 - 4}}{2}.$$

Here we have explicitly indicated the dependence of the trajectories upon the parameter $a$. It is now easy to verify that for all $0 < a \le 2$, the origin is a *stable node*; for $a > 2$, the origin is a *stable focus*. Thus, for all $a > 0$ the origin is an asymptotically stable equilibrium, i.e., the property of asymptotic stability of the origin is preserved for all movements in the family $\Sigma_a$ from $a \to \bar{a}$ if $a, \bar{a} > 0$. However, for $a = 0$ the origin ceases to be an asymptotically stable equilibrium and turns into a *neutrally stable center*. Thus, for any passage from a system $a > 0$ to the system $a = 0$, a *bifurcation* occurs in the sense that the property of interest, the asymptotic stability of the origin, is lost. In this situation we would say the system $a = 0$ is *structurally unstable* with respect to the continuous perturbation $a = 0 \to \bar{a} > 0$, and that the point $a = 0$ is a *bifurcation* point for the family $\Sigma_a$.

While there are many auxiliary notions associated with the general themes of Lyapunov and structural stability, Examples 1 and 2 illustrate in particularly transparent form the central issues involved. We now turn to a more detailed and technically precise consideration of these topics.

## II. LYAPUNOV STABILITY

Since the principal results surrounding Lyapunov stability have been extensively covered in the mathematical and engineering literature, we shall content ourselves with a presentation of only the most important and useful aspects of the theory. For the many refinements, extensions, and generalizations available, the reader is urged to consult the chapter notes and references.

We consider the system

$$\dot{x} = f(x, t), \qquad x(t_0) = x_0, \tag{$\Sigma$}$$

and assume the origin is an equilibrium for $\Sigma$, i.e., $f(0, t) = 0$. Let us further assume that $f$ is continuous in some neighborhood of the origin. Lyapunov's basic contribution was in the development of two methods to study the stability properties of $\Sigma$.

The first method of Lyapunov establishes a relationship between the properties of the zero solution of the linear system

$$\dot{z} = A(t)z \tag{6.1}$$

and the nonlinear system $\Sigma$ when $f(x, t) = A(t)x + g(x)$. In this situation, Lyapunov gave conditions on the function $g(\cdot)$ which ensure that the stability of the linear approximation to $\Sigma$ implies the stability of $\Sigma$.

Lyapunov's second, or direct, method is based on the idea that the rate of change of the energy of an autonomous system is an indicator of its stability characteristics. Through the introduction of generalized energy functions for $\Sigma$, termed *Lyapunov functions*, Lyapunov showed that the stability of the origin could be inferred from the properties of these energy functions. We now consider these two methods in greater detail.

**Definition 6.1** The equilibrium at the origin for the system $\Sigma$ is called *stable* in the sense of Lyapunov if for every $\epsilon > 0$, there exists a $\delta > 0$ such that $|x(t; x_0, t_0)| < \epsilon$ for all $t \geq t_0$ whenever $|x_0| < \delta(\epsilon)$. Geometrically, this definition means that if the system starts within a distance of $\delta$ from the origin, then the system trajectory always remains within some larger, but uniformly bounded, distance $\epsilon$ from the origin, and that $\delta$ depends upon the chosen bound $\epsilon$.

**Definition 6.2** The equilibrium of $\Sigma$ is *asymptotically stable* if it is stable and if $\lim_{t \to \infty} x(t; x_0, t_0) = 0$.

Our first results provides conditions under which stability of the linear approximation to $\Sigma$, Eq. (6.1), implies the stability of $\Sigma$. For simplicity, we consider only *autonomous* systems $\Sigma$, i.e., those for which $f(x, t)$ does not explicitly depend on $t$. In this case, without loss of generality we take $t_0 = 0$ in the linear system (6.1). Furthermore, we now have $f(x) = Ax + g(x)$, with $A$ a constant matrix (the linear part of $f$ at the origin).

The basic result relating the stability of $\Sigma$ to that of its linear approximation (6.1) is

**Theorem 6.1** *Assume that*

  (i) *$A$ is a stability matrix, i.e., the characteristic roots of $A$ all lie in the left half-plane;*
  (ii) *$\|g(x)\|/\|x\| \to 0$ as $\|x\| \to 0$, i.e., $g$ contains no constant or linear terms in the components of $x$;*
  (iii) *$\|x_0\|$ is sufficiently small;*
  (iv) *$f(\cdot)$ is continuous in some neighborhood of the origin. Then the origin is an asymptotically stable equilibrium for $\Sigma$.*

PROOF    From elementary matrix theory, we have that there exists a matrix
$T$ reducing $A$ to Jordan form

$$
J = T^{-1}AT = \begin{bmatrix} \lambda_1 & b_{12} & \cdots & b_{1n} \\ & \lambda_2 & & \\ & & \ddots & \\ 0 & & & \lambda_n \end{bmatrix},
$$

where $\lambda_i = i$th characteristic root of $A$, and $|b_{ij}| \leq \epsilon$, where $\epsilon$ is an arbitrary
number, $\epsilon > 0$.

Letting $z = Tx$ gives

$$
\frac{dx}{dt} = Jx + T^{-1}g(Tx) = Jx + \bar{g}(x).
$$

Here it is easy to see that $\bar{g}$ satisfies the same conditions as $g$.

Consider the quantity $\|x\|^2$. It is easy to verify that

$$
\frac{d}{dt}\|x\|^2 = 2(x, Jx) + 2(x, \bar{g}).
$$

Thus,

$$
\frac{1}{2}\frac{d}{dt}(\|x\|^2) \leq \mathrm{Re}\,\hat{\lambda}(J)\|x\|^2 + \epsilon\|x\|^2 + \|x\|\,\|\bar{g}\|,
$$

where $\hat{\lambda}(J)$ is the characteristic value of $J$ nearest the imaginary axis.

At $t = 0$, since $\mathrm{Re}\,\hat{\lambda}(J) < 0$ and $\|x(0)\|$ is sufficiently small, $\frac{1}{2}(d/dt)(\|x\|^2) < 0$.
Hence, $\|x\|^2$ is decreasing in a neighborhood of $t = 0$. By repeating this
argument, we obtain the inequality for all $t$,

$$
\|x\|^2 \leq \|x(0)\|^2 e^{-at}, \qquad a > 0.
$$

Thus, $x(t) \to 0$ as $t \to \infty$, completing the proof.

REMARK 1    The theorem gives no information on the global stability
properties of $\Sigma$.

REMARK 2    The theorem may be generalized to hold for nonautonomous
systems, i.e., when $A$ is time-varying, at the expense of imposing some sort
of uniformity condition on $A(t)$ (e.g., uniform boundedness, periodic, etc.).

REMARK 3    Under more restrictive hypotheses on $g$, the theorem can be
extended to show that if $A$ has $k < n$ characteristic values in the left half-
plane, then there is a $k$-parameter family of solutions of $\Sigma$ which approach
zero as $t \to \infty$.

Basically, Theorem 6.1 tells us that in the neighborhood of an equilibrium,
the stability properties of $\Sigma$ and the stability properties of the linear approxi-

mation to $\Sigma$ are identical, provided that certain conditions are imposed upon the linear part $A$, the nonlinearities $g$ and the distance from the origin. In actual point of fact, a much stronger result is true. Namely, that locally the trajectories of $\Sigma$ and those of its linear approximation are topologically equivalent as long as the linear part $A$ has no characteristic values on the imaginary axis. This result, called Hartman's theorem, we now state without proof for future reference.

**Theorem 6.2** (Hartman)   *Let the origin be a hyperbolic equilibrium for $\Sigma$, i.e , Re $\lambda_i(A) \neq 0$, $i = 1, \ldots, n$. Then there exists a neighborhood $U$ of $0$, such that the trajectories of $\Sigma$ and those of its linear approximation* (6.1) *are homeomorphic in $U$.*

As a consequence of Theorems 6.1 and 6.2, we can often employ linear analysis in the investigation of the local behavior of $\Sigma$ near an equilibrium point. However, many important cases fall outside the bounds of these theorems and their extensions, either because the local neighborhood of validity $U$ is too small, or because the requisite conditions on $A$ cannot be met. In such situations more powerful methods must be invoked. One such approach is to employ the so-called second, or *direct*, method of Lyapunov, which enables us to study the stability properties of $\Sigma$ (often globally) by analyzing the properties of an auxiliary energy function associated with $\Sigma$.

**Definition 6.3**   A scalar function $V(x, t)$ possessing the following properties is termed a *Lyapunov function* for the nonlinear system $\Sigma$:

(i)   $V(x, t)$ has continuous first-partial derivatives in $x$ and $t$ and is such that $V(0, t) = 0$;

(ii)   $V(x, t)$ is positive-definite, i.e., there exists a continuous, nondecreasing scalar function $h$ such that $h(0) = 0$ and for all $t$ and all $x \neq 0$,

$$0 < h(\|x\|) \leq V(x, t),$$

and $h(\|x\|) \to \infty$ as $\|x\| \to \infty$;

(iii)   there exists a continuous scalar function $g$ such that $g(0) = 0$ and the derivative $\dot{V}$ along the trajectory of $\Sigma$ satisfies

$$\frac{dV}{dt} \leq -g(\|x\|) < 0;$$

(iv)   there exists a continuous, nondecreasing scalar function $f$ such that $f(0) = 0$ and for all $t$,

$$V(x, t) \leq f(\|x\|).$$

The foregoing properties of $V$ generalize the ordinary concept of *total energy* associated with the system $\Sigma$. The following theorem of Lyapunov shows that the existence of such a function $V$ is necessary and sufficient for uniform, global asymptotic stability of the origin.

**Theorem 6.3**  *The origin is a uniform, globally asymptotically stable equilibrium for $\Sigma$ if and only if $\Sigma$ admits a Lyapunov function $V$.*

PROOF   See notes and references, especially the books by LaSalle and Lefschetz and Hahn.

An important special case of Theorem 6.3 is when $\Sigma$ is linear, i.e., $f(x) = Fx$. We then have

**Corollary 6.1**  *The origin is an asymptotically stable equilibrium for $\dot{x} = Fx$ if and only if for any matrix $Q > 0$, there exists a matrix $P > 0$ solving the Lyapunov matrix equation*

$$F'P + PF = -Q.$$

*In this case, the function $V(x) = (x, Px)$ is a Lyapunov function for the system.*

The difficulty in applying Lyapunov's second method is that the main theorem is not constructive, i.e., it provides no clear-cut systematic procedure for finding a suitable function $V(x, t)$. However, there are cases where by imposing structural assumptions on the system dynamics $f(x)$, an appropriate function $V(x, t)$ can be generated. Corollary 6.1 shows how to do this in the linear case $f(x) = Fx$. The following result, due to Krasovskii, shows how to do it for a broad class of interesting nonlinear systems.

**Theorem 6.4**   *Let $\dot{x} = f(x)$, with $f(0) = 0$, $f \in C^1$. Further, assume the Jacobian matrix $J(x) = (\partial f_i/\partial x_j)$ satisfies*

$$J(x) + J'(x) \leq -\epsilon I < 0,$$

*$\epsilon > 0$ arbitrary. Then the origin is asymptotically stable in the large and $V(x) = \|f(x)\|^2$ is a Lyapunov function.*

PROOF   Let $V(x) = \|f(x)\|^2$. Then

$$\frac{dV}{dt} = (x, \text{grad } V)$$

$$= 2 \sum_{j=1}^{n} \dot{x}_j \sum_{i=1}^{n} f_i(x) \frac{\partial f_i}{\partial x_j}(x)$$

$$= 2(f(x), J(x)\dot{x})$$

$$= (f(x), J(x)f(x))$$

$$\leq -\epsilon\|x\|^2 < 0.$$

Hence, $dV/dt$ is negative definite.

Let $c$ be a constant nonzero vector. The set $\{\alpha c : 0 \leq \alpha \leq 1\}$ is a straight line connecting the origin to $c$. Integrating along this ray

$$f_i(c) = \sum_{j=1}^{n} \left[ \int_0^1 c_j \frac{\partial f_i(\alpha c)}{\partial x_j} \, d\alpha \right].$$

Suppose $f(c) = 0$ for some $c \neq 0$. Then

$$0 = (c, f(c)) = \sum_{i=1}^{n} c_i f_i(c)$$

$$= \int_0^1 \left[ \sum_{i,j=1}^{n} c_i \frac{\partial f_i(\alpha c)}{\partial x_j} c_j \right] d\alpha$$

$$\leq -\epsilon \|c\|^2 / 2 < 0$$

which is a contradiction. Hence, $V$ is positive-definite. This argument also shows that $(x, f(\alpha x)) \to -\infty$ with $\alpha \to \infty$, for any $x \neq 0$. But this can happen only if at least one component of $f(x) \to \pm\infty$ as $\|x\| \to \infty$, completing the proof.

Theorems 6.3 and 6.4 have provided *global* asymptotic stability results, while the more general Theorem 6.1 was local. Use of Lyapunov functions, in addition to settling issues of asymptotic stability, also provide us with a tool for answering the question, "how local is local?" Probably the most complete results in this direction are contained in the work of V. Zubov. The essence of his procedure is contained in the following theorem.

**Theorem 6.5** *In order that the region $A \subset R^n$, containing the origin, be the domain of attraction for the system $\Sigma$, it is necessary and sufficient that there exist functions $V(x)$ and $\phi(x)$ such that*

(i)  *$V(x)$ is continuous in $A$ while $\phi(x)$ is continuous on $R^n$;*
(ii)  *$-1 < V(x) < 0$ for $x \in A$, $\phi(x) > 0$ for $x \in R^n$, $|x| \neq 0$;*
(iii)  *for any $\gamma_2 > 0$, there exists a $\gamma_1$ and $\alpha_1$ such that $V(x) < -\gamma_1$ for $|x| \geq \gamma_2$, $\phi(|x|) > \alpha_1$ for $|x| \geq \gamma_2$;*
(iv)  *$V(x)$ and $\phi(x) \to 0$ as $|x| \to 0$;*
(v)  *if $y \in \partial A$, $y \neq 0$, then $\lim_{x \to y} V(x) = -1$, while if $|x| \to +\infty$, $x \in A$, then $V(x) \to -1$;*
(vi)  *$dV/dt = \phi(x)(1 + V(x))[1 + \sum_{i=1}^{n} f_i^2]^{1/2}$.*

REMARK    The conditions of the theorem make $V(x)$ a Lyapunov function for the system $\Sigma$.

An important corollary for continuously differentiable $f$ is

**Corollary 6.2**  *If the origin is asymptotically stable, then the equation*

$$\sum_{i=1}^{n} \frac{\partial V(x)}{\partial x_i} f_i(x) = \phi(x)(1 + V(x)) \left[ 1 + \sum_{i=1}^{n} f_i^2 \right]^{1/2} \tag{6.2}$$

*has a unique $C^1$ solution defined by the condition $V(0) = 0$, for all $x \in A$. Furthermore, this solution satisfies all the conditions of Theorem 6.5 for any $\phi$ such that $\int_0^\infty \phi(x)dt < \infty$, for $|x_0|$ sufficiently small.*

**Example**  Let $\dot{x}_1 = -x_1 + 2x_1^2 x_2$, $\dot{x}_2 = -x_2$. Equation (6.2) for $V$ is

$$\frac{\partial V}{\partial x_1}(2x_1^2 x_2 - x_1) + \frac{\partial V}{\partial x_2}(-x_2) = (x_1^2 + x_2^2)(1 + V), \qquad (6.3)$$

obtained by the choice $\phi(x_1, x_2) = (x_1^2 + x_2^2)/(1 + \sum_{i=1}^2 f_i^2)^{1/2}$. It is easy to see that for $V(0) = 0$, Eq. (6.3) has the solution

$$V(x_1, x_2) = \exp\left[-x_2^2/2 - \frac{x_1^2}{2(1 - x_1 x_2)}\right] - 1.$$

From this it follows that the boundary of the region $A$ of asymptotic stability of the origin is the curve $x_1 x_2 = 1$.

Under the additional hypotheses that $f(x)$ is analytic, the procedure for finding the domain of attraction of the origin can be substantially improved. Let us assume that $f(x)$ is analytic and that the linear approximation to $\Sigma$ is stable, i.e., Re $\lambda_i(a) < 0$.

Under the foregoing assumptions, it is not hard to show that Eq. (6.2) has a solution of the form

$$V(x) = v_2(x) + v_3(x) + \cdots + v_m(x) + \cdots, \qquad (6.4)$$

where $v_m(x)$ is a homogeneous form of degree $m$ in $x$. If the system $\Sigma$ is analytic, then

$$f_s(x_1, x_2, \ldots, x_n) = \sum_{i=1}^n a_{si} x_i + \sum_{\Sigma m_i > 1} p_s(m_1, \ldots, m_n)x_1^{m_1}, \ldots, x_n^{m_n}.$$

Substituting this representation into Eq. (6.2), we obtain

$$\sum_{i=1}^n \left(\frac{\partial v_2}{\partial x_i}\right) \sum_{k=1}^n a_{ik} x_k = \phi(x_1, \ldots, x_n),$$

$$\sum_{i=1}^n \left(\frac{v_m}{x_i}\right) \sum_{k=1}^n a_{ik} x_k = R_m(x_1, \ldots, x_n), \qquad m = 3, 4, \ldots,$$

where $R_m$ is a *known* form of degree $m$, determined by knowledge of the forms $v_2, v_3, \ldots, v_{m-1}$.

The following properties of the series (6.4) have been established by Zubov:

1. $v_2(x)$ is negative definite;
2. the series converges in a neighborhood of the origin;

3. the function $V(x)$ defined by the series (6.4) may be analytically continued along any ray emanating from the origin and terminating on $\partial A$.

REMARK    The choice of $\phi$ influences the region of convergence for the series (6.4)

Zubov's approach to finding the domain of attraction of the origin is based upon using finite segments of the series (6.4) to successively approximat $A$. Consider the family of hypersurfaces $v_2(x) = -\mu$, $0 < \mu < \infty$. Let $\partial A$ be the true stability boundary. Then there exists some value $\bar{\mu}$ such that the surface $v_2(x) = -\bar{\mu}$ will be tangent to some point of $\partial A$. Thus, since the family $v_2(x) = -\mu$ fills up $R^n$, we let $\bar{\mu}$ be the largest such value of $\mu$. However, since $\partial A$ is unknown we proceed as follows. Let

$$W(x) = \frac{dv_2}{dt} = \sum_{i=1}^{n} \frac{\partial v_2}{\partial x_i} f_i(x)$$

and let $W_0 = \{x: W(x) = 0\}$. Now let

$$-\mu_0 = \max_x \{v_2(x): W(x) = 0\}.$$

Then we can show that the hypersurface $v_2(x) = -\mu_0$ is entirely contained in $A$.

The general algorithm based upon the foregoing idea is as follows:

1. Consider the hypersurface $S_n(x) = -\mu$, where $S_n(x) = v_2(x) + \cdots + v_n(x)$. Define

$$W_n(x) = \frac{dS_n}{dt}, \qquad W_{0n}(x) = \{x: W_n(x) = 0\}.$$

2. Let $-\mu_{0n} = \max_x \{S_n(x): x \in W_{0n}\}$.
3. The hypersurface $S_n = -\mu_{0n}$ will be entirely contained in $A$. Further, as $n \to \infty$, the regions $S_n = -\mu_{0n} \to A$.

Before leaving the topic of Lyapunov stability, we note that the basic results we presented are capable of an almost infinite variety of extensions, modifications, and generalizations. In regard to the question of using the linear approximation as a tool for studying $\Sigma$, a very elegant procedure due to V. M. Popov, called the circle criterion, has been used. This method involves using the properties of the transfer function for the linear part of $\Sigma$, together with some sector conditions on the nonlinear part to conclude asymptotic stability through use of a cleverly constructed Lyapunov function.

In another direction, work by Evans *et al.* based on Helmholtz's theorem involving the decomposition of vector fields into scalar and irrotational parts has provided a fresh look at the question of how to determine the region of stability $A$.

Finally, we note the important work of Sandberg, Zames, and others on the use of functional-analytic methods for studying the stability of systems governed by functional-differential equations. Some of these ideas are developed later in this chapter and in the Problems at the end of the chapter, while the remainder can be found in the chapter Notes and References.

### III. THE CENTER MANIFOLD THEOREM

In Section II, Hartman's theorem has shown that the linear part of $\Sigma$ determines the qualitative behavior of the system trajectories locally provided $\mathrm{Re}\,\lambda_i(A) \neq 0$. In other words, if the linear part of $\Sigma$ has no characteristic values lying on the imaginary axis, then in a neighborhood of the origin $\Sigma$ behaves as if it were a linear system. This result suggests that any essentially nonlinear behavior of $\Sigma$ (multiple equilibria, limit cycles, hysteresis effects, etc.) are strongly connected with the roots of $A$ lying on the imaginary axis. In this section we shall justify this conjecture, at least insofar as the stability properties of $\Sigma$ are concerned. The basic tool we employ is a generalization of the idea of decoupling systems of equations, termed the center manifold theorem.

To fix ideas, suppose we write $\Sigma$ in the form

$$\dot{z} = Nz + p(z, v),$$
$$\dot{v} = Mv + q(z, v), \tag{$\Sigma$}$$

where $z \in R^j$, $v \in R^m$, $j + m = n$, with $N$ and $M$ constant matrices such that $\mathrm{Re}\,\lambda_i(N) = 0$, $i = 1, 2, \ldots, j$. Further, assume $\mathrm{Re}\,\lambda_i(M) < 0$ and that $p$ and $q$ are smooth functions with $p(0,0) = q(0,0) = p'(0,0) = q'(0,0) = 0$, with $'$ denoting the Jacobian matrix.

If $p$ and $q$ are identically zero, then $\Sigma$ has two invariant manifolds, $z = 0$, $v = 0$. The manifold $v = 0$ is called the *stable* manifold since if we restrict the initial conditions $(z_0, v_0)$ to $z_0 = 0$, all solutions of $\Sigma$ tend to zero. The manifold $z = 0$ is called the *center* manifold. In general, if $v = h(z)$ is an invariant manifold for $\Sigma$ and $h$ is smooth, then $h$ is called a *center manifold* if $h(0) = h'(0) = 0$.

In the linear case when $p = q = 0$, all solutions of $\Sigma$ tend exponentially fast to solutions of $\dot{z} = Nz$. That is, the equation on the center manifold determines the asymptotic behavior of the entire system up to exponentially decaying terms. The center manifold theorem justifies extending this conclusion to the nonlinear case when $p$ and $q$ are nonzero.

The center manifold theorem consists of three parts:

(i)   a nonconstructive proof of the existence of $h$;

(ii)   a proof that the behavior on the center manifold determines the entire behavior of $\Sigma$;

(iii)   a construction enabling us to approximate the center manifold $h$ to any desired degree of accuracy. Since the proofs of these assertions are long, complicated, and readily available, we state only the final result.

**Theorem 6.6**   (Center Manifold Theorem)   1. *There exists a center manifold $v = h(z)$ for $\Sigma$ for $|z|$ sufficiently small. The behavior of $\Sigma$ on the center manifold is governed by the equation*

$$\dot{u} = Nu + p(u, h(u)); \tag{6.5}$$

2. *Suppose the origin is a stable (asymptotically stable, unstable) equilibrium for (6.5). Then the origin is also a stable (asymptotically stable, unstable) equilibrium for $\Sigma$. Furthermore, suppose the origin is stable for (6.5). Let $z, v$ be a solution of $\Sigma$ with $|z(0)|, |v(0)|$ sufficiently small. Then there exists a solution $u(t)$ of (6.5) such that*

$$z(t) = u(t) + O(e^{-\gamma t}),$$

$$v(t) = h(u(t)) + O(e^{-\gamma t}),$$

*as $t \to \infty$ for some $\gamma > 0$.*

3. *Let $\phi: R^j \to R^m$ be a $C^1$ function and let the operation $[K\phi](w)$ be defined as*

$$[K\phi](w) \doteq \phi'(w)\{Nw + p(w, \phi(w))\} - M\phi(w) - q(w, \phi(w)).$$

*Suppose $\phi(0) = \phi'(0) = 0$ and that as $w \to 0$, $[K\phi](w) = O(|w|^r)$ for some $r > 1$. Then as $w \to 0$, $|h(w) - \phi(w)| = O(|w|^r)$.*

Now let us consider the implications of this result:

1.   Existence of the center manifold $h$ means that there exists a transformation of the $z$ coordinates which enables us to express the $v$ coordinates solely in terms of the $z$ variables *locally*. Thus, we can locally replace the $v$ variables in the equation for $\dot{z}$, thereby decoupling the $z$ and $v$ equations.

2.   The second part of the theorem tells us that all the information needed to determine the asymptotic behavior of $\Sigma$ near the origin is contained in Eq. (6.5).

3.   If we substitute $v = h(z)$ into the second equation of $\Sigma$, we obtain

$$h'(z)\{Nz + p(z, h(z))\} = Mh(z) + q(z, h(z)).$$

This equation, together with the conditions $h(0) = h'(0) = 0$ determines $h$, *theoretically*. However, in general it is at least as difficult to solve as the original problem. The last part of the theorem tells us that we can approximate $h$ to terms $O(|z|^r)$ by letting $h(z) = \phi(z)$.

The best way to see the various implications of the center manifold theorem is by example. Consider the system

$$\dot{z} = zv + az^3 + bv^2 z,$$

$$\dot{v} = -v + cz^2 + dz^2 v,$$

$a, b, c, d$ constants.

By part 1 of the theorem, this system has a center manifold $v = h(z)$. To approximate $h$, set

$$[K\phi](z) = \phi'(z)[z\phi(z) + az^3 + bz\phi^2(z)] + \phi(z) - cz^2 - dz^2\phi(z).$$

For any function $\phi(z)$ such that $\phi(z) = O(|z|^2)$, $[K\phi](z) = \phi(z) - cz^2 + O(|z|^4)$. Thus, if we take $\phi(z) = cz^2$, then $[K\phi](z) = O(|z|^4)$ which, by part 3, gives $h(z) = cz^2 + O(|z|^4)$.

By part 2, the equation determining the stability of $\Sigma$ is

$$\dot{u} = uh(u) + au^3 + buh^2(u) = (a + c)u^3 + O(|u|^5).$$

Thus, the origin is stable if $(a + c) < 0$ and unstable if $(a + c) > 0$. If $(a + c) = 0$, then we have to obtain a better approximation of $h(z)$.

Suppose $a + c = 0$. Now let $\phi(z) = cz^2 + \psi(z)$, where $\psi(z) = O(|z|^4)$. Then

$$[K\phi](z) = \psi(z) - cdz^4 + O(|z|^6).$$

Thus, if $\phi(z) = cz^2 + cdz^4$, $[K\phi](z) = O(|z|^6)$ and, by part 3 of the theorem, $h(z) = cz^2 + cdz^4 + O(|z|^6)$. The equation governing the stability of $\Sigma$ is now

$$\dot{u} = uh(u) + au^3 + buh^2(u) = (cd + bc^2)u^5 + O(|u|^7).$$

Hence, if $a + c = 0$, the origin is stable if $cd + bc^2 < 0$ and unstable if $cd + bc^2 > 0$. Again, if $cd + bc^2 = 0$, we must then obtain a better approximation to $h$.

It is important to emphasize here again what the center manifold theorem has accomplished. By defining the new variables $v = h(z) \cong \phi(z)$, the asymptotic behavior of $\Sigma$ is reduced to the study of the asymptotic behavior of the much lower dimensional system of Eq. (6.5) in the variables $u$. Thus, the nonlinear coordinate change, $z \to h(z)$ decouples the system $\Sigma$ in such a way that the asymptotic behavior is determined only by the behavior of $\Sigma$ on the center manifold $v = h(z)$. We might then think of the center manifold theorem as a nonlinear and dynamical extension of the familiar matrix diagonalization procedure used to decouple a set of linear algebraic equations. We shall return to this theme in a nondynamical (equilibrium) setting in a later section.

## IV. FAMILIES OF VECTOR FIELDS AND NORMAL FORMS

We consider a parameterized family of vector fields generating the system

$$\dot{z} = F(z, \mu), \qquad\qquad (\Sigma)$$

where $F(0, \mu) = 0$, $z \in R^{n+m}$ and $\mu \in R^p$. Suppose that the linearized version of $\Sigma$ is

$$\dot{z} = A(\mu)z.$$

If the characteristic values of $A(0)$ all have nonzero real parts, then for $|\mu|$ small, solutions of $\Sigma$ locally behave like solutions of the linear approximation. Thus, the only possibility for $\Sigma$ to exhibit behavior that qualitatively differs from its linearization is for $\mathrm{Re}\ \lambda(A(0)) = 0$. In this case, the value $\mu = 0$ is called a *bifurcation point* for the system $\Sigma$.

Suppose $A(0)$ has $n$ purely imaginary roots and $m$ roots in the left half-plane (i.e., we consider bifurcation from stable behavior). We can rewrite $\Sigma$ as

$$\dot{x} = Fx + f(x, y, \mu),$$

$$\dot{y} = Gx + g(x, y, \mu), \qquad\qquad (\Sigma)$$

$$\dot{\mu} = 0,$$

where $f, g, f', g'$ vanish at $(x, y, \mu) = (0, 0, 0)$.

By the center manifold theorem, $\Sigma$ has a center manifold $y = h(x, \mu)$, for $|x|, |\mu|$ small. In addition, the behavior of small solutions of $\Sigma$ is governed by the equation

$$\dot{u} = Fu + f(u, h(u, \mu), \mu),$$

$$\dot{\mu} = 0,$$

where $u \in R^n$. Generally, $n = 1$ or $2$ so the reduction in dimensionality in studying the $u$-equation on the center manifold is substantial over studying $\Sigma$ on $R^{n+m}$. We wish to study the types of behavior that can emerge as $\mu$ passes through the bifurcation value $\mu = 0$. To carry out this investigation, it is useful to consider the reduction of $\Sigma$ to so-called *normal form*.

The problem of reducing $\Sigma$ to normal form revolves about the question of whether there exists a nonlinear change of coordinates (analytic or smooth) near a singularity of the vector field $f(x)$ such that the vector field is linear in the new coordinates. Necessary conditions for being able to solve this linearization problem come from solving for the Taylor coefficients at the singularity of the diffeomorphism defining the new coordinates. A recursive set of equations involving linear combinations of the characteristic values of the linear part of $f(0)$ are obtained. If a solution to this system is to exist, all of these linear combinations of characteristic values must be nonzero. If any one of these coefficients is zero, then the corresponding nonlinear term in the Taylor series of the vector field cannot be eliminated by a smooth co-ordinate change. In bifurcation theory, we are interested in the cases in which there are zero or purely imaginary characteristic values, and the linearization problem is definitely not solvable. We sketch the mathematics underlying this result.

Consider the family $U$ of all smooth vector fields $f(x)$ on a smooth mani-fold $M$. Under the Lie bracket operation, this family forms an infinite-dimensional Lie algebra £. Next, let $D$, the group of diffeomorphisms, act on £ through the Lie bracket action

$$g_* f(g^{-1}x) \doteq (ad_g f)(x), \qquad f \in U, \quad g \in D.$$

The problem of normal forms involves the orbits of the action of the group $D$ on $U$.

Suppose that in a fixed coordinate system near 0, the vector field $f$ has the local form

$$f(x) = Ax + \cdots,$$

while the diffeomorphism $g$ leaves $x = 0$ fixed and has the identity as its linear part at 0. Thus, the Taylor expansion of $g$ in the same coordinates near 0 has the form

$$g = I + h_2 + h_3 + \cdots = I + h,$$

where $h_i$ is a homogeneous polynomial in $x$ of degree $i$.

A simple calculation immediately leads to the expression

$$ad_{I+h}f = f + ad_h f + O(h^2),$$

where $ad_h f = [h, f]$ is the usual Lie bracket operation on $U$.

Now we investigate the orbit of the linear vector field $f(x) = Ax$. Thus, we want to study the conditions under which the following equation in $h$ is solvable

$$ad_{I+h}f = f + w,$$

where $f = Ax$ and $w$ is a nonlinear perturbation. By our earlier calculation, this means we must study the equation

$$ad_h f = w.$$

Since the operation $ad_h(\cdot)$ is linear, let us express this equation as

$$L_f(h) = w,$$

where $L_f$ is the operation of bracketing with the linear field $f = Ax$.

It is an easy exercise to verify that the linear operator $L_f$, acting on the space of vector fields with zero linear part into itself, leaves invariant the space of homogeneous polynomials of any degree when $f$ is linear. Thus, suppose for simplicity that our operator $A$ is diagonal, i.e., $A = \Lambda = \text{diag}(\lambda_1, \ldots, \lambda_n)$. Let the characteristic vector associated with $\lambda_i$ be denoted by $v_i$.

The following result of Poincaré describes this situation.

***Theorem 6.7*** *If the operator $\Lambda$ of the field $f(x) = \Lambda x$ is diagonal, then the operator $L_f$ of bracketing with $f$ is also diagonal. The characteristic vectors of $L_f$ are vector monomials $u^l v_i$ (where $u^l = u_1^{l_1} \cdots u_n^{l_n}$, with $u$ being the coordinates in the basis $\{x_i\}$). The characteristic values of $L_f$ are linear functions of the characteristic values of $\Lambda$ given by*

$$-L_f u^l v_i = [\lambda_i - (l, \lambda)] u^l v_i,$$

$$|l| = l_1 + \cdots + l_n \geq 2.$$

REMARK  If $\Lambda$ is not diagonal, then $L_f$ has Jordan blocks but the characteristic values are still given by the same formula.

Clearly, if the numbers $\alpha_i = [\lambda_i - (l, \lambda)] \neq 0$, then $L_f$ is invertible and our basic equation

$$L_f(h) = w$$

is uniquely solvable for $h$. In this case, we say there is no *resonance* between the values $\{\lambda_i\}$ and the field $f$ is *resonance-free*. Thus, any system $\Sigma$ whose linear part at 0 is resonance-free can be linearized to within terms of arbitrarily high degree by a polynomial change of variables obtained by truncating $h$ at a sufficiently long segment. By formally *inverting* $L_f$, we can also *completely* linearize the formal series $f(x) = \Lambda x + \cdots$ at the origin.

It is instructive to examine in more detail the explicit calculation of the elements $h_i$ in the formal series for $h$. Let $f(x) = f_1 + f_2 + \cdots$, where $f_1(x) = \Lambda x$. To linearize $f_1 + f_2$, set $h_2 = L_{f_1}^{-1} f_2$. To linearize $f_1 + f_2 + \cdots + f_{k+1}$, first linearize $f_1 + f_2 + \cdots + f_k$, i.e., find coordinates such that $f_1 + \cdots + f_{k+1}$ has the form $f_1 + w_{k+1}$. Then set $h_{k+1} = L_{f_1}^{-1} w_{k+1}$. Then the diffeomorphism $I + h_{k+1}$ takes $f_1$ into $f_1 + w_{k+1}$, and the inverse diffeomorphism linearizes $f_1 + w_{k+1}$.

In the case when some $\alpha_i = 0$, we cannot get rid of all the nonlinear terms in the Taylor expansion of $f$, but only those for which the characteristic values of $L_f$ are nonzero. As a result, instead of a linear normal form we can bring $\Sigma$ to the form

$$\dot{x}_i = x_i \Sigma c_{ik} x^k,$$

where $k$ ranges over all integer vectors satisfying $(\lambda, k) = 0$. Thus, the coefficients $c_{ik}$ are nonzero if $k_i \geq -1$, $k_j \geq 0$ $(i \neq j)$, $\Sigma k_m \geq 1$. Of course, such a reduction is possible if there are only a *finite* number of integer vectors $k$ satisfying the relation $(\lambda, k) = 0$. This observation leads to

**Definition 6.4**  A vector $\lambda$ of characteristic values belongs to the *Poincaré domain* if the convex hull of the points $(\lambda_1, \lambda_2, \ldots, \lambda_n)$ in the complex plane does not contain the origin. Otherwise, $\lambda$ belongs to the *Siegel domain*.

The importance of these two domains is expressed in the following result.

**Theorem 6.8**  *Let $A$ be the operator of the linear part of $f(x)$ at $0$. Let the characteristic values of $A$ belong to the Poincaré domain. Then $f(x)$ is smoothly equivalent to a polynomial vector field in which all the vector-valued monomials of degree greater than 1 are resonant.*

REMARK 1    If $\lambda$ belongs to the Siegel domain it may or may not be possible to smoothly reduce $f$ to linear, or even polynomial, form. For instance, the series leading to the normal form is divergent for even the simple system $\dot{x}_1 = x_1^2, \dot{x}_2 = -x_1 + x_2$.

REMARK 2    From the standpoint of *topological*, rather than smooth reductions, the above results are rather trivial if $f(x)$ is a real vector field. The Poincaré case can be encountered only when $\lambda$ lies in either the right or left half-plane, in which case $\Sigma$ is topologically equivalent to either $\dot{x} = x$ or $\dot{x} = -x$.

On the other hand, if there are no roots of $A$ on the imaginary axis, then Hartman's theorem implies that $\Sigma$ is topologically equivalent to a standard saddle. We shall take up the case of roots of $A$ on the imaginary axis in the next section.

## V.  ELEMENTARY BIFURCATIONS

We now return to the study of the family of vector fields, parameterized by a scalar $\mu$,

$$\dot{x} = f(x, \mu), \qquad x \in R^n, \quad \mu \subset R^1, \tag{$\Sigma$}$$

and consider the simplest way in which the equilibrium at the origin can fail to be hyperbolic, i.e., the simplest way in which the characteristic values of the linear part of $\Sigma$, $A(\mu)$, can cross the imaginary axis with variation in $\mu$. Those values of $\mu$ at which a root of $A(\mu)$ cross the imaginary axis are the bifurcation values of $\Sigma$. For each of the ways in which such a passage can occur, we shall embed the corresponding vector field in a one-parameter family of vector fields which *unfolds* the degeneracy. These one-parameter families have the property that when they are perturbed there will still be a parameter value at which a bifurcation occurs and this bifurcation is qualitatively similar to the original one.

The first case to consider is when $A(\mu)$ has the simple characteristic value zero at some value $\mu = \mu_0$, with no purely imaginary roots. To ensure that this happens in the simplest possible way, we must place conditions on the quadratic part of the Taylor series for $f(x, \mu_0)$. Basically, we require that the quadratic part of $f$ be nonzero in the direction of the degeneracy in $A(\mu_0)$. Under these assumptions, we have a so-called *saddle-node* bifurcation.

To understand the bifurcation behavior of the saddle node, we first note that by the center manifold theorem it suffices to consider a *scalar* family of vector fields. Furthermore, a normal form for such a family is given by

$$\dot{u} = \pm u^2 + \mu, \qquad u \in R^1, \quad \mu \in R^1.$$

As $\mu$ passes through the critical value $\mu = 0$, what happens depends on the sign: either two singular points (one stable and one unstable) annihilate one another ($\mu > 0$), or a pair of singular points is born ($\mu < 0$) and they immediately move apart (asymptotically to $\sqrt{|\mu|}$).

The only other way a single characteristic value of $A(\mu)$ can cross the imaginary axis is for a complex conjugate pair to go across the axis. This case leads to the so-called *Hopf bifurcation*.

Using the center manifold theorem, we can reduce the study of this case to a two-dimensional system. Furthermore, the coordinates in this system can be chosen so that the linear part of the dynamics is an infinitesimal rotation. Thus, we study the two-dimensional system

$$\dot{u}_1 = -\theta u_2 + \text{nonlinear terms},$$

$$\dot{u}_2 = \theta u_1 + \text{nonlinear terms}.$$

By using the theory of normal forms, we can find smooth coordinate transformations that will eliminate some of the nonlinear terms. Let us carry out the explicit details for the quadratic terms.

Consider the quadratic equations

$$\dot{x}_1 = -\theta x_2 + P_1(x_1, x_2),$$

$$\dot{x}_2 = \theta x_1 + P_2(x_1, x_2),$$

where $P_1$, $P_2$ are homogeneous quadratic polynomials. Introduce the new coordinates

$$y_1 = x_1 + Q_1(x_1, \ x_2),$$

$$y_2 = x_2 + Q_2(x_1, \ x_2),$$

with $Q_1$ and $Q_2$ quadratic. Then

$$\dot{y}_i = \dot{x}_i + \frac{\partial Q_i}{\partial x_1}\dot{x}_1 + \frac{\partial Q_i}{\partial x_2}\dot{x}_2$$

$$= \theta\left[(-1)^j x_j - \frac{\partial Q_i}{\partial x_1}x_2 + \frac{\partial Q_i}{\partial x_2}x_1\right] + P_i + \text{higher terms}$$

$$= \theta\left[(-1)^j y_j + (-1)^j Q_j - \frac{\partial Q_i}{\partial x_1}y_2 + \frac{\partial Q_i}{\partial x_2}y_1\right] + P_i + \text{higher terms}.$$

Here $i \neq j$, $i, j = 1, 2$. We calculate the quadratic terms in parentheses. If $Q_i(x_1, x_2) = \alpha_{i1}x_1^2 + \alpha_{i2}x_1 x_2 + \alpha_{i3}x_2^2$, then

$$Q_2 - \frac{\partial Q_1}{\partial x_1}x_2 + \frac{\partial Q_1}{\partial x_2}x_1$$

$$= (\alpha_{12} + \alpha_{21})x_1^2 + (-2\alpha_{11} + 2\alpha_{13} + \alpha_{22})x_1 x_2 + (-\alpha_{12} + \alpha_{23})x_2^2,$$

$$-Q_1 - \frac{\partial Q_2}{\partial x_1}x_2 + \frac{\partial Q_2}{\partial x_2}x_1$$

$$= (-\alpha_{11} + \alpha_{22})x_1^2 + (-\alpha_{12} - 2\alpha_{21} + 2\alpha_{23})x_1 x_2 + (-\alpha_{13} - \alpha_{22})x_2^2.$$

It requires only a bit of linear algebra to see that we can always choose $Q_1$ and $Q_2$ so that $P_i + [(-1)^j Q_j - (\partial Q_i/\partial x_1)x_2 + (\partial Q_i/\partial x_2)x_1)] = 0$. This calculation is the coordinate form of the Lie algebraic discussion given in Section IV.

As a result of the preceding calculations, we can always find coordinate transformations for which our system has the form

$$\dot{u}_1 = -u_2 + (au_1 - bu_2)(u_1^2 + u_2^2) + O(|u|^4),$$

$$\dot{u}_2 = u_1 + (au_1 + bu_2)(u_1^2 + u_2^2) + O(|u|^4),$$

In polar coordinates, this system takes the simpler form

$$\dot{r} = ar^3 + \text{higher terms},$$

$$\dot{\psi} = \theta + br^2 + \text{higher terms}.$$

The conditions we must impose so that the Hopf bifurcation occurs in the simplest possible fashion are, first of all, the coefficient $a \neq 0$. If $a > 0$, then the origin is a repellor; if $a < 0$, the origin is an attractor. The second condition is that we embed our system into a one-parameter family in such a way that the derivative of the real part of the characteristic values with respect to the parameter at the bifurcation point should be nonzero. Thus, a normal form for the Hopf bifurcation is

$$\dot{r} = \mu r + a r^3, \qquad a \neq 0,$$
$$\dot{\psi} = \theta.$$

We see that if $\mu a < 0$, then there is a periodic orbit defined by $r = \sqrt{-\mu/a}$. It is stable if $\mu > 0$ and repelling if $\mu < 0$. The interesting case in practice is when the origin is a stable equilibrium and loses its stability as a complex conjugate root of $A(\mu)$ passes through the imaginary axis in such a way that a *stable* periodic orbit is born. This orbit, termed a limit cycle, then becomes the attractor for the system with the origin now becoming an *unstable* equilibrium.

### A. Biomedical Example — Limit Cycles in Immune Response

A problem which illustrates most of the ideas we have presented arises in the study of the immune response to an antigen. A mathematical model of this process is given by the system

$$\epsilon \dot{x} = -[x^3 + (a - \tfrac{1}{2})x + (b - \tfrac{1}{2})],$$
$$\dot{a} = \tfrac{1}{2}\delta(1 - x) - a - \gamma_1 ab, \qquad\qquad \text{(IR)}$$
$$\dot{b} = -\gamma_1 ab + \gamma_2 b,$$

where $\epsilon, \delta, \gamma_1, \gamma_2$ are positive parameters. Here $a$ and $b$ represent concentrations of the antigens, while $x$ measures the stimulation of the immune system in response to the antigens. The stimulation is assumed to take place on a much faster time-scale than the antigen dynamics, so we take $\epsilon \ll 1$. Here we will employ the center manifold theory to show that the system (IR) has a periodic solution bifurcating from a fixed point for certain values of the parameters, i.e., there is a Hopf bifurcation.

Let $(x^*, a^*, b^*)$ be an equilibrium point for the system (IR). If $b^* \neq 0$, then $a^* = \gamma_2/\gamma_1$ and $x^*$ and $b^*$ satisfy the equations

$$x^{*3} + (\gamma_2/\gamma_1 - \tfrac{1}{2})x^* + b^* - \tfrac{1}{2} = 0,$$
$$\tfrac{1}{2}\delta(1 - x^*) - \gamma_2/\gamma_1 - \gamma_2 b^* = 0.$$

For the remainder of our discussion, assume that $a^* = \gamma_2/\gamma_1$.

If we let

$$y = a - a^*, \qquad z = b - b^*, \qquad w = -\psi(x - x^*) - x^* y - z$$

with

$$\psi = 3x^{*2} + a^* - \tfrac{1}{2},$$

then if $\psi \neq 0$,

$$\epsilon \dot{w} = g(w, y, z, \epsilon),$$
$$\dot{y} = f_2(w, y, z, \epsilon),$$
$$\dot{z} = f_3(w, y, z, \epsilon),$$

where

$$g(w, y, z, \epsilon) = f_1(w, y, z, \epsilon) - \epsilon x^* f_2(w, y, z, \epsilon) - \epsilon f_3(w, y, z, \epsilon),$$
$$f_1(w, y, z, \epsilon) = -\psi w + N(w + x^* y + z, y),$$
$$f_2(w, y, z, \epsilon) = (\delta \psi^{-1} x^*/2 - 1 - \gamma_1 b^*) y$$
$$+ \delta \psi^{-1}/2 - \gamma_2)z + \delta \psi^{-1}/2 - \gamma_1 yz, \qquad (6.6)$$
$$f_3(w, y, z, \epsilon) = -\gamma_1 b^* y - \gamma_1 yz,$$
$$N(\alpha, y) = -\psi^{-2}\alpha^3 + 3\psi^{-1}x^*\alpha^2 - y\alpha.$$

To put all equations of the system (6.6) on the same time-scale, let $s = t/\epsilon$ and now denoting differentiations with respect to $s$ by $'$, we can rewrite the $w$–$y$–$z$ system as

$$w' = g(w, y, z, \epsilon),$$
$$y' = \epsilon f_2(w, y, z, \epsilon),$$
$$z' = \epsilon f_3(w, y, z, \epsilon),$$
$$\epsilon' = 0.$$

Suppose $\psi > 0$. Then the linearized version of the system (6.6) has one negative characteristic value and three zero roots. Hence, by Theorem 6.6 there exists a center manifold

$$w = h(y, z, \epsilon).$$

Furthermore, the local behavior of the solution to the system is determined by the equation

$$y' = \epsilon f_2[h(y, z, \epsilon), y, z, \epsilon],$$
$$z' = \epsilon f_3[h(y, z, \epsilon), y, z, \epsilon],$$

or, in terms of the original time-scale,

$$\dot{y} = f_2[h(y, z, \epsilon), y, z, \epsilon],$$
$$\dot{z} = f_3[h(y, z, \epsilon), y, z, \epsilon]. \qquad (\#)$$

We must study the system ($\#$) to see about the possibility of a Hopf bifurcation.

The linear part of the ($\#$) system near $y = z = 0$ is given by

$$J(\epsilon) = \begin{bmatrix} \delta\psi^{-1}x^*/2 - 1 - \gamma_1 b^* & \delta\psi^{-1}/2 - \gamma_2 \\ -\gamma_1 b^* & 0 \end{bmatrix}.$$

If ($\#$) is to have a Hopf bifurcation, then we must have

$$\text{trace } J(\epsilon) = 0$$

and

$$\delta\psi^{-1}/2 - \gamma_2 > 0.$$

From the earlier analysis, we also know that $x^*$ and $b^*$ are solutions of the equilibrium equations and for the problem to make physical sense we must also have $|x^*| < 1, b^* > 0$, and $\psi > 0$. The satisfaction of these requirements is assured by the following result.

**_Lemma_** Let $\gamma_1/\gamma_2 < 2$. Then for each $\epsilon > 0$, there exists a $\delta(\epsilon)$, $x^*(\epsilon)$ and $b^*(\epsilon)$ such that $0 < x^*(\epsilon) < \frac{1}{2}$, $b^*(\epsilon) > 0$, $\delta(\epsilon)\psi^{-1} - 2\gamma_2 > 0$, $\psi > 0$, trace $J(\epsilon) = 0$ and the equilibrium equations for $x^*(\epsilon)$ and $b^*(\epsilon)$ are satisfied.

In other words, no matter what _fast–slow_ time-scale $\epsilon$ is employed, there always exists a value of $\delta$ which will send the immune response bifurcating into oscillatory behavior from an equilibrium.

The preceding example shows very clearly the power of center manifold theory to reduce the study of bifurcation phenomena from the original three-dimensional system to the associated two-dimensional center manifold system ($\#$).

Before leaving the topic of bifurcations, we point out that almost all of the material we have presented has its corresponding analogue for the case of _maps_, rather than continuous flows, i.e., for _discrete-time_ dynamical systems. It should also be noted that the results for point equilibria can be extended to the case of bifurcation from periodic orbits using much the same machinery, by introduction of the Poincaré _return map_. Since both of these situations have been extensively pursued in the literature, we shall confine our discussions to a few exercises in the Problem section of the chapter.

Saddle nodes and Hopf bifurcations exhaust the so-called elementary or _codimension one_ bifurcations, i.e., those which can be embedded into a one-parameter family of vector fields in a structurally stable way. There is, as yet, no general theory for codimension two and higher bifurcations, although a number of useful results are available for special cases. Rather than enter into this fairly treacherous territory, we refer the reader to the literature and shift our attention to the much simpler problem of studying families of *functions* rather than families of vector fields. This setting will provide us with a suitable background to discuss the theory of elementary *catastrophes* as developed by Thom, Arnol'd and Mather.

## VI. SINGULARITY THEORY AND THE ELEMENTARY CATASTROPHES

We have seen that the classification of vector fields by their normal forms is a somewhat tricky business, depending heavily on the notion of equivalence used. Even the coarsest classification, the topological case, involves several levels of subtlety and for a finer classification, using smooth coordinate changes, is filled with many essentially insurmountable technical difficulties. In contrast with vector fields, the study of smooth *functions* and their smooth classification, the so-called *singularity theory*, has had a remarkable degree of success and has spawned one of the most important streams of thought in modern applied mathematics, the theory of *catastrophes*. In this section, we shall give a brief account of these developments and show how the famous Thom classification theorem emerges as an outgrowth of the more general study of singularities of smooth functions.

Consider a smooth $(C^\infty)$ function $f: R^n \to R^m$ and assume that $f$ has a critical point at the origin, i.e., $df(0) = 0$. Singularity theory addresses the following questions:

(a) *Determinacy problem*—what is the *local* character of $f$ in a neighborhood of the origin? Basically, this question amounts to asking "at what point is it safe to truncate the Taylor series for $f$?"

(b) *Unfolding problem*—what are the *essential* perturbations of $f$? That is, what perturbations of $f$ can occur which change the qualitative nature of $f$ and which cannot be transformed away by a coordinate change?

(c) *Classification problem*—can we classify the types of singularities $f$ can have up to smooth coordinate changes?

Elementary catastrophe theory solves these problems when $m = 1$; its generalization to singularity theory solves the first two, and gives relatively complete information on the third for $n, m$ small. For the moment, we confine ourselves to the case $m = 1$ and outline the solutions of problems A–C in the elementary catastrophe theory setting.

The technically most efficient way to deal with these problems is to pass from functions to function *germs*, a germ being an equivalence *class* of functions agreeing on a suitable neighborhood of 0. Two functions $f_1$ and $f_2$ belong to the same germ if there exists a neighborhood $U$ of 0 such that $f_1$ and $f_2$ agree on $U$.

## A. Codimension

Let $E_n$ denote the set of all smooth germs $R^n \to R$. A *diffeomorphism germ* $\phi: R^n \to R^n$ satisfies $\phi(0) = 0$ and has an inverse $\phi^{-1}(x)$ for $x \in U$; $\phi$ is a smooth, invertible local coordinate change. A simple test for whether a given smooth $\phi$ is a diffeomorphism germ is provided by the inverse function theorem: $\phi$ is a diffeomorphism germ if and only if the Jacobian of $\phi$ is nonzero, i.e.,

$$\det \left[ \frac{\partial \phi_i}{\partial x_j} \right] (0) \neq 0.$$

Two function germs $f$, $g: R^n \to R$ are *right-equivalent* if there exists a diffeomorphism germ $\phi$ and a constant $\gamma \in R$ such that

$$g(x) = f(\phi(x)) + \gamma.$$

A *type* of a germ is a right-equivalence class. Each type forms a subset of $E_n$, and the main object of study in elementary catastrophe theory is to see how these types fit together.

Let $F_n$ be the set of formal power series in $x_1, x_2, \ldots, x_n$. Define the map $j: E_n \to F_n$ by the rule

$$jf = f(0) + \sum \frac{\partial f(0)}{\partial x_i} x_i + \frac{1}{2} \sum \frac{\partial^2 f(0)}{\partial x_i \partial x_j} x_i x_j + \cdots,$$

where the right side is the Taylor series, or *jet* of $f$. Note that no notions of convergence are involved here; we are dealing purely on the level of *formal* power series. The map $j$ is onto, linear (over $R$) and preserves products, $j(fg) = jf \cdot jg$.

Let $m_n = \{f \in E_n : f(0) = 0\}$. This set is an *ideal* of $E_n$ and its $k$th power, $m_n^k$, consists of all $f \in E_n$ such that

$$f(0) = df(0) = d^2 f(0) = \cdots = d_f^{k-1}(0) = 0.$$

In particular, $f$ has a singularity at 0 if and only if $f \in m_n^2$. Let $M_n = j(m_n)$, i.e., $M_n$ is the set of formal power series with zero constant term. Then $M_n^k = j(m_n^k)$, is the set of formal power series without terms of degree $\leq k - 1$. We have $\cap_k M_n^k = 0$, while $\cap_k m_n^k$ is the set $m_n^\infty$ of flat germs, having zero Taylor series.

The *Jacobian ideal* of $f$ is the set of all germs expressible in the form

$$g_1 \frac{\partial f}{\partial x_1} + g_2 \frac{\partial f}{\partial x_2} + \cdots + g_n \frac{\partial f}{\partial x_n},$$

for arbitrary germs $g_i$. Denote it by $\Delta(f)$. Since $df(0) = 0$, $\Delta(f) \subseteq m_n$. The *codimension* of $f$ is defined as

$$\text{cod}(f) = \dim_R m_n / \Delta(f).$$

Similarly, for formal power series we define

$$\text{cod}(jf) = \dim_R M_n / j\Delta(f).$$

Essentially, the codimension measures the number of independent directions in $E_n$ *missing* from $\Delta(f)$.

It can be shown that if either $\text{cod}(f)$ or $\text{cod}(jf)$ are finite, then so is the other and they are equal. Thus, the computation of $\text{cod}(f)$ may be carried out on the formal power series level where it is a combinatorial calculation. We note that it can be shown that if $\text{cod}(f) = c$, then under a small perturbation of $f$ at most $c + 1$ critical points can occur, i.e., under a small perturbation of $f$, the critical point at 0 can separate or *dissolve* into at most $c + 1$ critical points. Thus, $\text{cod}(f)$ is a measure of the degree of the degeneracy of the critical point at 0.

## B. Determinacy

Let $f \in E_n$ and define the *k-jet*, $j^k f$ of $f$ to be the Taylor series of $f$ at 0 up to and including terms of degree $k$. For example,

$$j^6(\cos x) = 1 - \frac{x^2}{2!} + \frac{x^4}{4!} - \frac{x^6}{6!}.$$

We say that $f$ is *k-determinate* if whenever $g \in E_n$ and $j^k g = j^k f$, then $g$ is right-equivalent to $f$. In other words, $f$ is *k-determinate* if for *every* $g$ whose $k$-jet agrees with that of $f$, we can find a change of coordinates (i.e., a diffeomorphism germ) such that $f$ is transformed into $g$ in the new coordinates. In particular, if $f$ is $k$-determinate we can take $g = j^k f$ and we then find that $f$ is equivalent under a change of variable to the terms through degree $k$ of its own Taylor series. Thus, the solution of the determinacy problem hinges upon finding ways to calculate the determinacy of $f$, in particular whether or not $f$ is *finitely determined*.

The basic results involving determinacy are summed up in the following theorem, basically due to Mather.

***Theorem 6.9***   *Let $\Delta$ be the Jacobian ideal of $f$. Then*

(i)   *if $m_n^k \subseteq m_n \Delta$, $f$ is k-determined;*
(ii)  *if $f$ is k-determined, then $m_n^{k+1} \subseteq m_n \Delta$;*
(iii) *$f$ is k-determined if and only if $m_n^{k+1} \subseteq m_n \Delta(f + g)$ for all $g \in m_n^{k+1}$.*

***Example a***   $f(x) = x_1^2 \pm x_2^2 \pm \cdots \pm x_n^2$. Then

$$\Delta = \{h \in E_n : h = \pm g_1 x_1 \pm \cdots \pm g_n x_n, g_i \in E_n\}.$$

It is easy to see that $\Delta = m_n$ and it then follows that $m_n \Delta = m_n^2$. Hence, by part (i) of the theorem, $f$ is 2-determined.

REMARK   This example shows that any 2-determined $f$ is right-equivalent to a nondegenerate quadratic, a reformulation of the well-known Morse's lemma.)

***Example b***   $f(x_1, x_2) = \frac{1}{3}x_1^3 + \frac{1}{4}x_2^4$. It is easy to see that

$$\Delta = \{h : h = g_1 x_1^2 + g_2 x_2^3, g_i \in E_n\}.$$

Thus, $m_n \Delta$ involves cubic and higher terms and a small calculation shows that $m_n \Delta \supseteq m_n^4$, but $m_n \not\supseteq m_n^5$. Thus, $f$ is 4-determined by part (i) of Theorem 6.9.

***Example c***   $f = x_1^2 x_2$. Here

$$\Delta = \{h : h = 2g_1 x_1 x_2 + g_2 x_1^2, g_i \in E_n\}.$$

After a steadfast algebraic effort, it soon becomes apparent that $m_n \Delta \not\supseteq m_n^k$ for *any* finite value of $k$. Thus, $f$ is not finitely determined and it is not safe to truncate the *tail* of the Taylor series of $f$ at any finite segment. The proof that $f$ is not finitely determined follows more easily from the next result, which relates the codimension of $f$ to its determinacy.

***Theorem 6.10***   *The following are equivalent*:

   (i)   $\text{cod}(f) < \infty$;
   (ii)   $f$ *is finitely determined*;
   (iii)   $m_n^t \subseteq \Delta$ *for some* $t < \infty$.

*Furthermore, we have the inequality*

$$\text{cod}(f) \geq (\text{determinacy } f) - 2.$$

The importance of Theorem 6.10 is that it allows us to replace a difficult calculation (the determinacy of $f$) by a simpler algebraic computation $(\text{cod}(f))$. In particular, returning to our last example, $f(x_1, x_2) = x_1^2 x_2$, it is easy to see that a basis for $m_n / \Delta(f)$ is given by the set $\{x_2, x_2^2, x_2^3, \ldots\}$. Thus, all the *directions* $x_2^i$, $i \geq 1$, are missing in $E_n$ and $\text{cod}(f) = \infty$. By Theorem 6.10, this implies that $f$ is not finitely determined.

   We have now solved our first major problem, the determinacy problem: it is safe, up to right-equivalence, to truncate a $k$-determined germ after terms of degree $k$ of its Taylor series.

Before moving on to the unfolding problem, it is useful for future reference to note the following result. Suppose $f$ is not 2-determinate, so that the Hessian matrix $H$ of $f$ is such that $\det H = 0$. Let $n - \text{rank } H = r$ and call $r$ the *corank H*. Our next result shows that for many purposes, it suffices to consider only $r$ of the $x$ variables.

**Theorem 6.11**  (Splitting Lemma)  *Let corank $H = r$. Then $f$ is right-equivalent to a germ of the form*

$$g(x_1, x_2, \ldots, x_r) \pm x_{r+1} \pm \cdots \pm x_n^2, \tag{6.7}$$

*where $g$ is order cubic or higher.*

In applications we can often ignore the quadratic terms in expression (6.7), focusing attention only upon $g$. We shall give examples of the efficiency of this *dimensionality reduction* idea later.

Since calculation of the codimension of $f$ involves the first derivatives of $f$, while the corank involves dependencies among the second derivatives, it is natural to expect that there may be some numerical relationship between these two numbers. As it turns out, the following inequality holds

$$r(r + 1)/2 \le \text{cod}(f).$$

Note that this result places a severe bound on the number $r$ of *essential* variables in $f$. For instance, if $\text{cod}(f) \le 5$, then $r \le 2$ implying that no matter how many variables $f$ depends on, if $\text{cod}(f) \le 5$ we can always find a coordinate system such that all but *at most* 2 of the new variables appear only in the nondegenerate quadratic form. This fact provides a basis for much of the utility and geometric intuition of elementary catastrophe theory.

## C.  Unfoldings

Now let us turn to our second main question, the identification of those perturbations of $f$ which cannot be transformed away by a coordinate change. For this we need the concept of an *unfolding*.

Let $f \in E_n$. Then an *l-parameter unfolding* of $f$ is a germ $F \in E_{n+l}$, such that $F(x, 0) = f(x)$, i.e., $F = F(x_1, x_2, \ldots, x_n; \alpha_1, \alpha_2, \ldots, \alpha_l) = F(x, \alpha)$, where $F(x, 0) = f(x)$. An unfolding $\bar{F}$ is said to be *induced* from $F$ if

$$\bar{F}(x, \delta) = F(P_\delta(x), \psi(\delta)) + \gamma(\delta),$$

where $\delta \in R^m, P_\delta : R^n \to R^n, \psi : R^m \to R^l, \gamma : R^m \to R$, and $F$ and $\bar{F}$ are *equivalent* if each can be induced from the other. In other words, $F$ and $\bar{F}$ are equivalent if we can transform the $x$ and $\alpha$ variables, using *coordinate* changes $P_\delta$ and $\psi$, such that $F$ and $\bar{F}$ differ only by a constant $\gamma$. We say an *l-parameter* unfolding is *versal* if all other unfoldings can be induced from it; it is *universal* if it is versal and $l$ is as small as possible, i.e., a universal unfolding is one which is equivalent to any other unfolding and which uses as few parameters as possible.

Now suppose $f$ has codimension equal to $c < \infty$. Let $u_1, u_2, \ldots, u_c$ be a basis for $m_n/\Delta(f)$. Then a *universal unfolding* of $f$ is given by the germ

$$F(x, \alpha) = f(x) + \alpha_1 u_1(x) + \alpha_2 u_2(x) + \cdots + \alpha_c u_c(x).$$

Note that the universal unfolding is linear in the $\alpha_i$. This is a theorem, not part of the definition of an unfolding.

***Example*** $f(x_1, x_2) = \frac{1}{3}x_1^3 + \frac{1}{4}x_2^4$. Here a basis for $m_2/\Delta(f)$ is given by the elements $\{x_1, x_2, x_1 x_2, x_2^2, x_1 x_2^2\}$. Thus $\text{cod}(f) = 5$ and a universal unfolding is given by

$$F(x, \alpha) = f(x) + \alpha_1 x_1 + \alpha_2 x_2 + \alpha_3 x_1 x_2 + \alpha_4 x_2^2 + \alpha_5 x_1 x_2^2.$$

Intuitively, we can think of the unfolding terms as the most general type of perturbation of $f$ that cannot be removed by a coordinate change. If we let

$$g(x) = f(x) + p(x),$$

where $p(x)$ is a smooth perturbation of $f$, we can always write

$$p(x) = z(x) + \sum_{i=1}^{c} \alpha_i u_i(x).$$

The basic theorem on unfoldings then states that $z(x) = 0$ in an appropriate coordinate system.

Another way of looking at the universal unfolding $F(x, \alpha)$ is to think of it as the smallest parameterized family of functions containing $f$, such that the *type* of the singularity displayed by $f$ cannot be removed by a small displacement of the family, i.e., by a perturbation of the family. The preceding ideas effectively answer our second main question, the unfolding problem.

## D. Classification

Let us now sketch how the preceding ideas enable us to classify germs $f$ of codimension no greater than 4. This will result in an informal proof of Thom's famous classification theorem.

Let $f \in E_n$ and, first of all, assume $df(0) \neq 0$. Then $f(x)$ is right-equivalent to $x_1$, by the Implicit Function Theorem. Now let $df(0) = 0$, but $\det[\partial^2 f(0)/\partial x_i \partial x_j] \neq 0$. Then by Morse's lemma, $f$ is right-equivalent to $\pm x_1^2 \pm x_2^2 \pm \cdots \pm x_n^2$. Otherwise, $\det[\partial^2 f(0)/\partial x_i \partial x_j] = 0$. Let this matrix have corank $r$ and use the Splitting Lemma to write $f$ as

$$f(x) = g(x_1, x_2, \ldots, x_r) \pm x_{r+1}^2 \pm x_{r+2}^2 \pm \cdots \pm x_n^2.$$

It can be shown that the classification of $f$ depends only upon a similar classification for $g$, so we now drop the quadratic terms. Note that this implies the first element in our classification scheme is the integer $r$.

The Taylor series of $g$ begins with terms of degree 3 or higher. First, suppose $r = 1$ and let the first nonzero jet of $g$ be $a_k x^k$. This is $k$-determined and can be scaled to $\pm x^k$ ($k$ even), $x^k$ ($k$ odd). The codimension is $k - 2$, so we can take $k = 3, 4, 5,$ or 6 if the codimension is to be no greater than 4. This covers all cases of corank 1, codimension $\leq 4$.

Now assume $r = 2$. and let

$$j^3 g(x_1, x_2) = ax_1^3 + bx_1^2 x_2 + cx_1 x_2^2 + dx_2^3.$$

By a linear change of variable, we may bring this cubic to the form $x_1^3 + x_1 x_2^2$, $x_1^3 - x_1 x_2^2$, $x_1^2 x_2$, or 0.

The forms $x_1^3 \pm x_1 x_2^2$ are 3-determinate and have codimension 3.

The form $x_1^2 x_2$ is not 3-determinate so we consider higher terms. A series of coordinate changes brings any higher order expansion to the form $x_1^2 x_2 \pm x_2^t$, which is $t$-determined and has codimension $t$. Only $t = 4$ is of interest for our classification.

No higher terms added to $x_1^3$ or 0 produces a codimension 4 result.

Finally, if $r \geq 3$, it can be seen from the inequality $r(r + 1)/2 \leq \operatorname{cod}(f)$ that cod $f \geq 6$ (actually, it can be shown that for $r \geq 3$, $\operatorname{cod}(f) \geq 7$). Thus, this case does not arise for us.

So, we can summarize with

**Theorem 6.12**   *Let $f$ be a germ with* $\operatorname{cod}(f) \leq 4$. *Then $f$ is right-equivalent to one of the following forms*:

(i)   $x_1$,
(ii)   $\pm x_1^2 \pm x_2^2 \pm \cdots \pm x_n^2$,
(iii)   $x_1^t + (M)$, $t = 3, 4, 5, 6$,
(iv)   $x_1^3 \pm x_1 x_2^2 + (N)$,
(v)   $x_1^3 + x_2^4 + (N)$,

*where* $(M) = \pm x_2^2 \pm \cdots \pm x_n^2$, $(N) = \pm x_3^2 \pm \cdots \pm x_n^2$.

The famous list of elementary catastrophes of Thom are the universal unfoldings of the above canonical forms, together with its extension to codimensions greater than 4.

Theorem 6.12 and its extension to higher codimensions resolves our final problem, the classification problem.

So far, we have considered only the case of functions, i.e., $f: R^n \to R^m$, with $m = 1$. The corresponding results for $m > 1$ are much more difficult to obtain and, in fact, are known only for certain *nice* combinations of $(n, m)$, e.g., $n = m = 2$. A treatment of these cases would take us too far afield for our purposes here, so we refer the reader to the chapter Notes and References for details.

## VII. APPLICATIONS OF CATASTROPHE THEORY

In practice, there are two different ways to apply catastrophe theory. In Thom's terms, the *physical way* and the *metaphysical way*, depending on whether the function $f(x)$ is known for the problem at hand. Generally speaking, in problems arising in physics, chemistry, and engineering, $f$ is known from one or another of the many laws and principles governing physical systems (conservation of energy, Fermat's principle, Hamilton's principle, etc.). In this case, the *physical way*, we can proceed as in Section VI, calculate the determinacy of $f$, find a universal unfolding, reduce $f$ to canonical form and, in the process, usually shed some new light on the structure of the problem under investigation. If $f$ is not known, then we are in the so-called *metaphysical case*, in which we must first postulate the existence of *some* $f$ relating the system variables. Of course, this is not too severe an assumption since, without it, we concede at the outset that *no* relationship exists linking the problem variables and, as a result, no modeling is possible *at all*. The next step is to arbitrarily isolate one of the problem variables and call it the system output, and to isolate some number $k \geq 1$ of the remaining variables and call them inputs. The remaining $n - k - 1$ variables are then suppressed.

This procedure is tantamount to *assuming* that the system variables are already in the canonical coordinate system and that the corank is 1, with the codimension being $k$. Under all of these assumptions, the normal form of the unknown $f$ can be read off from the standard Thom list of elementary catastrophes. Outrageous as this procedure appears, it actually works in a number of cases and is, in fact, the common approach to the use of catastrophe theory in the social and behavioral sciences. As we might expect, the biological sciences seem to occupy a place in between the two extremes. In what follows, we present a sequence of examples illustrating both approaches.

Before proceeding to examples, we pause to point out that the catastrophe theory machinery developed above applies to *dynamical* processes only in those cases when the dynamical system

$$\dot{x} = h(x) \tag{$\Sigma$}$$

is such that the *equilibria* of $\Sigma$ coincide with the set of *critical points* of the function $f(x)$. This will be the case only when $\Sigma$ is a so-called *gradient* system, i.e., when $h(x) = \operatorname{grad} f(x)$. Unfortunately, the condition that $\Sigma$ be a gradient system is a very strict one, holding only when $\partial h_i / \partial x_j = \partial h_j / \partial x_i$, where $h_k = k$th component of $h$. It can be shown, however, that if we are only interested in the equilibria of $\Sigma$, the catastrophe formalism can be used to study the larger class of *gradient-like* systems. Essentially, this class includes all $\Sigma$ having only point equilibria. We refer to the literature for details on how to make various extensions of these ideas to more complicated types of equilibria sets.

## Example 1:  Electric Power Systems

Consider an electrical power generation network with $n$ generators and zero transfer conductance. The dynamical equations describing the network are

$$M_i \frac{d\omega_i}{dt} + d_i\omega_i = \sum_{\substack{j=1 \\ j \neq i}}^{n} E_i E_j B_{ij}[\sin \delta_{ij}^* - \sin \delta_{ij}],$$

$$\frac{d\delta_i}{dt} = \omega_i, \qquad i = 1, 2, \ldots, n,$$

where

| | |
|---|---|
| $\omega_i$ | angular speed of rotor $i$, |
| $\delta_i$ | electrical torque angle of rotor $i$, |
| $M_i$ | angular momentum of rotor $i$, |
| $d_i$ | damping factor for rotor $i$, |
| $E_i$ | voltage of generator $i$, |
| $B_{ij}$ | short circuit admittance between generators $i$ and $j$, |
| $\delta_{ij}$ | $\delta_i - \delta_j$, |
| $\delta_{ij}^*$ | the stable steady-state value of $\delta_{ij}$, |
| $\omega_{ij}$ | $\omega_i - \omega_j$. |

If we define $a_{ij} = d_i - d_j$, $b_{ij} = E_i E_j B_{ij}$, it can be verified that the function

$$V(\omega_{ij}, \delta_{ij}) = \sum_{i=1}^{n-1} \sum_{k=i+1}^{n} \left[\tfrac{1}{2}M_i M_k \omega_{ik}^2 - a_{ik}\delta_{ik} - b_{ik}(M_i + M_k) \cos \delta_{ik}\right]$$

$$- \sum_{i=1}^{n} \sum_{\substack{j=1 \\ j \neq i}}^{n-1} \sum_{\substack{k=j+1 \\ k \neq i}}^{n} M_i b_{jk} \cos \delta_{jk} + K,$$

$K$ constant, is a Lyapunov function for the system. Thus, this is a gradient-like system and we take the function $V$ as our object of study.

Consider the simplest case when we have $n = 2$ generators. In this situation there are only two variables

$$x_1 \doteq \omega_{12}, \qquad x_2 \doteq \delta_{12}.$$

Our function $f(x_1, x_2)$ is then

$$f(x_1, x_2) = \tfrac{1}{2}M_1 M_2 x_1^2 - a_{12}x_2 - b_{12}(M_1 + M_2)\cos x_2 + K$$
$$\doteq \tfrac{1}{2}\alpha x_1^2 - \beta x_2 - \gamma \cos x_2 + K.$$

Since addition of the constant $K$ does not affect the structure of $f$, we set $K = 0$. The critical points of $f$ are at

$$x_1^* = 0, \qquad x_2^* = \sin^{-1}\beta/\gamma.$$

The 4-jet of $f$ at $x^*$ is

$$j^4 f(x_1, x_2) = -[\beta \sin^{-1}\beta/\gamma + \sqrt{\gamma^2 - \beta^2}]$$
$$+ \frac{1}{2}[\alpha x_1^2 - \sqrt{\gamma^2 - \beta^2}x_2^2] + \beta \frac{x_2^3}{3!} + \sqrt{\gamma^2 - \beta^2}\frac{x_2^4}{4!}.$$

Again we drop the constant term and we find that $f$ is 2-determinate with $\operatorname{cod}(f) = 0$ if $\alpha \neq 0$ and $\gamma \neq \pm\beta$. The condition $\alpha \neq 0$ is necessary for the problem to make sense, so the only possibility for a degeneracy in $f$ occurs when $\gamma = \pm\beta$. If $\gamma \neq \pm\beta$ then $f$ is equivalent to a Morse function near its critical point and $f$ can be replaced by its 2-jet

$$\tfrac{1}{2}\alpha x_1^2 - \sqrt{\gamma^2 - \beta^2}x_2^2,$$

a simple Morse saddle. So, let us now assume $\gamma = \pm\beta$.

The function $f$ now has the form

$$f(x_1, x_2) = \tfrac{1}{2}\alpha x_1^2 - \beta(x_2 + \cos x_2).$$

The Jacobian ideal of $f$ is

$$\Delta(f) = \{h : h = \alpha g_1 x_1 + \beta(-1 + \sin x_2)g_2, \; g_i \in E_2\}.$$

It is easy to see that the term $\{\cos x_2\}$ is a basis for $m_2/\Delta$, therefore $\operatorname{cod}(f) = 1$. At the critical point, we also see that

$$\left[\frac{\partial^2 f}{\partial x_i \partial x_j}\right] = \begin{bmatrix} \alpha & 0 \\ 0 & \beta \cos x_2 \end{bmatrix},$$

which, at the critical point $x_1^* = 0$, $x_2^* = \sin^{-1} 1$, has corank $r = 1$. By examination of $j^4 f$ when $\gamma = \beta$, we see that the single *essential* variable can be taken to be $x_2$. Thus, a universal unfolding of $f$ is

$$F = \frac{x_2^3}{3} + \alpha_1 \cos x_2 .$$

However, since $\operatorname{cod}(f) = 1$, $r = 1$, we also have from Thom's canonical list the fact that $f$ is equivalent to

$$\tilde{F} = \frac{x_2^3}{3} + t x_2 .$$

(This example illustrates the fact that the unfolding is *not* unique.)

In the canonical unfolding, the parameter $t$ depends on the physical variables of the problem $\alpha$, $\beta$, $\gamma$ and a change in system stability can only occur when $t$ passes through $t = 0$. We can see the structure more clearly if we examine the 3-jet of $f$ (neglecting the constant term)

$$J^3 f = \frac{1}{2}(\alpha x_1^2 - \sqrt{2\beta\epsilon + \epsilon^2} x_2^2) + \frac{x_2^3}{3!},$$

with $\gamma = \beta + \epsilon$. Neglecting the term in $x_1$, this is an unfolding of $x_2^3$ and can be brought into the standard form $\tilde{F}$ by a linear coordinate change. This change will then yield $t$ as a function of $\beta$ and $\gamma$.

### Example 2:  International Conflicts and Crises

It has been remarked that "a crisis is, in some way, a change of state in the flow of international political action." If we accept this interpretation, then catastrophe theory suggests itself as a language with which to distinguish crisis from noncrisis periods.

Since there is no readily identifiable function $f$ governing the dynamics of crisis emergence and resolution, we shall employ the *metaphysical way* of catastrophe theory and *postulate* the existence of such a function. Further, we assume that the coordinate system chosen to verbally describe the situation is chosen such that we can appeal to the Splitting Lemma and separate the many factors involved in a crisis into *essential* and *nonessential* variables. For this example, we consider the single essential variable, *military action*. This is equivalent to assuming that our postulated $f$ has corank 1. The control (or unfolding) parameters used in our model will be taken to be *decision time* and *perceived threat*. This choice implies we are assuming $f$ has codimension 2. Thus, by Thom's classification theorem, our unknown $f$ must be right-equivalent to the canonical *cusp* catastrophe. If we let $x$ be the level of military action, $\alpha_1$ the decision time, and $\alpha_2$ the perceived threat, then the canonical structure for $f$ is $f(x) = (x^4/4) + \alpha_1(x^2/2) + \alpha_2 x$. The geometry of the critical points of $f$ as a function of the controls is shown in Fig. 6.1.

The literature on crisis management indicates that the jump from noncrisis mode to crisis is distinct from the jump from crisis mode to noncrisis. Thus, it is appropriate to employ the so-called *delay rule* in interpreting Fig. 6.1.

The geometry of the figure strongly suggests that when the system is not already involved in military action, it will not choose to engage in such action until the threat is extremely high. But if military action is already being taken, the system will continue such action until the threat is fairly low (e.g., occupation forces). The actual levels of *high* and *low* can, of course, only be determined by empirical means.

An interesting extension of the model is to include an additional behavior variable termed *operational preparedness*, along with another control variable, *degree of uncertainty* (i.e., corank $f = 2$, cod $f = 3$). The original behavior variable, military action, acts as a measure of the influence of the system on its *external* environment. On the other hand, the new output, operational preparedness, acts as a measure of change in the *internal* environment of the system to meet the perceived threat.

The interrelationship of these control and behavior variables is canonically governed by the so-called *elliptic umbilic* catastrophe. The bifurcation set $B$,

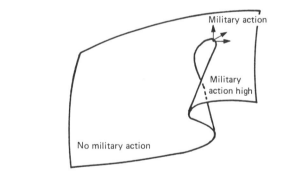

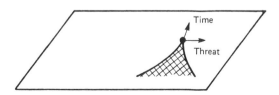

**FIG. 6.1**  Cusp model of crisis.

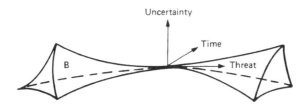

**FIG. 6.2**   Bifurcation set for the elliptic umbilic catastrophe.

which plays the same role for this catastrophe as the shaded region of Fig. 6.1 plays for the cusp, is displayed in Fig. 6.2.

To enter $B$ is to create potential crises, while to leave $B$ is to create a shift in behavior space, i.e., a crisis. Note, however, that the model distinguishes between a crisis and a crisis situation. A *crisis* is an instantaneous change in behavior, i.e., a behavioral discontinuity. A *crisis situation* places the system in a state of *alert*. Basically, any point of $B$ corresponds to a crisis situation, while crossing the boundary of $B$ may bring on the crisis.

### Example 3:  Land Use and Development

As an illustration of how the metaphysical way of catastrophe theory can be *souped-up* to mimic the physical way, consider an urban housing model, whose objective is to predict the development of a given residential area as a function of both the accessibility of the area and the number of vacant *units* remaining in the area (e.g., units could be land parcels suitable for construction or actual vacant dwellings).

Let $\dot{N}(t)$ be the *rate* of growth of housing units in the area at time $t$, $a$ the *excess* number of vacant units relative to the regional norm, and $b$ the *relative* accessibility of the area to the regional population. We assume that the dynamic underlying $N$ is such that for any fixed level of $a$ and $b$, $\dot{N}(t)$ moves to locally *maximize* some potential function $f$. This assumption, or its equivalent, is often employed in land development models of the so-called *gravity* type. In addition, we assume that for each fixed $a$ and $b$, the time scale of $\dot{N}$ is sufficiently faster than that of $a$ and $b$ that we observe only the steady-state level of $\dot{N}$, i.e., the transient dynamics of $\dot{N}$ are *fast* compared to the *slow* changes of $a$ and $b$.

Under these hypotheses, the metaphysical way of catastrophe theory implies the canonical geometry governing changes in the steady-state levels of $\dot{N}$ as a function of $a$ and $b$ is the *cusp*, having the universal unfolding $f(\dot{N}) = \pm(\frac{1}{4}\dot{N}^4 + \frac{1}{2}a\dot{N}^2 + b\dot{N})$. The geometric picture governing the situation is displayed in Fig. 6.3. We choose the negative sign for $f$, since it is more reasonable to assume that for a fixed level of vacancy and accessibility, the

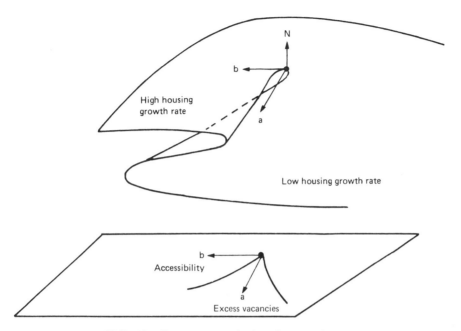

**FIG. 6.3**   Cusp geometry for housing growth rate.

region will develop at the fastest rather than slowest possible rate. Thus, our model is actually the *dual* cusp.

To transform this static model into a dynamical description, we can use the assumption that $\dot{N}(t)$ moves to maximize $f(\dot{N})$. This leads to the dynamical equation

$$\ddot{N} = \frac{d\dot{N}(t)}{dt} = -(\dot{N}^3 + a\dot{N} + b).$$

Now, of course, we also regard $a$ and $b$ as time-varying functions satisfying their own equations

$$\frac{da}{dt} = G_1(a, b, \dot{N}),$$

$$\frac{db}{dt} = G_2(a, b, \dot{N}).$$

The functions $G_1$ and $G_2$ are not dictated by catastrophe theory arguments and must be determined through understanding of the urban housing process (expert knowledge) and utilization of measured data (empirical knowledge). We note in closing that to have the dynamical model merge into the earlier static one, it is necessary to select the functions $G_1$ and $G_2$ so that the time scales of $\dot{N}$ and $a$ and $b$ differ significantly. In other words, we cannot use functions $G_1$ and $G_2$ that would cause $a$ and $b$ to change at more-or-less the same rate as $\dot{N}$. This constraint can easily be satisfied, however, by first selecting relevant $G_1$ and $G_2$, then multiplying these functions by a small parameter $\epsilon \ll 1$, which acts to slow down the time scale of $a$ and $b$.

## VIII. CHAOS AND STRANGE ATTRACTORS

Up to this point we have concerned ourselves only with attractors which are equilibria points or periodic orbits. Justification for this focus is provided by the $C^0$-density lemma which, roughly speaking, states that if $X$ is a smooth vector field on a smooth manifold $M$, making an arbitrarily small $C^0$ (continuous) perturbation of $X$, we can obtain a new vector field $\hat{X}$ which is structurally stable and that $\hat{X}$ has only fixed points ($=$ point equilibria) and closed orbits ($=$ limit cycles) as its attractors. Thus, up to continuous perturbations, all smooth dynamical systems have only fixed points and closed orbits as their steady-state behavior. However, in recent years, beginning with the work of Lorenz on atmospheric circulation, a number of systems of physical interest have been discovered that display vastly more complicated attractor sets. These sets, which have been labeled *strange attractors*, are the limit sets of dynamical behavior that has been termed *chaotic*, due to its indistinguishability from random motion. In this section we briefly explore the background and basic results in this area and show how the ideas of chaos lead to a description of the problem of the onset of hydrodynamic turbulence.

### A. Discrete-Time Processes

Chaotic behavior is used to describe the motion of dynamical systems exhibiting the following characteristics:

    (i)   a countable number of periodic trajectories;
   (ii)   an uncountable number of nonperiodic trajectories;
  (iii)   hyperbolicity (instability) of almost all trajectories.

The simplest example of a chaotic system arises by consideration of a single population with discrete generation which obeys the density-dependent law of growth

$$x_{t+1} = 4\mu x_t(1 - x_t) = f(x_t), \qquad x_t, \mu \in [0, 1],$$

where $x_t$ is the population at time $t$. Given the initial level $x_0$, the orbit

$\{f^i(x)\}_{i\geq 0}, x \in [0, 1]$ describes the evolution of the population. For $\mu > \frac{1}{4}$, $f(x)$ has one nontrivial fixed point $\bar{x} = f(\bar{x})$.

It is instructive to examine the local stability of the fixed point $\bar{x}$ as determined by the characteristic value of the map $f$ linearized about $\bar{x}$,

$$\lambda(\mu) = f'(\bar{x}) = 2(1 - 2\mu).$$

The fixed point is attracting for $\mu < \frac{1}{2}$. When $\mu$ is increased beyond $\frac{1}{2}$, however, $\bar{x}$ becomes repelling. To see what happens next, examine the second iterate of $f$: $f^{(2)} = f \circ f(\cdot)$. At $\mu = \frac{3}{4}$ the fixed point at $\bar{x} = \frac{2}{3}$ bifurcates into two new fixed points of period 2: $f^{(2)}(\bar{x}_i^{(2)}) = \bar{x}_i^{(2)}, i = 1, 2$. The period 2 orbit remains stable as long as the characteristic value of $f^{(2)}(\bar{x}_i^{(2)})$ has magnitude less than 1. But, by the chain rule

$$\lambda_i^{(2)}(\mu) = f'(\bar{x}_1^{(2)})f'(\bar{x}_2^{(2)}).$$

So, as $\mu$ is further increased, the period 2 orbit becomes unstable and a stable 4-point cycle appears whose stability is governed by $\lambda_i^{(4)} = \sum_{j=1}^{4} f'(\bar{x}_j^{(4)})$. By this mechanism cycles of length $2^k$, $k = 1, 2, \ldots$, are generated as $\mu$ increases. However, the range of $\mu$ values for which the $2^k$-point cycle is stable grows smaller as $k$ increases. Eventually, a critical value $\mu = \mu^*$ is reached where a second type of bifurcation occurs. When one of the minima of $f^{(k)}$, for some $k$, dips low enough to touch the line $x_t = x_{t+1}$, a bifurcation through $\lambda(\mu) = +1$ occurs, which creates a new fixed point at the point of tangency. This new fixed point promptly splits into two fixed points, one stable and one unstable. By a theorem of Li and Yorke (Theorem 6.13), when a period 3 cycle occurs, there then exist cycles of any length, as well as orbits which are aperiodic, i.e., which asymptotically approach neither an equilibrium nor a periodic orbit. For the simple, one-dimensional logistic growth map considered here, the following important features can be established:

(i)  there is at most one stable periodic orbit for each value of the parameter;
(ii)  the aperiodic points have nonzero measure only at $\mu = 1$.

When $\mu = 1$, then $f$ has no attracting periodic orbits (despite the fact that the periodic points are still dense in $[0, 1]$. The orbit of $f(x) = 4x(1 - x)$ does not asymptotically approach either an equilibrium or a periodic orbit, but rather approaches a much more complicated limit set, a *strange attractor*.

**Definition 6.5**  A *strange attractor* for a map $f$ is an infinite point set $\Omega$ with the following properties:

1.  $f(\Omega) = \Omega$, i.e., $\Omega$ is invariant under $f$;
2.  $f$ has an orbit which is dense in $\Omega$;

3. $\Omega$ has a neighborhood $N$ consisting of points whose orbits tend asymptotically to $\Omega$,

$$\lim_{t \to \infty} f^{(t)}(N) \subset \Omega.$$

The most important property of strange attractors is that orbits in or near such a limit set behave in an essentially chaotic fashion. Consequently, the dynamical behavior is described in statistical terms. For instance, we can give a statistical description of the map $f(x) = 4x(1 - x)$ by computing the density function giving the distribution of points on $[0, 1]$ after a large number of iterations. This density is

$$\rho(x) = \frac{1}{\pi \sqrt{x(1 - x)}}.$$

It can be shown that $f$ is topologically equivalent to the piecewise linear map

$$\hat{f}(x) = \begin{cases} 2x, & 0 \le x \le \tfrac{1}{2}, \\ -2x, & \tfrac{1}{2} \le x \le 1 \end{cases}$$

via the homeomorphism $h(x) = (2/\pi) \sin^{-1} \sqrt{x}$. If we count points in the left half of the unit interval as 0 and points in the right half as 1, then the orbit of $\hat{f}$ generates a sequence of 0's and 1's whose density function is uniform. Thus, the orbit of $\hat{f}$ is equivalent to a sequence of Bernoulli trials (i.e., flips of a fair coin). This example graphically illustrates the fact that the deterministic dynamics in a strange attractor can be literally as random as possible.

To summarize the situation for one-dimensional chaos, we have the famous *Period* 3 theorem of Li and Yorke.

**Theorem 6.13**    *Let $J$ be an interval and let $f$ be a continuous map $f : J \to R$. Suppose there exists a point of period 3 for the system* (*) $x_{t+1} = f(x_t)$. *Then*

(i)    *for each $k = 1, 2, \ldots$, there is a point of* (*) *having period $k$;*

(ii)    *there is an uncountable invariant set $S \subset J$ containing no periodic points, which satisfies*

$$\lim_{n \to \infty} \sup |f^{(n)}(p) - f^{(n)}(q)| > 0 \qquad \text{for all} \quad p, q \in S, p \ne q; \qquad \text{(a)}$$

*for every $p \in S$ and periodic point $q \in J$,*

$$\lim_{n \to \infty} \sup |f^{(n)}(p) - f^{(n)}(q)| > 0. \qquad \text{(b)}$$

*Furthermore,*

(iii)    *there is an uncountable subset $S_0 \in S$ such that*

$$\lim_{n \to \infty} \inf |f^{(n)}(p) - f^{(n)}(q)| = 0 \qquad \text{for all} \quad p, q \in S_0.$$

Simple examples show that the existence of a periodic point of period 3 does not suffice to produce chaos in higher dimensions. For instance, the system

$$x_{t+1} = (ax_t + by_t)(1 - ax_t - by_t),$$

$$y_{t+1} = x_t,$$

has a stable cycle of period 3 when $a = 1.9$ and $b = 2.1$, but chaotic behavior does not occur for those parameter values, although it does occur for different values.

To handle the higher dimensional situation

$$x_{t+1} = f(x_t), \qquad f: \; R^n \to R^n, \tag{†}$$

the notion of a *snap-back* repellor is useful.

**Definition 6.6**   Let $f: R^n \to R^n$ be continuously differentiable in some ball $B_r(z)$ about a fixed point $z$ of $f$. We say that $z$ is a *repelling fixed point* if all characteristic values of $Df(x)$ exceed 1 in norm for all $x \in B_r(z)$.

The repelling fixed point $z$ is called a *snap-back repellor* if there exists $x_0 \in B_r(z)$, $x_0 \neq z$, and an integer $M$ such that $f^{(M)}(x_0) = z$ and $|Df^{(M)}(x_0)| \neq 0$.

The following theorem, due to Marotto, generalizes the Li–Yorke result to higher dimensions.

**Theorem 6.14**   *Snap-back repellors imply chaos in $R^n$. More precisely, suppose $z$ is a snap-back repellor for $f$. Then*

(i)   *there is an integer $N$ such that for every $k > N$, there is a periodic point of (†) having period $k$.*

(ii)   *There exists an uncountable set $S \subset B_r(z)$ satisfying the conclusion (ii) of Theorem 6.13.*

PROOF   Since it is easy, we sketch the proof of part (i). Assume $x_0 \in B_r(z)$ but $f(x_0) \notin B_r(z)$. Let $x_k = f^k(x_0)$. We have $f^M(x_0) = z$ and $|Df^M(x_0)| \neq 0$. Hence, by the Inverse Function Theorem, there exists a ball $B_\epsilon(z)$ and a function $g: B_\epsilon(z) \to R^n$, such that $g(z) = x_0$ and $g|_{B_\epsilon(z)} = f^{-M}$.

Since $z$ is a repelling fixed point, there must exist an integer $J^*$ such that for $J > J^*$, $f^{-J}(Q) \subset B_\epsilon(z)$, where $Q = g(B_\epsilon(z))$. But,

$$f^{-J}(Q) = f^{-J}(f^{-M}(B_\epsilon(z)))$$

$$= f^{-(J+M)}(B_\epsilon(Z))$$

$$\subset B_\epsilon(z).$$

Thus, by the Brouwer fixed point theorem, there exists a fixed point of $f^{-(J+M)}$ in $B_\epsilon(z)$ for all $J > J^*$. Further, such a fixed point is automatically a fixed point of $f^{J+M}$, which establishes the result (i) using $N = M + J^*$.

## B. Continuous-Time Systems

As a consequence of the Poincaré–Bendixson theorem, strange attractors and chaotic limiting behavior cannot occur for continuous-time dynamical systems of dimension less than 3. However, in a pioneering paper devoted to the problem of turbulence in fluids, E. N. Lorenz discovered the three-dimensional chaotic system

$$\dot{x} = -\sigma x + \sigma y,$$

$$\dot{y} = -xz + rx - y,$$

$$\dot{z} = xy - bz, \qquad \sigma, r, b > 0$$

which exhibits strange attractors when

$$\sigma > b + 1$$

and

$$r > \sigma(\sigma + b + 3)/(\sigma - 1 - b).$$

To discuss strange attractors in more general terms, it is necessary to introduce the idea of an Axiom A attractor, first proposed by Smale.

***Axiom A***   A dynamical system satisfies Axiom A if its nonwandering set (a point $p$ is nonwandering if every neighborhood of $p$ intersects some orbit twice)

(a)   has hyperbolic structure, and
(b)   is the closure of the set of closed orbits of the system.

Part (a) implies that the system $f : M \to M$ is such that along a strange attractor there is a *good* splitting of $M$ into directions along which $f$ is contracting and those along which $f$ is expanding. Furthermore, Axiom A attractors are structurally stable in that perturbations of $f$ will yield attractors which have the same geometric properties.

The following result of Newhouse, Ruelle, and Takens shows that the Lorenz attractor is not unusual for nonplanar vector fields.

***Theorem 6.15***   *Let $v$ be a constant vector field on the torus $T^n = R^n/Z^n$. If $n \geq 3$, every $C^2$ neighborhood of $f$ contains a vector field $\bar{v}$ with a strange Axiom A attractor.*

Theorem 6.15 shows that in the space of all differential equations, those which have strange attractors form a set which contains a subset which is open in the $C^2$ topology. The closure of this open set contains the constant vector fields. However, we add a note of caution: this does *not* mean that the set is large in the measure-theoretic sense.

The presence of a strange attractor has been used in a variety of ways to provide deterministic models for the onset of turbulence in fluid flow. The initial attempt in this direction was made by Ruelle and Takens and relies upon Theorem 6.15. We examine their scenario in a bit more detail to see the reasoning behind why aperiodic orbits suggest themselves as candidates for representing turbulent motion. More recent scenarios competing with that of Ruelle and Takens are similar in spirit and a comparative account can be found in the chapter Notes and References.

The idea underlying the Ruelle–Takens route to turbulence is to describe a physically plausible set of assumptions that imply the conditions of Theorem 6.15 and hence its conclusion.

Assume the system

$$\dot{x} = f(x, \mu)$$

has a stable steady-state solution $x_\mu^*$ for $\mu < \mu_c$. Assume further that $x_\mu^*$ loses its stability through a Hopf bifurcation, i.e., a pair of complex conjugate characteristic values of $\partial f / \partial x |_{x = x_\mu^*}$ cross the imaginary axis. This means that the steady state (a constant flow or an equilibrium) becomes oscillatory, i.e., some system mode is destabilized. Assume that this happens *three* times in succession at values $\mu_c < \mu_c' < \mu_c''$ and that the three newly created modes are essentially independent. Schematically, we have the situation shown in Fig. 6.4. Under the foregoing assumptions, Theorem 6.15 asserts that a strange attractor *may* occur and is *likely* in the sense that if a property holds in an open set, namely the presence of a strange attractor, then if we vary the coefficients of the system a little, the attractor will persist; in other words, it is not exceptional.

We can now reformulate the Ruelle–Takens scenario as: if a system undergoes three Hopf bifurcations starting from a stationary solution as a parameter (e.g., the Reynolds number) is varied, then it is likely that the system possesses a strange attractor with sensitivity to the initial conditions after the third bifurcation.

The power spectrum (Fourier transform) of such a system will exhibit one, two, and possibly three independent basic frequencies. When the third frequency is about to appear, simultaneously some broad-band noise will

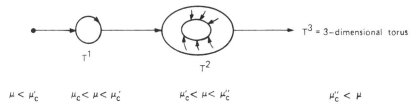

FIG. 6.4 Triple Hopf bifurcation to turbulence.

appear if there is a strange attractor. The Ruelle–Takens scenario interprets this as the onset of turbulent behavior of the system. Experiments have been performed on the formation of Taylor vortices between rotating cylinders and on the Rayleigh–Bénard convection. The results are in agreement with the Ruelle–Takens model.

### IX. CONTROL SYSTEMS AND FEEDBACK

One of the greatest triumphs of linear system theory is the famous Pole-Shifting Theorem, which expresses the degree to which a linear feedback control can alter the stability characteristics of the free dynamics of a linear system. Roughly speaking, the Pole-Shifting Theorem states that if the system is completely reachable, then the closed-loop system can be made to have its characteristic values at any predefined locations in the complex plane. In other words, the stability characteristics of the uncontrolled system can be *arbitrarily* altered by a suitable linear feedback control law.

Decoupling is another important problem that is essentially solved in the linear theory. We have a system

$$\dot{x} = Fx + Gu + Ew,$$

$$y = Hx,$$

$$z = Jx,$$

where $y$ is the measured output, $z$ is the part of the state we want to regulate, and $w$ is an external noise source. Our desire is to insulate the output $z$ from the noise $w$ by a linear feedback law depending upon the measured output $y$. When this can be accomplished is intimately tied to the controllability and observability structure of the system.

Finally, the linear theory also provides a complete solution to the so-called *regulator* problem in which we want to find a feedback control law minimizing

$$\frac{1}{2} \int_0^\infty [(x, Qx) + (u, Ru)] dt + \frac{1}{2}(x_0, Mx_0),$$

where

$$\dot{x} = Fx + Gu, \qquad x(0) = c.$$

Again, the reachability of the dynamics, together with the observability properties of the performance criterion, plays a central role in determination of the solvability of the regulator problem and in the properties of the optimal control law.

Each of these basic problems shares the feature that the feedback control law is used to modify the free dynamics of the system in some essential way.

Thus, the essence of each problem is to find conditions under which a structural modification of a certain type can take place and to express these conditions in computable form. In this section, we shall examine the way in which *nonlinear* feedback can be used to address similar questions. Of course, results as sharp and complete as in the linear case are not to be expected, given the vast expanse of possibilities inherent for nonlinear systems. Nonetheless, substantive progress has been made on providing nonlinear analogues of many of the main linear system results indicating that the essence of the matter is system-theoretic, rather than a particular artifact of linearity. Let us now take a look at a few of the more interesting results.

## A. Popov and Circle Criterion

We consider the nonlinear feedback system

$$\dot{x} = Fx - g\phi(\sigma), \qquad \sigma = h'x, \tag{$\Sigma$}$$

where $F$ is an $n \times n$ matrix and $g$, $h$ constant vectors. The system nonlinearity $\phi(\cdot)$ is assumed to be restricted to the first and third quadrants, i.e., $\sigma\phi(\sigma) > 0$. The system nonlinearity can either be regarded as an external nonlinear feedback control, or as a nonlinear perturbation of the linear system. In either case, interest centers upon the way in which the nonlinear term affects the *global* stability properties of the unperturbed linear system.

Considerable work has been done on this question which, in the control literature, is usually termed the *Lur'e problem*. The main results have been obtained using a Lyapunov function of the form

$$V(x) = (x, Qx) + \psi(x),$$

where $Q > 0$ and $\psi(\cdot)$ is a suitably chosen function, often an integral of $x$. Early in the study of the problem of Lur'e, it was conjectured by Aizerman that if

$$k_1 \leq \phi(\sigma)/\sigma \leq k_2,$$

with $k_1 \geq 0$ and $k_2 > 0$, and if $\Sigma$ were globally stable for all *linear* $\phi(\sigma) = h\sigma$, $k_1 \leq h \leq k_2$, then $\Sigma$ would be globally stable for every $\phi(\cdot)$ satisfying the quadrant condition above. A simple counterexample is the second-order system having transfer function

$$z(\lambda) = h'(\lambda I - F)^{-1}g = (\lambda + 1)/\lambda^2,$$

with

$$\phi(\sigma) = \begin{cases} \sigma/e(e + 1), & \sigma \leq 1, \\ \exp(-\sigma)/[1 + \exp(\sigma)], & \sigma \geq 1. \end{cases}$$

A new approach to the Lur'e problem was developed by Popov by expressing stability criteria for $\Sigma$ in terms of the frequency domain response of the linear part of $\Sigma$. The geometrical interpretation of the Popov stability criterion is in the form of an inequality, similar in spirit to the well-known Nyquist criterion for linear systems. Popov's famous result takes the following form.

**Theorem 6.16**   *The zero solution of $\Sigma$ is globally asymptotically stable if $\phi(\cdot)$ is a continuous function satisfying*

(i)   $\phi(0) = 0, 0 < \phi(\sigma) < K$ *for* $\sigma \neq 0$;
(ii)   *there exists a constant $\alpha$ such that the function*

$$J(\lambda) = (1 + \alpha\lambda)Z(\lambda) + \frac{1}{K}$$

*is positive real, i.e., $J(\cdot)$ has no poles with positive real parts, the poles of $J$ on the imaginary axis are simple and have real positive residues, and* $\operatorname{Re} J(i\omega) \geq 0$ *for all real $\omega$.*

Popov's result contains a number of features of practical importance:

1. the result, while only a sufficient condition, is a *global* stability condition;

2. it applies without restriction on the order of the system;

3. the criterion only involves the transfer function of the linear part of the system and need be checked only on its frequency response $J(i\omega)$;

4. the criterion does not require the precise mathematical form of the nonlinear feedback element $\phi$, only that the maximum and minimum values of the feedback gain be bounded.

The inequality $\operatorname{Re} J(i\omega) \geq 0$ has a very simple graphical interpretation which also enables us to find a constant $\alpha$ satisfying assumption (ii) of the Popov theorem. Consider the plot of

$$M(i\omega) = \operatorname{Re} Z(i\omega) + i\omega \operatorname{Im} Z(i\omega)$$

for $\omega > 0$. Then the condition $\operatorname{Re} J(i\omega) \geq 0$ means that there must exist a straight line through the point $\lambda^* = -(1/K) + 0i$, such that no point of the curve $M(i\omega)$ lies to the left of this line for $\omega > 0$ (see Fig. 6.5). The slope of this line is the reciprocal of the desired constant $\alpha$.

Before moving on to other frequency domain criteria for stability of feedback systems, it is worthwhile to note that the Popov criterion can be modified to determine a domain of attraction of the origin for systems which are not globally asymptotically stable. These and other extensions and generalizations of Theorem 6.16 can be found in the references.

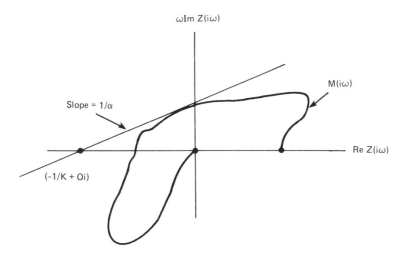

**FIG. 6.5**   Critical line for Popov criterion.

Now consider the system $\Sigma$ with the nonlinear feedback $\phi(\sigma) = -k(x)\sigma$, $\sigma = h'x$. Here the scalar function $k(x)$ is assumed to satisfy the bounds $k_1 < k(x) < k_2$, for all $x$. Thus the feedback control in such systems is linear feedback $h'x$, modified by the state-dependent scale factor $k(x)$. For such systems, we have

**Theorem 6.17** (Circle Criterion) *The origin is globally asymptotically stable for the system*

$$\dot{x} = Fx + gk(x)h'x,$$

*if $k_1 < k(x) < k_2$ for all $x$ and the function*

$$L(\lambda) = \frac{k_2 Z(\lambda) + 1}{k_1 Z(\lambda) + 1}$$

*is positive real.*

The above criterion is called the *circle* criterion for the following reason. Let the segment of the real axis between the points $-1/k_1$ and $-1/k_2$ determine the diameter of a circle $C$ in the complex plane. Furthermore, let $N$ be the Nyquist plot of the transfer function $Z(\lambda)$. Then the positive real criterion on $L(\lambda)$ means graphically that

(i)   if $k_1$ and $k_2$ have the *same sign*, then $N$ must encircle $C$ as many times in the counterclockwise direction as there are poles of $Z(\lambda)$ with positive real parts, i.e., unstable open-loop poles;

(ii)  if $k_1$ and $k_2$ are of *opposite sign*, then $N$ is contained entirely within the circle $C$.

Note that as $k_1 \to k_2$, the circle criterion tends to the Nyquist criterion, i.e., $C$ tends to the critical point $(-1/k, 0)$ of the Nyquist test for linear systems. Other circle criteria have been given for the case when $k$ is time-varying, i.e., $k = k(x, t)$, as well as *instability* criteria involving the circle $C$.

As an illustration of the use of Theorem 6.17, consider the third-order system

$$\dddot{x} + a_2\ddot{x} + a_1\dot{x} + a_0x + \gamma(\delta\dot{x} + x)^2(\ddot{x} + b\dot{x}) = 0.$$

Application of the circle criterion yields the following sufficient conditions for global asymptotic stability:

$$\gamma > 0, \qquad a_i, b \geq 0, \qquad b \leq a_2, \qquad a_0 \leq ba_1.$$

When $b \neq a_2$, these conditions are sharper than those obtained by linearizing the system about $x = 0$.

## B. Nonlinear Decoupling

Now we turn to another use of feedback control for the alteration of system structure. In decoupling, we are interested in conditions under which the observed system output can be made independent, or decoupled, from external disturbances (noise) in the system dynamics. This problem can take on many forms depending on assumptions made regarding what can be measured, the way in which the disturbances affect the dynamics, and so forth. Here we briefly treat a typical version of the problem as an indication of the type of results to expect.

Consider the system

$$\dot{x} = f(x) + g(x)u + p(x)w, \qquad x(0) = x_0,$$

$$y = x,$$

$$z = k(x),$$

where $x$, $y$, and $u$ are as usual, $w$ is the external noise, and $z$ is the output that is to be isolated from $w$. Here, for simplicity, we assume that the complete state is observable and we let $z$ be contained in some subset of $R^r$.

The goal is to find a feedback function $u = \alpha(x)$ so that the output $z$ is independent of $w$. The question we address here is when can we accomplish this task? It is clear that if we could find $\alpha(x)$ and a local coordinate change in

$x$ so that the new system took the block triangular form

$$\dot{x}_1 = \hat{f}_1(x_1),$$

$$\dot{x}_2 = \hat{f}_2(x_1, x_2) + p_2(x_1, x_2)w,$$

$$z = k(x_1),$$

with $\hat{f}(x) = f(x) + g(x)\alpha(x)$, then locally $z$ would not depend upon $w$. We focus upon conditions under which such a triangular decomposition is possible.

Let $V$ be an $(n - k)$-dimensional subset of $R^n$. $V$ defines a *foliation* of $R^n$ into submanifolds of the form $x + V$, i.e., the translates of $V$. The quotient $R^n/V$ is a linear space of dimension $k$ whose points are the translates of $V$, i.e., the *leaves* of the foliation.

Given the state manifold $M$, with a foliation, we want to construct a quotient manifold $\overline{M}$ whose points are the leaves of the foliation. This is not always possible for every $M$, but when it is the foliation is called *regular*. Suppose we have a regular foliation of $M$ so that in local coordinates the leaves of the foliation are given by the subsets $x_1 = c_1$ and that under suitable feedback $u \doteq \alpha(x)$, the dynamics are in the above block triangular form. Then we can regard the system as a model for the generation of $z$ with state space $\overline{M}$ with $z$ *decoupled* (in a regular fashion) from $w$.

Note that the triangular form is locally equivalent to the fact that if we start out at two different points on the same leaf (same $x_1(0)$) and follow the dynamics for the same amount of time $t$, then both trajectories end on the same leaf (same $x_1(t)$). That is, the foliation is *invariant* under the dynamics.

Now we return to the question of when there exists such a foliation. To answer this, suppose that at each point $x \in M$, we have a linear subspace of tangent vectors to $M$ denoted by $\Delta(x)$. Suppose $\Delta(x)$ has constant dimension $(n - k)$ and varies smoothly over $M$. In this case, we call $\Delta(x)$ an $(n - k)$-dimensional *distribution*. A submanifold $S$ of $M$ is an *integral submanifold* of $\Delta$ if for each $x \in S$, $\Delta(x)$ is the space of directions tangent to $S$ at $x$.

Every foliation of $M$ defines a distribution: let $\Delta(x)$ be the tangent vectors to the leaf of the foliation through $x$. The converse is also true if $\Delta$ is closed under the Lie bracket operation. Such distributions are called *involutive*. If $\Delta$ is an involutive distribution generating a regular foliation of $M$, then $\Delta$ is called *regular*. For example, if $V$ is a subspace of $R^n$, define the distribution $\Delta(x)$ on $R^n$ by $\Delta(x) = V$ for every $x \in R^n$. Then $\Delta$ is regular and the corresponding foliation is just the translates of $V$.

We have seen that decoupling involves finding a foliation invariant under the dynamics. We say $\Delta$ is *invariant* under $\dot{x} = f(x)$ if for every vector field $v \in \Delta$, $[f, v] \in \Delta$, where $[\cdot, \cdot]$ is the usual Lie bracket of two vector fields. It can be shown that a foliation is invariant under $f(x)$ if and only if the corresponding regular distribution is also invariant under $f(x)$.

However, we can modify the dynamics by feedback. Therefore, a distribution $\Delta$ is $(f, g)$ *invariant* if there exists an $\alpha(x)$ such that

$$[f + g\alpha, v] \in \Delta \qquad \text{for all} \quad v \in \Delta.$$

Finally, we have the decoupling result,

***Theorem 6.18*** *The noise w can be decoupled from the output z in a regular fashion if and only if there exists a regular $(f, g)$-invariant distribution $\Delta(x)$ which contains the columns of $p(x)$ and which is contained in the kernel of $dk(x)$, (i.e., the space of tangent vectors which annihilate* grad $k_i(x)$, $k_i = i$th *component of $k(x)$).*

This result is not quite satisfactory since the desired feedback law $\alpha$ is part of the definition of $(f, g)$-invariance. An alternate characterization is that $\Delta$ is *locally $(f, g)$-invariant* if and only if

(i)  $[g, v] \in \Delta(x)$,
(ii)  $[f, v] \in \Delta(x) +$ range $g(x)$,

for every $v \in \Delta$, where range $g(x)$ is the space generated by the columns of $g$.

Using this characterization of local $(f, g)$-invariance, the problem is reduced to finding maximal locally $(f, g)$-invariant distributions containing the columns of $p(x)$ and contained in ker $dk(x)$.


## C. Nonlinear Regulators

We conclude this section on the effect of feedback by considering a nonlinear version of one of the most well-studied problems in control theory—the regulator problem. Not only is this nonlinear extension of the classical *LQG* problem of interest in its own right, but it also provides an excellent illustration of the principle that, in an appropriate setting, virtually all of the major results of linear system theory can be transferred to nonlinear problems. We have seen this principle in action time and again throughout this book, so it seems only fitting that we conclude with a final illustration of its applicability.

From linear theory it is well known that if the single-input system

$$\dot{x} = Fx + gu$$

is optimized with respect to the criterion

$$J = \int_0^\infty [u^2 + (x, Qx)]dt, \qquad Q \geq 0,$$

then if $(f, g)$ is reachable and $(F, Q^{1/2})$ is observable, the optimal feedback control $u^*(x)$ is such that the optimal closed-loop dynamics are asymptotically stable. We consider the extension of this result to systems with dynamics and criteria nonlinear in $x$.

Consider the dynamics

$$\dot{x} = f(x) - Gu(t), \qquad (\Sigma)$$

which is to be optimized with respect to the criterion

$$J = \int_0^\infty [(u, u) + M(x)]dt,$$

where $M(x) \geq 0$, $M(0) = 0$, $f(0) = 0$. Further, for sake of exposition, let us assume that $f(\cdot)$ and $M(\cdot)$ are as smooth as needed to ensure that an optimal control exists and that $J$ satisfies the Hamilton–Jacobi equation. Under these conditions, it follows from standard Hamilton–Jacobi theory that the optimal feedback law $u^*(x)$ satisfies the relation

$$u^*(x) = -\tfrac{1}{2}G' \text{ grad } \phi,$$

where $\phi$ is a solution of

$$(\text{grad } \phi, f(x)) - \tfrac{1}{4}((\text{grad } \phi)G, (\text{grad } \phi)G) + M(x) = 0, \qquad \phi(0) = 0.$$

The question that we first want to address is under what circumstances the function $u^*(x)$ is such that the closed-loop dynamics

$$\dot{x}^* = (F - \tfrac{1}{2}GG' \text{ grad } \phi)x^*$$

are asymptotically stable. For this, we have

**Theorem 6.19** *If the system $\Sigma$ is (globally) completely controllable and (globally) completely observable, then the optimal closed-loop system is (globally) asymptotically stable.*

PROOF The proof is virtually identical to the linear case. From the Hamilton–Jacobi equation, the rate of change of $\phi$ along any optimal trajectory is given by

$$\frac{d\phi}{dt}(x^*(t)) = (\text{grad } \phi(x^*), f(x^*) - \tfrac{1}{2}GG' \text{ grad } \phi(x^*))$$

$$= -M(x^*) - \tfrac{1}{4}(\text{grad } \phi(x^*)G, \text{grad } \phi(x^*)G).$$

The observability assumption implies that $d\phi/dt \neq 0$, implying that $\phi(x^*)$ is a Lyapunov function for the optimal system.

In the linear theory, an important question is the inverse problem of optimal control, in which we are given a stable linear feedback law $\hat{u} = -Kx$, and ask under what circumstances there exists a quadratic criterion $J$ such that $\hat{u}$ optimizes $J$. A nonlinear version of this problem is expressed in the following result.

**Theorem 6.20**   Let $u(t) = -k(x)$ be an asymptotically stable control law for the completely controllable system $\Sigma$. Then $k(x)$ is optimal for some criterion of the form

$$\int_0^\infty [M(x) + (u, u)]dt, \qquad M(x) \geq 0,$$

if and only if $k(x)$ satisfies the return difference condition

$$\int_0^\infty [u + k(x)]'[u + k(x)]dt \geq \int_0^\infty [(u, u)]dt$$

for all square-integrable $u(\cdot)$, whenever $x(0) = 0$.

The proof of this result is a bit complicated so we shall leave it to the references. The important point to note here is that the condition on $k(x)$ reduces exactly to the classical return difference inequality

$$|1 + k'(i\omega I - F)^{-1}g| \geq 1,$$

when $k(x) = k'x$ and $f(x) = Fx$. This is most easily seen by converting the condition of the theorem to a frequency domain inequality, applying Parseval's inequality and using the arbitrary nature of $u$.

It is critical to the results of this section that the control appear quadratically in the performance criterion. These results would clearly extend to the case when the cost $(u, u)$ is replaced by $(u, Ru)$, $R > 0$; however, it is an open question as to what degree the ideas can be carried through for a more general cost function of the form $M(x) + r(u)$, with a positivity condition of some kind imposed on $r(u)$.

### PROBLEMS AND EXERCISES

1.   (a)   Consider the discrete-time linear system

$$x_{t+1} = Fx_t, \qquad x_0 \neq 0, \qquad t = 0, 1, \ldots.$$

Show that the origin is asymptotically stable if and only if the unique solution $P$ of the matrix equation

$$F'PF - F = -C, \qquad\qquad\qquad (*)$$

for all $C > 0$, is positive definite.

(b)   Show that the above requirement is equivalent to requiring the characteristic roots of $F$ to lie inside the unit circle, i.e., $|\lambda_i(F)| < 1$.

(c)  Prove that if $P$ is the solution of the *continuous-time* Lyapunov equation

$$PF + F'P = -C, \tag{$\dagger$}$$

then the Cayley transform $F' \to (I + F')(I - F')^{-1}, C \to 2(I - F')^{-1}C(I - F')$ converts ($\dagger$) into (∗), retaining the same solution $P$.

2.  (Floquet's theorem) Consider the matrix equation

$$\frac{dX}{dt} = P(t)X, \qquad X(0) = I,$$

where $P(t)$ is periodic with period $\tau$ and continuous for all $t$. Show that the solution has the form

$$X(t) = Q(t)e^{Bt},$$

where $B$ is constant and $Q(t)$ has period $\tau$.

3.  Assume that the nonlinear system

$$\dot{x} = f(x)$$

has a positive-definite first integral $V(x) = k \geq 0$. Show that $V(x)$ can be used as a Lyapunov function to conclude stability, but not asymptotic stability of the origin.

Apply this result to the gyroscope equations

$$a_1\dot{x}_1 + (a_3 - a_2)x_2x_3 = 0,$$
$$a_2\dot{x}_2 + (a_1 - a_3)x_3x_1 = 0,$$
$$a_3\dot{x}_3 + (a_2 - a_1)x_1x_2 = 0.$$

4.  Consider the system

$$\dot{x}_1 = \frac{2x_1(1 - x_1^2 + x_2^2)}{(x_1 + 1)^2 + x_2^2} + x_1x_2,$$

$$\dot{x}_2 = \frac{1 - x_1^2 + x_2^2}{2} - \frac{4x_1^2x_2}{(x_1 + 1)^2 + x_2^2},$$

having the equilibrium $x_1^* = 1, x_2^* = 0$. Use Zubov's Theorem 6.5 to conclude that the boundary of the domain of attraction $A$ of $x^*$ is the entire $x_2$ axis, i.e., $A$ is a right half-plane. Hint: Consider the Lyapunov function

$$V(x_1, x_2) = \frac{(x_1 - 1)^2 + x_2^2}{(x_1 + 1)^2 + x_2^2}.$$

5.  Consider the system

$$\dot{x} = F(x)x, \tag{∗∗}$$

where $F(\cdot)$ is a continuous matrix function of $x$. By Helmholtz's Theorem, the vector field $F(x)x$ can be resolved into an irrotational and rotational component. The irrotational component defines a scalar field $\phi$, which allows (**) to be written as

$$\dot{x} = -\operatorname{grad}\phi + \dot{y} = F(x)x.$$

The potential function $\phi$ can be derived from $F(x)$ by separating $F$ into its symmetric and skew-symmetric parts, $F_s$ and $F_a$, respectively.

(a)  Derive conditions on $F_s(x)$ which guarantee the existence and uniqueness of $\phi$.

(b)  Define the component of $\dot{x}$ along $-\operatorname{grad}\phi$ as

$$F_\phi = \left(\dot{x}, \left(\frac{-\operatorname{grad}\phi}{\|\operatorname{grad}\phi\|}\right)\right)\left(\frac{-\operatorname{grad}\phi}{\|\operatorname{grad}\phi\|}\right) = \left(\frac{d\phi}{dt}\right)\frac{\operatorname{grad}\phi}{\|\operatorname{grad}\phi\|^2}.$$

Show that if $F_\phi$ is directed into a closed $\phi$ contour containing a critical point $x^*$ of (**), then this $\phi$ contour is contained within the domain of attraction of $x^*$.

(c)  Apply the above result to the system

$$F_s(x) = \begin{bmatrix} 0 & 0 \\ 0 & -1 \end{bmatrix}, \qquad F_a(x) = \begin{bmatrix} 0 & x_1^2 + 1 \\ -(x_1^2 + 1) & 0 \end{bmatrix}.$$

**6.**  Consider the equations for a nonlinear passive $RLC$ electrical network

$$\frac{d\psi}{dt} = f(q), \qquad \frac{dq}{dt} = f(\psi),$$

where $\psi_i$ is the flux through inductor $i$, while $q_j$ is the charge on capacitor $j$, $i = 1, 2, \ldots, m$; $j = m + 1, m + 2, \ldots, n$. Denote the state variables as

$$x_i = \begin{cases} \psi_i, & i = 1, 2, \ldots, m, \\ q_i, & i = m + 1, \ldots, n. \end{cases}$$

If the system has an equilibrium at $x = 0$, show that the function

$$V(x) = \sum_{j=1}^{n} \int_0^{x_i} f_j(x_j)\, dx_j$$

is a Lyapunov function if

(i)  $x_j f(x_j) > 0$,

(ii)  $\displaystyle\int_0^\infty f_j(x_j)\, dx_j = \infty$,

(iii)  $\displaystyle\sum_{j=1}^{n} f_j(q_j)\, dq_j/dt < 0$.

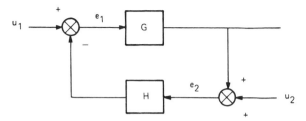

**FIG. 6.6**  Feedback connection.

**7.**  Consider a system described by the functional equations

$$e_1 = u_1 - He_2, \qquad e_2 = u_2 + Ge_1,$$

where $u_1, u_2, e_1, e_2$ belong to an extension $\hat{X}$ of a Banach space $X$, and the nonlinear operators $G, H: \hat{X} \to \hat{X}$. The above system can be thought of as a feedback connection with the operator $G$ representing the subsystem in the forward path, and $H$ representing the subsystem in the feedback path (see Fig. 6.6). We regard $u_1, u_2$ as *inputs*, $e_1, e_2$ as *error signals*, with $Ge_1$ and $He_2$ as *outputs*. The input–output stability question is: given $u_1, u_2 \in X$ and assuming the system has a solution $e_1, e_2$ in $\hat{X}$, do $e_1$ and $e_2$, in fact, belong to $X$?

Let $x_T(\cdot)$ denote the truncation to $[0, T]$ of an element $x(\cdot) \in \hat{X}$. Show that $e_1, e_2 \in X$ if there exist constants $k_1, k_2, m_1, m_2$ such that

$$\|(Gx)_T\| \le k_1\|x_T\| + m_1, \qquad \|(Hx)_T\| \le k_2\|x_T\| + m_2,$$

with $k_1 k_2 < 1$. That is, the system is stable if the product of the *gains* of the individual subsystems is less than one.

**8.**  Under the same conditions as Problem 7, but with $X$ a Hilbert space on $[0, \infty)$ with inner product $\langle \cdot, \cdot \rangle$, show that the system is stable if there exist constants $k, m_1, m_2, m_3, \delta$, and $\epsilon$ such that

$$\langle (Gx)_T, (Gx)_T \rangle \le k\langle x_T, x_T \rangle + m_1,$$

$$\langle x_T, (Gx)_T \rangle \ge \delta\langle x_T, x_T \rangle + m_2,$$

$$\langle x_T, (Hx)_T \rangle \ge \epsilon\langle (Hx)_T, (Hx)_T \rangle + m_3,$$

with $\delta + \epsilon > 0$.

**9.**  Consider the system

$$\dot{x}_1 = \epsilon x_1 - x_1^3 + x_1 x_2,$$

$$\dot{x}_2 = -x_2 + x_2^2 - x_1^2,$$

where $\epsilon$ is a real parameter.

(a)  Show that the linear part of this system near the origin has characteristic values $-1$ and $\epsilon$.

(b)  Show that by regarding $\epsilon$ as an additional state variable, the resulting three-dimensional system has a linear part with characteristic values $-1, 0, 0$.

(c)  Use the center manifold theorem to show that the three-dimensional system has a two-dimensional center manifold $x_2 = h(x_1, \epsilon)$ and that $h$ can be approximated by

$$x_2 = h = -x_1^2 + O(|x_1|^3, |\epsilon|^3).$$

Consequently, show that solutions near the origin are governed by the system

$$\dot{u} = \epsilon u - 2u^3 + O(|u|(u^3 + \epsilon^3))$$

$$\dot{\epsilon} = 0.$$

(d)  Determine the behavior of the solution to the original system near the origin for the cases $-\delta < \epsilon < 0$ and $0 < \epsilon < \delta, \delta > 0$.

**10.**  Consider the system

$$\dot{x}_1 = -x_1^3,$$

$$\dot{x}_2 = x_1^2 - x_2.$$

Assume that there exists a center manifold $x_2 = h(x_1)$, with $h$ analytic at the origin. Show that this implies

$$h(x_1) = \sum_{n=2}^{\infty} a_n x_1^n$$

for $|x|$ small, and that $a_{2n+1} = 0$ for all $n$, with $a_{n+2} = na_n$, $n = 2, 4, \ldots$, $a_2 = 1$. Hence, deduce that there exists no analytic center manifold for this system.

**11.**  What is the analogue of the center manifold theorem for the difference equation system

$$x_{t+1} = Nx_t + p(x_t, y_t),$$

$$y_{t+1} = My_t + q(x_t, y_t)?$$

**12.**  Prove that the generalized Lotka–Volterra system

$$\dot{x} = x(\alpha + ax + by),$$

$$\dot{y} = y(\beta + cx + dy),$$

has no limit cycles.

**13.**  Let $v(x_1, x_2)$ be a vector field in the plane and assume that $v(0, 0) = 0$ and that the linear part of $v$ has two real characteristic values $\lambda_1, \lambda_2$ satisfying the resonance condition $\lambda_1 = 2\lambda_2$. Show that $v$ can be formally reduced to the normal form

$$\dot{x}_1 = \lambda_1 x_1 + cx_2^2,$$

$$\dot{x}_2 = \lambda_2 x_2, \qquad c \quad \text{a constant.}$$

**14.** Show that the system

$$\dot{x} = x + o(|x|, |y|),$$

$$\dot{y} = -y + o(|x|, |y|),$$

cannot be linearized by a smooth coordinate change, as cubic terms of the form $\binom{x^2 y}{0}$ and $\binom{0}{xy^2}$ cannot be removed.

**15.** Show that the system

$$\ddot{x} + \mu\dot{x} + vx + x^2\dot{x} + x^3 = 0$$

undergoes a Hopf bifurcation on the lines $B_1 = \{\mu = 0, v > 0\}$ and $B_2 = \{\mu = v, \mu, v < 0\}$.

**16.** Consider the system

$$\dot{x}_1 = -x_2 + x_1[\alpha(1 - \alpha) - x_1^2 - x_2^2],$$

$$\dot{x}_2 = x_1 + x_2[\alpha(1 - \alpha) - x_1^2 - x_2^2],$$

$0 \le \alpha \le 1$. Show that this system undergoes a Hopf bifurcation at $\alpha = 0$ and $\alpha = 1$ and sketch the phase portraits in $(x_1, x_2, \alpha)$ space for $0 \le \alpha \le 1$.

**17.** Consider the scalar differential-delay equation

$$\dot{N} = -\mu N + vN(t - T)[1 - N(t - T)^z]^+,$$

where $\mu$, $v$, $T$, $z$ are positive constants, while $[X]^+ = X$ if $X > 0$, zero otherwise.

(a) Show that there is an equilibrium at

$$N^* = \left[\frac{(\alpha - 1)}{\alpha}\right]^{1/z},$$

where $\alpha = v/\mu$.

(b) Show that the linearized equation near $N^*$ is

$$\dot{y} = \lambda y + O(y),$$

where

$$\lambda = -\mu - [(v - \mu)z - \mu]e^{-\lambda T}.$$

(c) Define the normalized variables

$$\Lambda = \lambda/\mu, \qquad \tau = \mu T, \qquad b = (\alpha - 1)z - 1,$$

and show that $N^*$ is locally stable if

$$\tau < \frac{\pi - \cos^{-1}(1/b)}{(b^2 - 1)^{1/2}} \doteq \tau^*.$$

(d)  Show that $\tau = \tau^*$ a Hopf bifurcation occurs with a stable limit cycle emerging having a period

$$T^* = \frac{2\pi T}{\pi - \cos^{-1}(1/b)}.$$

**18.**  Consider the system

$$\dot{x}_1 = x_2,$$
$$\dot{x}_2 = \beta x_1 - \delta x_2 - \alpha x_1^3 + f \cos \theta,$$
$$\dot{\theta} = \omega,$$

and the Poincaré map $\sigma : \Sigma \to \Sigma$, where

$$\Sigma = \{(x_1, x_2, \theta) \in R^2 \times S^1 : \theta = 0, 2\pi/\omega, \ldots\},$$

i.e., $\sigma$ is the period $-1$ Poincaré map.

(a)  Let $f \equiv 0$. Show that the Poincaré map has a structure identical to the vector field of the two-dimensional system

$$\dot{x}_1 = x_2, \qquad \dot{x}_2 = \beta x_1 - \delta x_2 - \alpha x_1^3,$$

in the sense that the stable and unstable *manifolds* of the saddle $(0, 0)$ of $\sigma$ are curves identical to the stable and unstable *separatrices* of $(0, 0)$ for the vector field.

(b)  Show that for $f \equiv 0$ the above two-dimensional vector field is globally structurally stable and, hence, so is $\sigma$.

(c)  Let $\alpha = 1$, $\beta = 10$, $\delta = 100$, $\omega = 3.76$. Show that for $f \approx 0.79$, the stable and unstable manifolds of the saddle-point intersect, giving rise to infinitely many homoclinic points.

**19.**  The dynamical system

$$\dot{x}_1 = x_i \left[ k_i x_{i-1} - \sum_{j=1}^{n} k_j x_j x_{j-1} \right], \qquad i = 1, 2, \ldots, n$$

describes a *hypercycle*, a structure of considerable interest in studies of evolutionary development in biology, population genetics, and chemical reactions. We restrict attention to the invariant set $S_n = \{x \in R^n : x_i \geq 0, \sum_{i=1}^{n} x_i = 1\}$.

(a)  Show that the conditions

$$k_n x_n^* = k_2 x_1^* = \cdots = k_n x_{n-1}^*,$$

$$\sum_{i=1}^{n} x_i^* = 1$$

defines an equilibrium state $x^* = (x_1^*, x_2^*, \ldots, x_n^*)$ for the hypercycle.

(b)  Let $J(x^*)$ be the Jacobian matrix of the hypercycle. Prove that the characteristic values of $J(x^*)$ are given by

$$\lambda_i(J) = K \exp(j 2\pi i/n), \qquad j = 1, 2, \ldots, n-1,$$

where $K$ is a positive constant. (We remark that there are only $n - 1$ characteristic values, since one of them is dropped because attention is restricted to the $(n - 1)$-dimensional invariant set $S_n$.)

(c)  Prove that $x^*$ is globally asymptotically stable if and only if $n \le 4$.

(d)  Prove that for any hypercycle, there exists a $\delta > 0$ such that if $x_i(0) > 0, i = 1, 2, \ldots, n$, then $x_i(t) > \delta$ for $t$ sufficiently large, i.e., no *species* originally present can ever become extinct.

**20.**  Consider the function

$$f(x_1, x_2, x_3) = x_1^2 + \tfrac{3}{2}x_2^2 + x_2^3 - 3x_2 x_3^2.$$

(a)  Show that $f$ is 4-determined.

(b)  Prove that corank $f(0) = 1$.

(c)  Show that in appropriate coordinates, $f$ is right-equivalent to the function $\tfrac{3}{2}w^2 - \tfrac{3}{2}w^4$, up to an arbitrary quadratic form.

**21.**  Show that a universal unfolding of the function

$$f(x_1, x_2) = x_1^2 x_2 + x_2^p/p$$

is given by

$$f(x_1, x_2) + \sum_{j=1}^{p-2} \alpha_j x_2^j + \sum_{k=p-1}^{p} \alpha_k x_1^{k-p+2}.$$

**22.**  The van der Waals equation of state for an ideal gas is given by

$$[P + a/V^2][V - b] = RT,$$

where $P$ is the pressure, $V$ the volume, $T$ the absolute temperature, $R$ the gas constant, and $a$ and $b$ are constants characteristic of the gas.

(a)  Taking $V$ as the dependent variable, show that the van der Waals equation is cubic in $V$, hence diffeomorphic to the equilibrium surface of the canonical cusp catastrophe.

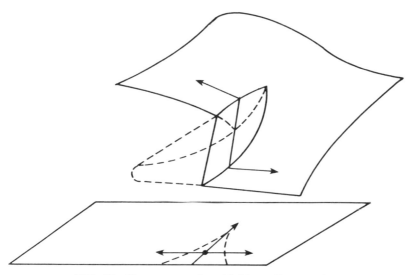

**FIG. 6.7**  Cusp catastrophe with Maxwell convention.

(b)  Taking $T$ and $P$ as control variables, interpret the behavior of $V$ as the cusp catastrophe with the Maxwell convention, i.e., $V$ always moves to the *global* minimum of the thermodynamic potential (see Fig. 6.7).

**23.**  The following equations are often used to represent the growth of a single species of microorganism:

$$\dot{x} = (\mu - D)x,$$

$$\dot{s} = D(s_r - s) - \mu x/Y,$$

$$\mu = \mu_m k_i s/(s^2 + k_i s + k_i k_s),$$

where $x$ is the biomass, $s$ the nutrient concentration, $D$ the dilution rate, and $\mu$ the specific growth rate. The other quantities are constant.

Assume the system is in equilibrium and that $D$ is then slowly increased. Show that the behavior of $x$ is then governed by the fold catastrophe.

**24.**  A vector field $v(x): R^n \to R^n$ is called *gradient* if $\partial v_i(x)/\partial x_j = \partial v_j(x)/\partial x_i$ for all $i, j = 1, 2, \ldots, n$. In this case, there exists a scalar potential function $V(x): R^n \to R$, such that the dynamical system

$$\dot{x} = v(x) = -\operatorname{grad} V(x).$$

(a)  Show that the system

$$\dot{x}_1 = x_1 x_2,$$

$$\dot{x}_2 = \tfrac{1}{2}(x_1^2 - x_2^2)$$

is gradient and find the potential function $V_0(x_1, x_2)$ associated with it.

(b)  Show that $V_0$ is the germ of the elliptic umbilic catastrophe.

**25.**  The following system of equations arises in the modeling of lake eutrophication:

$$\dot{p} = \left[ \frac{\mu(t)}{1 + p} - \frac{1}{x} \right] p,$$

$$\dot{\bar{p}} = p/x - \sigma \bar{p} x,$$

$$\dot{x} = \frac{\delta \mu(t) p}{1 + p} - \frac{1}{4} \alpha \sigma \bar{p} x + \gamma(t)(1 - x),$$

where $\sigma, \delta, \alpha$ are fixed constants having the values $\sigma = 1.2, \delta = 0.25, \alpha = 1.0$. The functions $\mu(t)$ and $\gamma(t)$ are given by

$$\mu(t) = 1.0 + b \sin^2 \left[ \frac{\pi(t - 20)}{150} \right],$$

$$\gamma(t) = \begin{cases} 0.01, & t \le 50, \quad t \ge 120, \\ 0.10, & 50 < t < 120. \end{cases}$$

Show that for $b > 7.0$ the system displays chaotic behavior.

**26.**  Consider the cubic map of $[-1, 1]$ to itself:

$$x \mapsto ax^3 + (1 - a)x.$$

Show that for $a > a^* = 1 + \frac{3}{2}\sqrt{3}$, the origin is a snap-back repellor and, hence, the dynamics

$$x_{n+1} = a^* x_n + (1 - a^*)x_n$$

are chaotic.

**27.**  The discrete version of the unforced Duffing equation $\ddot{x} - ax^3 - (1 - a)x - b\dot{x} = 0$ is given by

$$x_{n+1} = ax_n^3 + (1 - a)x_n + by_n,$$

$$y_{n+1} = x_n.$$

Show that if $a > a^*, b \ll 1$, then the system displays chaotic behavior.

**28.**  The Rössler attractor is given by the equations

$$\dot{x} = y - z,$$

$$\dot{y} = x + ey,$$

$$\dot{z} = f + xz - \mu z,$$

where $e, f, \mu$ are parameters. Fix $e = f = 0.2$. Show that period-doubling bifurcations occur for $z(t)$ at $\mu \cong 3.5$ and again at $\mu \cong 4.1$. Also, show that chaotic *bands* appear around these periodic orbits when $\mu > \mu_\infty \cong 4.23$.

**29.** Consider the two-dimensional map

$$\theta_{n+1} = 2\theta_n \bmod 2\pi, \qquad z_{n+1} = \lambda z_n + \cos\theta_n,$$

where $1 < \lambda < 2$, $0 \le \theta < 2\pi$. This map is not invertible since given $\theta_n$, there are two possibilities for $\theta_{n+1}$: $2\theta_n$ or $2(\theta_n - \pi)$.

(a) Show that the Jacobian of the map has characteristic values $\lambda$ and 2; hence almost all initial conditions generate orbits that go to either the attractor $z = +\infty$ or $z = -\infty$.

(b) Show that the boundary of the domain of attraction of $z = \pm\infty$ is given by the curve

$$f(\theta) = - \sum_{i=1}^{\infty} \lambda^{-(i+1)} \cos(2^i\theta),$$

in the sense that $z_0 \to +\infty$ if $z_0 > f(\theta_0)$, while $z_0 \to -\infty$ if $z_0 < f(\theta_0)$.

(c) Prove that $f(\theta)$ is nondifferentiable and that the curve $f(\theta)$ has infinite length and a *fractal* dimension $d = 2 - (\log\lambda)/\log 2$.

**30.** In classical economic models, the function

$$f(P) = AP^\beta(1 - P)^\gamma$$

is often used as a production function, where $P$ is the population, $A$, $\beta$, $\gamma$ are positive constants. If $\lambda$ represents the natural population growth rate, and $\sigma$ measures the subsistence level, it has been proposed that the population dynamics is governed by the equation

$$P_{t+1} = \min\{(1 + \lambda)P_t, AP_t^\beta(1 - P)^\gamma/\sigma\}.$$

Let $\beta = 1$, $\gamma \ll 1$. Show that the condition

$$A\left[(1 + \lambda)\left(\frac{1 - \lambda}{A}\right)^{1/\gamma} - \lambda\right]^\gamma \le \sigma/(1 + \lambda)^2$$

is sufficient for chaotic population fluctuations.

**31.** Consider the differential equation

$$p(D)x + f_1[q(D)x] + Dq(D)x \cdot f_2[q(D)x] = 0,$$

$(D = d/dt)$, with $f_1(0) = 0$, $p$, $q$ polynomials such that $\deg p > \deg q + 1$.

(a) Prove that the origin is globally asymptotically stable if there exists an $a > 0$ such that

(i) $(1 + as)q(s)/p(s)$ is positive-real;
(ii) $f_2(u) \ge 0$ for all $u$;
(iii) $uf_1(u) > 0$ for all $u \ne 0$.

(b) Use this criterion to find a necessary and sufficient condition for the global asymptotic stability of the origin for the system

$$\dot{x}_1 = x_2,$$
$$\dot{x}_2 = -kx_2 - [x_1 + g(x_1^2 + x_1^3)] - gx_1^2 x_2/k,$$

$g, k > 0$.

**32.**  Prove that the origin is uniformly globally asymptotically stable for the system

$$\dot{x}_1 = x_2,$$
$$\dot{x}_2 = -ax - f(x_1, x_2, t)x_1,$$

if there exist $k, \epsilon > 0$ such that

  (i)   $0 \le k \le f(x_1, x_2, t) \le (a + \sqrt{k})^2,$
  (ii)  $0 < k + \epsilon \le f(x_1, x_2, t) \le (a + \sqrt{k})^2 - \epsilon,$

for all $x_1, x_2$.

**33.**  Let $M$ be the three-dimensional solid torus

$$M = \{(w, z) : w, z \in \mathbb{C}, |w| = 1, |z| \le 1\}.$$

Define the embedding $f : M \to M$ by

$$f(w, z) = \{w^2, w/2 + z/4\}.$$

Let

$$\Lambda = \bigcap_{n > 0} f^n(M).$$

Show that $\Lambda$ is a strange attractor of $f$.

**34.**  Consider the homogeneous polynomial system

$$\dot{x}(t) = Fx(t)^{[p]} + \sum_{i=1}^{m} u_i(t)G_i x(t)^{[q_i]}, \qquad x(0) = x_0,$$

where the notation is as in Chapter 4.

Let it be desirable to minimize the performance criterion

$$J = \int_0^\infty \left[ v'x(t)^{[\mu]} + \sum_{i=1}^{m} u_i^2(t) \right] dt, \qquad v'x^{[\mu]} > 0.$$

Let $\mathcal{V}$ be an ideal in $R[s_1, s_2, \ldots, s_n]$ such that the reachable set of the system is contained in $V(\mathcal{V})$. Let $v'x^{[\mu]}$ be a positive-definite $\mu$-linear form on $V(\mathcal{V})$ and suppose that $\psi_0$ is a solution to the linear equation

$$F'_{[r]}\psi = -v,$$

such that $\psi_0'x^{[r]}$ is a positive-definite r-linear form on $V(\mathcal{V})$.

(a)   Show that for all $x_0 \in V(\mathscr{V})$, the feedback controls

$$u_i(t) = -\alpha' \psi_0 G_{i[r]} x(t)^{[q+r-1]}$$

are asymptotically stabilizing for any $\alpha > 0$.

(b)   Prove that the stabilizing control that minimizes $J$ is given by choosing $\alpha = (\frac{1}{2}, \frac{1}{2}, \ldots, \frac{1}{2})$.

(We remark that if $F$ is a stability matrix, $\psi_0$ is unique.)

## NOTES AND REFERENCES

**Section 6.I**   Some general references on classical Lyapunov-based stability theory are

W. Hahn, "Stability of Motion," Springer, New York, 1967.

R. Bellman, "Stability Theory of Differential Equations," McGraw-Hill, New York, 1973.

J. LaSalle and S. Lefschetz, "Stability by Lyapunov's Direct Method with Applications," Academic Press, New York, 1961.

Works of a more recent nature, emphasizing structural stability, rather than point stability include

M. Hirsch and S. Smale, "Differential Equations, Dynamical Systems and Linear Algebra," Academic Press, New York, 1974.

V. I. Arnol'd, "Ordinary Differential Equations," MIT Press, Cambridge, Massachusetts, 1973.

**Section 6.II**   Lyapunov's original works still make interesting reading. His monograph, originally published in Russian in 1892, then in French in 1907, was finally translated into English only in 1949.

A. M. Lyapunov, "The General Problem of the Stability of Motion," Princeton Univ. Press, Princeton, New Jersey, 1949.

There are literally hundreds, if not thousands of articles, books, surveys, etc., expanding on Lyapunov's basic idea. In addition to all of the works cited earlier, the following are good sources.

R. Kalman and J. Bertram, Control system analysis and design via the "Second method" of Lyapunov, I, II, *J. Basic Eng. Trans. ASME* **82** (1960), 371–393; 394–400.

Hartman's theorem or, as it is sometimes termed, the Hartman–Grobman theorem, is proved in

P. Hartman, "Ordinary Differential Equations," Wiley, New York, 1964.

This theorem essentially says that in the neighborhood of a noncritical equilibrium, all flows can be locally classified by a single *arithmetic* invariant, the number of roots of $Jf$ in the left half-plane. Thus, there are only $(n + 1)$ nonequivalent (up to *homeomorphism*) local flows near a noncritical equilibrium. As noted in the text, up to *diffeomorphism*, there are an uncountable number of classes, since the characteristic values of $Jf$ are diffeomorphism invariants.

The Hartman theorem is the analogue for dynamical systems of the well-known distinction in matrix theory between matrix *equivalence* and *similarity*. $A$ and $B$ are equivalent if $A = PBQ$, for some $P$, $Q$; they are similar if $A = TBT^{-1}$ for some $T$. In the first case, rank $A$ is the only invariant, while in the second, the characteristic values of $A$ are invariant.

The results of Zubov on calculating the domain of attraction are detailed in

V. I. Zubov, "Methods of A. M. Lyapunov and Their Application," Noordhoff, Groningen, 1964.

**Section 6.III**   Our treatment follows that of

J. Carr, "Applications of Centre Manifold Theory," Springer, New York, 1981.

where proofs are given of the various assertions made in the text. See also

J. Marsden and M. McCracken, "The Hopf Bifurcation and Its Applications," Springer, New York, 1976.

**Section 6.IV**   The normal form discussion follows that in

V. I. Arnol'd, "Geometrical Methods in the Theory of Ordinary Differential Equations," Springer, New York, 1983.

Additional results are in

V. I. Arnol'd, Lectures on bifurcations in versal families, *Russian Math Surveys* **27** (1972), 54–123.
J. Guckenheimer and P. Holmes, "Nonlinear Oscillations, Dynamical Systems, and Bifurcations of Vector Fields," Springer, New York, 1983.

**Section 6.V**   In addition to the books of Guckenheimer–Holmes, Marsden–McCracken, and Arnol'd cited earlier, see the following for more details on bifurcations of flows and maps.

P. Holmes, ed., "New Approaches to Nonlinear Problems in Dynamics," SIAM Publications, Philadelphia, 1980.
Bifurcations theory and applications in scientific disciplines, *in* "Ann. New York Acad. Sci., Vol. 316, New York, 1979.

**Section 6.VI**   One of the most accessible treatments of singularity theory, especially for maps $X \to Y$, rather than just for functions $X \to R$, is

Y. C. Lu, "Singularity Theory and an Introduction to Catastrophe Theory," Springer, New York, 1976.

A more technical discussion is given by

M. Golubitsky and V. Guillemin, *Stable Mappings and their Singularities*, Springer, New York, 1973.

See also

V. I. Arnol'd, "Singularity Theory," Cambridge University Press, Cambridge, 1981.
J. Martinet, *Singularities of Smooth Functions and Maps*, Cambridge Univ. Press, Cambridge, 1982.

The classical paper that sparked off the entire field of singularity theory is

H. Whitney, On singularities of Euclidean spaces. I. Mappings of the plane into the plane, *Ann. of Math.* **62** (1955), 374–410.

Catastrophe theory and a proof of Thom's classification theorem, can be found in

E. C. Zeeman, "Catastrophe Theory: Selected Papers: 1972–1977," Addison-Wesley, Reading, Massachusetts, 1977.

Another source, valuable for its geometric treatment of the basic ideas as well as an extended bibliography, is

T. Poston and I. Stewart, "Catastrophe Theory and Its Applications," Pitman, London, 1978.

An elementary and very readable introduction is

P. T. Saunders, "An Introduction to Catastrophe Theory," Cambridge Univ. Press, Cambridge, 1980.

**Section 6.VII**    There have been several critiques given of the *metaphysical* way of catastrophe theory. Among the most well known is

H. Sussman and R. Zahler, Catastrophe theory as applied to the social and biological sciences: A Critique, *Synthese*, **37** (1978), 117–217.

By and large, most of the so-called *objections* revolved about semantical interpretations and have been unlamentably buried and forgotten.

Many of the examples of this section first appeared in

J. Casti, Topological methods for social and behavioral systems, *Internat. J. Gen. Systems* **8** (1982), 187–210.

**Section 6.VIII**    The work that serves as the precursor to much of the current studies of chaotic dynamics is

P. R. Stein and S. M. Ulam, Non-linear transformation studies on electronic computers, *Rozprawy Matewatyczne* **39** (1964), 1–66 (reprinted in "Stanislaw Ulam: Sets, Numbers and Universes" (W. Beyer, J. Mycielski, and G. C. Rota, eds.), MIT Press, Cambridge, Massachusetts, 1974).

The original problem that has led to today's explosion of literature on chaos was Lorenz's study of atmospheric circulation. See

E. N. Lorenz, Deterministic non-periodic flow, *J. Atmospheric Sci.* **20** (1963), 130–141.

An extensive recent summary of work done with Lorenz's model is

C. Sparrow, "The Lorenz Equations: Bifurcations, Chaos, and Strange Attractors," Springer, New York, 1982.

The mathematical basis for much of the material in this section was formed in the papers

J. Li and J. Yorke, Period three implies chaos, *Amer. Math. Monthly* **82** (1975), 985–992.
M. Feigenbaum, Universal behavior in nonlinear systems, *Los Alamos Sci.* **1** (1980), 4–27.
F. Marotto, Snap-back repellers imply chaos in $R^n$, *J. Math. Anal. Appl.* **63** (1978), 199–223.

The use of chaos to model turbulence fluid flow is surveyed in

J. P. Eckman, Roads to turbulence in dissipative dynamical systems, *Rev. Modern Phys.* **53** (1981), 643–654.

A truly extraordinary survey of the field through 1980, together with an extensive bibliography, is

R. H. G. Helleman, Self-generated chaotic behavior in nonlinear mechanics, *in* "Fundamental Problems in Statistical Mechanics V" (E. Cohen, ed.), North-Holland, Amsterdam, 1980.

**Section 6.IX**   The Popov and Circle criterion are discussed in detail in

J. Willems, "Stability Theory of Dynamical Systems," Wiley, New York, 1970.

See also the classic papers of Popov and others reprinted in

J. Aggarwal and M. Vidyasagar, eds., "Nonlinear Systems," Dowden, Hutchinson, and Ross, Stroudsburg, Pennsylvania, 1977.

The linear decoupling problem is extensively treated in

W. M. Wonham, Linear multivariable control, *in* "Lectures Notes in Economics and Mathematical Systems," Vol. 101, Springer, Berlin, 1974.

The nonlinear revision presented here was first studied by

A. Krener, A heuristic view of nonlinear decoupling, *in* "Proceedings, 13th Asilomar Conference on Circuits, Systems and Computers," Asilomar, 1979.

See also

P. K. Sinha, State feedback decoupling of nonlinear systems, *IEEE Trans. Automat. Control* **AC-22** (1977), 487–489.

Our treatment of the nonlinear regulator follows that in

P. Moylan and B. D. O. Anderson, Nonlinear regulator theory and an inverse optimal control problem, *IEEE Trans. Automat. Control* **AC-18** (1973), 460–465.

# Index